Web Programming with Visual Basic®

Web Programming with Visual Basic®

by Craig Eddy with Brad Haasch

201 West 103rd Street, Indianapolis, Indiana 46290

I would like to dedicate this work to my wife, Susan, and my children, Madeline and Bobby, who encouraged me through many late nights and long days. If not for their love and dedication this book would have never been possible.

—Craig Eddy

Copyright © 1996 by Sams Publishing

FIRST EDITION

International Standard Book Number:

1-57521-106-8

Library of Congress Catalog Card Number: 96-67959

99 98 97 96 4 3 2 1

Interpretation of the printing code: the rightmost double-digit number is the year of the book's printing; the rightmost single-digit, the number of the book's printing. For example, a printing code of 96-1 shows that the first printing of the book occurred in 1996.

Composed in AGaramond and MCPdigital by Macmillan Computer Publishing

Printed in the United States of America

Publisher and President: *Richard K. Swadley*
Publishing Team Leader: *Dean Miller*
Managing Editor: *Cindy Morrow*
Director of Marketing: *John Pierce*
Assistant Marketing Managers: *Kristina Perry*, *Rachel Wolfe*

Acquisitions Editor
Kim Spilker

Development Editor
Brian-Kent Proffit

Software Development Specialist
Cari Skaggs

Production Editors
Johnna L. VanHoose
Marla Reece

Copy Editor
Marla Reece

Indexer
Cheryl Dietsch

Technical Reviewer
Ricardo Birmele

Editorial Coordinator
Bill Whitmer

Technical Edit Coordinator
Lynette Quinn

Editorial Assistants
Carol Ackerman
Andi Richter
Rhonda Tinch-Mize

Cover Designer
Tim Amrhein

Book Designer
Alyssa Yesh

Copy Writer
Peter Fuller

Production Team Supervisor
Brad Chinn

Production
Stephen Adams, Debra Bolhuis, Jeanne Clark, Mike Dietsch, Jason Hand, Daniel Harris, Clint Lahnen, Chris Livengood, Ryan Oldfather, Casey Price, Erich Richter, Laura Robbins, Mark Walchle

Overview

Contents

Acknowledgments

This book came together through the efforts of many people. The team at Sams.net was phenomenal: Kim, Marla, Johnna, Cari, and Brian. I would especially like to thank Marla, who was always able to inject a bit of humor into her editorial queries. The technical editor, Ricardo Birmele, was instrumental in making sure all the code in this book works as advertised.

Personally, I have many people to thank: My wife Susan for always encouraging me; my parents for always pushing me to give life my best effort; Bernard Jones for kindling the fire of excitement I experienced when I first discovered the Internet. Finally, to the team at Pipestream Technologies for putting up with a grouchy senior developer, who had stayed up most of the previous night writing, and to Ken Banks, president of Pipestream Technologies, who had the vision to add as much Web capability to our sales force automation product as possible. This vision made my experimentation with Web programming possible.

—Craig Eddy

About the Author

Craig Eddy has been a Visual Basic programmer for five years and holds a degree in electrical engineering. He is senior developer and Webmaster for Pipestream Technologies, Inc., a software development company in Richmond, VA. He was an author for *Access 95 Unleashed* and *Microsoft Office Unleashed*, both by Sams Publishing. Craig can be reached via e-mail at `craige@richmond.infi.net` (or `CraigE@PIPESTREAM.ipctech.com`) and some of his Web creations can be seen at `http://pipestream.ipctech.com`.

Tell Us What You Think!

As a reader, you are the most important critic and commentator of our books. We value your opinion and want to know what we're doing right, what we could do better, what areas you'd like to see us publish in, and any other words of wisdom you're willing to pass our way. You can help us make strong books that meet your needs and give you the computer guidance you require.

Do you have access to CompuServe or the World Wide Web? Then check out our CompuServe forum by typing **GO SAMS** at any prompt. If you prefer the World Wide Web, visit our site at `http://www.mcp.com`.

NOTE:

If you have a technical question about this book, call the technical support line at (800) 571-5840, ext. 3668.

As the team leader of the group that created this book, I welcome your comments. You can fax, e-mail, or write me directly to let me know what you did or didn't like about this book—as well as what we can do to make our books stronger. Here's the information:

FAX: 317/581-4669

E-mail: opsys_mgr@sams.mcp.com

Mail: Dean Miller
Comments Department
Sams Publishing
201 W. 103rd Street
Indianapolis, IN 46290

Chapter 1

Introduction

Welcome to Web Programming with Visual Basic. As you can probably tell by the title of the book, the topic here is the integration of Visual Basic and the World Wide Web.

To start off, we'll go into reasons to use the Web as an information source and why you should choose Visual Basic as a Web development tool.

Then we'll go over the structure of the book—where you can find specific information. From there, you're on your way to becoming a Web-savvy Visual Basic developer.

Why the World Wide Web?

You may ask, "Besides all the hype, what good is the Web?"

The answer is simple: The Web allows for the distribution of information over a wide area, to a wide audience at a low cost (compared to a WAN). This network of networks enables users from across the world to access data on any computer whose administrator has deemed that the data should be made public using the Web.

This opens up a lot of possibilities for both providing and gathering information. Couple the Web with the other features of the Internet (e-mail, network news, file repositories), and it's easy to see all the potential applications of the Web.

Here are a few ideas to get your mind going: first, a Web-based order entry form. This gives a remote salesman using a Web browser on a notebook computer the ability to place orders minutes after a deal is made. Another potential application is to provide a Visual Basic search engine that scans Web-based databases of résumés for keywords. Finally, a custom Web browser that you provide to your customers. The browser allows access only to your Web site and even provides the ability to personalize the information on your Web server to match the customer.

The applications are as wide open as the Web itself, and I'm sure that as more people jump on the Web bandwagon, more and more applications will spring up.

Why Choose Visual Basic as a Web Programming Tool?

An important question at the start of any software design project is the choice of a language or languages to use. When you think about designing applications that use Web-based information, the question still applies: "Why should I use Visual Basic?"

Visual Basic makes sense for the following reasons:

- Database Connectivity—By using ODBC or RDO, you can easily wrap database accessibility into a Visual Basic Web application. The question is no longer what can be done via the current set of Web tools but what can be done using Visual Basic.

- Up-to-date custom controls—The market for third party custom controls in Visual Basic is huge. At least 10 different companies currently make OCXs or VBXs for Internet programming. This is reassuring because a change in an Internet specification used somewhere in your application doesn't mandate a change in the application's code. Instead, it means upgrading a custom control and then performing the much easier task of verifying that the control works as intended with the application.
- OLE—The ability to control and to access data from other applications is a big plus to application development. Not only can a Visual Basic application control several OLE-enabled Web Browsers, but you can also relay information from the Web to an OLE-enabled application.
- The Windows user interface—The usability of a Windows application far exceeds the current set of HTML tags that allow for textboxes, comboboxes, and buttons. This, coupled with the large Windows install base, ensures that the learning curve of a properly designed Visual Basic application will be close to that of any other Windows application.

Combining Visual Basic and the Web

The merging of Visual Basic and the ability to tie into real-time, distributed information using the Internet produces an interesting and very powerful tool. In the constant flux of the Internet, Visual Basic becomes a very practical choice for Web application development thanks to Visual Basic's rapid application development aspect.

Visual Basic can be used to create both *client-side* and *server-side* Web applications. A Web browser such as Microsoft's Internet Explorer is one example of a client-side application. It is used to "surf" the Web—browsing the Web pages at a Web site and moving to other pages or to a completely different Web site by using the hyperlinks provided on most Web pages. Another example of a client-side application is an application that retrieves stock quotes from a quote provider's Web sites and provides the quotes to the user in some fashion. This application is not a Web browser but does access Web-based information.

Server-side applications run alongside a Web server, such as Microsoft's Internet Information Server. The server-side application is executed under the direction of the Web server, typically in response to a request made by a client-side application such as a Web browser. Server-side applications typically serve as *gateways* between a user's Web browser and information stored on the Web server that is not typically accessible using a Web browser. Such information can include database tables, information-providing machines attached to the server, and even OLE-enabled applications to which the server has access.

Past, Present, and Future

In the beginning, the Web was predominantly used by, maintained by, and programmed under the UNIX platform. The reasons for this are simple: First, UNIX was designed from the ground up to allow computers to easily communicate with one another and, second, UNIX has always been available for a wide variety of hardware platforms. Additionally, the TCP/IP protocol on which the Web is based was initially designed with the UNIX operating system in mind.

For these reasons, integrating the Web with Visual Basic was very impractical, if not outright impossible. Then recently, with the standardized Windows sockets (or *Winsock* for short) interface, things got a lot easier. The Winsocket interface is a layer that resides between the Windows operating system and the TCP/IP protocol. By making API calls to the Winsock interface, the Windows programmer can avoid the complexities of the TCP/IP protocol and instead concentrate on developing services and tools that run over TCP/IP networks.

Built atop the Winsock interface is a large group of tools that abstract the messy details of TCP/IP and the Internet protocols. With these tools, Web programming became a very practical solution to most distributed information programming tasks. As you'll see throughout this book, many custom controls and other tools exist that the Visual Basic programmer can use to further remove the application code from the complexities of the TCP/IP protocol.

What will the future hold? One thing that I can guarantee about the future is change. The Internet is still a very cutting-edge and young technology. Not only does this mean that this book will serve as a funny 'snapshot in time' five years from now, but it means that your work as an Internet programmer will be a "work in progress" for a long time to come. Unlike COBOL programming, Web programming will be a skill that requires frequent reading and training to keep up-to-date.

What You Should Know

As with many technical books, it's easy to get blown away unless you come into them well prepared. Although the main topic of this book is the World Wide Web, we aren't assuming more than a user level knowledge of the Web.

We've targeted this book to Visual Basic programmers who are familiar with the Internet, but who are by no means Internet experts. You don't need to know every function exposed in the `Winsock.DLL`, but you should have some experience with Netscape, Internet e-mail, and perhaps transferring files via ftp.

If you get stuck, don't worry, the very source of your frustration may be your salvation as well. A decent number of Web sites are dedicated to Visual Basic, and a listing of them is covered in Appendix D, "Bibliography and Cool Web Sites."

A Mild Warning to the Web Developer

While all this new technology seems great, there are a few things to watch out for.

First and foremost is that any time you retrieve information over the Internet, you are using someone else's equipment. Although you have their implicit permission to do so doesn't mean programs you write should repeatedly access another site without permission from the owner. Also be wary of any automated Web programs that you write (See Chapter 11, "A Brief Introduction to Web Spiders and Agents," for a complete description). The last thing you want to do is anger a system administrator by overwhelming his or her server with requests. As always, test on a server where you're the administrator, or on a server you have permission to test programs on before actually putting it into distribution.

The other warning is that even with the knowledge obtained from reading this book, your learning about Web programming is just beginning. The Web and Visual Basic are continually changing entities, which means that to stay current and up-to-date requires keeping up on the latest tools, gadgets, and specifications. While this may seem like an incredible hassle compared to learning something more stable, most of its excitement comes from being one of the first to explore this new technology.

What's Inside?

In this book you'll start with the HTTP protocol. Unfortunately, the publisher couldn't attach two aspirin underneath the accompanying CD-ROM in the back of the book, but take it slow—it isn't too bad. The material is covered in Chapter 2, "HTTP: How to Speak on the Web," which can be read from beginning to end and can also serve as a reference guide to the HTTP protocol.

We then move into DDE and OLE control of the Netscape browser in Chapter 3, "Interfacing to the Web with DDE and OLE." Although the chapter covers Navigator exclusively, other browsers (Spry's Mosaic and Microsoft's Internet Explorer, for example) are also controllable using DDE and OLE. However, their implementations of DDE and OLE are not covered in this book.

Chapter 4, "Using Web Browser Custom Controls," introduces a few of the many custom controls available to interface Visual Basic with the World Wide Web.

Next is coverage of CGI applications. If you don't know what CGI is, turn to Chapter 6, "The Win/CGI Interface," which covers the interface between Windows and CGI applications. In Chapter 7, "Creating CGI Applications in Visual Basic," you'll put this knowledge to use writing actual Win/CGI applications for Windows- or Windows NT-based Web servers.

One of the previously mentioned reasons to choose Visual Basic for Internet development included database accessibility. This is covered in detail in Chapter 8, "Database Connectivity: The

WebGuest Application." In this chapter you design a complete guest book application similar to ones seen on most Web sites. In addition to entering information, users of the WebGuest application can also list and search information entered by previous registrants.

Chapter 9, "Connecting to OLE Servers: Using the Web as a Front-End to Schedule Plus," covers using OLE to link the Web and Visual Basic to other OLE-enabled applications. The application example presented in this chapter allows a doctor's office to accept and schedule appointments using their Web site. As appointments are created by the doctor's patients, they are entered into the Schedule Plus database for use by any other machine with access to the Schedule Plus data.

Chapter 10 continues the coverage of server-side applications with "Using OLEISAPI with the Microsoft Internet Information Server."

Chapter 11 provides a brief introduction to the role of Web Spiders and Robots and serves as the start of the section of the book covering client-side applications.

The first chapter in this section is Chapter 12, "QuoteWatcher: An Interactive Web Agent." In this chapter you create an application that retrieves price quotes for specified stocks and mutual funds. The quotes are obtained from a Web server that typically provides quotes in response to user input on one of the server's HTML forms. The QuoteWatcher application bypasses the need to use a Web browser and fill in those forms, however, by sending the proper requests to the Web server.

In Chapter 13, "Building an E-Mail Signature Generator," you build an application that constructs an e-mail signature file based on random quotations obtained from one of the many random quotation generators available on the Web. This signature file can then be used by your e-mail application to attach the newly generated signature to your outgoing e-mail.

Chapter 14, "WebSearcher: A Simple Search Tool," brings the concept of popular Web-based search engines to a client-side application. A simple search tool is developed that allows you to specify a Web page to search and the keyword for which to search. The WebSearcher then searches the specified page and any page to which it links for the keyword, providing a list of any "hits" it finds.

Finally, Chapter 15, "LinkChecker: A Spider that Checks for Broken Links," shows how to check a specified Web page for hyperlinks to resources that aren't accessible. This is useful if you administer a Web site and want to ensure that any hyperlink you place on your Web pages is valid.

Conventions Used in the Book

NOTE

Note boxes highlight important or explanatory information that compliments the topic at hand.

TIP

These tips give you helpful suggestions and shortcuts to improve your Visual Basic programming.

CAUTION

If you're about to do something that could damage your system, these warnings guide you through so this won't happen.

http://www.anything.com

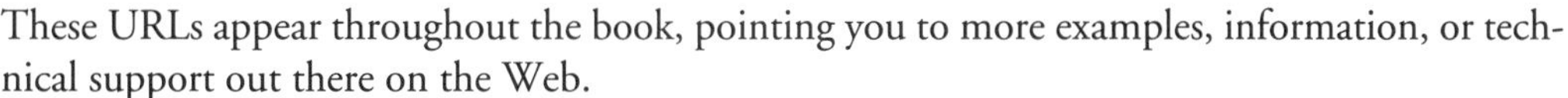

These URLs appear throughout the book, pointing you to more examples, information, or technical support out there on the Web.

This book also uses `computer` type to denote sections of code and other application design elements, such as property names, property values, etc. *`Italic computer type`* refers to a placeholder that should be filled with the actual number, variable, or value represented.

And Away We Go...

Now that you know why Visual Basic is a fantastic Web development tool, it's time to get started on your road to Web programming mastery.

I would suggest starting with Chapter 2. This chapter serves as the foundation for many other chapters in the book. Although it can also serve as a great reference, if you don't read it in its entirety you should at least skim it for the general content before proceeding.

From there, you can choose to continue, reading straight through, or you can narrow your reading to cover either client-side or server-side applications. If you choose the former, start with Chapters 4 and 5, then move to Chapter 11, and move on from there. If you choose to cover server-side applications, start at Chapter 6, and work your way to Chapter 10.

And, if you develop some snazzy applications after reading this book, drop us a line. We'd love to hear how this book has helped you. Craig can be reached at craige@richmond.infi.net and Brad's address is haasch@execpc.com.

2

HTTP: How to Speak on the Web

- Introduction to HTTP
- HTTP as a Client/Server Protocol
- Addressing on the Web
- HTTP Messages
- HTTP Request Messages
- HTTP Response Messages
- The Entity Portion of HTTP Messages
- Authentication Through HTTP

The global Internet, a "network of networks," is possible for one reason: the adherence to standard communications protocols. These protocols define how the computers and applications running on the network communicate with one another. They allow computers running on different hardware platforms and different operating systems to share information. These protocols include the Simple Mail Transfer Protocol (SMTP) and Post Office Protocol (POP) for e-mail, the File Transfer Protocol (FTP) for file transfer, and the Network News Transfer Protocol (NNTP) for reading and posting to Internet newsgroups.

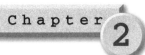

The World Wide Web (Web for short) uses a protocol named the Hypertext Transfer Protocol (HTTP) to transfer hypermedia documents and other resources between server and client computers. These *hypermedia* documents are often referred to as Web pages and can contain links to other Web pages (hence the term *hypertext*). Figure 2.1 shows an example of a hypermedia document. The screen shot illustrates many of the features of the Web: hyperlinks (the underlined text) which can transport the user to another page; embedded data objects (such as the Under Construction picture); and embedded applications (the LED banner is actually an application transferred from the server and executed on the client machine).

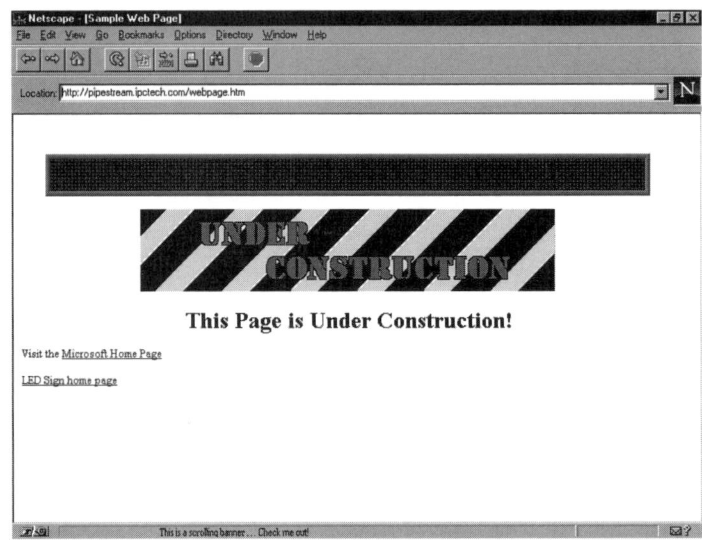

Figure 2.1.
An example of a Web document.

This chapter discusses the HTTP protocol in enough depth that Visual Basic programmers should be able to proficiently write applications that run on both HTTP server and client machines. Although some of the material may seem to be beyond the scope of a typical Visual Basic programming book, the concepts are necessary to correctly communicate on the Web.

It is important to understand the structure and operation of HTTP messages. For applications that will serve as user agents (retrieving information from HTTP servers), the proper request messages must be generated. This is necessary not only to assure that proper information is presented to the user, but also to limit the load on the network. Likewise, when developing server-side applications, you need to make sure the proper status, header, and entity information is returned to the client. This chapter, though not exhaustive on the subject, gives you an understanding of the proper use of HTTP messaging so you can effectively write both types of applications.

Introduction to HTTP

The HTTP protocol defines how client and server applications communicate in order to transfer hypertext documents and other resources located on the network. The protocol does not attempt to define what types of resources are transferred. The data may be text, sound, full-motion video, even applications to be executed on the client machine. Although the protocol is commonly used for communicating on a TCP/IP network (such as the Internet), it can be used with any network topology.

http://www.ietf.cnri.reston.va.us/ids.by.wg/http.html

Even though the HTTP protocol has been in use since 1990, it is still evolving. As of this writing, the protocol is in Internet-Draft form. Internet-Drafts are working documents of a group known as the Internet Engineering Task Force (IETF). The Internet-Draft for the HTTP protocol is authored by the HTTP Working Group, which includes Tim Bernes-Lee (who originally proposed the hypertext protocol in 1989), Roy Fielding, and Henrik Frystyk Nielsen. The protocol is currently being referred to as HTTP/1.0. The Internet-Draft was last published on February 19, 1996, and expires on August 19, 1996. You should refer to this document if you desire an in-depth coverage of the HTTP specification. We will rely heavily on it throughout this chapter. A link to this Internet-Draft and a list of other HTTP-related Internet-Drafts can be found at `http://www.ietf.cnri.reston.va.us/ids.by.wg/http.html`.

According to the minutes of a recent meeting of the HTTP Working Group, the next release of the protocol, HTTP/1.1, is slated to be available in August 1996. A protocol called HTTP/NG ("next generation") is slated to be released as a Proposed Standard in December 1996.

The HTTP/1.0 Internet-Draft defines the HTTP protocol as "an application-level protocol with the lightness and speed necessary for distributed, collaborative, hypermedia information systems. It is a generic, stateless, object-oriented protocol which can be used for many tasks...."

Many of these terms and concepts are defined and discussed in the remainder of this chapter. Table 2.1 gives some brief definitions of the common terms used when discussing the HTTP protocol and Web communications.

Table 2.1. Web and protocol terminology.

Term	*Definition*
Connection	A "virtual circuit" connecting two programs and allowing these programs to communicate with one another.
Message	A structured sequence of characters transmitted using an open connection.
Request	A message from a client application to a server application, typically for retrieving a resource from an HTTP server.
Response	A message from a server application to a client application, typically containing a hypermedia file that was requested by the client application.
Resource	An object of data residing on the network or a service available on the network, which can be identified by a unique address.
Entity	Defined in the HTTP/1.0 Internet-Draft as "A particular representation or rendition of a data resource, or reply from a service resource, that may be enclosed within a request or response message." An entity is essentially the data from a file or service that is "wrapped" within an HTTP message.
User Agent	The application that initiates a request message. Typically Web browsers, spiders, agents, or other client-side tools.
Server	The application that listens on a network and responds to HTTP request messages.

HTTP as a Client/Server Protocol

As you can probably guess from Table 2.1, the HTTP protocol defines a client/server model. The difference between HTTP and typical client/server protocols, however, is that either role can be played by either computer involved in the conversation. The role a given computer plays during the conversation depends on the resource being accessed and possibly the HTML contained by the resource.

Another very important difference is the fact that the HTTP is a stateless protocol. Users are not required to go through a logon process, which is typical of most client/server systems. In fact, the majority of HTTP data transfers are completely anonymous—beyond the machine address of the client, the server has no knowledge of who is retrieving data from it. In addition to the lack of user information, the HTTP protocol provides no mechanism for tracking how long a client may actually utilize information it has retrieved or for knowing what a client may have done before requesting a resource from the server.

The typical HTTP conversation contains the following steps, which are illustrated in Figure 2.2.

1. A client opens a connection with a server. Recall that any computer can act as a client, even if the computer is running a server application.
2. The client sends a request to the server. This request consists of a request method, a resource or service address, and possibly other header fields, and body content. These concepts are discussed in the following sections.
3. The server returns to the client a status line, possible header information, and (usually) an entity section.
4. The server closes the connection.

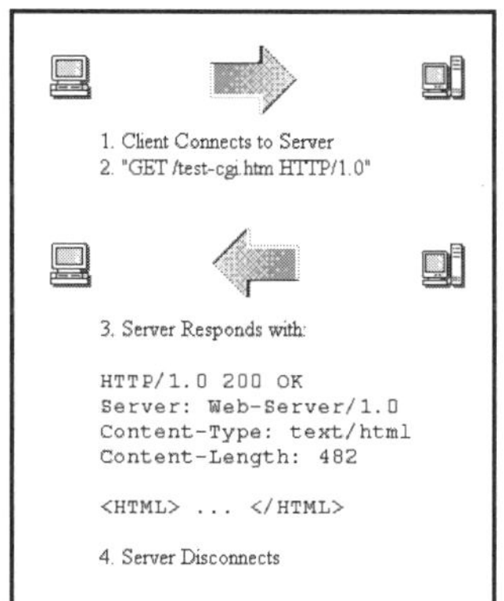

Figure 2.2.
Illustrating the request-response nature of HTTP.

There is always the possibility on the global Internet that a connection can fail at any time. The HTTP protocol provides that both the client and server applications must be prepared for such a situation. The loss of connection can occur due to user interaction, a communication time-out, or an application failure. A loss of connection is considered to terminate the client's current request. This means that, regardless of the state of the request when the termination occurs, the client must restart the entire process to properly attempt to access the resource again.

In addition to this drawback, the HTTP protocol allows for only a single resource to be transferred during a connection. This means that if a hypertext page has embedded references to other resources (such as images), the client must retrieve each resource individually through separate connections. For example, to construct the Web page of Figure 2.1, the Web browser had to make three connections. One to retrieve the HTML file, another to retrieve the embedded Java applet, and a third to retrieve the Under Construction picture. This shortcoming of HTTP has often been blamed for the slow response time of the Web.

Addressing on the Web

As mentioned in the preceding section, HTTP is used to transfer data objects from a server machine to a client. In order to make this transfer happen, the two applications involved in the conversation must recognize a common addressing mechanism. This addressing mechanism must uniquely identify every data object available not only on the server application machine, but also on the entire network the applications are using for communication. The addressing scheme must also be familiar to programmers and publishers on the Web because addresses must be used both to gather and to publish information or services on the Web.

The Web uses a form of address known as a *Universal Resource Identifier* (URI) to identify data objects on servers. The URI for an object is independent of which protocol is used to access the data. An object's URI also provides no real clue as to what type of data is being identified. However, most URIs include a filename extension (similar to the DOS filename extension) that can be used by the client application as a clue to how the object should be presented to the user. For example, a Web site dedicated to gardening may have a file named `roses.htm`, which is most likely an HTML document, and perhaps a file named `roses.gif`, which is probably a picture of roses.

The more common form of a URI is known as a *Universal Resource Locator* (URL). This is typically what is specified when you see a list of Web pages. A URL is a URI that contains protocol information specifying how the data object should be retrieved from the server. The difference is subtle but important. Here are a few examples that should clear up any confusion you may have:

URI: `//myserver.com/user1/default.htm`

URL: `http://myserver.com/user1/default.htm`

URI: `//ftp.myserver.com/demos/demo.zip`

URL: `ftp://ftp.myserver.com/demos/demo.zip`

The first two examples illustrate the crucial difference between a URI and a URL. The URL informs the machine at address `myserver.com` to retrieve a file named `default.htm` for its `/user1` directory and return it to the client using the HTTP protocol. The URI merely defines the location of the file; whereas, the URL specifies how it should be retrieved.

Similar to DOS, the URI can contain either absolute or relative addressing. For instance, if you are viewing (or creating) a Web-based document with a URI of `//myserver.com/user1/default.htm`, you can use the following addressing mechanisms within the document:

- `//myserver.com/home/file2.htm` would specify an absolute path.
- `file3.htm` would specify a relative path equivalent to `//myserver.com/user1/file3.htm`.
- `/file4.htm` would specify a relative path equivalent to `//myserver.com/file4.htm`.

Another similarity to DOS in specifying a URI is that the URI cannot contain any spaces and must encode certain reserved characters. If whitespace is required within a URI, you must encode the space as the string `"%20"`. So, a directory named `"My Documents"` if used in a URI would appear as `"My%20Documents"`. Similarly, there are several reserved characters that have special meanings

within a URI. These are outlined in Table 2.2. These reserved characters, if actually meant to appear within a URI, must be encoded using the ISO Latin-1 character set.

Table 2.2. Reserved characters in URIs.

Character	*Usage in URIs*
`%` (percent)	Identifies encoded characters.
`/` (forward slash)	Used to separate path- and filenames.
`#` (pound)	Used to separate the URI of an object from a placeholder within the object. Often used to mark off sections of a document into different portions.
`?` (question mark)	Identifies a query to a data object. Text after the question mark is the search term(s) to be applied to the data object.
`*`, `!`, `^`, `¦`, `~`	Reserved for special circumstances.

The HTTP URL

The HTTP URL has a specific format that identifies data resources available on a network. The format is:

```
http://<host>[:<port>]/[<path>][?<search_text>]
```

The `http` portion is used to indicate that the resource is to be retrieved using the HTTP protocol. The `<host>` is the Internet hostname or IP address for the machine on which the resource resides. The port, which is a numeric value, is an optional parameter necessary if the server is not listening on TCP port 80 (which is the value assumed if `<port>` is not specified). The `<path>` portion is either an absolute path or relative path locating the resource within the server's file structure. If the `<path>` is not specified, the server should respond with a default HTML file. This method is typically used to access the site's home page. You can specify the `<path>`, however, if you know the exact URL for the resource you're interested in. The default file's location is typically set up in the server software's setup or configuration program. If the resource can be searched, the `?<search_text>` portion can be provided to instruct the server on how the resource should be searched. This item is both server and resource specific. Later chapters address these searchable resources in-depth.

HTTP Messages

As most programmers familiar with Windows programming are aware, applications can communicate with one another only when there exists an agreed-upon language. When computer applications converse, they use messages that must conform to predefined rules and formats.

Similarly, all conversations that take place using the HTTP protocol use a message-based system. The message format is nearly identical for both client and server sides of the conversation. This section discusses the Backus-Naur Form (a method of documenting rules and syntax) and the general format of HTTP messages. The following sections discuss the portions of HTTP messages that are of particular importance to programmers designing Web-based applications.

Using Backus-Naur Form

The HTTP/1.0 Internet-Draft document makes heavy use of a notation known as the *Backus-Naur Form* (BNF) to specify how the HTTP protocol operates. This section illustrates the Backus-Naur Form in enough detail to help you understand the notation. The BNF is compact and easy to read and understand. Most programmers have no problem understanding the format, but some introduction to it may still be necessary.

Basic Notation

The basic notation for defining a rule using the BNF is

```
name = definition
```

The name of a rule is simply the name itself (no enclosing < or > characters). The = sign is used to separate the rule from its definition. Whitespace (spaces, tabs, new lines, and so on) has no meaning within a rule except that indentation indicates that a definition spans multiple lines. The < and > signs can be used within a definition to help separate element names. There are certain basic rules that appear in uppercase characters (`SP` to indicate a space, `DIGIT` to indicate a numeric character, and so forth).

To represent a literal character within a rule, place quotation marks around it:

```
"literal"
```

Use of quotation marks is reserved for marking literal characters. The text is generally not case-sensitive (unless otherwise noted).

To denote an either/or rule, use

```
rule1 ¦ rule2
```

The pipe character denotes that either element can be used. For example, `0 ¦ 1` states that either `0` or `1` is acceptable.

Parentheses are used to group elements that are considered as a single element:

```
(rule1 rule2)
```

For example, `(x (and ¦ or) y)` allows for `(x and y)` or `(x or y)` to be accepted.

To indicate a repeating rule or element, use

```
*rule
```

The asterisk character (*) indicates repetition of an element. The notation is also expressed as <n>*<m>element. This indicates that at least <n> and at most <m> repetitions of the element are permitted. The default for <n> is 0; the default for <m> is infinity. For example, 1*element indicates that at least one element must appear. The rule 1*5element indicates that at least one but at most five of element can appear.

The square brackets ([]) are used to indicate elements that are optional:

```
[rule]
```

This is identical to the notation used in the Visual Basic documentation to indicate optional parameters in function calls.

To indicate a specific number of repetitions of an element or rule, use

```
N rule
```

which indicates that the rule must appear N times. This notation is identical to <n>*<n>rule defined above. For example, 2DIGIT indicates a two-digit number.

To indicate a list of elements, the notation

```
#rule
```

is used. This notation is similar to *rule defined earlier. A more complete form is <n>#<m>element where <n> indicates the minimum number of list items acceptable and <m> indicates the maximum number of list items. The defaults are 0 and infinity.

To separate rules from comments, use a semicolon character, as in

```
; comment
```

The comment starts with the semicolon and continues to the end of the current line.

Basic Rules

Some of the basic rules you'll encounter in this chapter are listed in the following lines:

```
OCTET = <any 8-bit sequence of data>
CHAR = <any ASCII character>
ALPHA = <any character in the range "A"…"Z" or "a"…"z">
DIGIT = <any digit "0"…"9">
CR = <the ASCII carriage return (Chr$(13))>
LF = <the ASCII line feed (Chr$(10))>
CRLF = CR LF
SP = <the ASCII space (Chr$(32))>
TEXT = <used for describing values that won't be parsed by the applications>
```

The Format of an HTTP Message

As mentioned previously, the client request message and the server response message use a similar format. In fact, the formats are practically identical. This section introduces the Backus-Naur Form for the two messages.

NOTE:

Remember, the role of client (requester) and server (responder) can belong to either machine involved in a conversation at any given time during the conversation. However, during a given connection the roles will not change.

HTTP messages can take either a *full* request/response or a *simple* request/response message format. HTTP/1.0 clients and servers use the simple request/response format to communicate with clients and servers using previous versions (specifically HTTP/0.9) of the HTTP protocol. When a client makes a simple request, the server *must* use the simple response format. Simple requests can also be used by the client application in instances where the available HTTP headers and content negotiation would be merely unnecessary overhead.

The syntax of the full request is illustrated in the following lines:

```
<Method> SP <URI> SP <HTTP-Version> CRLF
     *( <General-Header>
     | <Request-Header>
     | <Entity-Header> )
CRLF
[<Entity-Body>]
```

The format specifies that the first line of the full request contains three required elements: a method, a URI, and the HTTP version. The elements are separated by a space, and the line is terminated with a carriage return and line feed. The methods include `GET`, `HEAD`, `POST`, and others discussed in the next few sections. The `<HTTP-Version>` element is defined by the following BNF rule: `"HTTP/" 1*DIGIT "." 1*DIGIT`. The current version would have an `<HTTP-Version>` element of `"HTTP/1.0"`.

The header fields are optional fields, which are discussed shortly. Header fields are defined by the following rule:

```
HTTP-Header = <Header-Field-Name> ":" [<Value>] CRLF
```

There can be any number of headers, and they can appear in any order. The headers are typically sent General-Header fields first, then Request/Response-Headers, then Entity-Header fields. The headers can span multiple lines as long as each line is preceded with whitespace. A request can also include an entity body if separated from the headers and initial request line by a `CRLF` on a line by itself. For example, the request message includes an entity portion if the request is a `POST` from an HTML form.

The full response message looks like this:

```
<HTTP-Version> SP <Status-Code> SP <Reason-Phrase> CRLF
    *( <General-Header>
     | <Response-Header>
     | <Entity-Header> )
CRLF
[<Entity-Body>]
```

As I have stated, the response is very similar to the request. The first line of the format and the use of `<Response-Header>` are the only differences. The first line of the response consists of the `<HTTP-Version>` element, a status code, and a reason phrase. The status codes and reason phrases defined by the protocol are discussed later in this chapter.

A simple request looks like the following line:

```
"GET" SP <URI> CRLF
```

The simple response (which must be returned if the server receives a simple request) contains only the entity body (the HTML document itself, for example). The server is not permitted to return any header fields and cannot identify the media type of the data being returned.

General Message Header Fields

The `<General-Header>` fields are common to both request and response messages. They are optional headers that apply only to the individual messages themselves and not to the applications, machines, or users involved, or the data being transferred.

Date

The `Date` header specifies the date and time the message was transferred. The value must be a valid HTTP date. There are three generally accepted formats. See the HTTP/1.0 Internet-Draft document for the full definition of the HTTP date formats. The following is an example of the header field in the preferred format:

```
Date: Mon, 18 Mar 1996 10:05:00 GMT
```

The `Date` header should always be sent in full response messages in order to allow clients to properly cache data. Clients should send the `Date` field in request messages when sending requests that include an entity body (such as `PUT` and `POST` requests).

Pragma

The `Pragma` header is used for implementation-specific directives that may be of value to either the requester or the responder.

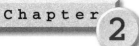

Forwarded

Used by proxy machines when the message travels between origin and destination through other machines, the `Forwarded` header is used mainly to trace the route of an HTTP message through proxy servers. It is of limited use to Visual Basic programmers except in debugging problems involving a firewall (which is a machine that, for security reasons, sits between the global Internet and an organization's local area network).

Message-ID

The `Message-ID` field is used to attempt to uniquely identify a message but not the contents of the message. The `Message-ID` is intended to be valid for a longer time period than the message itself. The value typically consists of a string that is unique at the originating machine followed by the `@` character and the fully-qualified domain name of the originating machine. Many methods are available for generating the ID, but the following is an example:

```
Message-ID: <9603181005123@myserver.com>
```

NOTE:

The `Forwarded` and `Message-ID` header fields have appeared in some texts covering HTTP but do not appear in the current version of the Internet-Draft for HTTP/1.0

HTTP Request Messages

The HTTP Request message is the mechanism used to retrieve a data resource from a server. In order to maintain backward compatibility with the previous version of the HTTP protocol, the HTTP/1.0 protocol provides for both a full request (for HTTP/1.0) and a simple request (for HTTP/0.9) style of message. If an HTTP/1.0 server receives a simple request message, it must respond with an HTTP/0.9-compatible simple response message. Likewise, an HTTP/1.0 client should always generate a full request message.

Request Methods

As mentioned in the previous section, the syntax of the full-request message includes an element named `<Method>`, which has the following rule:

```
Method = "GET" ¦ "HEAD" ¦ "POST" ¦ <extension-method>
```

The `<Method>` element indicates what operation should be performed on the data resource specified by the `<URI>` element. The acceptable methods for a given resource can change at any time. If a method is not allowed for a resource, the client receives notification of this in the `<Status-Code>` and `<Reason-Phrase>` elements of the response message.

The following sections describe the named methods. The `<extension-method>` element allows for extensions to the HTTP/1.0 protocol. Both client and server must recognize these extended methods or the server will likely return a `<Status-Code>` of 501 (not implemented).

The GET Method

As perhaps the easiest method to understand, the `GET` method merely instructs the server to return to the client the resource indicated by the `<URI>` element of the request message. If the `<URI>` points to a server application, the server returns the data output by the application, not the application itself.

Also, a `Request-Header` field named `If-Modified-Since` creates a conditional `GET` request. If the resource has been modified since the time value specified in the header, the resource is returned. If it has not been modified since that time, the server responds with a status code of 304 (not modified) and with no entity in the response message. This header field is used to perform client-side caching and to reduce network load.

The HEAD Method

The `HEAD` method is nearly identical to the `GET` method. The very important difference, however, is that the server must return only HTTP header information related to the resource. The resource (entity) itself must never be returned in response to a `HEAD` request.

The `HEAD` method allows spiders and agents operating on the Web to retrieve only necessary header information *about* a particular resource. This can be useful when checking the validity of hypertext links or checking a resource to see whether it has been modified since a particular date.

The POST Method

The `POST` method is used when sending entity information to a server. For instance, `POST` is used when filling out an HTML form on a Web page. The Submit button on the form typically performs a `POST` request and appends the form's field values to the request message as the `<Entity-Body>` element.

The `POST` method is usually performed on some type of application resource as opposed to a document resource. A successful `POST` request does not require the server to return an `<Entity-Body>` element in the response message. In some cases, the action may not produce a resource that can be identified by a URI. If no `<Entity-Body>` is returned, the server should indicate a `<Status-Code>` of 200 (okay) or 204 (no content). If the action does produce an `<Entity-Body>`, the `<Status-Code>` should return as 201 (created) and, of course, the `<Entity-Body>` should be transmitted to the client.

An entity header field called `Content-Length` is required on all `POST` messages. If it is invalid or missing, the server returns a `<Status-Code>` or 400 (bad request).

Request Message Header Fields

The full-request message can contain any number of header fields that can be used to qualify the request or to provide information about the client making the request. The syntax for the request header is

```
Request-Header = Authorization ¦ From ¦ If-Modified-Since ¦ Referer ¦ User-Agent
```

Additional field names can be added only if all applications involved in a conversation recognize them as request header fields. Otherwise, unrecognized fields are considered `Entity-Headers`.

Authorization

The `Authorization` request-header field is used by user agents that wish to present some sort of credentials to the server. The format of the field is

```
Authorization = "Authorization:" <credentials>
```

More on authentication appears in the last section of this chapter.

From

The `From` request-header field is sent by a user agent that wishes to provide the e-mail address of the person who is at the helm. The address should be a valid mailbox and should be sent only with the user's express knowledge and permission. This field should always be used by Web robots and crawlers to provide the e-mail address of the person who started the robot. The format of the field is as follows:

```
From = "From:" <mailbox>
```

If-Modified-Since

As mentioned in the section titled "The `GET` Method," the `If-Modified-Since` header field is used to produce a conditional `GET` request. The field uses this format:

```
If-Modified-Since = "If-Modified-Since:" <HTTP-date>
```

The resource is returned to the client only if the resource has been modified since the date specified in the `<HTTP-date>` element. If the `<HTTP-date>` element specifies an invalid date or if the date is later than the server's current date, the server essentially ignores the header field and returns the resource as though it is responding to a normal `GET` request.

Referer

The `Referer` header field specifies the URI of the resource from which the request message's `<URI>` element was obtained. This field must be sent only if the `<URI>` field has actually been obtained

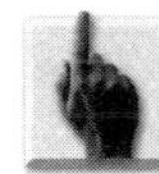

from a source that has an address. If a user has generated the `<URI>` element value (by typing in the address or selecting from a bookmark list, for example), this field must not be sent. It uses this format:

```
Referer = "Referer:" <referer-URI>
```

User-Agent

`User-Agent` contains information about the user agent that generated the request message. This request-header field is useful to the server in logging server activity and also for creating responses that are specific for the given user agent. The field is not required but should be sent as a courtesy to the server, using this format:

```
User-Agent = "User-Agent:" 1*( <product> ¦ <comment>)
```

The convention for the `<product>` element is to list the information in order of significance. Typically, this field's values include the product name of the user agent, the product version, and sometimes the operating system the user agent is running under.

HTTP Response Messages

The HTTP response message is really where the bulk of the information transmitted on the Web is contained. After the server receives a request message, the server processes it and determines what should be returned to the client.

The Status Line of HTTP Responses

The first line of the response message, as previously shown, includes the `<HTTP-version>`, `<Status-Code>`, and `<Reason-Phrase>` elements. The `<HTTP-version>` element has been discussed in previous sections of this chapter. It is identical in this usage to the previous usages.

The `<Status-Code>` element consists of a three-digit integer code. This code is meant to be used by the client application to determine the status of the response message. The first digit of the code indicates the category into which the response message falls:

- `1xx: Informational`—Reserved for future use.
- `2xx: Success`—The request succeeded.
- `3xx: Redirection`—Further action is required to complete the request.
- `4xx: Client Error`—The request is invalid or cannot be fulfilled.
- `5xx: Server Error`—The server failed to fulfill the request.

The `<Reason-Phrase>` element is a textual message intended for the user. It attempts to explain the `<Status-Code>` in language meaningful to a human reader. The client application is not required to display the `<Reason-Phrase>` element, but typical user agents do anyway.

Table 2.3 lists the possible `<Status-Code>` values and typical corresponding `<Reason-Phrase>` values.

Table 2.3. Response message status codes and reason phrases.

Status Code	*Reason Phrase*
200	OK
201	Created
202	Accepted
204	No content
301	Moved permanently
302	Moved temporarily
304	Not modified
400	Bad request
401	Unauthorized
403	Forbidden
404	Not found
500	Internal server error
501	Not implemented
502	Bad gateway
503	Service unavailable

Response Message Header Fields

Just as the request message can send header fields that qualify or provide additional information about the request being submitted, the HTTP protocol provides the opportunity for the response message to send the client additional information about the response. If new header fields are added, they must either accompany a change in the HTTP protocol version, or all parties in a conversation must recognize them as response header fields.

The syntax of the `<Response-Header>` element is

```
Response-Header = Location ¦ Server ¦ WWW-Authenticate
```

Location

If the `<Response-Header>` contains a `Location` element, defined as

```
Location = "Location:" <absoluteURI>
```

this defines an absolute address that the client should be redirected to. It is used in cases where the `<Status-Code>` is of the `3xx` variety (indicating redirection), such as when a resource has moved to a new location. The `<Entity-Body>` element of the response message typically includes a short note explaining the redirection and offering a hyperlink to the URI specified in the `Location` field's value.

Server

The `Server` header field is the response message's equivalent to the request message's `User-Agent` header field. It provides information to the client about the server application and version, using the format:

```
Server = "Server:" 1*(<product> ¦ <comment>)
```

As with the `User-Agent` header field, the `Server` field's values are listed in order of their significance in identifying the server software.

WWW-Authenticate

If the `<Status-Code>` in the response message is 401 (unauthorized), the `WWW-Authenticate` header field must be included in the message. This response message basically issues an authentication challenge to the user agent. The user agent must then provide authentication information to the server. The `WWW-Authenticate` header uses the format:

```
WWW-Authenticate = "WWW-Authenticate:" 1#<challenge>
```

The issue of authentication is taken up in the final section of this chapter, "Authentication Through HTTP."

The Entity Portion of HTTP Messages

The bulk of response messages and a few types of request messages include an `<Entity-Body>` element and can also include an `<Entity-Header>` element. In a response message, the `<Entity-Body>` portion is the actual data resource that is being transferred. For instance, if the request message `GET //myserver.com/home.html HTTP/1.0` is received by a server, the entity portion of the response message will be the file `home.html` located in the Web server's root directory.

In a request message, the `<Entity-Body>` element is used for `POST`ing information to a Web server. This is used typically for submitting information entered into an HTML form by a human user or for queries being performed by some automated user-agent application.

The remainder of this section discusses the `<Entity-Header>` element.

Entity Header Fields

The <Entity-Header> element's fields provide additional information about the <Entity-Body> or, if the <Entity-Body> is not present (as in the case of HEAD requests), about the resource requested. These headers are optional. If sent <Entity-Header> element fields are returned, they generally follow the <Response-Header> fields.

The following line shows the format for the <Entity-Header> element:

```
Entity-Header = Allow ¦ Content-Encoding ¦ Content-Length ¦ Content-Type ¦
                Expires ¦ Last-Modified ¦ <extension-header>
```

The <extension-header> element provides for the addition of new <Entity-Header> element fields without changing the entire protocol. However, if a user agent does not recognize an <Entity-Header> element field it is (and should be) ignored.

Allow

The Allow field is used to indicate which methods are supported by the resource requested in the request message. The format of the header field is

```
Allow = "Allow:" 1#method
```

An example is Allow: GET, HEAD. This header field is used to inform the user agent of which methods are valid for the resource being requested. However, it does not specify which methods are implemented by the server. Also, the use of this field does not prevent the user agent from attempting to perform other methods upon the resource. Nevertheless, it is good practice to follow the advice of this header field.

Content-Type, Content-Encoding, and Content-Length

These header fields indicate the type of resource being returned, how it is encoded, and the size of the <Entity-Body> being returned. The following lines show the respective formats for these headers:

```
Content-Type = "Content-Type:" <media-type>
Content-Encoding = "Content-Encoding:" <content-coding>
Content-Length = "Content-Length:" 1*DIGIT
```

The Content-Type header indicates the media type used for the <Entity-Body> element. It essentially documents the format of the entity being transferred. The typical HTML document is sent with a Content-Type of text/html. If the request method is HEAD, the Content-Type represents the media type that would be returned if the request is a GET.

The Content-Type field can be used by the user agent to determine how to present the resource to the user. The content types are used by Web browsers when setting up helper applications that are external applications used to display specific file types (also known as media types). For instance, a Content-Type of audio/basic represents a sound file that the typical Web browser has to present to the user through an external application.

The `Content-Encoding` field is a modifier to the `Content-Type` header and indicates whether and how a resource has been encoded before transmission. This is used when a resource has been compressed, for example. The user agent must use the encoding information in order to decode the data received before presenting it to the human user.

The `Content-Length` indicates the size of the `<Entity-Body>` element. It is used in both request and response messages and is, in fact, required in request messages. The size is the number of octets sent to the recipient. If the message is a response to a `HEAD` request, the `Content-Length` field indicates the size that would have been returned by a response to a `GET` request on the same resource.

Expires

As the name of this header field indicates, the `Expires` entity header indicates the date after which the entity should be considered expired or invalid. This can be returned by applications that are generating real-time data, for example, to indicate the date (and time) after which the entity should be considered as old news. Caches should not retain the entity after the date specified.

The presence of an `Expires` header does not mean that the resource will change or no longer exist after the value specified, but simply that it will be "stale" (to use the wording from the Internet-Draft). If the value specified is `0` or is an invalid HTTP date, the resource should be considered as immediately expired and should not be cached in any way.

The format for the `Expires` header is

```
Expires = "Expires:" <HTTP-date>
```

Last-Modified

The `Last-Modified` header field indicates the date that the server believes the resource was last changed. The value is interpreted differently depending on the nature of the resource being transferred. This header can be used to determine whether a new copy of a resource should be retrieved or if the user should be notified that the resource has been changed. For a file resource, it is most likely to be the date that the file was last saved. For a database resource, this field can be used to indicate the date a record was last updated. The possibilities are endless.

The format for the `Last-Modified` header is

```
Last-Modified = "Last-Modified:" <HTTP-date>
```

When you write server-side applications, it is important to think about how this field should be used if the resource is time-sensitive. If you're writing a user-agent application, take care when attempting to interpret this field's value.

Authentication Through HTTP

The HTTP/1.0 protocol provides a simple method for user authentication. This can be used to provide subscription-based services or to limit access to data and resources to specific individuals. The mechanism is a challenge-response cycle in which the server issues a challenge to the user agent and the user agent responds with the proper authentication information.

When a user agent attempts to access a resource that is in a protected space, the server responds with a message with a `<Status-Code>` of 401 (Unauthorized) and a `WWW-Authenticate` response header field. The `WWW-Authenticate` header will contain a `<realm>` element, which can be displayed to the user in order to obtain a user-ID and password. After the user agent determines the user-ID and password to be used, it issues another request message to the server. This time the request includes an `Authorization` request header field. The value used for the field is a base64 encoded string. The string contains the user-ID and password separated by a colon. Borrowing the example from the HTTP/1.0 Internet-Draft, if the user-ID is "Aladdin" and the password is "open sesame," the `Authorization` header would be the following string:

```
Authorization: Basic QWxhZGRpbjpvcGVuIHNlc2FtZQ==
```

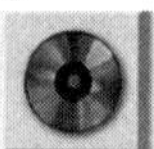

NOTE:

Information on base64 encoding can be found in the Internet Request-For-Comments (RFC) 1521 (this is included on the CD-ROM).

If the server determines that either the user-ID or password sent with the request is invalid, it responds with a `<Status-Code>` of 403 (forbidden). The user agent can then prompt the user to re-enter the credentials. However, this cycle should not be allowed to repeat indefinitely.

CAUTION:

This HTTP authentication method is a *clear text* method. No encryption is performed on the user-ID and password that is transmitted. Care must be taken by the user not to use sensitive passwords for this authentication method. If any programs you write allow access to sites requiring authentication, you may wish to inform the user through some sort of warning message that the passwords they enter will be sent unencrypted.

Summary

This chapter probably made for dry reading. However, it will serve as a valuable reference throughout the remainder of this book. Most of the applications we'll delve into use HTTP messaging in one form or another. In some of those chapters, you'll expand on some of the topics covered here. In others, you'll simply refer back to this chapter to refresh your memory of this fascinating topic.

If you'd like to delve deeper into the HTTP protocol, I encourage you to follow the work of the HTTP Working Group. Relevant links can be found in Appendix D, "Bibliography and Cool Web Sites."

Chapter 3

Interfacing to the Web with DDE and OLE

- Manipulating Netscape Navigator Using DDE
- Grabbing the URL and Page Name from Netscape Using DDE
- Using OLE Automation to Control Netscape Navigator

Much like other Windows-based applications, most Web browsers support OLE automation and DDE control. In this chapter, we go through the methods and syntax of controlling the Netscape Web browser from a Visual Basic program using these technologies. The most typical uses for this are to retrieve the current URL from the browser or to cause the browser to load a specific URL.

This chapter assumes you have some knowledge of both DDE and OLE Automation. If you need a refresher, there are many introductory texts that go into detail on these topics. Likewise, the VB help file provides a good introduction to both topics.

Manipulating Netscape Navigator Using DDE

The complete documentation (as of March 22, 1995) of Netscape's DDE Implementation can be found at `http://home.netscape.com/newsref/std/ddeapi.html`. In the following sections, I describe and outline the DDE topics (which are simply names for data elements available via DDE) exposed by Netscape Navigator.

Netscape can act as both a DDE client and a server, depending on which topics are used. It is important to remember that if you use any of the topics that make use of Netscape as the *client*, your application needs to register itself as a DDE server. The service name used for Netscape Navigator during DDE conversations is `NETSCAPE`.

WWW_Activate

The `WWW_Activate` topic maximizes Netscape if it is minimized, or it brings a Netscape window to the front of all other applications and gives it focus.

WWW_Alert

In this topic, Netscape acts as the client. Netscape passes to the server application three parameters, `qcsMessage`, `dwType`, and `dwButtons`:

- **`qcsMessage`**: The text message that should be displayed to the user.
- **`dwType`**: The type of alert box that should be displayed. The values and types are as follows:

  `0x0` Error Alert Dialog
  `0x1` Warning Alert Dialog
  `0x2` Question Alert Dialog
  `0x3` Status Alert Dialog

- **`dwButtons`**: A flag variable indicating which buttons should be contained in the alert dialog box; these are the valid values and types:

  `0x0` OK button only
  `0x1` OK and Cancel buttons
  `0x2` Yes/No buttons
  `0x3` Yes/No/Cancel buttons

The value returned by `WWW_Alert` is held in `dwAnswer`; the valid responses are:

`0x0` Error : the alert box could not be displayed
`0x1` The OK button was pressed
`0x2` The Cancel button was pressed
`0x3` The No button was pressed
`0x4` The Yes button was pressed

WWW_BeginProgress

In the `WWW_BeginProgress` topic, Netscape acts as the client. The two arguments, `dwWindowID`, the ID of the Netscape window that is loading a document, and `qcsInitialMessage`, which is a message that the DDE server displays to indicate that Netscape has begun to load the document.

When a DDE application provides Netscape with a DDE server name in the `WWW_OpenURL` topic, Netscape sends progress indicators to that DDE server.

This topic returns the ID of the window that replies with progress topics that are used in other progress topics that will be sent to the DDE server. If `WWW_BeginProgress` returns `0X0`, the DDE server no longer accepts other progress topics from Netscape

WWW_CancelProgress

The single argument to `WWW_CancelProgress` topic is the `Transaction ID`. The `Transaction ID` is the return value from the `WWW_BeginProgress` topic. The `WWW_CancelProgress` topic tells Netscape to cancel the download for that specific `Transaction ID`.

WWW_EndProgress

`WWW_EndProgress` notifies the DDE server that Netscape is finished loading a URL. This does not necessarily mean that Netscape has completely loaded the URL, rather that Netscape has quit trying to load the URL either due to an error or that the URL has been completely loaded.

WWW_Exit

WWW_Exit causes Netscape to attempt to exit. Netscape exits unless an OLE Automation application is blocking Netscape from exiting. Netscape windows that aren't involved in the OLE operation will close, however. Any argument passed to the WWW_Exit topic is not ignored.

WWW_GetWindowInfo

The argument to WWW_GetWindowInfo is the Netscape window ID or 0xFFFFFFFF (that's eight "efs") that specifies the last active Netscape window. This returns the URL and the title of the page that is currently loaded in the Netscape window.

WWW_ListWindows

WWW_ListWindows returns an array of double length words holding the window IDs. The array is terminated by the null character (0x0). If a Netscape window is minimized, it is not reported as a window. Any argument provided to the WWW_ListWindows topic is ignored.

WWW_MakingProgress

In this topic, Netscape passes the following parameters to the DDE server application:

- dwTransactionID: The ID from the initial call to WWW_BeginProgress.
- qcsMessage: Message from Netscape reporting on the progress of loading the current URL.
- DWProgress: A double word that holds a value between 0x0 (no progress) and the maximum value, which is set by using the WWW_SetProgressRange topic.

The DDE server application should return a Boolean value: True if Netscape should stop loading that URL, False otherwise.

WWW_OpenURL

The WWW_OpenURL is called as both a client and a server topic between Netscape and the other DDE-enabled application. When Netscape acts as the server, the following are the arguments sent by the client application:

- The URL Netscape should attempt to load.
- The filename to which Netscape should save the URL. This is an optional argument, and if not specified, the URL isn't saved to a file.

- The Netscape window ID that should display the loaded URL. If the value is `0x0`, Netscape creates a new window for the document. If the value is `0xFFFFFFFF`, Netscape uses the last active browser window or creates a new one if a browser window doesn't already exist.
- A flag variable containing one of the following values:

  `0x1` Ignore the cached documents when loading the URL.

  `0x2` Ignore the cached images when loading the URL.

  `0x4` Load the URL in the background.

- The data that should be posted to the form via the HTTP `POST` method. Again, this is an optional argument, and if not specified, no data is sent.
- The MIME type of the data to be posted if any.
- The name of the DDE server to which Netscape should send progress updates. See the earlier discussion of `WWW_BeginProgress` for the usage of this argument.

Netscape returns the window ID of the Netscape window that is servicing the request to open the URL. A return value of `0x0` indicates failure; `0xFFFFFFFF` indicates that the data loaded is of a MIME type that Netscape cannot display.

Netscape, acting as a client, can also use `WWW_OpenURL` to request that a DDE application load a URL. The following are the arguments sent from the Netscape window to the DDE application:

- The URL to load.
- The file to which the URL should be saved. This is an optional argument; if it isn't specified, the URL doesn't need to be saved to a file.
- The Netscape window ID that is making the request.
- The form data to be posted, if any.
- The MIME type of the form data to be posted.
- The name of the DDE application that should be notified with progress updates.

The DDE application should return `0x0` if the operation failed, `0xFFFFFFFF` if the URL data was not accepted by the DDE application, and any other value to indicate to Netscape that the operation has been successful.

WWW_ParseAnchor

In the `WWW_ParseAnchor` topic, the absolute URL and relative URL is sent to Netscape, which acts as the DDE server. Then Netscape returns the combined URL to the DDE client application.

WWW_QueryURLFile

Here, Netscape acts as the DDE server. The client application passes Netscape a path and filename that might have been loaded by Netscape during that session. Netscape returns the URL of that file if it was loaded during that session. If the file was not loaded, the topic fails.

WWW_QueryViewer

In `WWW_QueryViewer`, Netscape sends the URL that it is currently loading and the MIME content type of the URL. The DDE server application should return to Netscape the fully qualified path and filename to which Netscape should save the file.

WWW_RegisterProtocol

`WWW_RegisterProtocol` is used by the DDE client application to tell Netscape that it will handle URLs of a certain protocol type. The first argument passed is the DDE server that will be handling the URL for the specified protocol. The second argument is the protocol to be handled. Netscape returns a Boolean value indicating success or failure of registration. The topic fails if a DDE server is currently registered to handle that protocol.

Whenever Netscape encounters a URL using the protocol specified, it acts as a DDE client and uses the `WWW_OpenURL` topic to request that the registered server load the URL.

WWW_RegisterURLEcho

This topic from the DDE client application notifies Netscape that it should send `WWW_URLEcho` topics when they occur. The single argument to Netscape is the name of the DDE server application that will be notified.

WWW_RegisterViewer

`WWW_RegisterViewer` allows a DDE application to register itself with Netscape to receive data of a specified MIME type.

The DDE application sends Netscape the following arguments:

- The DDE server to receive the specified MIME type.
- The MIME type that the DDE server wants to handle.
- A flag containing one of the following values:

  `0x1` Indicates that the data received should be saved to a temporary file, and then the routine `ShellExecute()` should be called.

`0x2`	Finds the filename to use for storing the data received by using the `WWW_QueryViewer` topic.
`0x4`	Saves the data received to a temporary file, and then calls the `WWW_ViewDocFile` topic.
`0x8`	`WWW_ViewDocData¦WWW_ViewDocCache…` (Undefined as yet.)

Netscape either returns a Boolean `True` or `False`: `True` indicates that the registration process has completed successfully. `False` means that there is already another DDE server application registered to receive that MIME type.

WWW_RegisterWindowChange

In `WWW_RegisterWindowChange`, the DDE application sends two arguments to Netscape: first, the name of the DDE server that wants to be informed of Netscape window changes and second, the Netscape window ID that will be "watched" for changes.

Netscape returns a double word holding the window ID of the Netscape window that informs the DDE application of changes. This is usually the same as the window ID that is passed as the second argument to the topic.

WWW_SetProgressRange

In the `WWW_SetProgressRange` topic, Netscape sends to the DDE application two arguments:

- The transaction ID from the original call to the `WWW_BeginProgress` topic.
- A double word holding the value of the maximum value of progress messages. This maximum can be used with progress updates to calculate a percent completed number or progress bar.

The DDE application doesn't need to furnish Netscape with a return value.

WWW_ShowFile

In the `WWW_ShowFile` topic, the DDE application sends to Netscape the following arguments:

- The filename Netscape should attempt to load.
- The MIME type of the file to be loaded.
- The window ID of Netscape—a value of `0xFFFFFFFF` indicates that Netscape should use the most recently active Netscape window; a value of `0x0` indicates that Netscape should open a new window to display the file.
- The URL of the file—this allows Netscape to reload the file if necessary.

Netscape returns the window ID of the Netscape window that is loading the file. If `0x0` is returned, this indicates that the call to the `ShowFile` topic failed. If `0xFFFFFFFF` is returned by Netscape, the file is not of a MIME type that Netscape can display.

WWW_UnRegisterProtocol

In `WWW_UnRegisterProtocol`, the DDE application passes to Netscape the name of the server application that no longer wants to handle a protocol, and the second parameter is the protocol type. Netscape returns a Boolean `True` if the topic has been successful; `False` otherwise.

WWW_UnRegisterURLEcho

With `WWW_UnRegisterURLEcho`, the DDE application passes to Netscape the name of the server application that no longer wants to receive `WWW_URLEcho` topic notifications from Netscape. There are no return arguments.

WWW_UnRegisterViewer

In `WWW_UnRegisterViewer`, the DDE application sends to Netscape the name of the server that should be unregistered for a given MIME type. The second argument is that MIME type. Netscape returns a Boolean value: `True`, if the operation has been successful; `False` otherwise.

WWW_UnRegisterWindowChange

The DDE application sends to Netscape, the server that doesn't want `WWW_WindowChange` topics sent to it and the window ID of the Netscape window that should no longer be monitored.

Netscape replies with Boolean `True` if the topic has been successful; `False` otherwise.

WWW_URLEcho

Each time Netscape loads a URL, it sends `WWW_URLEcho` to all DDE server applications that are registered via `WWW_RegisterURLEcho`.

Netscape sends the following arguments:

- The URL that Netscape has just tried to load.
- The MIME type of that URL.
- The window ID of the Netscape window.
- The referring URL which is the URL that contains an anchor and led to this current URL.

WWW_Version

WWW_Version allows the DDE application to query Netscape about its version. Any argument the DDE application sends to Netscape is ignored. Netscape replies with a double word holding the version of the API currently in use by Netscape.

WWW_ViewDocFile

In WWW_ViewDocFile, Netscape sends to the DDE application the following arguments:

- The filename of the viewer that is registered in the WWW_RegisterViewer topic.
- The URL to view.
- The MIME type of the filename in the first argument.
- The window ID of the Netscape window that loaded the URL.

WWW_WindowChange

WWW_WindowChange can treat Netscape as both a DDE client and a DDE server. When Netscape acts as the client, Netscape sends to the DDE server application the following arguments:

- The window ID of the Netscape window that has changed.
- A flag variable holding one of the following values:

0x00000001	The Netscape window has changed position or size, or both.
0x00000002	The Netscape window has been maximized.
0x00000004	The Netscape window has been normalized.
0x00000008	The Netscape window has been minimized.
0x00000010	The Netscape window has been closed.
0x00010000	The Netscape window is attempting to exit.

- The X position of the Netscape window as a double word.
- The Y position of the Netscape window as a double word.
- The new width of the Netscape window as a double word.
- The new height of the Netscape window as a double word.

When Netscape acts as the server application, the DDE client can request the window to do any of the following: move, resize, minimize, maximize, or close.

The arguments to Netscape using the WWW_WindowChange topic are

- The Netscape window ID to be changed.

- A flag value holding one of the following:

`0x00000001`	Netscape should change position to the values contained in following arguments.
`0x00000002`	The Netscape window should maximize.
`0x00000004`	The Netscape window should normalize.
`0x00000008`	The Netscape window should minimize.
`0x00000010`	The Netscape window should close.

The following arguments must be specified if the operation on the Netscape window is to reposition or resize the window:

- The new X position for the Netscape window.
- The new Y position for the Netscape window.
- The new width of the Netscape window.
- The new height of the Netscape window.

Grabbing the URL and Page Name from Netscape Using DDE

An example of using DDE would be to retrieve the currently loaded URL and page name from Netscape into a textbox. You can accomplish this by the following sample application.

Start with a plain form and add a textbox and a command button, as shown in Figure 3.1.

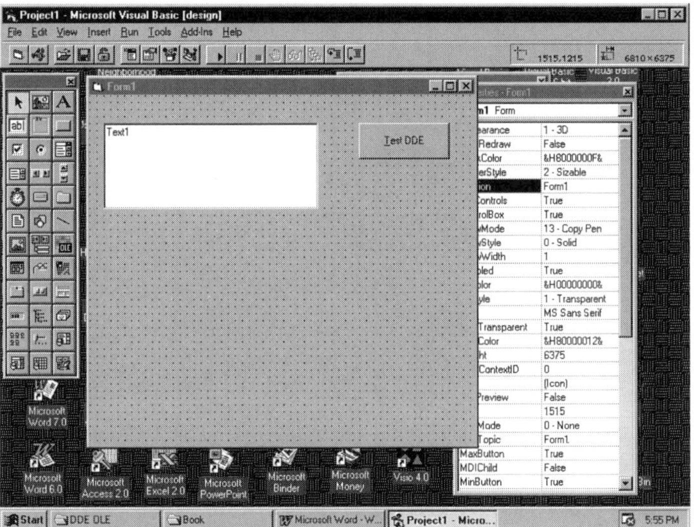

Figure 3.1.
Design-time view of the Netscape-DDE test application.

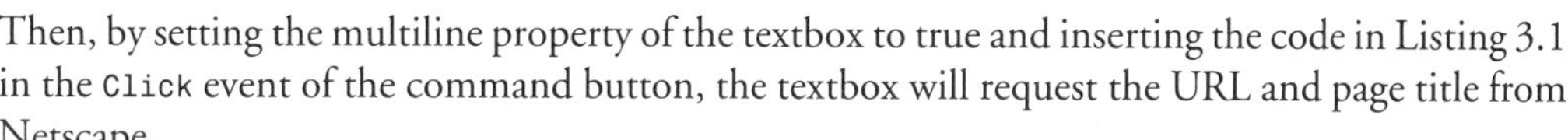

Then, by setting the multiline property of the textbox to true and inserting the code in Listing 3.1 in the `Click` event of the command button, the textbox will request the URL and page title from Netscape.

Listing 3.1. The command button's **Click** event.

```
Text1.LinkTopic = "NETSCAPE¦WWW_GetWindowInfo"
Text1.LinkItem = &HFFFFFFFF
Text1.LinkMode = 2
Text1.LinkRequest
```

Figure 3.2 shows what is displayed when Netscape has loaded the Netscape home page and the command button of the Visual Basic application has been pressed.

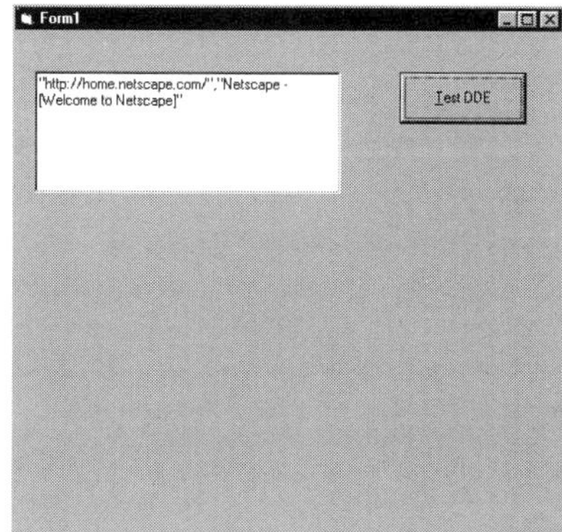

Figure 3.2.
Runtime view of the Netscape-DDE test application.

Although it is possible to write Visual Basic applications that control Netscape using DDE, the preferred method is using OLE Automation. The remainder of this chapter looks into using OLE Automation to add control of Netscape to your applications.

Using OLE Automation to Control Netscape Navigator

In the beginning, there was DDE—and only DDE—for Windows interprocess communication. Its successor, OLE Automation, is a much nicer solution to this problem of getting applications to work cooperatively.

Exposing Netscape in Visual Basic 4.0

To get a look at the methods exposed by Netscape, select Tools | References, click on Browse, and then select the `NETSCAPE.TLB` file in the Netscape Program directory.

Then open the Object Browser and select Netscape from the drop-down combobox. The classes and modules for Netscape then appear, as shown in Figure 3.3.

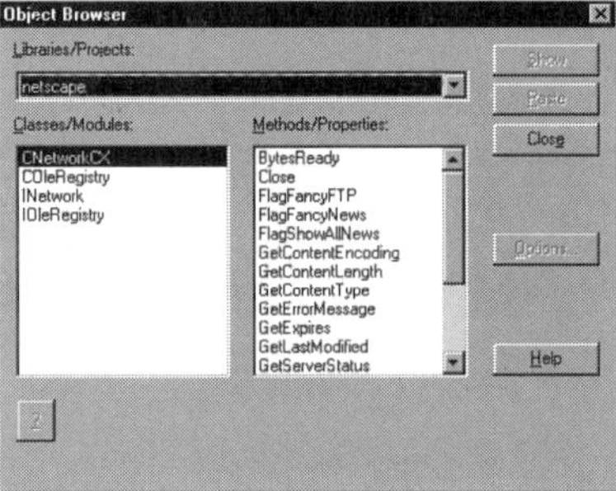

Figure 3.3.
Netscape's TLB file as viewed by the Object Browser.

Notice that the following items appear in the Classes/Modules box of the Object Browser: `CNetworkCX`, `COleRegistry`, `INetwork`, and `IOleRegistry`.

Now, if you look in the documentation, available at `http://home.mcom.com/newsref/std/oleapi.html`, the documented classes are `Network.1` and `Registry.1`.

NOTE:

Confused yet? For some reason, the classes exposed in the `NETSCAPE.TLB` file do not line up with the documentation. The classes in the documentation work fine, so ignore the information in the Object Browser and go with what the documentation says.

A possible reason for this may be a syntax change between Netscape 1.1 and Personal Netscape 2.01. The documentation was written for 1.1; the author has 2.01.

So, stick with what's documented, and everything should work just fine.

The OLE-Exposed Classes and Functions of Netscape

The two classes Netscape exposes via OLE are `Netscape.Network.1` and `Netscape.Registry.1`. The Network grouping of methods provides foreign applications the ability to use the functionality of

Netscape from within that application. The Registry grouping of functions allows non-Netscape programs to register themselves as Netscape plug-ins to handle specific MIME types.

The Methods of the `Netscape.Network.1` Class

This section describes the methods exposed by the `Netscape.Network.1` class.

`BytesReady()`

The `BytesReady()` function is passed no arguments. Netscape returns a short integer containing the number of bytes that are available to be read from Netscape using the `Read()` function.

`Close()`

The `Close()` function, which is passed with no arguments and returns nothing, disconnects any active Netscape connections and resets the `Netscape.Network.1` object.

This function is used either to terminate an active download or to indicate when the application is finished with the load from a previous call to the `Open()` function.

`GetConnectEncoding()`

`GetConnectEncoding()` passes no arguments and returns a string containing the MIME type of the currently loaded or loading document. This function should only be called if `Open()` is successful.

`GetContentLength()`

`GetContentLength()` returns the total length of the currently loaded document in bytes as a long integer. This function should only be called if `Open()` is successful.

`GetContentType()`

`GetContentType()` returns the MIME type of the currently loaded document as a string. This function should only be called if `Open()` is successful.

`GetErrorMessage()`

If a call to `GetStatus()` indicates that an error has occurred, use `GetErrorMessage()` to retrieve the Netscape-generated error message. The error message is returned as a string.

GetExpires()

The return value of `GetExpires()` is the time and date of when the data received by the current load is no longer considered valid.

GetFlagFancyFTP()

A call to `GetFlagFancyFTP()` returns a Boolean value: `True` if FTP output contains the additional listing information (file size, file type, last modified date, and so forth), `False` otherwise.

GetFlagFancyNews()

This function returns a Boolean value: `True` if Netscape displays only newsgroups with descriptions, `False` to display all newsgroups.

GetFlagShowAllNews()

`GetFlagShowAllNews()` returns a Boolean value: `True` to list all news articles, `False` to list only unread articles.

GetLastModified()

A call to `GetLastModified()` returns a string containing the time and date that the current load was last modified.

GetPassword()

`GetPassword()` returns a string—the currently set password from a previous call to `SetPassword()`. A null string is returned if no password has been specified.

GetServerStatus()

If a server error occurs, which can be detected by a call to `GetStatus()`, use `GetServerStatus()` to retrieve the error code reported by the server.

The function call returns the error code from the server as a short integer. The values of these error codes are dependent on the protocol that is being used.

`GetStatus()`

This function returns the status of the current load as a long integer. The `GetStatus()` function is only useable between the time of the call to `Open()` and the call to `Close()`.

The return value is a long integer that contains a masked variable. The following are the individual components that make up the masked values and their respective meanings:

`0x0000`	Everything is normal.
`0x0001`	Netscape has requested a user name.
`0x0002`	Netscape has requested a user password.
`0x0100`	Netscape is busy; the operation can be retried.
`0x0200`	The server has reported an error; make a call to `GetServerStatus()` for the error code.
`0x0400`	An internal load error has occurred; the attempted contact to the server failed.
`0x0800`	Netscape has raised an internal error; use a call to `GetErrorMessage()` for the details.

`GetUserName()`

A call to `GetUserName()` returns the currently set user name as a string. Unless this value has been set by a call to `SetUsername()`, this function returns the null string.

`IsFinished()`

This function returns a Boolean value: `True` if the load is complete, `False` otherwise.

`Open()`

The `Open()` method causes Netscape to attempt to open an URL. The parameters passed to the function are as follows:

- The URL to load.
- The HTTP method to retrieve the URL with these valid values:

`0x0`	GET
`0x1`	POST
`0x2`	HEAD

- The data to post to the application—this value is ignored if `POST` is not the selected method in argument two.

- The size of the data to be posted—again, this argument is ignored if `POST` is not the selected method.
- The additional headers to be posted if the HTTP method being used is `POST`. The default header is `Content-type: application/x-www-form-urlencoded`.

The function call returns a Boolean `True` if the operation has been successful; `False` otherwise.

Read()

`Read()` is used to collect the data retrieved by Netscape. The arguments to the `Read()` function are

- The buffer to hold the information read.
- The maximum amount of information (in bytes) to hold in the buffer.

The `Read()` function returns a short integer containing the amount of data in bytes that was read from Netscape.

Resolve()

This function builds a fully qualified URL from the base and relative URLs. The following are the arguments to the `Resolve()` function:

- The base URL.
- The relative URL.

The function returns a string containing the fully qualified URL.

SetFlagFancyFTP()

This function takes a single Boolean argument. `True` informs Netscape that the FTP file listings contain the extra FTP information; `False` indicates that only the filenames are listed.

SetFlagFancyNews()

The `SetFlagFancyNews()` function takes a single Boolean argument. `True` tells Netscape that it should include the newsgroup descriptions. `False` leaves them out.

SetFlagShowAllNews()

`SetFlagShowAllNews()` takes a single Boolean argument. `True` tells Netscape to display both read and unread news articles; `False` makes Netscape display only the unread articles.

`SetPassword()`

The `SetPassword()` function takes a single string argument. This password value is used by Netscape for any loads that require user name/password authentication.

`SetUsername()`

`SetUsername()` sets the user name used for authentication. The argument is passed to the function as a string.

The Methods of the **Netscape.Registry.1** Class

This section discusses the methods for the Registry class. This class performs functions similar to the DDE topics `WWW_RegisterViewer` and `WWW_RegisterProtocol`.

`RegisterViewer()`

The `RegisterViewer()` method is used by an OLE Automation Server to notify Netscape that an external viewer will be handling certain MIME types. The arguments to this function include the following:

- The MIME type to be handled.
- The name of the OLE Automation Server that will handle this MIME type.

The function returns a Boolean `True` if the registration has been successful; it returns `False` if a server already is registered for that MIME type.

`RegisterProtocol()`

The `RegisterProtocol()` function acts like the `RegisterViewer()` function. The one difference is that `RegisterProtocol()` registers an OLE server to handle a specific protocol instead of a MIME type. The arguments to the `RegisterProtocol()` function are

- The protocol type (news, gopher, or other type).
- The name of the OLE automation server that will handle this protocol.

Summary

By using OLE or DDE, you can add control of the user's browser into your Visual Basic application. The potential applications are as wide open as the Web itself. You could easily use OLE to use a Visual Basic program to monitor the sites a user visits during the browsing session or to ensure that the person using the browser doesn't visit specified URLs. (Could you imagine if every boss had a list of the pages his or her employees visited?)

What's Next?

From here, we move on to harnessing the power of the Internet by using custom controls. In Chapter 4, "Using Web Browser Custom Controls," you learn about third-party tools that enable your Visual Basic application to harness the power of the Internet. Then, in Chapter 5, "Retrieving Information from the Web," we look into using the `dsSocket` control to retrieve Web content. In later chapters, you'll use those controls to integrate the content of the Web into our own applications.

Chapter 4

Using Web Browser Custom Controls

- Sax Webster Control
- Coding a Simple Application with the Webster Control
- Microsoft HTML Control
- Comparing the ICP and the Sax Webster HTML Controls
- Crescent CIHTML Control

If the concept of spending hours poring over proposed standards, working Internet drafts, and trying to adhere to the HTTP protocol specification aren't your ideas of a good time, but you still want to use the resources of the World Wide Web in your Visual Basic application, help is now available. Since version 1.0 of Visual Basic, custom controls have been available for databases, and with the advent of OLE objects and Visual Basic 4.0, easy-to-use custom controls for the Web are here.

In this chapter I'll go over the functionality of each tool, and give some examples of their uses.

Sax Webster Control

When I began searching for HTML-compatible browser controls, the first one I found was the Webster control. Originally written by an independent developer, the Webster control has since been bought and enhanced by Sax Software. A demo version of the control can be found at their Web site (`http://www.saxsoft.com`).

http://www.saxsoft.com

The Sax Webster control abstracts away the HTTP protocol, leaving the programmer with enough properties, events, and methods to incorporate a web browser into an application. For example, to set the browser's default home page, change the value of the `HomePage` property to the desired URL. To load a specific URL, change the value of the `PageURL` property to the URL. The loading and displaying of the page are taken care of by the Webster control.

The Webster manual claims that the control is a complete WWW browser in a single custom control. After I installed the software, I started a new project in Visual Basic, added the custom control to the toolbox, and dragged the Webster control onto the form. When I ran the application and clicked the Webster control's Home Page (House) icon, up came Sax's WWW page in the browser window, as shown in Figure 4.1. As advertised, a complete Web browser in a single control!

The fun begins when you modify the values of the Webster control. By adding a status bar, a button bar, a few textboxes and comboboxes, a proficient programmer can produce a full-featured browser with a minimal of coding effort.

The applications for this tool are as limitless as the World Wide Web itself. These are a few examples: up-to-date online help via your companies Web site, Intranet access using a custom browser, or offline reading of HTML files. This section provides an overview of the properties, methods, and events available with the Webster control and then develops a custom browser using the control.

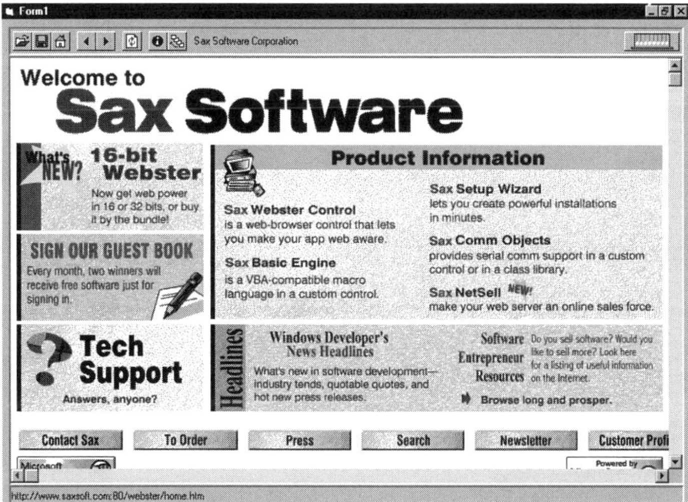

Figure 4.1.
The Sax Webster Browser displaying the Sax home page.

Webster Properties, Methods, and Events

The following are some properties and methods essential to the Webster control and its function. Only the major properties, methods, and events are covered here. In addition to these properties, methods, and events are most of the standard Visual Basic control properties, as well as properties to control the fonts of the headings, URLs, menus, and so on. The help file provided with the Webster control gives a complete listing of the properties, methods, and events.

`PageURL` Property

Assigning a new value to this string property is equivalent to entering a URL in a browser's GoTo window and hitting Enter. Webster will search for the URL and try to load it. The control will display either the Web page (if located) or an appropriate error code if the URL could not be loaded.

`HomePage` Property

The `HomePage` property is a string that sets the URL that is loaded when the user clicks on the House icon of the Webster control's default toolbar. The default is `http://www.saxsoft.com` (the Sax home page).

`DownloadDir` Property

The `DownloadDir` property specifies a valid path name where files will be placed when the user elects to save them locally. It can be specified by users when they save a file, or it can be set by the program.

AuthenticName and AuthenticPassword Properties

Some sites require a basic user name/password combination to gain access. The AuthenticName and AuthenticPassword properties can be set for that authentication process.

BrowserName Property

The BrowserName property sets the string that will be placed in the HTTP request message's User-Agent field whenever the Webster control accesses a Web resource. As noted in Chapter 2, "HTTP: How to Speak on the Web," this field identifies the browser to the HTTP server. It can be used for logging purposes or for providing Web site customization based on the browser that is being used to access the Web site.

Enabled Property

This property is similar to the standard Visual Basic Enabled property. When Enabled is set to false, the Webster control does not respond to user-driven events, such as clicking on the toolbar.

IgnoreBaseInFile Property

Setting the IgnoreBaseInFile to False instructs the browser to ignore the <BASE> tags in HTML files. The <BASE> tag provides relative path resolution for links within an HTML file that use relative paths. If your server is named www.myserver.com and you have a link coded as `<A HREF="/path1/document.htm">` this would usually generate a URL of http://www.myserver.com/path1/document.htm. By specifying a <BASE> tag somewhere within the HTML file that contains this link, you can modify the URL that is generated. For example, if you have, in the same document as the above <A HREF> tag, a <BASE="/foo">, the URL generated would be http://www.myserver.com/foo/path1/document.htm (note the addition of /foo to the URL).

The IgnoreBaseInFile property, then, allows the user to copy an entire Web site to disk and browse the site locally without worry of a <BASE> tag referring to a URL on the Internet.

FromName Property

The FromName property corresponds to the HTTP From field. The From request message field, as defined in the HTTP specification, provides the e-mail address of the person using the Web browser. It is another logging mechanism similar to the User Agent field but is rarely used due to privacy concerns.

`ImageCacheKB` Property

This sets the amount of memory the application can use for storing inline images. The larger the number is, the more memory your application takes, but the user viewing a cached page does not have to wait for the images to be retrieved from the remote site.

`LoadImages` Property

The `LoadImages` Boolean value determines whether the Webster control automatically loads inline images embedded within the Web pages it's loading.

`LoadStatus` Property

The `LoadStatus` property is a read-only property which provides the current status of the browser. The possible values are shown in Table 4.1.

Table 4.1. The possible values of `LoadStatus`.

Setting	*Description*
0	Page load is complete
1	Connecting to host
2	Connected, waiting
3	Page text is loading
4	Images are loading
5	Load failure
6	Unknown—URL failed to load

`MaxPageLoads` Property

The value of the `MaxPageLoads` property determines the number of concurrent HTTP requests that can take place at one time.

`MaxSockets` Property

The setting in `MaxSockets` determines the maximum number of active TCP/IP *sockets* the Webster control can use. The term socket refers simply to a single specific connection between two computers on the network that are using a network service.

PageTitle Property

PageTitle returns the HTML title of the current page.

PagesToCache Property

The PagesToCache setting determines how many previously visited pages to hold in memory. The greater the number set here, the more memory the browser uses; however having pages cached reduces load time if the user goes back to pages previously loaded.

ProxyPortHTTP and ProxyServerHTTP Properties

The ProxyPortHTTP and ProxyServerHTTP properties determine the proxy port and proxy server names.

ShowRefer Property

The ShowRefer Boolean property determines whether the HTTP Referer request header field introduced in Chapter 2 is sent to the server when a document is retrieved. The Referer field specifies the URI of the resource from which the request message was generated. For example, if you are on a Web page whose URL is http://www.myserver.com and you click a hyperlink to another Web page, the Referer field sent within the message requesting the page you clicked on will contain the string http://www.myserver.com. When this property is set to False, the Webster control will not use the Referer field in its request messages.

TitleWindowStyle Property

You determine the look of the title window by the settings in TitleWindowStyle. Table 4.2 lists the valid settings and their descriptions.

Table 4.2. Values for the TitleWindowStyle property.

Setting	*Description*
0	Does not display the title window.
1	Displays the title window at the Top of the control (default).
2	Displays the title window at the bottom of the control.

`UrlWindowStyle` Property

The `UrlWindowStyle` setting determines the visibility and location of the current URL window using the values shown in Table 4.3.

Table 4.3. Values for the `UrlWindowStyle` property.

Setting	*Description*
0	The URL is not displayed.
1	Displays the URL window at the top of the control.
2	Displays the URL window at the bottom of the control (default).

`DoClickURL` Event

The `DoClickURL` event is fired every time the user clicks on a hyperlink. The parameters are

`SelectedURL` (string)—The URL pointed to by the link that was clicked.

`Cancel` (Boolean)—If set to `True`, the link will not load. Setting `Cancel` to `True` is good for limiting access to certain URLs.

`DoLoadImage` Event

`DoLoadImage` indicates to the Webster control's container that an image is about to be loaded. The parameters are

`ImageURL` (string)—The URL of the image to be loaded.

`Cancel` (Boolean)—If this value is set to `True`, the image will not be loaded.

`HyperlinkTransition` Event

The `HyperlinkTransition` event fires a link when the mouse pointer is moved over a hyperlink. A potential use for this is updating a status bar with the URL of the link that would be loaded if the user clicked on the hypertext. The parameters provided to the event are

`URL` (string)—The URL of the hyperlink.

`IsOverLink` (Boolean)—If `True`, the mouse pointer is directly over the hyperlink. Otherwise, the pointer has moved off of the hyperlink.

`LoadComplete` Event

The `LoadComplete` event is fired when the requested Web page text has been completely loaded or when the load request fails. The parameters are the URL of the loaded page as a string, and an integer that indicates the status of the page. The values and their meanings are the same as the `LoadStatus` property discussed earlier in this section.

`AboutBox` Method

Calling the `AboutBox` method displays the Sax Webster About box.

`Cancel` Method

`Cancel` stops the loading of the current page.

`DismissPage` Method

`DismissPage` removes a specified page from the memory cache.

NOTE:

Any method that accepts a page's URL as a parameter will accept either the URL to any page contained within the Webster page cache or an empty string to signify the currently loaded page.

`GetContent` Method

The `GetContent` method returns raw data from either the currently loaded page or from a page within the cache. You specify the byte offset within the page to begin and the number of bytes to return.

`GetContentSize` Method

This method returns the size in bytes for a document, as specified by the `Content Size` HTTP header field. If the `Content Size` HTTP header field is not present, returns `0`.

`GetContentSizeRead` Method

The `GetContentSizeRead` method returns the number of bytes that have currently been for a document. This is useful while a document is being loaded to determine load status.

GetContentType Method

The `GetContentType` method returns the `Content Type` HTTP header field for a document.

GetHiddenFlag, SetHiddenFlag Methods

The `GetHiddenFlag` method returns a Boolean which indicates whether or not the page specified as a parameter to the method is currently hidden or visible. The `SetHiddenFlag` method is used to set a specific page to be either hidden or visible.

GetLinkCount, GetLinkURL Methods

The `GetLinkCount` method returns a count of the URLs contained on the page specified as a parameter to the method. The `GetLinkURL` returns the URL of the link specified by the method's `Index` parameter. For example, to add all of the current page's links to a listbox, use the following code:

```
For I% = 0 to Webster1.GetLinkCount("")
    List1.AddItem Webster1.GetLinkURL("", I%)
Next
```

GetRedirectedURL Method

This method returns the translated URL in cases where HTTP redirections have taken place.

GetStatus Method

The `GetStatus` method returns a status code for the specified URL. For the possible values returned, see the `LoadStatus` property discussed earlier.

GetText, GetTextSize Methods

The `GetText` and `GetTextSize` methods return the pure text and the byte count for the pure text for a specified page. Note that HTML tags and hyperlinks are not considered text as far as these methods are concerned.

GetTitle Method

Returns the page title for the specified page. The page is what is specified within the `<TITLE>` tags in the HTML file.

GoHome Method

The GoHome method causes Webster to load the page specified by the HomePage property.

LoadPage Method

The LoadPage method causes Webster to load a specified page. The method also has a Hidden parameter where you instruct Webster on whether or not the page should be hidden or visible after it is loaded (see the GetHiddenFlag and SetHiddenFlag methods discussed earlier for more details).

PageBack, PageForth Methods

These methods instruct Webster to load either the previous or the next page in the control's history list.

Refresh Method

The Refresh method repaints the control, but does not reload the current document from its Web server.

Reload Method

The Reload method reloads the current page from the Web server.

SaveToDisk Method

This method saves the current page to the directory specified by the SaveDir property.

ShowDir Method

The ShowDir method displays the directory page, which allows the user to select and display an HTML file that has been saved to disk.

ShowHistory Method

This method displays the history page, which contains a log of all the URLs the user has loaded during the current session.

ShowStatus Method

The `ShowStatus` method displays the status page, which displays the status for the currently loaded page.

Coding a Simple Application with the Webster Control

This section discusses the creation of a simple Web browser using the Sax Webster control. Although the Webster control can operate as a good Web browser by itself, you'll want to add some of the functionality present in the commercially available browsers.

This simple application allows you to enter a URL directly into a textbox. The Webster control is then used to load the Web page pointed to by the URL. Further, you can store the URL in a bookmark database and retrieve it later using a drop-down combobox on the form. To accomplish these tasks, the following controls are used:

- A textbox where users can directly type in the URL they wish to load.
- A data-bound combobox that contains the user's favorite URLs.
- A status bar that displays the time, and when the mouse is pointed over a link, the URL for that link is displayed in the status bar.

Designing the Form

To get all this done, you need to add a data control, a data-bound combobox that holds the title of the page that you want to load, a textbox for the URL, and a Button to add the current page to the Access database that's used to store the URLs of sites you've visited. You also need a status bar control to give the user feedback about hyperlinks and the status of the Webster control.

Let's start by looking at the layout of the form with the Webster control and the additional controls. Figure 4.2 shows the form in the Visual Basic's design mode.

One important form-level action your code must perform is that on a resize of the client window the Webster control should be resized as well. This means moving the Webster control, as well as the support controls around it, as shown in Listing 4.1.

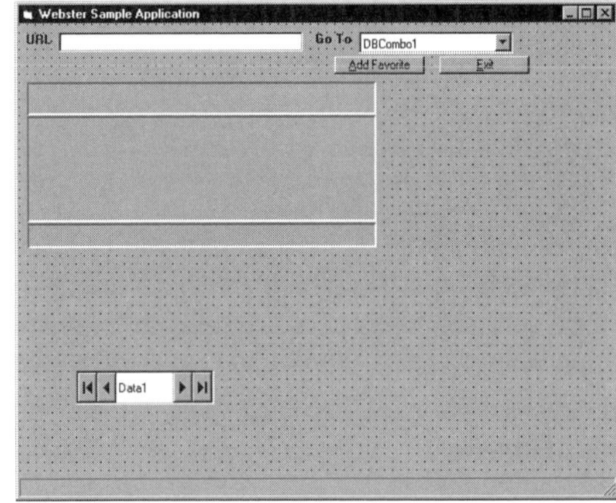

Figure 4.2.
Design mode view of the custom browser.

Listing 4.1. The `Form_Resize` Event

```
'make room for the added controls
Webster1.Top = 840
Webster1.Left = 0
'make room for status bar
Webster1.Width = ScaleWidth
If ScaleHeight > 490 Then
    Webster1.Height = ScaleHeight - 490
End If
```

By setting the `Top` property of the Webster object to `840`, you give yourself room for the additional controls you add to the top of the form. If the new height is greater than 490 twips, you assign the `ScaleHeight—490` value to the `Height` property of the Webster control to make room for the status bar. If the new height is less than 490, and you subtract 490, this results in a negative number, which is invalid for the `Height` property of any control.

Setting the Initial Properties of the Webster Control

One property you may want to set at form level or in design mode is the URL of the home page. The home page is the URL loaded when the user clicks on the small House icon in the toolbar. To do this, you add to the `Form Load` routine. The default home page is Sax Software's home page.

At this point, you could also specify the settings for the fonts used within the browser window, as well as any other tasks that need to be done at application startup, such as whether you wish to provide all of the toolbar buttons Webster makes available.

Setting Up the Access Database

For this limited sample application you will use a single table, two field Access database. The database name is `tblUrl`, the fields are `urlTitle` and `urlAddress`. The `urlTitle` and `urlAddress` fields are text, 50 characters long. The `urlTitle` field holds the user-supplied title of the page; the `urlAddress` holds the URL of the page.

Front-Ending the Access Database

This section describes how to set up the controls that interact with the database. You need to set the properties of the data control and the data-bound combobox. This is done by setting the properties of the controls as follows:

1. Set the properties for `Data1` — the single data control object you use by selecting the control on the form.
2. Set the `DatabaseName` property to the path of the Access database created earlier. The path could be stored and retrieved from the Windows registry if you wanted to get real fancy. However, in this example, set it at design time to a local `.MDB` file on the hard drive.
3. Set the `DataSource` property to `tblUrl`.
4. Set the `Visible` property to `False`—you don't need user interaction with the data control, so you make it invisible.
5. Select `DBCombo1`—the data-bound combo box that holds the title of the page the user wants to access.
6. Give the control a more descriptive name, such as `cboTitle`.
7. Set the control's `DataSource` and `RowSource` properties to `Data1` and set the `DataField`, `ListField`, and `BoundColumn` properties to `urlTitle` (the name of the field that holds the user-entered titles).
8. Select the textbox. Give it a more informative name, such as `txtURL`.

You also add the following code to the data control's `Validate` event:

```
Save=False
```

This prevents the dynaset from being overwritten when new records are selected with the combobox. However, it also makes it impossible to add records using the `Update` method. You will see how to get around this when you write the code for the `Add Favorite` button.

Using the StatusBar Control

In this example, you use the simple text flavor of the Visual Basic 4.0 `StatusBar` Control. By dragging the control onto the form, setting the `Style` property to `1` (single panel, simple text), you get a very basic, one-panel status bar. You change the text of the panel by setting its `SimpleText` property in the events of the Webster control (see Listing 4.2):

Listing 4.2. Webster event procedure code.

```
Private Sub Webster1_DoClickURL(SelectedURL As String, Cancel As Boolean)
    StatusBar1.SimpleText = "Loading " & SelectedURL
End Sub
Private Sub Webster1_HyperlinkTransition(URL As String, ByVal IsOverLink As Boolean)
    StatusBar1.SimpleText = URL
 End Sub
Private Sub Webster1_LoadComplete(URL As String, ByVal Status As Integer)
    StatusBar1.SimpleText = URL & " Loaded."
End Sub
```

This gives users some much-needed feedback as they use the Webster control: Moving over a hypertext link causes the status bar to display that hyperlink's URL, and the user is also notified when loading is in process and when the page text is completely loaded.

Programming the Data-Bound Combobox

On the `Click` event, you want two things to happen: The first is setting the `Bookmark` property of the data control's `Recordset` object equal to the value returned by the combobox's `SelectedItem` property.

The second is to set the `PageURL` property of the Webster control equal to the URL contained in the database for the item chosen by `cboTitle`. The code in Listing 4.3 demonstrates how these are accomplished.

Listing 4.3. Code for the `cboTitle_Click` event.

```
Private Sub cboTitle_Click(Area As Integer)

    If Area = dbcAreaList Then
        If Not (IsEmpty(cboTitle.SelectedItem)) Then
            Data1.Recordset.Bookmark = cboTitle.SelectedItem
            Webster1.PageURL = Data1.Recordset!urlAddress
        End If
    End If

End Sub
```

Note the two `If...Then` statements at the beginning of the procedure. The first checks to make sure the user has clicked within the list area of the data-bound drop-down combobox. The `Area` parameter specifies where the user has clicked. The `Click` event is fired no matter where the user clicks within the drop-down combobox, so you have to filter out clicks that don't really affect this program.

The second `If...Then` statement makes sure a valid record is being pointed to by the data-bound combobox. If an empty record is somehow selected, the `SelectedItem` property returns the special value `Empty`. A run-time error results if you attempt to assign this to the data control's `Bookmark` property.

Programming the Add Favorites Button

You need to have the Add Favorites button perform two things: First get a title for the page to be added from the user; second, write the URL and title to the Access database. For this example, you can use an `InputBox$()` function to gather the title.

1. First, drag a button onto the form.
2. Set the `Caption` to `&Add Favorite` and the `Name` to `cmdAddFav`.
3. With these in place, you can write the code in Listing 4.4. for the `cmdAddFav_Click` event. This code causes the input box to be displayed whenever the user clicks the Add Favorite button, as shown in Figure 4.3.

Listing 4.4. The `Click` event code for the `cmdAddFav` button.

```
Private Sub cmdAddFav_Click()

Dim strTitle As String
Dim strUrl As String

    strTitle = InputBox$("Please Enter a Title for the Page.", "Add Favorite")
    strUrl = txtURL.Text
    Data1.Recordset.AddNew
    Data1.Recordset!URLTitle = strTitle
    Data1.Recordset!urlAddress = strUrl
    Data1.Recordset.Update
    Data1.Recordset.Bookmark = Data1.Recordset.LastModified

End Sub
```

Programming the Exit Button

For the Exit button (`cmdExit`), use the single statement `Unload Me`, which unloads the single form, and thus the application.

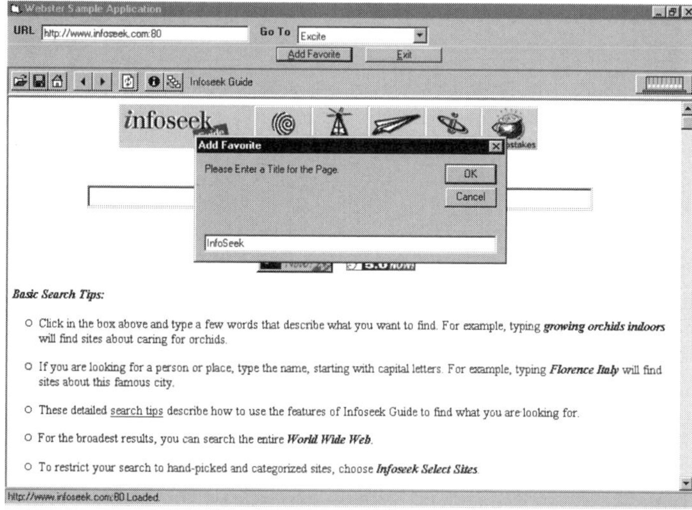

Figure 4.3.
Runtime view of the custom browser with the Input box.

Summary

This section guided you through the creations of a Web browser with the basic capabilities I outlined at the beginning of the section. As you can see, creating a stand-alone browser, or adding a browser to another application is a simple task with the Webster control. The running application with the Excite Web Search page loaded is shown in Figure 4.4.

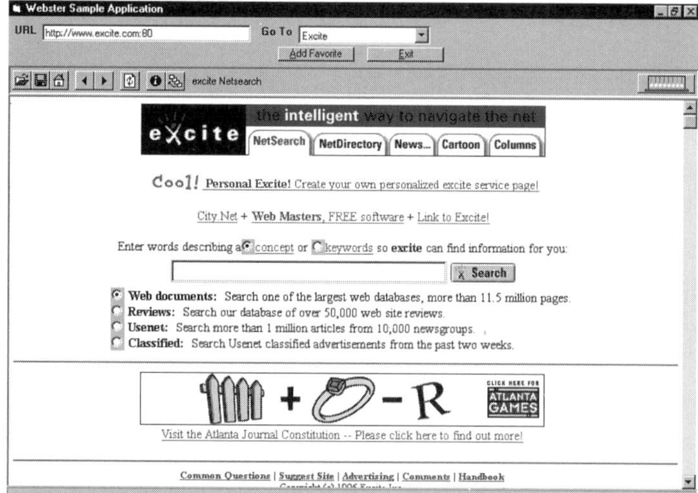

Figure 4.4.
Runtime view of the custom browser.

Microsoft HTML Control

Unless you live under a large, heavy rock, you've heard of Microsoft's ActiveX controls. These 32-bit OLE controls are Microsoft's attempt to integrate applications development, the Microsoft Internet Explorer, and the Internet.

http://www.microsoft.com/icp

The Internet Control Pack (ICP) ActiveX controls are a set of Internet tools. Included are tools for handling the following Internet protocols: FTP, HTML, HTTP, NNTP, SMTP, and POP3. The controls are currently in beta and available via Microsoft's Web site at `http://www.microsoft.com/icp`.

Overview of MS HTML's Properties, Methods, and Events

The following sections describe the various properties, methods, and events supported by the Microsoft ICP's HTML control beta. The text following property names provides the data type of the property.

BackImage Property (URL as a String)

The `BackImage` property sets the default background displayed in the browser window. This can be overridden by the HTML `<BODY BACKGROUND>` tag in the page being viewed.

BaseURL Property (URL as a String)

`BaseURL` is set to the URL contained in the `<BASE>` tag of the current page. If no base URL is specified, `BaseURL` is set to the URL of the current page.

DeferRetrieval Property (Boolean)

The `DeferRetrieval` property determines if inline images are loaded. A `False` value tells the browser to load the images; `True` turns off the loading of inline images.

DocBackColorProperty (Long)

This property is read-only at run-time and not available during design. `DocBackColorProperty` returns the value of the background color of the HTML document.

DocForeColor Property (Long)

The DocForeColor property is read only at runtime and not available during design. It returns the value of the foreground (text) color of the HTML document.

DocInput Property (DocInput)

The DocInput property returns a reference to the DocInput object. Again, it is read-only during runtime and unavailable during design-time. It enables the programmer to access the properties, methods, and events of the embedded DocInput object of the HTML control.

DocLinkColor Property (Long)

The DocLinkColor property returns the value of the color of the hypertext links that have not been accessed within the HTML document. Like other Doc-related properties, it is read only at runtime and not available during design.

DocOutput Property (DocOutput)

The DocOutput property returns a reference to the DocOutput object, is read-only during runtime, and is unavailable during design-time. It enables the programmer to access the properties, methods, and events of the embedded DocOutput object of the HTML control.

DocVisitedColor Property (Long)

The DocVisitedColor property (read-only at runtime and not available during design) returns the value of the color of the hypertext links that have been accessed in the HTML document.

ElemNotification Property (Boolean)

The ElemNotification property is read/write at design- and runtime. When set to true, it triggers the DoNewElement event during HTML parsing.

EnableTimer Property (Boolean)

The setting of EnableTimer determines the behavior of the TimeOut event. The three timeout conditions that can be set via the EnableTimer property are

prcConnectTimeout—The timeout allotment for connecting to the host.

prcReceiveTimeout—Time allotted for receiving data from the host.

prcUserTimeout—This is the user-defined timeout.

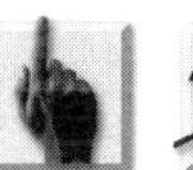

If any of the timeout times are surpassed without either a connection, receipt of data, or the user-defined event, the timeout event occurs.

The following code demonstrates how to set the `EnableTimer` property of each of these:

```
MSHTML1.EnableTimer(prcConnectTimeout)= True
MSHTML1.EnableTimer(prcReceiveTimeout)= True
MSHTML1.EnableTimer(prcUserTimeout)= True
```

FixedFont Property (Font as a String)

The `FixedFont` property is read/write at design- and runtime and is the font used to display fixed-width fonts in the HTML page.

Forms Property (HTML Forms)

This property is read-only and returns a reference to the HTML forms collection.

Heading#Font Property (Font as String)

The six properties `Heading1Font`, `Heading2Font`, and so on through `Heading6Font` are the fonts used by the HTML control to display text of the corresponding heading level that appears in the HTML file.

LayoutDone Property (Boolean)

`LayoutDone` is a read-only at runtime property. It is set to true when the HTML page layout is complete.

LinkColor Property (RGB Value)

`LinkColor` sets or returns the default link color that will be displayed. It can be overridden by the `DocLinkColor` property if the `UseDocColors` property is `True`.

ParseDone Property (Boolean)

The `ParseDone` value is set to false when an HTML file begins loading and is set to `True` when the HTML file is completely parsed.

Redraw Property (Boolean)

The `Redraw` property determines whether the data should be redrawn whenever the data in the HTML document changes or the user scrolls the browser window.

RequestURL Property (URL as a String)

RequestURL is a read-only property available only at runtime that returns the string value of the URL of the new document that has been requested.

RetainSource Property (Boolean)

The RetainSource value determines whether the HTML control should make the source HTML code available via the SourceText property.

RetrieveBytesDone Property (Long)

This read-only property is available only at runtime and returns the number of bytes that have been retrieved. RetrieveBytesDone returns a value of zero if no retrieval is in progress.

RetrieveBytesTotal Property (Long)

The RetrieveBytesTotal property is a read-only property, available only at runtime, that returns the total number of bytes of the HTML document and its embedded objects.

SourceText Property (String)

If the RetainSource property is true, the SourceText property returns the HTML source of the currently loaded URL.

TimeOut Property (Long)

The TimeOut returns or sets the timeout value in seconds. The timeout period begins when a document is requested. If the document is not received in the number of seconds set in the TimeOut property the TimeOut event is implemented.

TotalHeight Property (Long)

TotalHeight is a runtime, read-only property that returns the height of the current document in pixels.

TotalWidth Property (Long)

Similar to the TotalHeight property, TotalWidth applies to the width of the document.

`UnderlineLinks` Property (Boolean)

If `UnderlineLinks` is set to `True`, the browser displays hyperlinks with underline formatting; if `False`, no underlining of hyperlinks appears.

`URL` Property (URL as a String)

Returns the URL of the currently loaded document.

NOTE:

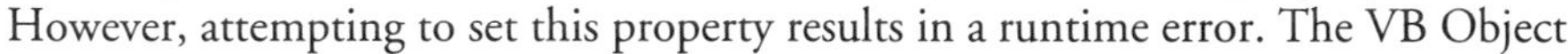

The Help file included with Beta 2 of the ICP indicates that this property is read/write. However, attempting to set this property results in a runtime error. The VB Object Browser correctly describes this property as I've described above.

`UseDocColors` Property (Boolean)

When `UseDocColors` is set to `True`, the document displays itself using the colors defined by the `DocColors` properties. If `Fasle`, it's displayed using the default properties for each element in the page.

`ViewSource` Property (Boolean)

Setting the `ViewSource` property to `True` displays the HTML for the current document.

`VisitedColor` Property (RGB)

`VisitedColor` determines the default color for visited links.

`Cancel` Method

The `Cancel` method, called without any parameters, causes any current requests for the calling control to be canceled.

`RequestAllEmbedded` Method

`RequestAllEmbedded` generates a request for all the embedded objects in the current document.

RequestDoc Method

The RequestDoc method has a single argument: the URL that is to be requested. After the request, the HTML control begins loading the requested URL.

BeginRetrieval Event

The BeginRetrieval event is implemented when the document retrieval begins.

DocInput Event

The properties and events of the DocInput method can be used to determine the current status while loading a URL. The event is fired when data is received by the HTML control.

DocOutput Event

DocOutput acts much like the DocInput event but is fired when data is being transferred from the control to a URL.

DoNewElement Event

The DoNewElement event is fired when a new element is encountered while an HTML document is being parsed. The parameters are

ElemType as a string

EndTag as a Boolean

Attrs as HTMLAttrs

Text as a string

EnableDefault as a Boolean

The ElemType is the HTML element type of the parsed source. It returns an empty string for character data. The EndTag Boolean value is True if the element is an end tag, False otherwise. The Attrs is the collection of HTML attributes. Text is the character data—Text is empty if the parsed data is a tag. EnableDefault is a Boolean that, if False, causes the control to continue parsing and ignore the current element, instead of attempting to render it on the control's window. If it is set to True, the element will be rendered using the control's standard processing.

`DoRequestDoc` Event

The `DoRequestDoc` event is fired when a new URL is requested. The parameters are

`URL` as a string

`Element` as an HTML element

`DocInput` as `DocInput`

`EnableDefault` as a Boolean

The `URL` is the requested document. The `Element` is not currently implemented but will identify the anchor of the link selected by the user. `DocInput` causes the control to accept input from another source. The Boolean `EnableDefault` enables or disables default processing. The default action varies depending on the type of file being retrieved. For HTTP and File URL, a new instance of the `DocInput` object is created, and the document is placed in that object. For other URL types, the `DocInput` property is set.

`DoRequestEmbedded` Event

`DoRequestEmbedded` is fired when an image or other embedded object is requested for display. The parameters are the same as for the `DoRequestDoc` event.

`DoRequestSubmit` Event

When the user clicks on the Submit button on a form, the `DoRequestSubmit` event is implemented. The parameters for the event are

`URL` as a string

`Form` as an HTML Form

`DocOutput` as `DocOutput`

`EnableDefault` as a Boolean

The `URL` and `EnableDefault` variables behave just as they do in the other `DoRequest` events. The `Form` parameter identifies the HTML form being submitted from the form's collection. The `DocOutput` object can be used with the `EnableDefault` to reroute the submission to something other than the HTTP reply by setting it to the `DocInput` property of another control.

`EndRetrieval` Event

The `EndRetrieval` event is fired when the text and inline images of the HTML document are completely retrieved.

LayoutComplete Event

As you may have guessed, LayoutComplete is implemented when the layout of the HTML document is complete.

ParseComplete Event

ParseComplete is fired when the entire HTML document has been parsed.

TimeOut Event

This event is fired when the amount of specified time in the TimeOut property passes without the corresponding event having occurred. The parameters for the TimeOut event are

Event as Integer

Continue as a Boolean

The Event argument is the process that caused the current TimeOut, as defined by:

prcConnectTimeout (1)	A connection was not established within the timeout period.
prcReceiveTimeout (2)	No data arrived within the timeout period.
prcUserTimeout (65)	Timeout for a user defined event. User should use prcUserTimeout + [Integer] range for custom timeout events.

This event fires only if EnableTimer for the specific event is set to True.

When Continue is set to True, the TimeOut condition is passed and normal processing resumes.

UpdateRetrieval Event

The UpdateRetrieval event happens periodically during the retrieval of text and images. The RetrieveBytesTotal and RetrieveBytesDone properties can be used during this event. These values can be used to generate user feedback about the progression of the retrieval of the page. For example:

```
Sub HTML1_UpdateRetrieval()
    StatusBar1.SimpleText = "Retrieved " & HTML1.RetrieveBytesDone & _
                            " of " & HTML1.RetrieveBytesTotal & " bytes."
End Sub
```

Designing the Form

After installing the controls, the help file appears in the Windows 95 Start menu, and the controls can be added under the Custom Controls menu item (CTRL-T) in Visual Basic 4. The controls are currently still in beta, and the help files are not yet complete. Keeping this in mind, I'll show you a basic Web browser that could be used for online help, an Intranet application, or to limit the sites the user can visit.

To start, you add the Microsoft HTML client control; the control appears in the toolbox. Next, size the tool to the desired size for the browser's viewing window. To round off the browser, add a label indicating the current location, a status bar for user feedback, and a control array of command buttons that enable users to access specific sites or exit the application. The form should look similar to Figure 4.5.

Figure 4.5.
A design-time view of the browser.

To accommodate the users' resizing of the form during runtime, add the code in Listing 4.5 to the `Form_Resize` event:

Listing 4.5. Code for the `Form_Resize` event.

```
HTML1.Top = 1000
HTML1.Left = 50
If ScaleWidth > 2000 Then
    HTML1.Width = ScaleWidth - 1600
    For x = 0 To 6
        cmdGo(x).Left = ScaleWidth - 1400
    Next x
End If
If ScaleHeight > 490 Then
    HTML1.Height = ScaleHeight - 1490
End If
```

The first two lines allow for an unused area to the left of the browser, and the 1000 twips at the top of the form are reserved for the label and textbox that indicate the current URL. The first

If...Then block checks to see whether the width has been reduced to a size too small for the buttons. If the new size is large enough, the buttons are moved also. The last three lines of code in Listing 4.5 check the height and resize to make room for the status bar.

Programming the Textbox

You want this textbox to behave in two directions, both as a method for user entry of the desired URL to visit, and as a display of the current URL. Thus, if a user types a URL and presses Enter, that URL is loaded and displayed. When the user follows a hyperlink on that page, the URL of the page followed is displayed. With the Microsoft HTML control, this is a relatively easy task. The code for the textboxes follows.

For the keypress event of the textbox, you want the following code:

```
If KeyAscii = 13 Then
    SendKeys "{TAB}"
End If
```

This causes the Tab key to be "pressed," if the user hits the Enter key. The side effect of the Tab being pressed is the LostFocus event, which has the following code:

```
HTML1.RequestDoc txtUrl.Text
```

The RequestDoc method of the Microsoft HTML control takes a string as its single argument. This string must be a valid URL or HTML file. With this in place, the control begins to load and display the URL.

Programming the Command Buttons

As you may have guessed with the simplicity of the RequestDoc method of the ICP HTML control, placing command buttons that load a specific site is an elementary task. The code for the Click event of the control array of command buttons is shown in Listing 4.6.

Listing 4.6. The cmdGo_Click event procedure code.

```
Private Sub cmdGo_Click(Index As Integer)

Select Case Index
        Case 0  'home
            HTML1.RequestDoc "http://execpc.com/~haasch"
        Case 1  'yahoo
            HTML1.RequestDoc "http://www.yahoo.com"
        Case 2  'Microsoft
            HTML1.RequestDoc "http://www.microsoft.com"
        Case 3  'Espn
            HTML1.RequestDoc "http://espnet.sportszone.com"
```

```
        Case 4  'ZD
            HTML1.RequestDoc "http://www.zd.com"
        Case 5  'Excite
            HTML1.RequestDoc "http://www.excite.com"
        Case 6
            Unload Me
    End Select

End Sub
```

Melding the Status Bar and the HTML Control

Like the Webster application earlier in the chapter, you'll want to provide the user with feedback about the state of the browser. You can use the events of the HTML control to set the `SimpleText` property of the status bar.

After setting the `Style` property of the status bar control to `1`—single panel, simple text—you can change the `SimpleText` property of the status bar in the corresponding events of the HTML control. The procedures involved are shown in Listing 4.7.

Listing 4.7. `HTML1` event procedure code.

```
Private Sub HTML1_BeginRetrieval()
    txtUrl = HTML1.URL
    StatusBar1.SimpleText = "Retrieving " & txtUrl
End Sub

Private Sub HTML1_EndRetrieval()
    StatusBar1.SimpleText = "Completed Loading " & HTML1.URL
End Sub

Private Sub HTML1_UpdateRetrieval()
    StatusBar1.SimpleText = "Retrieved " & HTML1.RetrieveBytesDone & _
                         " of " & HTML1.RetrieveBytesTotal & " bytes."
End Sub
```

As you can see, this event also updates the URL displayed in this textbox to the URL currently being retrieved.

With this code in place, you have a working browser based on the Microsoft HTML control. The running application is shown in Figure 4.6.

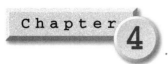

Figure 4.6.
The runtime view of the browser using the Microsoft HTML Control.

Comparing The ICP And The Sax Webster HTML Controls

As you have seen, both of these controls can add a World Wide Web browser to your application in a matter of minutes. Both are relatively new controls, and although only two are available at this time, Web browser controls will become more widespread soon.

Unfortunately, with only a beta and no documentation of the Microsoft HTML control, I was pretty limited in evaluating it. However, it did prove to work well and provided enough functionality to build a simple browser.

The `Forms` collection contained in the Microsoft control is very handy if you're designing applications that use HTML-based forms. You can use the `DoRequestSubmit` event to trap the user clicking the Submit button and then use the `Forms` collection to determine what the user has entered on the form. What you do with this information is entirely up to you and your needs, but it leaves the imagination with lots of possibilities, especially for Intranet applications.

The Webster control evaluated was version 1.07. This update to the 1.0 version fixed several small bugs and allows the `PageURL` to be set to a string without the `http://` in front of it. I had some problems with certain graphics displaying correctly, but the incidence of this was in less than 10 percent of the pages I visited.

The Webster control offers a lot of functionality to the programmer. For a quick application, leave the Sax toolbar in place. This accomplishes most of the work with no code. On the other extreme, if you want to make it a truly custom browser, the Webster control provides enough properties, methods, and events to make it a serious tool for adding a browser to any application.

Crescent **CIHTML** Control

Crescent has also thrown its hat into the Internet game with its Internet ToolPak. This set of controls includes an FTP client control, a Web control that provides accessibility to Web documents, a mail control that includes SMTP and POP3 compatibility, a news control (NNTP protocol), and a TCP/IP control.

Crescent's `CIHTML` control does not claim to be a browser in a control. Rather, it focuses on Web information retrieval and manipulation.

Properties, Events, and Methods of the **CIHTTP** Control

In this summary of properties, methods, and events, I only cover those that are specific to the `CIHTTP` control. For information on the standard Visual Basic properties, methods, and events, consult your manuals or help file.

AnchorListBoxName Property (String)

`AnchorListBoxName` is an optional property. If a listbox name is assigned to it and a page is retrieved, the anchors of the retrieved page appear in the listbox.

EventState Property (Integer)

The `EventState` property returns the value of the event currently taking place. The events supported are

ListBoxes Populated	`120`
HTTPServer Connection	`121`
Socket Closed	`122`
HTTPServer Connection Closed	`123`
File Closed	`124`

HostAddress Property (String)

The `HostAddress` property can be set with or returns the value of the Internet host's IP address (for example, `156.46.10.10`).

Either the `HostAddress` or the host name must be specified. The host name takes the more popular Domain Name Server (DNS) name (`www.mycompany.com`) and uses that to derive the IP address.

If going through a server proxy/firewall (a machine that, for security reasons, sits between the global Internet and an organizations local area network), a `ProxyServerName` or `ProxyServerAddress` must also be specified.

`HostName` Property (String)

`HostName` is similar to the `HostAddress` property, but the host is specified by its DNS name rather than its IP address.

`HTMLPageTextWithoutTags` Property (String)

`HTMLPageTextWithoutTags` is a read-only at runtime property that returns the HTML page without the formatting tags.

`HTMLPageTextWithTags` Property (String)

`HTMLPageTextWithTags` works much like the `HTMLPageTextWithoutTags` property, but leaves the HTML tags intact. The `ParseIncomingData` property (described below) must be `True` for this to work correctly.

`HTTPPort` Property (Integer)

The `HTTPPort` property, which defaults to `80`, sets the port used for HTTP communications.

`ImageFileListBoxName` Property (ListBox)

The `ImageFileListBoxName` property corresponds to the `AnchorListBoxName` property. However, instead of storing the names of anchors, it stores the names of images.

`LocalFileName` Property (String)

The path/filename combination in `LocalFileName` is the location where information retrieved via the `CIHTTP GET` method is stored.

`MethodState` Property (Integer)

`MethodState` works similar to the `EventState` property but applies to the `GET`, `HEAD`, and `POST` methods. The properties possible values are:

```
GET    14
HEAD   15
POST   16
```

ParseIncomingData Property (Boolean)

If the value of ParseIncomingData is True, the control parses the data; otherwise, the control assumes the information is binary.

ProxyServerAddress Property (String)

If the user is going through a server proxy (firewall) either the IP address or the name of the firewall must be stored in either the ProxyServerAddress property (IP Address) or the ProxyServerName property (DNS Name).

ProxyServerName Property (String)

The DNS name of the user's firewall (if any) must be stored in the ProxyServerName property or the firewall's IP address stored in the ProxyServerAddress property.

TagListBoxName Property (ListBox)

TagListBoxName works similar to its ImageFileListBoxName and AnchorListBoxName counterparts: While the CIHTTP control parses the incoming page, the HTML tags are placed in the specified listbox.

URL Property (String)

This sets or retrieves the URL of the currently loading, or loaded request.

WWWSiteName Property (String)

The WWWSiteName property contains the title of the currently loaded page. The title is retrieved from the <TITLE> element of the HTML file.

CleanupConnection Method

Use CleanupConnection to clear any errors that occur when a GET, HEAD, or POST method occurs, or if the control is having problems reopening a socket.

ConnectToHTTPServer Method

Once the HostName or HostAddress properties are set (ProxyServerName/ProxyServerAddress if necessary), ConnectToHTTPServer attempts to connect to the specified server. If successful, it returns the socket number opened for the connection as an integer. If failed, it returns 0 and fires the WSAError event.

GET Method

After connecting to the Web server and setting the URL, the GET method retrieves the page specified by the URL.

HEAD Method

The HEAD method retrieves the page information from the specified URL.

POST Method

After the URL is set, the POST method sends the text to that URL.

SendHTTPCommand Method

The SendHTTPCommand method enables you to issue HTTP commands other than GET, HEAD, and POST. The method's single argument is the HTTP command that is to be sent. This can be used to talk to servers that support HTTP request message extension methods as described in the "HTTP Request Messages" section of Chapter 2, "HTTP: How to Speak on the Web."

EventStateChanged Event

This event fires when the EventState property changes.

FileClosed Event

The FileClosed event is implemented when the file specified by the LocalFileName property is closed.

HTTPServerConnectionClosed Event

HTTPServerConnectionClosed is fired when a connection to a Web server is closed.

ListBoxesPopulated Event

This event fires after all of the AnchorListBox, ImageListBox, and TagListBox listboxes have been filled.

MethodStateChanged Event

MethodStateChanged occurs when the MethodState property changes.

`MethodStateChanged` Event

The `MethodStateChanged` event is implemented when a packet is received from the connected Web server.

`PacketSent` Event

`PacketSent` takes place when a packet is sent to the connected Web server.

`SocketClosed` Event

The `SocketClosed` event fires when the socket your control is using is closed. This should happen only after your application is done running. If `SocketClosed` occurs, the application should re-open a socket and retry the command that caused the error.

`TotalFileBytesReceived` Event

The single parameter in the `TotalFileBytesReceived` event is the `bytes_in` value. This value is incremented each time a packet is received from the server.

`WSAError` Event

`WSAError` fires when a Winsock error occurs. The single argument `error_number` is the Winsock error.

Summary

The Webster control is the first-released browser-in-a-box ready to be popped into any Visual Basic application. Its inclusion of command buttons and easy property manipulation makes it a breeze to use.

Microsoft's HTML client control, although in Alpha stages, looks promising. It, too, is an integrated browser, but look for future releases of the control to support VB Script, OLE, and a host of other Internet technologies that Microsoft has up its sleeve.

Crescent's `CIHTTP` control takes a different approach, offering a way to retrieve and easily parse HTML files. This can be used to create agents, spiders, and custom applications that draw off of information available via the World Wide Web.

The three tools you looked at are the first "Web-aware" tools to appear in the marketplace. As time progresses, I'm sure the tools will evolve as user demand and evolution of the Web protocols continue. Now it is up to the developers to find useful applications for these Web tools.

Chapter 5

Retrieving Information from the Web

- HTTP's **GET** and **HEAD** Methods Reviewed
- Introduction to **dsSocket** OCX
- Microsoft's Internet Control Pack HTTP Client Control
- Off and Surfing: Some Basic Examples

Thus far I have discussed the HTTP protocol, using DDE and OLE automation to control a few popular Web browsers, and using HTML custom controls. This chapter builds on the material about the HTTP protocol found in Chapter 2, "HTTP: How to Speak on the Web".

This chapter briefly reviews a few elements of the HTTP protocol. The HTTP request message methods are discussed, then the `dsSocket` OLE control is introduced. This control, in combination with the Windows Sockets (WinSock) interface, allows programs to connect to other machines on a TCP/IP network (the Internet, for example). With the `dsSocket` control you can create server and client applications using any Internet protocol. The control allows you to connect to a server or to listen on a TCP/IP network and send and receive data over the network. The control creates the TCP/IP packet messages, the Visual Basic program controls what data is sent. A demo version of this control is provided on the CD-ROM accompanying this book. You can also download the latest version of the control from the Dolphin Systems Web site at `http://www.dolphinsys.com`.

http://www.dolphinsys.com

Next, the HTTP OLE control found in Microsoft's Internet Control Pack is introduced. This control is a client-side control that uses the HTTP protocol for retrieving data from Web servers or for posting information to a Web resource. The latest version of the Internet Control Pack can be downloaded from the Microsoft Web site at `http://www.microsoft.com/icp/`.

http://www.microsoft.com/icp/

Finally, the chapter concludes by presenting a few examples using these two OLE controls. These examples demonstrate how easy it is to retrieve information from the Web using the OLE controls. They don't include any elaborate error or timeout handling so they should only be used in a controlled environment.

HTTP's **GET** and **HEAD** Methods Reviewed

For complete coverage of HTTP messaging, refer to Chapter 2 or to the HTTP Internet-Draft document that Chapter 2 is based on. The example programs later in this chapter use both of these methods to retrieve information from HTTP servers.

The `GET` and `HEAD` methods are used for retrieving information from an HTTP server. The `GET` method retrieves the entire content of a resource on the server. The `HEAD` method retrieves only the header information about a resource on the server. The two methods both have their places when creating Visual Basic applications to access Web-based information.

The GET Method

Applications that utilize or retrieve Web-based resources use the GET method the majority of the time. The HTTP protocol provides the GET method as a way of retrieving data resources (such as HTML documents and images) from network servers. When a client application (also referred to as a *user agent*) needs to parse information from an HTML file or to display an image file, the GET request method is used.

The HTTP/1.0 protocol defines two different GET requests. One is known as the *simple request.* This style of request is used to retrieve only the contents of a resource. No header information about the resource is returned from the server. When an HTTP/1.0-compliant server receives a simple request message, it must not send any header information within its reply message.

The other style is known as the *full request* message. This type of request message can itself contain header information that refines the request. When an HTTP/1.0-compliant server receives a full request message, it should reply with a *full response* message containing header information regarding the resource being retrieved in addition to the contents of the resource.

The formats for GET request messages are

```
Simple-Request = "GET" SP <Request-URI> CRLF

Full-Request = <Request-Line> *(<General-Header> ¦
                      <Request-Header> ¦ <Entity-Header>)
    CRLF
    [ <Entity-Body> ]

Request-Line = "GET" SP <Request-URI> SP <HTTP-Version> CRLF
```

The HEAD Method

The HTTP/1.0 specification also defines a HEAD request message. The HEAD request instructs an HTTP server to return only the header information about the specified resource. The contents of the resource itself are not returned. This method can be used when designing user agents that catalog Web documents, for example, to obtain information about a document without having to retrieve the entire document.

To use the HEAD method, you must issue a full-request message. The format for the message is

```
Full-Request = <Request-Line> *(<General-Header> ¦
               <Request-Header> ¦ <Entity-Header>)
    CRLF
    [ <Entity-Body> ]

Request-Line = "HEAD" SP <Request-URI> SP <HTTP-Version> CRLF
```

When the server responds to a HEAD message, it does not return an <Entity-Body> element (which, for a GET request, would contain the contents of the resource). Only the response message header information will be returned.

Introduction to **dsSocket** OCX

There are many TCP/IP controls available to the Visual Basic programmer. They range from controls that are not protocol-specific to controls that work only with specific protocols (such as FTP, NNTP, and SMTP).

The dsSocket custom control, produced by Dolphin Systems, is a Windows socket control (TCP/IP communications take place utilizing connections known as *sockets*). It is not protocol-specific. Instead, it allows you to create any type of application to communicate over a TCP/IP network. Applications developed using the control can, of course, use any of the Internet protocols, but they are not limited to a specific protocol.

Each connection you wish to establish using dsSocket must have its own instance of the dsSocket control on the Visual Basic form. For example, if the application will run as both a client and a server application and you expect to be able to listen and talk at the same time, you must have two dsSocket controls on your form. As a further example, some Web browsers use multiple connections to construct Web pages. If a Web page contains many pictures, for instance, the browser can use one connection for each picture it has to retrieve. This way, it can retrieve and display these images concurrently—it doesn't have to wait for each image to be read in a sequential manner. Coding this situation would again require one dsSocket instance for each concurrent connection to be made.

This chapter discusses using the dsSocket control to retrieve data from HTTP servers. The programs will, obviously, use the HTTP protocol discussed in Chapter 2 to retrieve this data. Other possible uses of the dsSocket control include using the SMTP protocol to send Internet mail from within Win/CGI applications (which are introduced in Chapter 6, "The Win/CGI Interface").

This section discusses some of the properties, methods, and events of the dsSocket control. The help file included with the control provides a complete reference to the entire set of properties, methods, and events. This discussion is limited to those that will be used in this book.

Properties

The control's properties provide the parameters to be used during the communication session. It can be set up to act as either a server or client, depending on the property settings. The control also uses an Action property that, incredibly enough, causes the connections and communication to happen.

The custom property page allows you to set up most of the important properties in one place. The property page is shown in Figure 5.1.

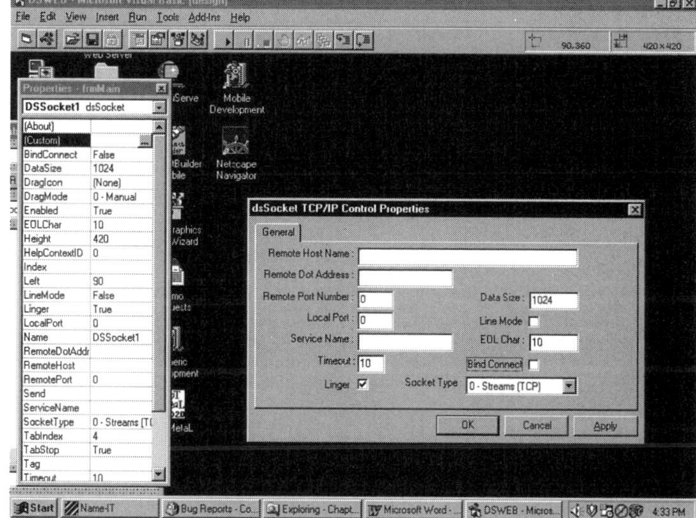

Figure 5.1.
The custom property page for the `dsSocket` control.

`RemoteHost` and `RemoteDotAddr`

These properties contain the IP address and (if available) the host name for the remote computer. If the `RemoteHost` property is set, either a name resolution service (which translates a host name into an IP address) must be available or a matching entry must exist in the Windows `hosts` file. This is necessary because connections are actually made using the standard IP *dot address* format.

By using either the `FwdLookup` method or setting the `Action` property to 6 (`SOCK_ACTION_FWDLOOKUP`), the value in `RemoteHost` is translated using forward lookup to an IP address and stored in the `RemoteDotAddr` property. Likewise, using the `RevLookup` method or setting `Action` to `7` (`SOCK_ACTION_REVLOOKUP`) converts the `RemoteDotAddr` property to a host name using reverse lookup and stores it in `RemoteHost`. If the name services are not available, these actions simply do not fill the corresponding properties.

Whenever multiple connections to the same server are required, a great deal of performance can be gained by using the `RemoteDotAddr` property. Internet hosts are typically named using host names (such as `www.myserver.com`) instead of IP addresses. To resolve the host name into an IP address, use the forward lookup method described previously. This translates the host name into an IP address to be stored in the `RemoteDotAddr` property. This only has to be done once for each assignment to the `RemoteHost` property.

RemotePort

This integer property specifies the port to be connected to on the remote computer. There are a number of well-known port assignments. These define standard port numbers to be used by specific services. For example, the well-known port for HTTP servers is 80.

The value specified must correspond to a port number on which the computer specified by `RemoteHost/RemoteDotAddr` is actively listening. If this property is set to zero, the `ServiceName` property is used to determine the port number on which to connect.

LocalDotAddr and LocalName

These properties set and retrieve the IP address and host name, respectively, of the machine on which the control is operating. The default values for these properties are determined by the TCP/IP settings for the machine. These settings are found in the Network Properties page (either in Control Panel or the Network Neighborhood folders). The properties are available only at runtime. Setting these properties to an empty string causes the property to be set to the default values.

LocalPort

When creating a server application, you should set the `LocalPort` property to the port number on which the application will listen. If you are implementing a standard protocol server (such as FTP or SMTP), you should use the well-known port number. Likewise, if you are creating both the client and server applications and they are not using a standard protocol, you should avoid using any of the well-known port numbers. This will prevent applications that are using a standard protocol connecting to your server accidentally.

DataSize

This property defines the maximum number of bytes that will be transferred to the `Receive` event. The default value is `2048`, the minimum value is `100`, and the maximum value is `32767`.

LineMode and EOLChar

The `LineMode` property determines how data is received by the control. When `LineMode` is set to True, the control's `Receive` event is fired whenever when the character specified by the `EOLChar` property is received. If `LineMode` is True and the character specified in `EOLChar` is not found in the incoming data, the `Receive` event is fired after the number of bytes specified in the `DataSize` property are received.

If `LineMode` is False, data is transferred to the control as it is received from the network.

Action

Once the connection properties have been set up using the other properties, the `Action` property is used to change the state of the communication socket. Table 5.1 lists the available values for the property.

Table 5.1. `Action` Property Values.

Constant	*Value*	*Action*
`SOCK_ACTION_CLOSE`	1	Closes an open connection
`SOCK_ACTION_CONNECT`	2	Establishes (opens) a connection
`SOCK_ACTION_LISTEN`	3	Listens for incoming connection
`SOCK_ACTION_FWDLOOKUP`	6	Converts host name to IP address
`SOCK_ACTION_REVLOOKUP`	7	Converts IP address to host name

The three values we'll use most often are `SOCK_ACTION_CONNECT`, `SOCK_ACTION_LISTEN`, and `SOCK_ACTION_CLOSE`.

The `SOCK_ACTION_CONNECT` value is used when creating a client application. When the `Action` property is assigned this value, the control connects to the server specified in the `RemoteHost` or `RemoteDotAddr` properties. The port (or socket) used is specified by the `Port` property. Assigning this value is identical to using the `Connect` method.

The `SOCK_ACTION_LISTEN` value is used when creating a server application. When the `Action` property is assigned this value, the control begins listening on the port specified by the `Port` property for any incoming connections. Assigning this value is identical to using the `Listen` method.

The `SOCK_ACTION_CLOSE` value is used to close an open connection. Assigning this value is identical to using the `Close` method.

Send

This string property sets the data to be sent to the remote machine. The control must be connected to the remote machine or a runtime error occurs. The data is sent immediately unless the network is not ready. If the network is not ready, a runtime error occurs. In this case, the `SendReady` event is fired when the network is available, at which time the program should set the `Send` property again.

State

This property specifies the current status of the control. The property is set after setting the `Action` property. If an error occurs (firing the `Exception` event), the value of this property does not change to reflect the the error condition. The possible values for the property are listed in Table 5.2.

Table 5.2. `State` Property Values.

Constant	*Value*	*State*
SOCK_STATE_CLOSED	1	There is no open connection
SOCK_STATE_CONNECTED	2	There is an open connection
SOCK_STATE_LISTENING	3	The control is listening for a connection
SOCK_STATE_CONNECTING	4	Waiting for a connection to be completed
SOCK_STATE_ERROR	5	There is an error
SOCK_STATE_CLOSING	6	The connection is closing
SOCK_STATE_UNKNOWN	7	The status is unknown
SOCK_STATE_BUSY	8	The network is busy

Methods

This section describes the methods available to the `dsSocket` control. All of these methods duplicate functions that can also be activated by setting the `Action` property.

Connect

Using the `Connect` method starts an attempt to connect to the machine specified by the `RemoteHost/RemoteDotAddr` on the port specified. The connection is not completed until the `Connect` event is fired. This method is synonymous with setting the `Action` property to `SOCK_ACTION_CONNECT`.

Close

The `Close` method closes an open connection. Using this method is identical to setting the `Action` property to `SOCK_ACTION_CLOSE`.

Listen

This method opens a port to listen for incoming connections. The `Accept` event fires when an incoming connection request is received. If the control is actively listening, it cannot be used for

sending data until the Listen is canceled. This method is identical to setting the Action property to SOCK_ACTION_LISTEN.

FwdLookup and RevLookup

These methods are used for doing forward and reverse name resolution. These concepts have previously been discussed with the Action, RemoteDotAddr, and RemoteHost properties. Using these methods is synonymous with setting the Action property to SOCK_ACTION_FWDLOOKUP and SOCK_ACTION_REVLOOKUP, respectively.

Events

The dsSocket events are fired whenever the state of the control changes. If there is no code for a specific event, the change of state is simply ignored. This section discusses the events in the order in which they take place when issuing an HTTP GET request (which is demonstrated by the example programs at the end of the chapter).

Connect

This event is fired after a connection is established with the remote machine. The connection sequence begins either by setting the Action property to SOCK_ACTION_CONNECT or by invoking the Connect method. Once the connection is established, the control can then exchange data with the server machine.

SendReady

This event indicates that the network is ready to receive data. The event is fired after a connection is established and also after the network changes from a not-ready state to a ready state.

It is possible that, when attempting to send data, the network is not in a position to transfer data. If this occurs, the Exception event will fire with the error code SOCK_ERR_WOULDBLOCK (error number 21035). The program must then wait for the SendReady event to fire, at which time the program can resend the data.

Receive

The Receive event fires whenever the control receives data from the machine to which it is connected. If the LineMode property is set to True, the event will not fire until the character specified in EOLChar is received. This feature is useful when communicating with line-mode protocols such as HTTP, SMTP and POP. All messages in these protocols have carriage-return and line-feed characters as the last characters of each line.

The data received is passed to the event using the event's `ReceiveData` parameter. The length of the data passed never exceeds the value of the `DataSize` property.

The usual processing for the `Receive` event is to append the received data to some data container (such as a string variable or a file) until a certain condition is met or the connection closes. The HTTP examples presented at the end of the chapter write the received data to a file and also append it to a textbox on the form. This continues until the HTTP server closes the connection, signalling the end of the resource being retrieved.

Close

This event occurs whenever an open connection closes. The event provides two parameters, `ErrorCode` and `ErrorDesc`, that specify whether the socket closed with errors. If there were no errors, the value of `ErrorCode` is zero and the value of `ErrorDesc` is "Socket closed." If an error did occur while the socket was closing, the `ErrorCode` parameter indicates the error number and the `ErrorDesc` provides a string description of the error.

Exception

The `Exception` event fires whenever an asynchronous error occurs. The event provides the `ErrorCode` and `ErrorDesc` parameters as described for the `Close` event.

If an active connection is aborted, the `Exception` event is fired instead of the `Close` event to signify that the connection closed prematurely.

Errors occurring while setting control properties are still trapped using the standard `Err` and `Error` variables.

Listen

The `Listen` event occurs whenever the `Action` property has been set to `SOCK_ACTION_LISTEN` or the `Listen` method was invoked and the control is now set to actively listen on the network. The event signifies that the control is now able to receive incoming connections from client machines.

Accept

This event fires whenever a control that is actively listening receives a connection request. This event passes a `SocketID` parameter which should be assigned to the `Socket` property of an available `dsSocket` control. This topic is covered in the control's manual and won't be used in this book.

Microsoft's Internet Control Pack HTTP Client Control

Microsoft has recently introduced a set of controls known as the ActiveX Internet Control Pack (ICP). These controls are each designed to handle a specific Internet protocol. The controls hide the implementation details of the protocol from the programmer. In so doing, a program can be written to access a specific type of server with just a few lines of code. This section discusses the HTTP client control.

Unlike accessing HTTP servers using the `dsSocket` control, the ICP's HTTP control handles creating and sending the request messages. The Visual Basic program merely specifies the URL to be retrieved, invokes the `GetDoc` method, then uses the `DocOutput` event to receive the incoming document. In addition to this, if the program is merely going to save the resource to a local file, the program simply sets the `Filename` property before invoking `GetDoc`. Then the HTTP control automatically writes the received data to the file specified without firing the `DocOutput` event. No further data processing is required of the program.

The HTTP control provides no mechanism for parsing or displaying the retrieved data. It is up to the application to determine what to do with the data that is received. Microsoft has provided the HTML control to act as a complete HTML browser.

CAUTION:

The Internet Control Pack was still in beta testing at the time of this writing. The material covered here may not be accurate for later releases of these controls. As an example, the documentation shipped with the ICP listed a method called `PerformRequest`. This method, however, was not actually implemented in the control. Most of the discussion here is of a general enough nature to be fairly accurate.

Properties

The HTTP control's properties specify the server to connect to, the document to be retrieved, and the means to be used in retrieving that document.

RemoteHost and RemotePort

The `RemoteHost` property specifies either the host name or the IP address of the machine containing the document to be retrieved. The value can be set to either addressing style (IP dot address or host name).

The RemotePort property specifies the port number to connect to on the remote machine. For the HTTP control, the default port number is 80.

Document

This string property sets or returns the name of the document to be retrieved. By combining the Document property with the RemoteHost property, you can construct the URL for the document.

URL

This property can be used instead of the RemoteHost and Document to specify the document to be retrieved. For the HTTP control, the protocol identifier can be omitted from the URL. If this is the case, it will default to http:.

Method

This property specifies the HTTP request method to be used for the transfer. These methods are discussed in detail in Chapter 2. The values available are listed in Table 5.3.

Table 5.3. Method Property Values.

Constant	*Value*	*Method*
prcGet	1	Get (default)
prcHead	2	Head
prcPost	3	Post
prcPut	4	Put

NotificationMode

This property is similar to the LineMode property found in the dsSocket control. Instead of searching for an end-of-line character, setting the NotificationMode property to zero (the default) delays notification of data received until the entire response message is received. If the property is set to one, an event is fired for each received piece of data. For most operations, it is best to leave the property at its default value and parse the retrieved data after it is completely received.

DocOutput

The `DocOutput` property provides a reference to the control's `DocOutput` object. The `DocOutput` object contains information about the document being received. A reference to the `DocOutput` object is also passed as a parameter to the `DocOutput` event.

The properties of this object include `BytesTotal` and `BytesTransferred`, which provide the total size of the file and the number of bytes that have currently been transferred, respectively.

The object also contains a `DocHeader` collection. The collection is referred to by the `Headers` property of the `DocOutput` object. This collection contains the HTTP header fields returned by the server. The items in the collection have only two properties: `Name` and `Value`. The collection is used by referring to the collection's `Item` collection. The `Headers` collection has a `Count` property which provides a count of the number of headers that exist.

For example, a header field may be accessed with

```
Debug.Print HTTP1.DocOutput.Headers.Item("content-type").Value
```

which prints the value of the `Content-Type` header field to the Visual Basic Debug window. Or, to print all the headers to the debug window, use

```
with HTTP1.DocOutput.Headers
    for x% = 1 to .Count
        Debug.Print.Item(x%).Name & ": " & .Item(x%).Value
    next
end with
```

Another useful property of the `DocOutput` object is `FileName`. If this property is assigned a valid filename and the HTTP control's `GetDoc` method is invoked, the document retrieved is stored in the specified file. No further processing is required by the program; the HTTP control handles the entire process automatically. This property is illustrated in one of the examples at the end of this chapter.

The `State` property indicates the status of the current transfer. The property is read-only and is always set to one of the values listed in Table 5.4.

Table 5.4. `State` Property Values.

Constant	*Value*	*State*
`icDocNone`	`0`	No transfer is in progress
`icDocBegin`	`1`	Transfer is being initiated
`icDocHeaders`	`2`	Headers are transferred (or requested)
`icDocData`	`3`	Data is available (or requested)
`icDocError`	`4`	An error has occurred
`icDocEnd`	`5`	Transfer is complete

Methods

The GetDoc method discussed next is invoked most often. This method provides the means for retrieving HTTP server-based documents. A few other methods are available but don't warrant discussion here. The second method discussed (GetData) is a method of the DocOutput object contained within the HTTP control.

GetDoc

Invoking this method initiates a request message to retrieve a document. The document to be retrieved can be specified using the method's optional parameters. If the parameters are not specified, the values of the URL, Headers, and DocOutput's OutputFile properties are used. The syntax for this method is

```
object.GetDoc [URL,] [Headers,] [OutputFile]
```

The URL parameter specifies the complete URL for the document to be retrieved. The URL includes the server's host name or IP address, the port number, and the document name. The Headers parameter contains a reference to the Headers collection of the HTTP control's DocInput object. It is of type DocHeaders. The Headers parameter is used to specify request message header fields for the request being issued. If the OutputFile parameter is provided, it specifies a local file into which the document being retrieved is placed. Similar to the OutputFile property of the DocOutput object, if this parameter is specified the DocOutput event is not fired when data is received. Instead, the data is placed into the specified file.

When data is received by the HTTP control in response to a GetDoc, the DocOutput event is fired. The program should then check the State property of the DocOutput object to determine the control's status. If the status indicates that data is available, the GetData method of the DocOutput object is invoked to actually retrieve the data.

GetData

The DocOutput object provides a GetData method which is used to retrieve the data from the receive buffer. This method can only be invoked from within the DocOutput event. When data is available (State = icDocData) this method is used to fetch the data into a variable. The syntax is

```
object.GetData data, [type]
```

The data parameter is where the retrieved data is stored. The variable can be of any data type. The optional Type parameter is a Long which specifies the type of data to be retrieved. The values use the intrinsic variables for specifying Visual Basic data types (vbInteger and vbString, for example).

Events

When using the HTTP control, there are a few events that are used most often. Of course, depending on the application you're developing, you may need to use *all* of the events the control provides. The examples at the end of this chapter are not meant to be commercial-quality applications. They only use most of the control's events to provide feedback to the user — in a "real" application the code should include more robust error and timeout handling.

The events discussed in this section are `DocOutput`, `Error`, `StateChanged`, and `TimeOut`.

DocOutput

The HTTP control's `DocOutput` event is analogous to the `dsSocket` control's receive event. The `DocOutput` event is fired whenever data has been received by the HTTP control.

The event passes one parameter, also named `DocOutput`, to the Visual Basic program. This `DocOutput` parameter is simply a reference to the control's `DocOutput` property. The `State` property of this `DocOutput` object should be examined to determine the status of the data stream. The possible values for the `State` property are listed in Table 5.4.

There is a property of the HTTP control named `NotificationMode` which controls how often this event is fired. If `NotificationMode` is set to zero (the default value), the `DocOutput` event does not fire until an entire portion of the HTTP response message is received by the control. For example, the event fires once after all the header fields have been received. In this case, the `DocOutput.State` property is set to `icDocHeaders` and the `Headers` collection of `DocOutput` is available. The event fires again when all the entity body portion of the response message has been received. The `State` in this case will be `icDocData` and the `GetData` method of `DocOutput` should be invoked to retrieve the data.

If `NotificationMode` is set to one, however, the `DocOutput` event fires continuously as data is received by the control.

Error

This event occurs whenever there is an error in background data processing. The event provides quite a few parameters describing the error and that determine how the appropriate error message will be displayed.

StateChanged

This event fires whenever there is a change-of-state in the control. The event provides a parameter named `State` which provides the current state. The possible values of this parameter are explained in Table 5.5.

This event is useful for updating status feedback controls such as status bars. It can also be useful when developing tightly controlled state-machine driven applications.

Table 5.5. `State` Parameter Values.

Constant	*Value*	*State*
`prcConnecting`	1	Connect requested, waiting for acknowledgement from the server
`prcResolvingHost`	2	Resolving host name to IP address
`prcHostResolved`	3	Resolved the host name
`prcConnected`	4	Connection established
`prcDisconnecting`	5	Close/disconnect has been initiated
`prcDisconnected`	6	Not connected

Off and Surfing: Some Basic Examples

The examples presented in this chapter are fairly simple. However, they do illustrate the key concepts that are necessary when creating a user agent that accesses Web-based information. These concepts include parsing the provided URL to extract the remote host name, the remote port number, and the resource name, as well as properly formatting the HTTP request message to allow the Web server to properly process the request.

Both examples allow the user to enter a URL and retrieve the resource it represents. The user can choose the `GET`, `HEAD`, or `POST` request method and whether or not to save the resource to a local file. The first example utilizes the `dsSocket` control and is the more complex of the two. This should not be surprising if you have read the previous two sections of this chapter. The second example utilizes the Microsoft HTTP Client control to accomplish the same feats. The code required, however, is much smaller than with the `dsSocket` control.

These examples don't include a lot of error handling or timeout processing. You should only use them in a tightly controlled environment until you feel comfortable with them. For example, as I write I am running the WebSite HTTP server and Visual Basic on a laptop. All my URLs reference `localhost` which is defined in the laptop's HOSTS file as IP address 127.0.0.1. This is the standard "loopback" IP address that refers to the local machine.

Example Using the **dsSocket** Control

The example using the `dsSocket` control (see Figure 5.2) is based on the dsWeb sample project that is shipped with the `dsSocket` control. I have added quite a bit to the code, however, to demonstrate the available HTTP/1.0 protocol features, as well as the ability to save the resource locally.

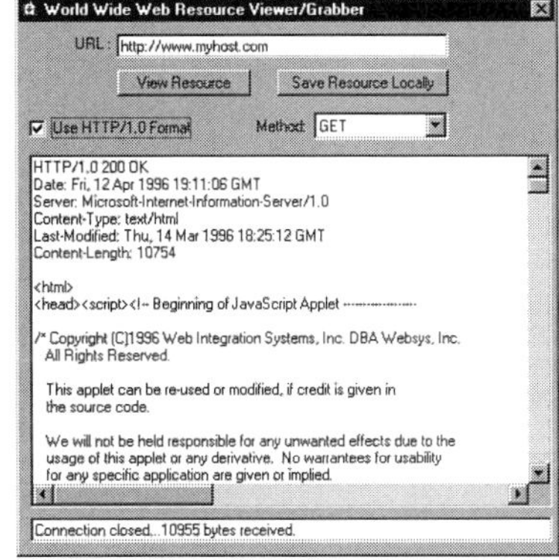

Figure 5.2.
The `dsSocket` example application's form.

Designing the Form

The form layout is shown in Figure 5.2. Beyond the standard Visual Basic controls, the project requires the `dsSocket` control and the Microsoft Common Dialog control. The form definition is given in Listing 5.1. Place the controls on your form and assign the properties as specified in Listing 5.1.

Listing 5.1. Form definition.

```
Begin VB.Form frmMain
   BorderStyle     =   3  'Fixed Dialog
   Caption         =   "World Wide Web Resource Viewer/Grabber"
   ClientHeight    =   6045
   ClientLeft      =   1155
   ClientTop       =   420
   ClientWidth     =   5175
   ForeColor       =   &H80000008&
   Height          =   6450
   KeyPreview      =   -1  'True
   Left            =   1095
   LinkTopic       =   "Form1"
   MaxButton       =   0   'False
   MinButton       =   0   'False
   ScaleHeight     =   6045
   ScaleWidth      =   5175
   ShowInTaskbar   =   0   'False
   Top             =   75
   Width           =   5295
```

continues

Listing 5.1. continued

```
   Begin VB.TextBox Text1
      Height          =   4035
      Left            =   120
      MultiLine       =   -1  'True
      ScrollBars      =   3  'Both
      TabIndex        =   5
      Top             =   1500
      Width           =   4875
   End
   Begin VB.CommandButton btnGetFile
      Appearance      =   0  'Flat
      BackColor       =   &H80000005&
      Caption         =   "Save Resource Locally"
      Height          =   300
      Index           =   1
      Left            =   3000
      TabIndex        =   9
      Top             =   540
      Width           =   1995
   End
   Begin VB.ComboBox cboMethod
      Appearance      =   0  'Flat
      Height          =   315
      Left            =   3420
      Style           =   2  'Dropdown List
      TabIndex        =   7
      Top             =   1020
      Width           =   1575
   End
   Begin VB.CheckBox chkProtocol
      Caption         =   "Use HTTP/1.0 Format"
      Height          =   255
      Left            =   120
      TabIndex        =   6
      Top             =   1080
      Value           =   1  'Checked
      Width           =   2355
   End
   Begin VB.TextBox txtStatus
      Height          =   285
      Left            =   120
      TabIndex        =   3
      Top             =   5640
      Width           =   4935
   End
   Begin VB.CommandButton btnGetFile
      Appearance      =   0  'Flat
      BackColor       =   &H80000005&
      Caption         =   "View Resource"
      Height          =   300
      Index           =   0
      Left            =   1140
      TabIndex        =   2
      Top             =   540
      Width           =   1545
   End
```

```
Begin VB.TextBox txtURL
   Height          =   285
   Left            =   1125
   TabIndex        =   0
   Text            =   "http://localhost/"
   Top             =   120
   Width           =   3870
End
Begin MSComDlg.CommonDialog dlgFileSave
   Left            =   5220
   Top             =   600
   _Version        =   65536
   _ExtentX        =   847
   _ExtentY        =   847
   _StockProps     =   0
   CancelError     =   -1  'True
   DialogTitle     =   "Save Resource As..."
End
Begin VB.Label Label2
   Alignment       =   1  'Right Justify
   Caption         =   "Method: "
   Height          =   255
   Left            =   2640
   TabIndex        =   8
   Top             =   1080
   Width           =   735
End
Begin dsSocketLib.dsSocket DSSocket1
   Height          =   420
   Left            =   90
   TabIndex        =   4
   Top             =   360
   Width           =   420
   _version        =   65542
   _extentx        =   741
   _extenty        =   741
   _stockprops     =   64
   localport       =   0
   remotehost      =   ""
   remoteport      =   0
   servicename     =   ""
   remotedotaddr   =   ""
   linger          =   -1   'True
   timeout         =   10
   linemode        =   0    'False
   eolchar         =   10
   bindconnect     =   0    'False
   sockettype      =   0
End
Begin VB.Label Label1
   Alignment       =   1  'Right Justify
   Appearance      =   0  'Flat
   BackColor       =   &H00C0C0C0&
   Caption         =   "URL :"
   ForeColor       =   &H80000008&
   Height          =   195
   Left            =   240
   TabIndex        =   1
```

continues

Listing 5.1. continued

```
        Top             =   135
        Width           =   825
    End
End
```

The combobox cboMethod allows the user to select which of the HTTP/1.0 request methods to use. The GET and HEAD methods require no user input apart from the URL. The list items are added to the combobox in the Form_Load event. Then the cboMethod.ListIndex property is set to the "GET" item.

The POST method requires that the user enter data in the large textbox. The data entered when performing a POST should be form encoded, meaning that it looks like the data sent when a Web browser performs a POST request. This format contains the field name, an equal sign, and the field value. If more than one field is present, the fields are separated by ampersand characters. The line

```
Name1=Craig&Name2=Susan&Fetch=Water
```

contains three fields, Name1, Name2, and Fetch; each with their respective values. When the line is sent to the HTTP server, it is terminated with a NULL character (Chr$(0)).

The checkbox chkProtocol allows the user to select between using the HTTP/1.0 protocol and the HTTP/0.9 protocol. The versions of the HTTP protocol prior to HTTP/1.0 provide only the GET request method. Therefore, when the checkbox is not checked, the drop-down listbox is disabled. The program only uses a simple request message.

The textbox txtURL is where the user enters the address of the resource to be retrieved. The URL should be in the form

```
http://www.myhost.com/resource.htm
```

or (to retrieve the server's default document)

```
http://www.myhost.com/
```

to be a valid URL. There are two functions that parse the entered URL into a host name (www.myhost.com) and a filename (resource.htm). These routines are discussed in the next section.

The textbox txtStatus is used to provide status information to the user. This includes informing the user that a connection has been established, that the program is waiting to receive data from the server, or that an Exception event has occurred.

The GetHostFromURL() and GetFileFromURL() Functions

These two routines are taken from the dsWeb sample that ships with the `dsSocket` control. They are used to parse the host and filenames from a URL. The routines depend on the URL being valid. If the URL is invalid, the routines return an empty string.

The `GetHostFromURL()` (Listing 5.2) retrieves the host name from the URL. The host name is the portion of the URL that occurs between the "//" and the first "/" characters. If the "//" is not present, `GetHostFromURL()` considers the URL to be invalid and returns an empty string.

Listing 5.2. `GetHostFromURL()` function.

```
Private Function GetHostFromURL(szURL As String) As String
    '   parse out the hostname from a valid URL
    '   the URL should be of the format: http://www.microsoft.com/index.html
    '   the returned hostname would then be: www.microsoft.com

    Dim szHost      As String
    Dim lPos%
    szHost = szURL
    '   invalid URL
    If InStr(szHost, "//") = 0 Then
        GetHostFromURL = ""
        Exit Function
    End If
    szHost = Mid(szHost, InStr(szHost, "//") + 2)
    lPos% = InStr(szHost, "/")
    If lPos% = 0 Then
        GetHostFromURL = szHost
        Exit Function
    Else
        GetHostFromURL = Left(szHost, lPos% - 1)
        Exit Function
    End If
End Function
```

The `GetFileFromURL()` function parses the resource's filename from the supplied URL. If the name is not provided, an empty string is returned. The function is shown in Listing 5.3. The routine first validates the URL. The URL must contain the "//" characters. A temporary string (`szFile`) is used to hold the filename. The portion of the `szURL` parameter up to and including the "//" is removed from the string. Finally, the function searches the string for the first occurrence of a single slash ("/"). If one is found, the portion of the string following the slash is returned. If a slash is not found, an empty string is returned. This situation is possible for URLs attempting to retrieve the default resource of a Web server.

Listing 5.3. GetFileFromURL() function.

```
Private Function GetFileFromURL(szURL As String) As String
    '   parse out the filename from a valid URL
    '   the URL should be of the format: http://www.microsoft.com/index.html
    '   the returned filename would then be: index.html

    Dim szFile      As String

    szFile = szURL
    '   invalid URL
    If InStr(szFile, "//") = 0 Then
        GetFileFromURL = ""
        Exit Function
    End If
    szFile = Mid(szFile, InStr(szFile, "//") + 2)
    If InStr(szFile, "/") = 0 Then
        GetFileFromURL = ""
        Exit Function
    Else
        GetFileFromURL = Mid(szFile, InStr(szFile, "/") + 1)
        Exit Function
    End If
End Function
```

The Form's Declarations Section

The declarations section for the form defines some constants and the form-level variables the program uses. These are shown in Listing 5.4 but the variables won't be discussed until the sections in which they are used are covered.

Listing 5.4. Declarations.

```
Option Explicit

'   Declare the constants used to set the Action property
'   and check the State of the socket

Const SOCK_STATE_CLOSED = 1
Const SOCK_STATE_CONNECTED = 2
Const SOCK_STATE_LISTENING = 3
Const SOCK_STATE_CONNECTING = 4
Const SOCK_STATE_ERROR = 5
Const SOCK_STATE_CLOSING = 6
Const SOCK_STATE_UNKNOWN = 7
Const SOCK_STATE_BUSY = 8

Const SOCK_ACTION_CLOSE = 1
Const SOCK_ACTION_CONNECT = 2
Const SOCK_ACTION_LISTEN = 3
```

```
Dim lBytesRcvd  As Long
Dim bGettingContent As Integer
Dim iFileHandle As Integer
Dim fSaveToFile As Integer
```

Miscellaneous Routines

This section contains the code for the many miscellaneous routines contained in the application. These are all event procedures and don't warrant much discussion. They are all contained in Listing 5.5.

Listing 5.5. Various event procedures.

```
Private Sub cboMethod_Click()

    'don't allow local save for HEAD method
    If cboMethod.ListIndex = 1 Then
        btnGetFile(1).Enabled = False
    Else
        btnGetFile(1).Enabled = True
    End If

End Sub

Private Sub chkProtocol_Click()

    'the request method can only be specified if
    'we're using HTTP/1.0
    If chkProtocol.Value = 1 Then
        cboMethod.Enabled = True
    Else
        cboMethod.Enabled = False
    End If

End Sub

Private Sub txtURL_KeyPress(KeyAscii As Integer)

    If KeyAscii = vbKeyReturn Then
        Call btnGetFile_Click(0)
        KeyAscii = 0
    End If

End Sub

Private Sub Form_KeyPress(KeyAscii As Integer)

    If KeyAscii = vbKeyEscape Then
        If dsSocket1.State = SOCK_STATE_CONNECTED Then
            dsSocket1.Close
            txtStatus = "Connection cancelled..."
```

continues

Listing 5.5. continued

```
        End If
        KeyAscii = 0
    End If

End Sub

Private Sub Form_Load()

    'add the methods to the combo box
    cboMethod.AddItem "GET"
    cboMethod.AddItem "HEAD"
    cboMethod.AddItem "POST"
    cboMethod.ListIndex = 0

End Sub
```

The `cboMethod_Click` procedure disables the Save Resource Locally command button if the selected method is `HEAD`. This is necessary because the contents of the resource are not returned in response to a `HEAD` request—the server returns only the response message header fields.

The `chkProtocol_Click` procedure disables the `cboMethod` combobox if the checkbox is not checked. This is necessary because the versions of the HTTP protocol prior to HTTP/1.0 only support the `GET` method.

The `txtURL_KeyPress` event is used to trigger the View Resource command button if the Enter key is pressed. Although this could also have been accomplished by setting the command button's `Default` property to `True`, I chose this method to prevent firing the command button by pressing the Enter key while in the Text1 textbox. Recall that for a `POST` request text must be entered into Text1.

The `Form_KeyPress` event is used to abort an open connection if the Escape key is pressed. If the HTTP server is not responding, it is necessary to close the connection. Otherwise, further attempts to retrieve resources would result in an error because the `dsSocket` control would already have an open connection.

Finally, the `Form_Load` event simply adds the available methods to the `cboMethod` combobox and sets the `ListIndex` property of the combobox to the first item (`GET`).

The Command Buttons in Action

The two command buttons on the form are the principal means the user has to retrieve the resource specified in the URL textbox. The user can also press the `Enter` key while the URL textbox has focus. This action activates the View Resource button.

The command buttons are part of a control array. The Save Resource Locally button (`Index` = 1) utilizes the same code as the View Resource button (`Index` = 0) and merely adds the code that handles the opening of the output file into which the resource will be saved.

The code is given in Listing 5.6. It's pretty straightforward so I'll just highlight the basics of what's going on here.

Listing 5.6. The `btnGetFile Click` event.

```
Private Sub btnGetFile_Click(index As Integer)

    Dim szHost As String, tmp$

    On Error Resume Next

    If index = 1 Then
        fSaveToFile = True
        iFileHandle = FreeFile
        'the file name to use is after the last "/"
        tmp$ = GetFileFromURL(txtURL)
        While InStr(tmp$, "/")
            tmp$ = Mid$(tmp$, InStr(tmp$, "/") + 1)
        Wend
        dlgFileSave.filename = tmp$
        dlgFileSave.Flags = cdlOFNExplorer + cdlOFNLongNames + _
                cdlOFNNoReadOnlyReturn + cdlOFNOverwritePrompt
        dlgFileSave.Action = 2
        If Err Then
            fSaveToFile = False
            If Err <> cdlCancel Then
                MsgBox "An error occurred opening the file: " & Error$
            End If
        Else
            Kill dlgFileSave.filename
            Err = 0              'clear any errors caused during Kill
            Open dlgFileSave.filename For Binary Access Write As #iFileHandle
            If Err Then
                Err = 0
                fSaveToFile = False
                MsgBox "An error occurred opening the file: " & Error$
            End If
 End If
        bGettingContent = False
    Else
        fSaveToFile = False
    End If

    lBytesRcvd = 0

    '   set to line mode for incoming data
    dsSocket1.LineMode = True
    dsSocket1.EOLChar = 10

    szHost = GetHostFromURL(txtURL)
    If (szHost = "") Then
        MsgBox "Invalid URL supplied."
        Exit Sub
    End If
```

continues

Listing 5.6. continued

```
    dsSocket1.RemoteHost = szHost
    dsSocket1.RemotePort = 80        ' use the default port

    txtStatus = "Connecting..."
    '   connect the socket, Connect or SendReady event will
    '   signify it's ok to send data
    dsSocket1.Connect

    If (Err > 0) Then
        MsgBox "Error connecting to host" & Chr(13) & Format(Err) & ":" & Error
    End If

End Sub
```

If the `Index` parameter is 1, the user has clicked the Save Resource Locally button. In this case, the code sets the `fSaveToFile` flag to `True`. This flag is used in other places to determine if data should be written to the file specified by `iFileHandle`. After a value is obtained for `iFileHandle`, the filename of the resource is parsed from the URL. Because the value returned by `GetFileFromURL()` may contain some server-based directory information, the routine uses only the portion of the filename *after* the last slash character.

The program next prompts the user for a local file in which to save the resource. This is done using the Visual Basic Common Dialog control (`dlgFileSave`). The Save As dialog will be used. The parsed filename the code just obtained is used as the initial filename for the common dialog. The `Flags` property is set to use the Explorer style dialog (`cdlOFNExplorer`), to allow long filenames (`cdlOFNLongNames`), to not allow read-only files (`cdlOFNNoReadOnlyReturn`), and to verify an overwrite attempt if the user selected an existing file (`cdlOFNOverwritePrompt`).

The `Action` property is then set to `2` to open the Save As dialog. The `dlgFileSave` control's `CancelError` property is set to `True` to produce a runtime error if the user presses the Cancel button on the dialog. If there is no error set after setting the `Action` property, the `Filename` property contains the full path to the file the user specified. If `Err` has a value greater than zero but not equal to `cdlCancel` (the value assigned when the Cancel button is pressed), a message box is displayed. If an error occurs, the `fSaveToFile` flag is set back to `False`.

If the user has chosen a valid filename, the program next attempts to open that file for output. The first step is to delete the file. This is done using the `Kill` statement. If the file does not exist, an error occurs. In this situation, however, it doesn't really matter because the program is just going to overwrite it anyway. So the code resets `Err` to `0`. Next, the code opens the file for binary write access. Binary is used because the user may not be retrieving a character-based resource. The URL may specify a GIF image or a sound file for example. The use of binary access allows the program to store any type of data within the file.

Finally, the flag `bGettingContent` is reset to `False`. This flag is used in the `dsSocket`'s `Receive` event.

If the `Index` parameter was not `1`, the `fSaveToFile` flag is set to `False`.

The program uses a variable called lBytesReceived to keep track of the number of bytes that have been received. This variable is reset to zero.

The next two lines of code set up the receive mode of the socket control. Most HTTP data is transmitted in complete lines that end with line feed characters (Chr$(10)). The LineMode property is set to True. This causes the Receive event to be fired only after the character specified by the EOLChar property is received. The EOLChar property is set to 10.

The next step is to get the host name from the URL. This is done using GetHostFromURL(). If an invalid URL was specified, a message box is opened and the procedure is aborted. The host name is assigned to the RemoteHost property, and the RemotePort property is set to the default HTTP port (80).

Finally, the Connect method of the dsSocket control is invoked. If the user specified a host name that cannot be resolved to an IP address, a runtime error occurs. The last section of code displays such an error.

Note that the Connect method returns immediately. If a timeout occurs, it will be handled in the Exception event. The only errors returned by the Connect method are those that prevent a connection from taking place. These include invalid IP addresses as well as the server refusing the connection.

When the program successfully connects to the specified server, the Connect and SendReady events fire. The SendReady event is where the program constructs and transmits the HTTP request message.

Miscellaneous dsSocket Events

Several of the dsSocket events are used to present status information to the user. They represent changes of protocol state during the retrieval process. All of them update the txtStatus textbox with a description of the socket's current state. Listing 5.7 contains the code for these events.

Listing 5.7. The miscellaneous dsSocket events.

```
Private Sub dsSocket1_Connect()

    txtStatus = "Connected..."

End Sub

Private Sub dsSocket1_Close(ErrorCode As Integer, ErrorDesc As String)

    txtStatus = "Connection closed..." & lBytesRcvd & " bytes received."
```

continues

Listing 5.7. continued

```
    If fSaveToFile Then
        bGettingContent = False
        Close #iFileHandle
    End If

End Sub

Private Sub dsSocket1_Exception(ErrorCode As Integer, ErrorDesc As String)

    txtStatus = "dsSocket1 Error : " & ErrorCode & ":" & ErrorDesc

End Sub
```

The first event encountered is the `Connect` event. This event is fired when the connection to the server has been completed. The event merely changes the text in the status box to "Connected..."

The `Close` event is fired when the HTTP server closes the connection. This signifies the end of the server's response message. The code updates the status box to inform the user that the retrieval has been completed. It also provides the total number of bytes received from the server. If the resource was being saved to a local file, the file is closed.

Any communication errors occurring after the `dsSocket` control has connected to the server cause the `Exception` event to be fired. The code in this event merely displays the error information in the status box. A more complete application would attempt to make sense of the error condition and take appropriate action.

The dsSocket SendReady Event

After the control has connected to the server and the network is prepared to send data, the `SendReady` event is fired. This signifies that the program can now proceed to send the HTTP request message. The code for the event is given in Listing 5.8.

Listing 5.8. The `dsSocket SendReady` event.

```
Private Sub dsSocket1_SendReady()

    Dim szFile      As String

    On Error Resume Next

    szFile = GetFileFromURL(txtURL)

    '   send the URL request
    If chkProtocol.Value Then
        dsSocket1.Send = cboMethod.Text & " /" & szFile & " HTTP/1.0" & vbCrLf
        'use the Accept header to make sure the server will send us everything:
        dsSocket1.Send = "Accept: */*" & vbCrLf
```

```
        If cboMethod.Text = "POST" Then
            dsSocket1.Send = "Content-Type: application/x-www-form-urlencoded" _
                             & vbCrLf
            dsSocket1.Send = "Content-Length: " & _
                        Trim$(Str$(Len(Text1.Text) + 2)) & vbCrLf & vbCrLf
            dsSocket1.Send = Text1.Text & Chr$(0) & vbCrLf
        Else
            dsSocket1.Send = vbCrLf
        End If
    Else
        bGettingContent = True
        dsSocket1.Send = "GET /" & szFile & vbCrLf
    End If
    Text1.Text = ""
    txtStatus = "Waiting for reply..."

End Sub
```

Once the housekeeping tasks of defining variables, setting the error handling method, and updating the status box are out of the way, the real work of this application begins.

The first step is to parse the resource's filename from the URL the user entered. This is accomplished using `GetFileFromURL()`.

The code then checks the state of the `chkProtocol` checkbox. If the checkbox is checked, the user has indicated that the request message should conform to the HTTP/1.0 protocol (the request message format is reviewed earlier in this chapter). Otherwise, a simple request message will be transmitted.

Outgoing characters are assigned to the `dsSocket`'s `Send` property. For the HTTP/1.0 message, the `cboMethod` combobox's current setting is used as the request method. The code then appends a slash (/) and the resource's filename. This is followed by the string "HTTP/1.0," which indicates an HTTP/1.0 request is being made. All lines in HTTP messages end with the carriage return/line feed combination (`vbCrLf`).

Next, the request is modified by adding a request header field to the message. The `Accept` header field informs the server which content types are acceptable to the client. In this application, the server should return the resource regardless of its content type. Therefore, the code sets the value of the `Accept` header to */*. The `vbCrLf` is added to indicate the end of this header field.

If the method specified in `cboMethod` is `POST` there are a few more pieces to transmit. First, for a `POST` request the client must specify the `Content-Type` and `Content-Length` entity body header fields. The code assumes `Content-Type` is `x-www-form-urlencoded` (which is a standard method of encoding HTML form data). The value of the `Content-Length` header field is the length of the text in the Text1 textbox plus two (one for the NULL character and one for the line feed). After these entity body header fields are sent, an extra `vbCrLf` is transmitted. This separates the request headers from the entity body. Finally, the contents of the `Text1` textbox are sent, followed by a NULL character (`chr$(0)`) and `vbCrLf`.

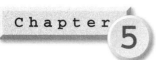

If the user left the chkProtocol checkbox unchecked, the program constructs a simple request message. This consists of the GET string followed by the filename of the resource, and ending up with vbCrLf.

Once the message is completed, the Text1 textbox is cleared and the status box is updated to Waiting for reply.... The program is now awaiting the firing of the Receive event which occurs after the first complete line of the response message is received from the server.

The dsSocket Receive Event

The Receive event is where the incoming data is processed, presented to the user, and, possibly, saved to disk. It's also the final piece of code for the application. The code in the Receive event is very basic. As Listing 5.9 shows, the only parameter for the event is a string called ReceiveData. This string contains the data just received from the server. Remember that the control is working in line mode so it only fires the event after a complete line is received.

The first step is to update the status box to reflect the fact that data is being received. Next, the ReceiveData is appended to the contents of Text1 for display purposes.

The HTTP/1.0 response message contains header information that precedes the actual body of the resource. When the program is saving the retrieved resource locally, only the body of the resource is stored to the local file, not the header information. If the HTTP header information were stored in an image file, the file would be invalid and unusable. The bGettingContent flag is used to signify that all the header information has been received and the program is now receiving the <Entity-Body> portion of the HTTP response message.

The code checks the state of bGettingContent and fSaveToFile. If both are true, the ReceiveData is written to the file specified by iFileHandle. The line of code that starts with "If ReceiveData = vbCrLf" is where the program decides that the incoming data is now the entity body portion of the response message. Recall that the response message format requires that the header portion and the entity body be separated with an empty line. This is received at the client as vbCrLf by itself. Once this string is received, the remainder of the response message is assumed to be the entity body. The bGettingContent is therefore set to True to indicate this state.

Finally, the value of lBytesReceived is updated to include the latest data.

Listing 5.9. The dsSocket Receive event.

```
Private Sub dsSocket1_Receive(ReceiveData As String)

    txtStatus = "Receiving data..."

    '   display the incoming html data
    Text1.Text = Text1.Text & ReceiveData
    If bGettingContent And fSaveToFile Then
        Put #iFileHandle, , ReceiveData
    End If
```

```
    If ReceiveData = vbCrLf And bGettingContent = False Then
        bGettingContent = True
    End If

    '   add the byte count to the total
    lBytesRcvd = lBytesRcvd + Len(ReceiveData)

End Sub
```

Testing the **dsSocket** Application

Now that the form has been set up and all of the code entered, it's time to test the application. Select Run | Start from the Visual Basic menu. The application loads and the form is displayed.

The first step is to enter a valid URL in the URL textbox. The URL should point to an HTML document for now. Leave the checkbox checked and the method drop-down set for `GET`. Click the View Resource button. The status box is updated as the retrieval proceeds. Once the document retrieval starts, the textbox begins filling with the HTML text. After the document has been fully received, the server closes the connection. This is signaled by changing the text in the status box. Figure 5.3 shows an example of how the screen will look.

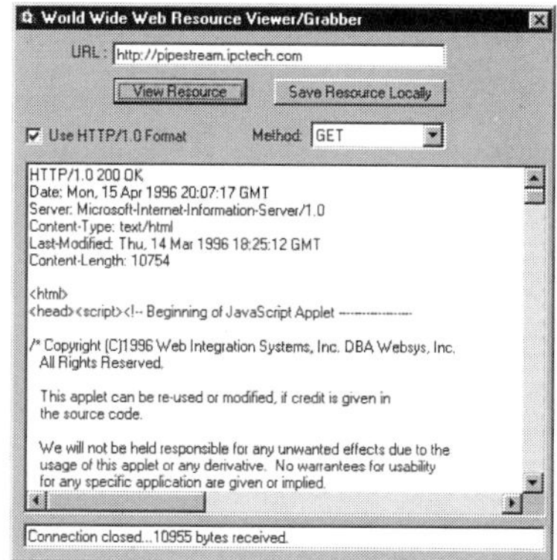

Figure 5.3.
A screen from the `dsSocket` example.

Note the text at the beginning of the textbox up to the first blank line. These lines are the response message header fields that were returned by the server.

After the document has been received, click Save Resource Locally. When the Save As dialog box appears, enter a valid filename to use when saving the resource. Click the OK button. The document appears in the textbox as before. This time, however, the program also stores the HTML text in the file you specified. To verify this, open the Windows Explorer and locate the file. View the file by whatever means you wish. If you retrieved an HTML document and have a Web browser such as Netscape Navigator or the Internet Explorer installed, you can double-click the filename to load it.

Next, change the method to HEAD. The Save Resource Locally command button should be disabled. Click View Resource. This time only the header lines are returned by the server. These should match the header lines received in our previous retrievals. Figure 5.4 illustrates this.

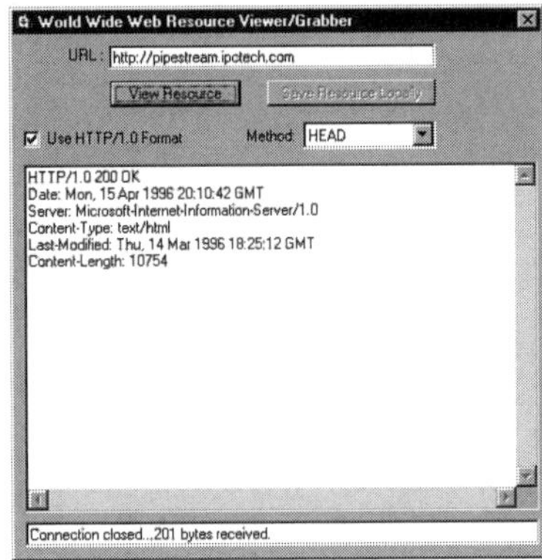

Figure 5.4.
An example of using the HEAD method.

The POST method is a little more complicated to use. You must enter into the textbox the field names and values that the resource is expecting to receive when you perform a POST. The best way to find these out is to view the source of an HTML form that also POSTs to the resource. For example, the sample Win/CGI application presented in Chapter 6 uses three fields: Name1, Name2, and Fetch. When entering data into the textbox, the fields are separated from their values using the equal sign. The field/value pairs are separated using an ampersand character. Spaces appearing within field values should be replaced with a plus sign. The text entered would then resemble Name1=Craig&Name2=Susan&Fetch=Water. If you know of a resource that accepts POST requests, and you know which fields the resource is expecting, you can enter the string into the textbox and retrieve the resource. Typically, the resource informs you (through the document which is received by the dsSocket control) if any fields are missing or invalid.

Example Using the Internet Control Pack HTTP Client Control

If you waded through the example in the previous section, you're probably wishing there wasn't another example. However, you'll be pleasantly surprised at how little code is necessary when using the HTTP Client control. Unlike the dsSocket control, the HTTP Client control is specifically designed to retrieve resources from an HTTP server. The control takes care of making the connection to the server, creating the request message and receiving the data returned. It also parses the header information from the content information. Because your application doesn't need to generate the HTTP request method, the code contained in the dsSocket's SendReady event of the previous example is unnecessary.

To create this example, start with the form from the previous example. Copy the form files and the project file to a different directory. Open the new copy of the project file in Visual Basic. The first step is to delete the `dsSocket` control from the form. You can leave the code if you desire. This allows you to compare the code required for the two controls.

Next you need to add the HTTP Client control to the project. Open the Custom Controls dialog using the Tools | Custom Controls menu. Scroll through the list until you locate Microsoft HTTP Client Control. Select it using the checkbox. You can also remove the `dsSocket` entry as long as the control has been deleted from the form. Click OK.

NOTE:

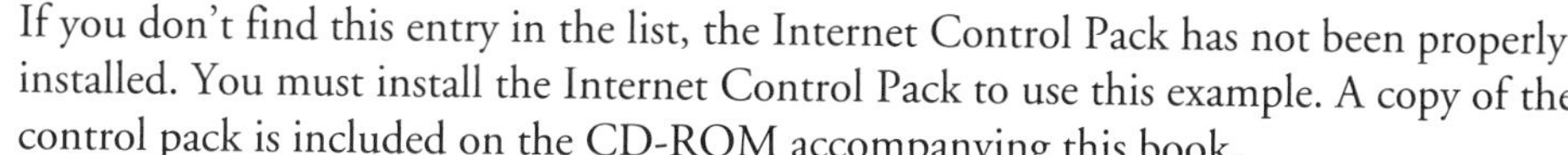

If you don't find this entry in the list, the Internet Control Pack has not been properly installed. You must install the Internet Control Pack to use this example. A copy of the control pack is included on the CD-ROM accompanying this book.

The code used in this example also requires us to provide a reference to the Microsoft Internet Support Objects. To set this up, open the References dialog using the Tools | References menu. Scroll through the list until you locate Microsoft Internet Support Objects. Select this item and click OK.

Add the HTTP Client control to the form. Change its name from the default to HTTP1 (just to have a shorter name).

The HTTP Client control does not provide a way to use the message format of previous versions of the HTTP protocol. Therefore, you can delete the chkProtocol checkbox from the form. It does provide a `Method` property that allows you to specify the HTTP request method to be used when retrieving a resource. So leave the `cboMethod` drop-down listbox on the form.

NOTE:

Despite many attempts, up to the time of this writing I have been unable to make a `POST` request work using the HTTP Client control. Even when the `Method` property is set to `prcPost`, the control always sends `GET` in the request message. I'm assuming this is a bug in the control that will be fixed in a future release. I have left the `POST` entry in the `cboMethod` drop-down listbox in anticipation of this.

In this example you'll use a listbox to display the header fields. Add a standard listbox to the form and name it `lstHeaders`.

The remainder of this section provides the code for any new routines (such as the HTTP control's event procedures) and also for any routines that have changed (such as `Form_KeyPress`). The rest of the routines will be used unmodified.

The Form_KeyPress Procedure

The Form_KeyPress event is where the Esc key press is captured. Pressing this key causes the document retrieval to be aborted. Listing 5.10 provides the new code for this event procedure.

The code has not changed much from the previous example. Now the HTTP1.State property is compared against the constant prcConnected to determine if the control is currently connected. If it is connected, the Cancel method of the HTTP control is invoked to cancel the transfer.

Note that the HTTP control also provides a built-in timeout mechanism. This can be used to automatically cancel the transfer if the server has not responded in a timely fashion. This feature is discussed in the following section covering the btnGetFile_Click event.

Listing 5.10. Form_KeyPress for the HTTP control example.

```
Private Sub Form_KeyPress(KeyAscii As Integer)

    If KeyAscii = vbKeyEscape Then
        If HTTP1.State = prcConnected Then
            HTTP1.Cancel
            txtStatus = "Connection cancelled..."
        End If
        KeyAscii = 0
    End If

End Sub
```

The btnGetFile Click Event

This event procedure is where the bulk of the work in this program is performed. The code is very similar to the dsSocket example's code but does not require as many lines. Listing 5.11 provides the code.

If the user clicks the Save Resource Locally command button (Index = 1), the code must obtain a filename to use when storing the resource to disk. The HTTP control can automatically send the retrieved document to a file if the DocOutput object's Filename property is set to a valid filename on the local machine. It is not necessary for the program to actually open a file and place the received data into it as was necessary when using the dsSocket control.

The code in Listing 5.11 obtains the filename from the user in the same manner as in the previous example. However, instead of opening the file for output, the code simply assigns HTTP1.DocOutput.Filename to the filename provided.

If the user clicks the View Resource command button (Index = 0), the HTTP1.DocOutput.Filename property is set to an empty string.

The HTTP control provides a `URL` property which accepts the URL of the resource to be retrieved. You don't need to parse the URL into host name, port number, and filename. The HTTP control handles this for you. The code simply assigns the contents of the `txtURL` textbox to the HTTP control's `URL` property.

The next two lines of code set up and enable the timeout feature of the control. The `TimeOut` and `EnableTimer` arrays provide for two predefined entries (`prcConnectTimeout` and `prcReceiveTimeout`) as well as user-defined entries (any value equal to or greater than `prcUserTimeout`). If one of the timers is enabled for a period equal to the value of the corresponding `TimeOut` property, the `TimeOut` event fires. This event has a parameter named `Event`, which specifies which of the timeouts has occurred. The `prcConnectTimeout` timer is disabled after a connection is made; the `prcReceiveTimeout` is disabled when the control receives data. The user-defined timeouts must be disabled with code to prevent the `TimeOut` event from firing. In this example, only the `prcReceiveTimeout` is used.

Next, the `Method` property is set to match the method chosen in the `cboMethod` drop-down listbox.

Finally, the `GetDoc` method is invoked. This starts the document transfer process. Note that the code tests for the use of the `POST` method but doesn't do anything differently. This is because, as mentioned in the Note above, I was unable to make the `POST` method work with the version of the HTTP control I had at the time of this writing.

Listing 5.11. `btnGetFile_Click` for the HTTP control example.

```
Private Sub btnGetFile_Click(index As Integer)

    Dim tmp$

    On Error Resume Next

    If index = 1 Then
        'the file name to use is after the last "/"
        tmp$ = GetFileFromURL(txtURL)
        While InStr(tmp$, "/")
            tmp$ = Mid$(tmp$, InStr(tmp$, "/") + 1)
        Wend
        dlgFileSave.filename = tmp$
        dlgFileSave.Flags = cdlOFNExplorer + cdlOFNLongNames + _
                cdlOFNNoReadOnlyReturn + cdlOFNOverwritePrompt
        dlgFileSave.Action = 2
        If Err Then
            If Err <> cdlCancel Then
                MsgBox "An error occurred opening the file: " & Error$
            End If
        Else
            HTTP1.DocOutput.filename = dlgFileSave.filename
        End If
    Else
        HTTP1.DocOutput.filename = ""
    End If
```

continues

Listing 5.11. continued

```
    'assign the URL
    HTTP1.URL = txtURL

    'set up the timer to catch timeouts
    HTTP1.Timeout(prcReceiveTimeout) = 120 * 1000
    HTTP1.EnableTimer(prcReceiveTimeout) = True

    'set up the request method
    HTTP1.Method = cboMethod.ListIndex + 1
    If cboMethod.Text = "POST" Then
        'some code must go here to output the data
        '
        HTTP1.GetDoc
    Else
        HTTP1.GetDoc
    End If

    txtStatus = "Connecting..."

End Sub
```

The HTTP1_DocOutput Event

The `HTTP1_DocOutput` event is fired when the control has received data. The code is presented in Listing 5.12. The `DocOutput` parameter passed to the event is a reference to the HTTP control's `DocOutput` object. It can be used in place of `HTTP1.DocOutput`.

Note that a property named `NotificationMode` determines when the `DocOutput` event is fired. The default setting is `0`, which indicates that the event should be fired only after all data has been received by the control. Setting this property to `1` causes the event to be fired continuously while data is received from the server. This is similar to the operation of the `dsSocket Receive` event.

The `State` property of the `DocOutput` object specifies the current state of the document transfer. The event code uses the `Select Case` construct to decide which code to execute.

When `State = icDocHeaders`, the header fields have been received. The `DocOutput.Headers` collection contains all the header fields received. The collection provides a `Count` property as well as an `Item` array. The properties of the `Item` array are `Name`, which is the header field, and `Value`, which is the value of the field. The code in the `DocOutput` event iterates through the `Item` array and adds each header field received to the `lstHeaders` listbox.

The `icDocBegin` and `icDocEnd` states mark the beginning and the end of the document transfer. These are used to update the status box text with an appropriate message. The `BytesTransferred` property of the `DocOutput` object provides a count of the number of bytes received. This property is valid throughout the document retrieval property, but I've used it only to provide the final byte count when the document transfer has been completed.

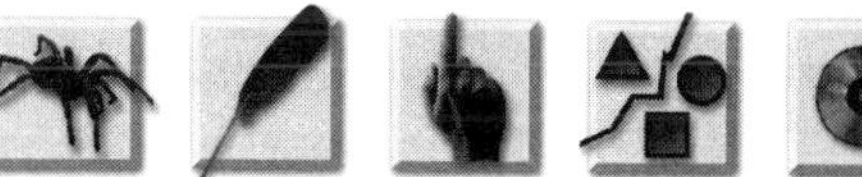

The `icDocData` state occurs when document content data has been received. Like the previous example, the code simply appends the data received to the `Text1` textbox.

Finally, the `icDocError` state indicates that an error occurred during the transfer.

Listing 5.12. The `HTTP1_DocOutput` event.

```
Private Sub HTTP1_DocOutput(ByVal DocOutput As DocOutput)

    Dim i%, vtData

    Select Case DocOutput.State
    Case icDocHeaders
        For i% = 1 To DocOutput.Headers.Count
            lstHeaders.AddItem DocOutput.Headers.Item(i%).Name _
               & ": " & DocOutput.Headers.Item(i%).Value
        Next

    Case icDocBegin
        Text1.Text = ""
        lstHeaders.Clear

    Case icDocEnd
        txtStatus = "Done... " & Str$(DocOutput.BytesTransferred) & _
              " bytes received"

    Case icDocData
        DocOutput.GetData vtData
        Text1.Text = Text1.Text & vtData

    Case icDocError
        MsgBox "Reply Code: " & HTTP1.ReplyCode
    End Select

End Sub
```

The **Error**, **StateChanged**, and **Timeout** Events

These three events are used to provide feedback to the user about the status of the transfer. The code for all three is contained in Listing 5.13.

Note that the `prcDisconnected` state is not handled. The `StateChanged` event fires with this state *after* the `DocOutput`'s `icDocEnd` state occurs. If text were written to the status box now, it would overwrite what was written during the `DocOutput` event.

Listing 5.13. The `Error`, `StateChanged`, and `Timeout` events.

```
Private Sub HTTP1_Error(Number As Integer, Description As String,
     Scode As Long, Source As String, HelpFile As String, HelpContext As Long,
     CancelDisplay As Boolean)

    If HTTP1.ReplyCode Then
        MsgBox "Server Reply Code: " & HTTP1.ReplyCode _
               & Chr$(13) & HTTP1.ReplyString
    Else
        MsgBox "Error: " & Description
    End If

End Sub

Private Sub HTTP1_StateChanged(ByVal State As Integer)

    Select Case State
    Case prcConnecting
        txtStatus = "Connecting..."
    Case prcResolvingHost
        txtStatus = "Resolving host name..."
    Case prcHostResolved
        txtStatus = "Host name resolved..."
    Case prcConnected
        txtStatus = "Connected..."
    Case prcDisconnecting
        txtStatus = "Disconnecting..."
    Case prcDisconnected

    End Select

End Sub

Private Sub HTTP1_Timeout(ByVal event As Integer, Continue As Boolean)

    Select Case event
    Case prcConnectTimeout

    Case prcReceiveTimeout
        MsgBox "Server did not respond. Try again later."

    End Select

End Sub
```

Testing the HTTP Control Application

This application (with the exception of `POST` requests as noted above) should operate just like the `dsSocket` control's example. See the section titled "Testing the `dsSocket` Application."

Summary

This chapter covered the basics of retrieving information from the Web using custom controls. The `dsSocket` control is a generic TCP/IP control that can be used whenever you want to have *complete* control over the HTTP messages that are sent to the server. The Microsoft HTTP Client control is a specialized control that sacrifices ultimate control for ease-of-use. Both of these controls have a place in your programming toolbox as you develop Web-based applications.

The information presented in this chapter is pretty basic. The first few sections were designed to serve as a reference to the `dsSocket` and HTTP Client controls. The last section presented basic but working examples that retrieve information from Web servers. Later chapters build on the knowledge you gained in this chapter by creating useful Web-based information gathering tools (such as the QuoteWatcher application in Chapter 12, "QuoteWatcher: An Interactive Web Agent") and spiders.

Chapter 6

The Win/CGI Interface

Anyone who has spent much time exploring the vast reaches of the World Wide Web has more than likely launched a CGI (Common Gateway Interface) application. Chances are just as good that that person wasn't even aware of having done such a thing. CGI applications perform all sorts of tasks on the Web: access counting, information gathering, database searching, online ordering, connecting to information appliances (such as soda machines, weather instruments, cameras, and the like), and almost any other imaginable function. Unlike static Web pages, a CGI application enables a webmaster to display real-time, dynamic information to the client. CGI applications also allow Web clients to access information that is not in a format usually readable by a Web client. This is why the term *gateway* is used—the CGI application serves as a gateway between an external information source and the Web server.

The most common uses for CGI applications are information gathering and database searching. Figure 6.1 shows a typical registration form that could be found on any Web site. The form is coded using HTML (see Appendix A, "Basic HTML Tags") and provides input controls into which the user enters data. These HTML forms are analogous to data entry forms in a Visual Basic database application except that the HTML forms are used only for data input. HTML forms are not typically used for displaying data to the user.

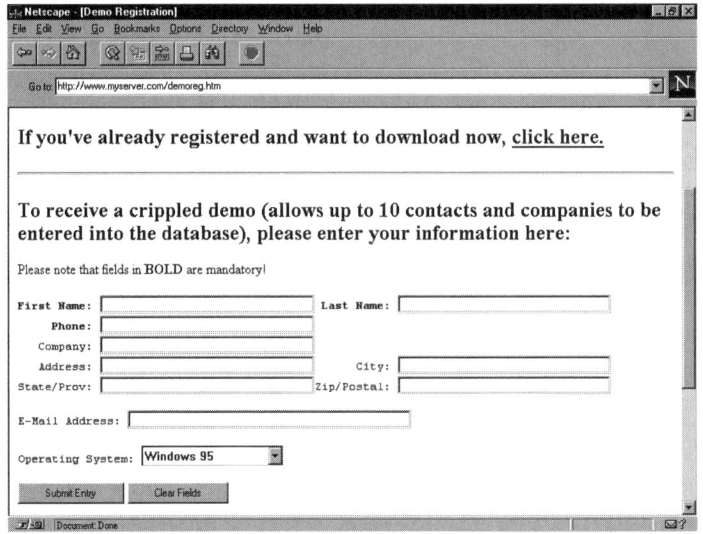

Figure 6.1.
A sample HTML form used with a CGI application.

The form in Figure 6.1 contains a button labeled "Submit Entry." This button instructs the Web browser application to send an HTTP request message to the server. Forms typically use the `POST` method in the request message. The resource specified in the request message for this form is a CGI application. The server launches the specified application. The application processes the data from the form and then produces some sort of output, which the server returns to the Web browser in the `<Entity-Body>` portion of the response message. The Web browser then displays this

output to the user. (See Figure 6.2.) After the user clicks the Submit button, the entire process that takes place is transparent to the user. Unless an error occurs, the user typically has no knowledge of what takes place "behind the scenes."

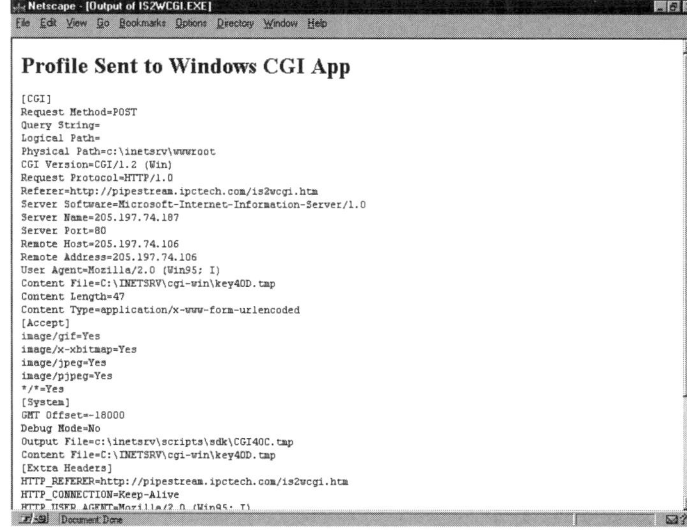

Figure 6.2.
Output of IS2WCGI.EXE.

NOTE:

Chapter 2, "HTTP: How to Speak on the Web," covers the details of the HTTP protocol, including HTTP messages and methods.

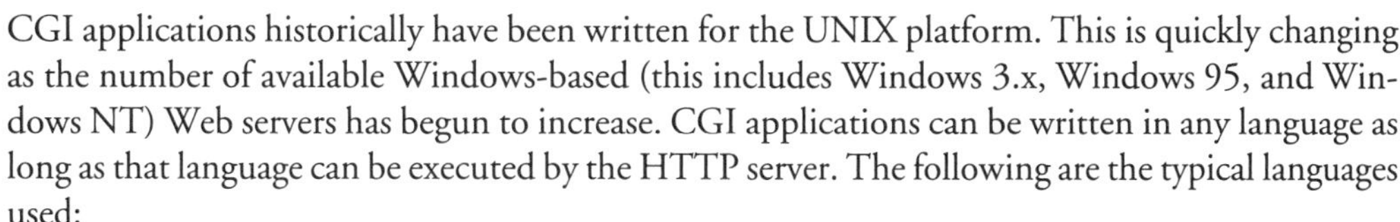

CGI applications historically have been written for the UNIX platform. This is quickly changing as the number of available Windows-based (this includes Windows 3.x, Windows 95, and Windows NT) Web servers has begun to increase. CGI applications can be written in any language as long as that language can be executed by the HTTP server. The following are the typical languages used:

- C/C++
- Perl (a UNIX scripting language)
- UNIX shell scripts
- Visual Basic
- AppleScript

Applications written to run on Windows-based platforms use a special interface known as the Windows CGI (or Win/CGI) interface. The difference between Win/CGI and UNIX CGI applications lies essentially in how the data is passed from the HTTP server to the application and then back to the server.

This chapter discusses the Win/CGI interface in detail. Subsequent chapters build on the material contained here to assist you in building Win/CGI applications that can be run on your own Windows-based Web server.

NOTE:

The Win/CGI interface specification is not a formal Internet specification. It is authored by Robert Denny, who wrote the Windows-based Web server application now sold by O'Reilly and Associates as WebSite. The specification is currently at version 1.3a and can be found at `http://website.ora.com/wsdocs/32demo/windows-cgi.html`. The WebSite demo version can be found on the CD-ROM accompanying this book.

How CGI Data Is Handled

When writing a CGI application, the developer has the same two concerns that developers of all applications have: data input and data output. This section discusses how data is input into a CGI application. The closing section of the chapter ("Returning the Results to the Client") discusses how data is output by the application.

In the UNIX environment, CGI applications receive their data from command line arguments, environment variables, and the standard input (known as `stdin` to C programmers). By querying the value of one of a predefined set of these variables, the UNIX CGI application can determine the server context that it has been run under and the data that was entered at the client side. The application then returns its data to the server using the standard output (`stdout`).

In the various Windows environments (Windows 3.x, Windows 95, and Windows NT), the operating system makes the use of environment variables and the standard input/output difficult. For this reason, the Win/CGI interface uses a spooling paradigm for passing data between the server and the CGI application. Before executing the CGI application, the server creates a CGI data file. This file contains the same data fields that are used in UNIX CGI applications, along with fields specific to Win/CGI. The name of the data file is passed to the CGI application as a command line argument. Likewise, the CGI application places its output into a file whose location the server specifies in one of the fields of the CGI data file.

Decoding the HTML Form

As you learned in Chapter 2, the client is not limited to simply retrieving resources from HTTP servers. There are also two HTTP request methods that allow the client to interact in some way with a resource.

The first method uses a `GET` request message that includes search terms in the resource address:

```
GET //myserver.com/cgi-win/search.exe?last=smith+first=jim
```

This request message could have been generated by clicking the Submit button of a form or by some sort of user agent. Likewise, the user of a Web browser such as Netscape could enter the address portion of this string into the text box provided for Web addresses. Any of these three actions causes the HTTP server to launch search.exe and pass it the search text that appears after the "?".

The second method uses a `POST` request message. The difference between a `POST` message and the `GET` message illustrated previously is that the `POST` message uses the `<Entity-Body>` portion of the message to transfer the form data. This method is used by the Submit button or by a user agent. Because the form data entered on the HTML form is sent in the `<Entity-Body>`, it cannot be entered into the address box of a Web browser.

With the second method, the Win/CGI interface requires that the server parse the HTML form data from the POST message it received. This data is then stored in either the CGI data file previously discussed or in an external file. In the later case, the server places an entry in the CGI data file that specifies the filename and length of this external file. The client application uses the `Content-Type` entity header to specify how the data is encoded in the `<Entity-Body>`. There are two `Content-Types` used: `application/x-www-urlencoded` and `multipart/form-data`. The first is the `Content-Type` used in most cases. The second `Content-Type` provides for uploading files from the client by using a multipart MIME message. To date, multipart MIME messages are not widely used in HTTP messages. The `Content-Type` header is passed to the CGI application as one of the fields in the CGI data file.

Launching the Application

When a client application or user agent requests a CGI application resource, the server must launch the application. This section discusses how the application is launched and the environment that is available to it. Because this chapter discusses the Win/CGI interface, I won't be covering the intricacies involved in running UNIX applications. I will instead concentrate on the Windows applications.

Special Considerations When Using Win/CGI

You should keep in mind several considerations when writing Win/CGI applications. These considerations are extremely important to the health of your Web server machine as well as to the user's experience with your Web site. Failure to take into account some of these considerations can have disastrous consequences for your computer.

The first consideration involves keeping your server and its data secure. It is of utmost importance for you to remember that, by opening a CGI application to the Internet, anyone can run the application on your machine. Make sure you don't leave any "back doors" open in the application. You should also make sure the application is installed into a special directory set up to specifically house CGI applications. The documentation for your Web server application should tell you how to set up this directory. Also, make sure that you limit the application's use of system resources, such as printers, network resources, and directories. Some people on the Internet make a hobby of trying to infiltrate the systems of others and exploit weaknesses they find. The havoc that they can wreak in an unprotected system is far worse than what a virus can accomplish, so use caution.

The second thing you should keep in mind is that while your application is running, the user is wondering what's taking it so long to finish. No matter how quickly a developer feels the application executes, the user always wants it to move along faster. Even if your application produces a Web page with valuable information for the user, the user might never see it if he or she decides to click that "Stop" button on the Web browser. Although this action won't directly affect your application (in fact, because of the statelessness of HTTP, the application won't even be aware that the Stop has happened), you do lose the opportunity to present the output to the user. If your application is collecting information, you might want to limit the CGI application merely to storing the data in a table. If there is further processing to be performed on the data and that processing doesn't have to be completed before producing the output page the client will see, it is best to leave the processing to a batch process that runs at a later time.

The third consideration is that when the server launches a CGI application, it creates a separate process on the machine. For each concurrent request made, another concurrent process is created. This consumes both memory and processing time, and it can also affect the ability of the operating system to share resources that may be needed by the CGI application. Therefore, you should attempt to limit the maximum number of concurrent connections to your server. Most HTTP server applications provide an option for specifying the maximum number of concurrent connections. You should pick a number that is a compromise between the number of people you'd like to have viewing your static Web documents and the number you'll allow to run applications.

The Win/CGI Command Line

When the server launches the CGI application, it does so using the `CreateProcess()` API function. It then monitors this process to detect when the process has finished (that is, when the application has completed execution). Typically during the time the application is running, the TCP/IP connection between the client machine and the server machine is left open. The client application typically displays a busy indicator to the user. When the CGI application exits, the server then transfers its output to the client in the form of an HTTP response message.

CAUTION:

The server may (and probably will) detect that the CGI application's process has ended *before* the application has been completely shut down. Do *not* rely on the program exiting for the closing of files and other resources—you should explicitly close them before the program ends. Visual Basic closes any open files when an application ends, but you should not rely on this "feature;" otherwise, your CGI application more than likely will not function correctly.

The command line used to execute the CGI application depends on the HTTP server. The current version of the CGI interface calls for the following command line:

```
<CGI-application-path> SP <cgi-data-file-path>
```

Both paths must be absolute paths. The server must not rely on the current directory (which has no meaning to the new process) or to the `PATH` environment variable.

Older versions of Windows-based HTTP servers used a command line with a few more parameters:

```
<CGI-application-path> SP <cgi-data-file-path> SP <Input-File>
➥SP <Output-File> SP <URL-parameters>
```

If your application will be executed only on servers using the simpler command line, there is no need to look for the rest of the command-line parameters. If, however, you plan to distribute your application publicly or aren't sure of the HTTP server's capabilities, you should plan for both possibilities.

The following section covers the CGI data file in depth.

Retrieving the CGI Data

Before the server launches a CGI application, it creates a CGI data file. This file contains information about the server and the client that submitted the request, as well as any data that is associated with the request (the HTML form data filled in by the user).

The file is formatted as a Windows initialization file. Therefore, the CGI application can use API calls such as `GetPrivateProfileString()` to retrieve the data. Listing 6.1 shows a portion of what this file might look like. In the next chapter we'll actually write the program that produced this Web page. If you've reviewed Chapter 2, a lot of the fields shown in Listing 6.1 will look familiar to you—they're the values of many of the HTTP request message header fields.

Listing 6.1. A sample CGI data file.

```
[CGI]
Request Protocol=HTTP/1.0
Request Method=POST
Query String=
Logical Path=
Request Keep-Alive=No
Executable Path=/cgi-win/project7.exe
Server Software=WebSite/1.1 (demo version)
Server Name=www.myserver.com
Server Port=80
Server Admin=webmaster@myserver.com
CGI Version=CGI/1.2 (Win)
Remote Address=127.0.0.1
```

continues

Listing 6.1. continued

```
Content Type=application/x-www-form-urlencoded
Content Length=25

[Accept]
image/gif=Yes
image/x-bitmap=Yes
image/jpeg=Yes
image/pjpeg=Yes
*/*=Yes

[System]
GMT Offset=-18000
Debug Mode=Yes
Output File=C:\WebSite\cgi-temp\3ews.out
Content File=C:\WEBSITE\CGI-TEMP\3EWS.INP

[Form Literal]
Name1=Craig
```

The remainder of this section discusses the different sections of the data file and the fields they contain. Some of the fields discussed in these sections aren't shown in Listing 6.1. This is because the server that generated this CGI data file is compliant with version 1.2 of the CGI interface. Also, if a field's value is empty, the interface is defined such that it should be omitted from the file. Obviously the server that generated this data file does not fully comply with the Win/CGI interface! This chapter discusses the current version (1.3a) and highlights the differences between the versions.

The `[CGI]` Section

The `[CGI]` section contains the fields that provide information about the client and server that are executing the application. Most of the fields in the data file are contained in this section.

Request Method

This field provides the value of the `<method>` portion of the HTTP request message. The standard methods are `GET`, `POST`, and `HEAD`. The HTTP protocol provides for additional methods as long as both the client and server applications both recognize them as request methods.

Query String

If the CGI application was launched in response to a `GET` or `HEAD` request containing search text in the URI, the portion of the URI appearing after the `?` is contained in the value of the `Query String`

field. The server does not attempt to decode the string in any way (recall from Chapter 2 that reserved characters are encoded using escape characters such as %20 for a space).

The value of this field also contains the HTML form data if the form's `ACTION` tag is defined as `GET` (see Appendix A for information on HTML forms). The format of the URI in this case is:

```
"//myserver.com/cgi-win/myapp.exe?key=value&key=value..."
```

Logical Path and Physical Path

If the request message includes additional path information, the server passes this to the CGI application using the `Logical Path` and `Physical Path` fields. The logical path is relative to the path space that is active for the server. The physical path is an absolute path that the application can always use. If the URI contained in the request uses an encoded path, the server must decode it before placing it in the CGI data file. The UNIX CGI specification calls these fields `PATH_INFO` and `PATH_TRANSLATED` respectively.

CGI Version

This field specifies the version of the CGI specification the server operates under. Listing 6.1 shows that the server is using version 1.2 of the Win/CGI specification. The format is `"CGI/"<version>`. The UNIX CGI specification calls this field `GATEWAY_INTERFACE`.

Request Protocol

This field specifies the protocol the request message used. This is the `<HTTP-Version>` element for an HTTP/1.0 request message. This field should be used when creating the output file to determine if you can send a complete response message. If the value is *not* HTTP/1.0, you should return only the entity portion (that is, the HTML) and no additional header fields. UNIX uses `SERVER_PROTOCOL`.

Referer

This field specifies the URI of the resource that contained the link to the CGI application. The value can be either an absolute or relative URI. This field can be used for *back-linking* to the resource that ran the application (back-linking refers to placing a link to the resource in the output document).

Server Software

This field holds the name and version number of the server software that received the request message and launched the application. The format is `<name> "/" <version>`. The example from Listing 6.1 specifies the demo version of WebSite 1.1.

Server Name and Server Port

The `Server Name` and `Server Port` fields specify the full host name (or IP address) and TCP port the server is listening on. These fields are used to create self-referencing URLs for the output file. They can also be used for logging purposes if the application accesses a database used by multiple servers.

Remote Host and Remote Address

These fields contain the host name and IP network address of the remote client that produced the request message. The remote host name may not always be available. These fields are used for logging purposes and can be used to compare CGI usage to the usage of other logged resources.

Content File, Content Type, and Content Length

If the request has data associated with it, these fields specify how the data can be retrieved. The `Content File` field specifies the full path to a file that holds the data. The `Content Type` field specifies the MIME type of the data. Its format is `<type> "/" <subtype>`. The `Content Length` specifies the length of the content (in bytes).

Document Root

This is the physical path to the server's logical root directory (referred to as /) as defined in the server setup. For example, the server at `myserver.com` may be set up to recognize `c:\wwwroot` as the root directory for Web services. A client that requests the document `//myserver.com/index.htm` is sent the file `c:\wwwroot\index.htm`. This field is new to version 1.3a of the specification.

Executable Path

`Executable Path` is the logical path that points to the CGI application. This is the path that the HTTP server recognizes but may not be the physical path. It is relative to the server's root HTTP directory as defined in the server setup.

User Agent

This field holds the value of the `User Agent` request message header field. The value specifies the client application that generated the request. Not all user agents generate this field.

From

The `From` field is the value of the `From` request message header field. The value specifies the e-mail address of the user that generated the request. This is in the HTTP specification but is typically not used due to privacy issues.

Server Admin

This field specifies the e-mail address of the server's administrator. It can be used in output files when an error occurs (use the `mailto:` link) or for sending mail to the administrator from within the CGI application.

Authentication Method and Authentication Realm

These fields are present if the request message was for a resource that the server requires to be authenticated. The `Authentication Method` field specifies the method being used to authenticate the user. The `Authentication Realm` specifies the server "realm" that describes the address space for the secure area of the server. Chapter 2 describes HTTP authentication to some extent, but the HTTP/1.0 Internet Draft document provides a complete description.

The server must provide these fields to the CGI application if they were included in the request message, even if the resource did not require authentication.

Authenticated Username and Authenticated Password

These are the username and password specified in the request message. They make up a valid and authenticated combination. If the user had failed the authentication process (by entering an invalid username/password combination), the server would not have launched the CGI application. It would have sent a response message with a status code of 401 (unauthorized).

The server must provide these fields to the CGI application if they were included in the request message, even if the resource did not require authentication.

The [Accept] Section

This section contains the client's acceptable MIME types. These are taken from the request message's `Accept` header field. Listing 6.1 illustrates five different values. The format of the `Accept` header field is

```
"Accept:" 1#(<type> "/" <subtype> [";" "q=" ("0" ¦ "1" ¦ FLOAT )] [";" "mxb=" 1*DIGIT])
```

The CGI data file enumerates each of the `Accept` header fields in the `[Accept]` section. The value is `Yes` unless the optional `q` parameter is present. The value of the `q` parameter becomes the value used in the CGI data file. The `q` parameter specifies the user's preference for the specified MIME type. For example:

```
"Accept: text/plain; q=0.5, text/html, text/x-div; q=0.4"
```

specifies that the client prefers HTML text but will accept plain text or `x-div` encoded text if HTML is not available. The client prefers plain text over `x-div` text if both are available.

TIP:

To retrieve all the values in the `[Accept]` section, make a call to the `GetPrivateProfileString()` with a `NULL` value in the key name parameter. This places all the fields from the `[Accept]` section in the string buffer provided. Each substring ends with a null character (`Chr$(0)`), and the entire returned string has two nulls at the end.

The [System] Section

The fields in this section are fields used by the Windows implementations of CGI. They are not found in UNIX CGI systems. This section defines these fields.

GMT Offset

This is the number of seconds to be added to Greenwich Mean Time (GMT) to obtain the local time. For Eastern Standard Time, the value is -18000.

Debug Mode

This field defaults to `No` unless the server has enabled CGI script tracing. The value is `Yes` if it is enabled. This can be used for conditional tracing in a CGI application. On some Web servers (such as WebSite), turning CGI tracing on also causes the server to leave all CGI data files intact after the CGI application ends. Usually these files would be deleted.

Output File

This field provides the full path to the file the application should use for its output. The server generates a unique filename to be used for this purpose. When the CGI application ends, the server sends this file to the client in (or in place of, depending on the contents of the file) the response message.

Content File

This field contains the filename of the file containing any content sent to the server in the request message.

The [Extra Headers] Section

This section contains any additional header fields sent with the request message. The keys and values must be decoded by the server if they included reserved characters.

TIP:

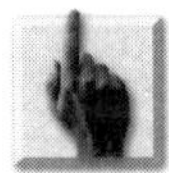

To retrieve all the values in the `[Extra Headers]` section, make a call to the `GetPrivateProfileString()` with a `NULL` value in the key name parameter. This places all the fields from the `[Extra Headers]` section in the string buffer provided. Each substring will end with a null character (`Chr$(0)`) and the entire returned string will have two nulls at the end.

The [Form Literal] Section

If the application was launched in response to a `POST` from an HTML form, this section contains the decoded form data. Each form element has an entry in this section. Listing 6.1 shows several fields in the form of `key=value`. The `key` element is the `NAME` tag from the HTML form element that produced the data.

If the HTML form contains any `SELECT MULTIPLE` elements, the `[Form Literal]` section contains multiple occurrences of the key. The server generates a `key=value` field for the first occurrence. Subsequent appearances of the element in the form data cause a sequence number to be appended to the key (`key1=value` for example). The CGI application must be aware of this possibility in order to properly use these form elements.

Generally the CGI application is designed to expect certain key values from the request message. The application is typically written alongside the HTML form, similar to the way Visual Basic applications are designed.

The [Form External] Section

If the form data contained any fields longer than 254 characters, control characters, or double-quotes, the server places this data in a file. The name of the file is then specified along with the form element that produced the data. The format is

```
key=pathname length
```

The `length` is the length in bytes. The file should be opened as binary unless you're sure that the contents of the field is text only.

The [Form Huge] Section

If a form data element is longer than 65,535 bytes, the server does not decode the element from the content file. Instead, it produces an entry in the `[Form Huge]` section as follows:

```
key=offset length
```

where `key` is the form element name, `offset` is the byte offset from the beginning of the content file, and `length` is the length in bytes of the value. In the application, you would use the `Seek` statement on the open content file to move the file pointer to the start of the value string. You would then read *length* bytes to retrieve the entire value.

As with the `[Form External]` section, you should open the content file as binary unless you're positive it contains only text data.

The [Form File] Section

This section contains a list of files where uploaded file data has been placed. This is used only if the content was sent as multipart/form-data content. The format of the entries in this section is

```
key="["<pathname>"]" SP <length> SP <type> SP <xfer> SP "[" <filename> "]"
```

The `<pathname>` element specifies the path to the file stored on the server. The square brackets are used to delimit the filenames in case they contain spaces. The `<length>` element is the length of the file in bytes. The `<type>` element indicates the MIME content type of the file, and `<xfer>` specifies the transfer encoding of the file. Finally, `<filename>` specifies the original filename of the uploaded file.

Returning the Results to the Client

The goal of a CGI application is to return some sort of response to the user. Even if the application is a guest book registration application, the user should still be informed of the fact that the entry was or wasn't added to the guest book. This section explains how data is returned to the client by the CGI application and the server.

The server is responsible for actually creating the HTTP response message sent to the client. The server is also typically responsible for adding the proper HTTP header fields to the response message. However, you can format the output such that the CGI application specifies these header fields. This is discussed below.

The body of the output file typically (but not necessarily) contains HTML formatted text. The body is displayed by the user's Web browser using the specified `Content-Type` header (discussed below). Several examples are given at the end of this section.

How Header Fields Are Handled

The header section consists of one or more lines of text. It is separated from the body of the message by a blank line. There are several header fields that may be placed in the application's output file.

If the application will be returning data to the client and you aren't using the direct return method discussed in following sections, the first line is used to specify the MIME type of the body. It should read as

```
Content-Type: <type>/<subtype>
```

If the application won't be returning data, but desires to send the user another file, or send them to another resource, the `URI:` header is used. It specifies a resource to be returned to the user in place of the body that would have been produced by the CGI application. The format is

```
"URI:" "<" <URI> ">"
```

Note that the URI is enclosed in angled brackets. If the URI points to a local file, the server sends this file within the response message. If the URI is a full URL, the server set the response message status to 401 (redirect), which informs the client that it should retrieve the URI directly.

The `Location:` header is used for the same reason as `URI:` but the address must *not* be enclosed in angled brackets.

If you wish to specify the response message's status, use the `Status:` header. The format is

```
"Status:" SP <Status-Code> SP <Reason-Text>
```

The `<Status-Code>` and `<Reason-Text>` elements should follow the definitions given for those elements in Chapter 2. However, the HTTP protocol does not require these elements to have any specific value. They should, though, follow the general classifications given in Chapter 2.

If the CGI application places any other header fields before the body, the server passes them unmodified to the client. Care must be taken to ensure that these headers do not conflict with any other response message headers the server may be using in the response message.

Creating the Complete HTTP Response Message

If you desire to create the entire response message, bypassing the server's creation of the message, you can do so. The output file would contain the complete HTTP response message (see Chapter

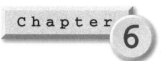

2 for details). This message *must* be a valid HTTP response or the user will likely not be able to interpret the results of the application.

To create the entire response message with the CGI application, begin the first line of the output file with HTTP/1.0. If the server sees this, it assumes the application is creating the response message. The server then returns the entire output file to the client without any modification.

Example Output Files

The following file would be returned by the server in the `<Entity-Body>` portion of the response message. It is an HTML document.

```
Content-Type: text/html
                                                    <== header/body separator (blank
line)
<html><head><title>Entry Submitted</title></head>
<body><H1>Entry Submitted!</H1>
Your entry has been submitted to the Guest Book.<br>
Thank you for your support!<br><hr>
<a href="/home.htm">Return Home</a></body></html>
```

The next example uses the Location feature to redirect the client to another resource. In this case, the resource is located on an ftp server.

```
Location: ftp://ftp.myserver.com/pub/demo/demo.zip
                                                      <== blank line
```

Finally, this example produces the entire HTTP response message, including some additional response message header fields.

```
HTTP/1.0 200 OK                                     <== start of HTTP header
Date: Mon, 25 Mar 1996 05:23:01 GMT
Server: Microsoft-Internet-Information-Server/1.0
Content-Type: text/html
Content-Length: 3202
Expires: Mon, 25 Mar 1996 13:23:01 GMT
                                                    <== header/body separator (blank
line)
<html><head><title>Query Results</title></head>
(etc.)
```

Summary

This chapter has presented the basics of using the Win/CGI interface to write server-side applications. You'll apply this information in the next chapter where you'll build a basic Win/CGI application. Subsequent chapters expand on this information in even greater detail.

Chapter 7

Creating CGI Applications in Visual Basic

- How CGI Apps Differ form "Typical" Visual Basic Apps
- Designing Some Oft-Used Routines
- Creating the HTML Form
- Installing the Application on Your Web Server
- WinCGI's Version of `Hello World`
- The CGI `StoryTeller`

Now that you've been properly introduced to both Chapter 2, "HTTP: How to Speak on the Web" and Chapter 6, "The Win/CGI Interface," it's time to build your first server-side Visual Basic application. Although this process builds on the Visual Basic experience you already have, if you've never developed an application that runs asynchronously at a random point in time and allows no interactivity, you're in for a treat!

In this chapter we'll discuss the differences between the "typical" Visual Basic application (if there is such a beast) and a CGI application. Then, after introducing some code you'll use throughout the remainder of the book, you'll build a few simple CGI applications, including the application that was used to create the Web page shown in Figure 6.2.

How CGI Apps Differ from "Typical" Visual Basic Apps

As I mentioned in the introduction to this chapter, writing CGI applications is a completely different animal than writing most Visual Basic applications. This section discusses some of the major differences that you must keep in mind when writing an application that your Web server will launch. If you forget these differences, your application will probably leave the Web surfer wondering why the browser displays the `Document returned no data` message when the Submit button is clicked!

Waiting For Response...

One of the most important things to keep in mind is that while your program is executing happily on the server machine, the user is staring at what might as well be a blank screen. The typical Web browser application (also referred to as a *user agent*), displays a message in its status panel to the effect of `Connected to` *`www.xyz.com`*`...Waiting for response....` The cursor is the hourglass cursor, further emphasizing to users that they're on hold. Therefore, CGI applications must do their thing and return control to the Web server as quickly as possible. The program should avoid using any but the quickest methods of accomplishing what needs to be accomplished.

For instance, you should avoid attempting to start a slow OLE automation server. If the application attempts to create an Excel spreadsheet object, stuff data into it, analyze the data, export the spreadsheet to a Word document, and then return the Word document to the user, the client will probably produce a time-out error—unless, of course, your Web server is running on a machine with an ultra-fast motherboard and hard drives. Unfortunately, there are no "rules of thumb" for what you should and shouldn't do. Only experimentation with the application will reveal how fast or slow it operates.

The Sluggish Net

Another item to keep in mind while we're discussing speed is the speed of the user's connection. If your application returns complicated Web pages with lots of graphics on them, you'll want to connect to the server and try the application using a 14.4Kbps modem. This simulates not only the typical user's connection, but also a fast T-1 connection from across the country. As the Internet becomes more and more crowded, even fast access points slow down as the user traverses the continent, hopping from network to network before finally reaching your server.

This is not a concern for CGI applications only—when designing a Web site, you should attempt to design for the lowest common denominator. If you can afford separate sets of pages for users with fast and slow connections, the effort is usually very much appreciated.

Do Not Allow for Interactivity

Perhaps the most important item to keep in mind is this: No one is there to click the OK button on a message box that a CGI application might open. This is particularly true on Windows NT Web servers that run as a system service. For debugging on a Windows 3.*x* or Windows 95 Web server, such interactivity might work. However, unless you want to sit by the machine while the Web server is operating and click OK, make sure you remove all possibility of having a message box appear.

If you're running a Windows NT Web server, such as the Microsoft Internet Information Server, the problem is even more severe. A CGI application that causes a message box also more than likely causes a time-out error on the client or returns no data if the server realizes the app is effectively dead in the water and times out first.

If you use common code modules, comb through them to make sure they contain no user interface code.

Use Tighter, Centralized Error Control

Make sure error trapping is turned on in the `Sub Main` routine and that, if errors are trapped separately in procedure and function calls, that no message boxes will display! It is best to use a central error trapping mechanism: The only `ON ERROR...` statement should be in the `Sub Main` procedure. This provides you with the ability to control exactly what code is executed when an error occurs. It also helps eliminate the possibility of an object requiring interaction being opened. The examples you'll build later use this type of error trapping.

TIP:

Unless the application requires user-interface controls for some reason, don't use any forms in your application. Use `Sub Main` in a module instead, for the startup. This decreases the size and load time of your application.

Synchronizing with HTML Forms

When designing an application that accepts input from the user (such as a guest book registration or search engine), you must keep CGI data in the application and input elements on the HTML forms in synch. If you change a form input element's `NAME` tag, for instance, you must update the CGI code to reflect this change. This becomes more apparent when you start into the examples.

For example, you wouldn't try to access a textbox named `Text1` in a typical application if it didn't exist. Likewise, you can't get meaningful data from a CGI field named `Text1` if one doesn't exist on the HTML form that serves as the user interface for a CGI application.

Formatting Output for HTML Browsers

Just as you have to be conscious of HTML forms for inputting data, you must also take care with HTML when outputting data to the client. Although HTML is an Internet standard, each Web browser renders an HTML document slightly (or, in some cases, grossly) different. You should limit what you try to accomplish with the output page in order to serve the most number of browsers possible.

http://www.research.digital.com/nsl/formtest/home.html

There is an HTTP header field and a corresponding CGI data field called `UserAgent` (in the CGI data file it's in the `[CGI]` system as `User Agent`). This field is where the Web client that generated the request message specifies its name and version. This *could* be useful for determining what to output to the client. However, there are so many different values used for this field that trying to make sense of it can be more trouble than it's worth. For a demonstration of this, visit the HTML Form-Testing Home at `http://www.research.digital.com/nsl/formtest/home.html` and follow the `Test Results Sorted by Browser` link. This will provide a *long* list of all the `UserAgent` values that have been tested by the site.

We hope a future version of HTTP (and Win/CGI) will provide a field for specifying HTML conformance and the graphical capabilities of client applications. This type of field would provide meaningful information to server-side applications when those applications produce HTML output.

Leave No Objects or Files Open

When the CGI program is ready to end, make sure you close all open files and any objects that have been created. The mechanism the server uses to monitor when your program exits has been known to trigger before the program has completely cleaned itself up. As most VB programmers are aware, VB cleans up behind an application if it leaves files or databases open. However, doing so in the CGI environment may cause unexpected results. This is particularly true with the CGI output file. If it is not explicitly closed before the server attempts to open it for transmission to the client, you're in for big trouble! The server may actually read all that's available in the file but miss the last segment of it. This could happen if VB has to close the file after the application exits—the last pieces of data the app wrote to it won't actually make it to the disk until the file is closed.

Use AutoNumber Fields for Access Databases

Because of the tremendous concurrency issues that arise on Web servers, you should always allow the database engine to specify primary keys. This ensures that two concurrently running CGI applications that add records to a table won't pick the same key.

Designing Some Oft-Used Routines

Well, now that all the dire warnings of the previous section are out of the way, it's time to actually write some code! This section provides a few routines that you'll use in the examples of this chapter, as well as throughout the remainder of the book. This section won't give all the routines used in the book, though. You'll add more as you go along.

For now, we'll examine two code modules: `FUNCS.BAS`, which houses common routines that might be used in any application, and `CGI.BAS`, which houses routines specific to Win/CGI and CGI applications. This section provides the complete code for the routines we'll cover. However, because all the code is on the CD-ROM for your use and modification, don't expect to see full code segments throughout the rest of the book.

The Code from `FUNCS.BAS`

This module is used for general-purpose routines that could be used in any application. Some of the routines are stupidly simple, others can be pretty neat to dissect and use.

This section discusses two of the routines that you'll use quite often: `tReplaceChars()` and `ParseString`.

tReplaceChars()

This routine is used to replace a given string within another string with a third string. You use this routine mostly when generating database SQL statements to replace single quote characters with two single quote characters.

For example, if you attempted to update a text field in a database using the SQL statement `UPDATE MyTable SET LastName = 'O'Neil'`, you'd get a syntax error due to unmatched quote characters. The correct SQL for this situation is `UPDATE MyTable SET LastName = 'O''Neil'`. How does `tReplaceChars()` correct this?

The following is some code that calls `tReplaceChars()`:

```
tName$ = "O'Neil"
tName$ = tReplaceChars(tName$,"'","''")
lSQL$ = "UPDATE MyTable SET LastName = '" & tName$ & "'"
```

The final value of `tName$` is `"O''Neil"`, and thus the SQL statement contained in `lSQL$` is valid.

`tReplaceChars()` not only replaces single-character strings; it can also replace entire words contained within a string. The possible uses for this routine are endless. So, without further ado, Listing 7.1 contains the code for `tReplaceChars()`.

Listing 7.1. `tReplaceChars()`.

```
Function tReplaceChars(ptInputStr As String, ptLookFor As String, _
                        ptReplaceWith As String) As String

    lsloc% = InStr(1, ptInputStr, ptLookFor, 1)
    If lsloc% = 0 Or Len(ptLookFor) = 0 Then
        tReplaceChars = ptInputStr
        Exit Function
    End If

    lRLen% = Len(ptReplaceWith)
    lLLen% = Len(ptLookFor)

    lxx$ = ptInputStr

    Do Until lsloc% = 0
        lxx$ = Mid$(lxx$, 1, lsloc% - 1) + ptReplaceWith + _
               Mid$(lxx$, lsloc% + lLLen%, Len(lxx$) - lLLen% - lsloc% + 1)
        lsloc% = InStr(lsloc% + lRLen%, lxx$, ptLookFor, 1)
    Loop

    tReplaceChars = lxx$

End Function
```

Briefly, here's how `tReplaceChars()` works. The first line of the function tests to see if `ptLookFor` (the string to be replaced) exists in `ptInputStr` (the input string). The `Instr()` function is called with its final parameter being `1`. This causes a case-insensitive search. If the `Instr()` function returns a value of `0`, `ptLookFor` is not in `ptInputStr`, and the function returns the input string. (There is nothing to replace so the output string is the same as the input string.) If there is an occurrence of `ptLookFor` within `ptInputStr`, the local variable `lsloc%` contains the start of the first occurrence. The value of `ptInputStr` is stored in a temporary string (`lxx$`).

The `Do_Until_lsloc% = 0` loop is where all the replacement takes place. The first line of the loop takes the portion of the temporary string up to the first occurrence of `ptLookFor`, appends the `ptReplaceWith` string, and then appends the portion of the temporary string that appears after the END of the searched-for string. Finally, you look for `ptLookFor` again and assign its starting position to `lsloc%`. When there are no more occurrences of `ptLookFor`, `lsloc%` will be `0` (zero), and the `Do Until` will be met, causing the loop to end. The final line assigns the temporary string to the function's output.

Here are some samples:

```
tReplaceChars("Quick Brown Fox", "Brown", "Red") = "Quick Red Fox"
```

This call replaces the "Brown" in "Quick Brown Fox" with "Red", as you can see from the results. The following replaces every occurrence of "BB" with "DD" in the string "ABBBCBBC":

```
tReplaceChars("ABBBCBBC", "BB", "DD") = "ADDBCDDC"
```

Finally, the following shows how the introduction of a space at the end of the string to be replaced can affect the results:

```
tReplaceChars("A BBB C BB C", "BB ", "DD ") = "A BBB C DD C"
```

ParseString

The `ParseString` procedure takes a delimited string and makes an array out of the delimited elements. For example, if you have a string that looks like: `"Jim,John,Jack"` and want an array of all the names contained in the string, you would call `ParseString(NameArray, "Jim,John,Jack", ",")` and, when the procedure returned, `NameArray` would contain three elements:

```
NameArray(1) = "Jim"
NameArray(2) = "John"
NameArray(3) = "Jack"
```

You'll use this procedure extensively to enumerate the fields contained within the CGI data file. Listing 7.2 contains the code for this procedure.

Listing 7.2. ParseString.

```
Sub ParseString(ptArray() As String, ptString As String, ptDelim As String)

'lPos is an array containing the positions of the delimiters and
'the start and end of the string
Dim lPos() As Integer
ReDim lPos(1)
lPos(0) = 1
lPos(1) = InStr(1, ptString, ptDelim)
lNum% = 1

If lPos(1) <> 0 Then
    Do
        lNum% = lNum% + 1
        ReDim Preserve lPos(lNum%)
        lPos(lNum%) = InStr(lPos(lNum% - 1) + 1, ptString, ptDelim)
    Loop Until lPos(lNum%) = 0
End If
lPos(lNum%) = Len(ptString)

ReDim ptArray(lNum%)
If lNum% > 1 Then
    For ln% = 1 To lNum%
        Select Case ln%
        Case 1      'First substring
            ptArray(ln%) = Mid$(ptString, lPos(ln% - 1), _
                (lPos(ln%) - lPos(ln% - 1)))

        Case lNum%  'Last substring
            ptArray(ln%) = Mid$(ptString, lPos(ln% - 1) + 1, _
                (lPos(ln%) - lPos(ln% - 1)))

        Case Else   'All other substrings
            ptArray(ln%) = Mid$(ptString, lPos(ln% - 1) + 1, _
                (lPos(ln%) - lPos(ln% - 1) - 1))

        End Select
    Next ln%
Else
    ptArray(1) = Mid$(ptString, 1, lPos(lNum%) + 1)
End If

End Sub
```

This code is pretty straightforward. The first section creates an array that contains the positions of the occurrences of the delimiter (`ptDelim`) within the string (`ptString`) and keeps track of how many delimiters were encountered (`lNum%`). The second section steps through the position array and pulls out each substring from `ptString`. Each substring is then placed into the array (`ptArray`) that was passed to `ParseString`.

The Code from CGI32.BAS

The file `CGI32.BAS` is used as a common code module by all of the CGI applications you develop in this book. It contains the data types, global variables, functions, and procedures that you'll use in creating your CGI applications.

The CGIData Type

The first thing you'll code is a user-defined data type. The `CGIData` type is used to store all the standard CGI data fields that the server passes to CGI applications.

The `CGIData` type includes an array element named `FormSmallFields`. This element is of type `CGI_FormFieldType`, which is defined in Listing 7.3. This type allows storage of the form or the URL's input field name (`key`) as well as the value specified on the form or URL (`value`).

Listing 7.3. The `CGI_FormFieldType` data type.

```
Type CGI_FormFieldType
    key As String
    value As String
End Type
```

Listing 7.4 provides the code for the `CGIData` user-defined type.

Listing 7.4. The `CGIData` type.

```
Type CGIData                    'used to access the CGI data file
    ProfileFile As String           'complete path to the CGI data file
    RequestMethod As String
    QueryString As String
    DocumentRoot As String
    LogicalPath As String
    PhysicalPath As String
    ExecutablePath As String
    CGIVersion As String
    RequestProtocol As String
    Referer As String
    ServerSoftware As String
    ServerName As String
    ServerPort As String
    ServerAdmin As String
    UserAgent As String
    RemoteHost As String
    RemoteAddress As String
    ContentFile As String
    ContentLength As Long
    ContentType As String
    GMTOffset As Variant            'time serial
    DebugModeOn As Integer          'False if Debug Mode=No, True otherwise
```

continues

Listing 7.4. continued

```
    OutputFileName As String       'Output File field from [System]
    OutputFileHandle As Integer    'file handle used for output
    FormFieldCount As Integer      'how many data fields?
    FormSmallFields() As CGI_FormFieldType    'holds all data fields
End Type
```

Most of the fields are defined in Chapter 6. However, a few fields have been added.

The `ProfileFile` field is where you'll store the name of the CGI data file. This is passed to the application as the first (and maybe only) command-line parameter.

The `OutputFileHandle` is the file handle to use when writing information to the output file. The output file path is specified in `OutputFileName`.

The `FormSmallFields` array contains most of the fields either from the HTML form that causes the application to launch, or from the URL used in an HTTP `GET` request message. The field `FormFieldCount` holds a count of the number of fields contained in `FormSmallFields`. The array holds fields that were found in the `[Form Literal]` and `[Form External]` sections of the CGI data. These are the only sections we cover in this chapter. The other sections contain fields that you'll rarely encounter when writing CGI applications.

The global variable `guCGIData` is of type `CGIData` and is used to store the CGI data.

The GetKeyValue() Function

The `GetKeyValue()` function is used to retrieve data from the CGI data file. It can retrieve either a specific field or all of the fields from the specified section. The function uses the value of `guCGIData.ProfileFile` to determine which file to use as the CGI data file. The function is defined in Listing 7.5.

The string parameter `ptSection` is the section you'll be getting data from. The values you'll pass with this parameter include `"CGI"`, `"Accept"`, `"System"`, `"Extra Headers"`, and `"Form Literal"`, to match the possible sections contained in the CGI data file. The parameter `ptKey` specifies the field to be retrieved. If `ptKey` is passed as an empty string, all the field names present in the section `ptSection` are returned. This feature is used to retrieve all the items in the `[Accept]` section and all of the fields in the `[Form Literal]` and `[Form External]` sections, for example.

The function works by calling the Windows API function `GetPrivateProfileString()`. `GetPrivateProfileString()` reads Windows initialization files and stuffs the value read into a string buffer provided to it. It returns a count of the number of characters placed in that string. The string is terminated with a `NULL` character (`CHR$(0)`). `GetKeyValue()` truncates the string to the length specified by the return value of `GetPrivateProfileString()` before returning it.

Listing 7.5. GetKeyValue() function.

```
Public Function GetKeyValue(ptSection As String, _
        ptKey As String, piLength As Long) As String
Dim bucket$, res&

bucket$ = Space$(piLength + 1)
If Len(ptKey) Then
    'return the specfied key
    res& = GetPrivateProfileString(ptSection, ptKey, "", _
           bucket$, piLength, guCGIData.ProfileFile)
Else
    'return all keys contained in ptSection
    res& = GetPrivateProfileString(ptSection, 0&, "", _
           bucket$, piLength, guCGIData.ProfileFile)
End If
bucket$ = Left$(bucket$, res&)
GetKeyValue = bucket$

End Function
```

CAUTION:

`GetPrivateProfileString()` removes single and double quotes that surround the value being read. So, if the CGI data file contains

```
[Form External]
LastName='Jones'
```

`GetKeyValue()` would return only the string `"Jones"`.

The LoadCGIData() Function and the LoadFields Procedure

The `LoadCGIData()` function is where the vast majority of the CGI data is retrieved. The function uses the value of `guCGIData.ProfileFile` as the path to the file that contains the CGI data. Then, the values of the many CGI fields are placed into the other elements of the `guCGIData` record variable. The function also obtains a file handle to be used for the application's output (`guCGIData.OutpuFileHandle`) and opens the output file for `Write` access. The code for `LoadCGIData()` is given in Listing 7.6.

The optional parameter `piLoadFields` informs the routine not to retrieve any of the `[Form Literal]` and `[Form External]` fields. This is useful in applications where a large number of fields are passed to the application but not all fields are used by the application. By setting the `piLoadFields` parameter to `False` when calling `LoadCGIData()`, you can save the time required to read all the fields. However, you have to call either the `GetKeyValue()` or `GetPrivateProfileString()` functions to retrieve the field values individually.

Listing 7.6. The `LoadCGIData()` function.

```
Public Function LoadCGIData(Optional piLoadFields As Variant) As Integer
'Input: (Optional) piLoadFields = TRUE or not present:
'        load [Form Literal] and [Form External]
'                                = FALSE: don't load the sections
'   Also, must have guCGIData.ProfileFile set to the path of the CGI data file
'Output: TRUE if successful, FALSE otherwise

LoadCGIData = False 'initial value

With guCGIData
    'if the ProfileFile element has not been defined, error out
    If Len(Trim$(.ProfileFile)) = 0 Then Exit Function

    .OutputFileName = GetKeyValue("System", "Output File", 255)
    .RequestMethod = GetKeyValue("CGI", "Request Method", 255)
    .QueryString = GetKeyValue("CGI", "Query String", 255)
    .DocumentRoot = GetKeyValue("CGI", "Document Root", 255)
    .LogicalPath = GetKeyValue("CGI", "Logical Path", 255)
    .PhysicalPath = GetKeyValue("CGI", "Physical Path", 255)
    .ExecutablePath = GetKeyValue("CGI", "Executable Path", 255)
    .CGIVersion = GetKeyValue("CGI", "CGI Version", 255)
    .RequestProtocol = GetKeyValue("CGI", "Request Profile", 255)
    .Referer = GetKeyValue("CGI", "Referer", 255)
    .ServerSoftware = GetKeyValue("CGI", "Server Software", 255)
    .ServerName = GetKeyValue("CGI", "Server Name", 255)
    .ServerPort = GetKeyValue("CGI", "Server Port", 255)
    .ServerAdmin = GetKeyValue("CGI", "Server Admin", 255)
    .UserAgent = GetKeyValue("CGI", "User Agent", 255)
    .RemoteHost = GetKeyValue("CGI", "Remote Host", 255)
    .RemoteAddress = GetKeyValue("CGI", "Remote Address", 255)
    .ContentFile = GetKeyValue("CGI", "Content File", 255)
    .ContentLength = Val(GetKeyValue("CGI", "Content Length", 255))
    .ContentType = GetKeyValue("CGI", "Content Type", 255)

    buf = GetKeyValue("System", "GMT Offset", 255)
    If buf <> "" Then
        .GMTOffset = CVDate(Val(buf) / 86400#)
    Else
        .GMTOffset = 0
    End If

    .DebugModeOn = (UCase$(GetKeyValue("System", _
                   "DebugModeOn", 255)) = "YES")

    'get an output file handle and open the output file
    .OutputFileHandle = FreeFile
    Open .OutputFileName For Output Access Write As #.OutputFileHandle

End With

'if piLoadFields was not passed, load the fields
If IsMissing(piLoadFields) Then
    Call LoadFields
Else
    'otherwise, check piLoadFields to determine if
    'we should load the fields
```

```
    If piLoadFields Then Call LoadFields
End If

LoadCGIData = True

End Function
```

If `piLoadFields` is `True` or is not passed to the function, `GetCGIData()` calls the `LoadFields` procedure. This procedure, shown in Listing 7.7, retrieves the fields from `[Form Literal]` and those referenced in `[Form External]` into the `guCGIData.FormSmallFields` array. Recall from Chapter 6 that the format for these sections is as follows:

```
[Form Literal]
FormFieldName=Value
[Form External]
FormFieldName=filename filelength
```

For the `[Form Literal]` section, `LoadField` first retrieves all of the `FormFieldNames` contained in the section. It then calls `ParseString()` to place these names into an array. Finally, it iterates through this array and assigns the `FormFieldNames` to the `.key` element of `guCGIData.FormSmallFields` and calls `GetKeyValue()` to get the value from the CGI data file to assign to the `.value` element.

For the `[Form External]` section, the procedure retrieves the field names in the same manner as the `[Form Literal]` section. The `.value` element, however, is contained in the file specified by the filename element in the value portion of the field's entry in the `[Form External]` section (see above). So, as the procedure iterates through each key in the section, it opens the file specified (using `Binary` access just in case the data is not textual) and reads its contents into the `.value` element.

Finally, the `LoadFields` procedure sets the value of `guCGIData.FormFieldCount`.

Listing 7.7. The `LoadFields` procedure.

```
Public Sub LoadFields()
    Dim tString$, iCount%
    Dim tmpArray() As String

    guCGIData.FormFieldCount = 0

    'get the Form Literal section
    tString$ = GetKeyValue("Form Literal", "", 4096)
    'tString$ is now "key1" & chr$(0) & "key2" & chr$(0) ... & chr$(0) & chr$(0)
    If Len(tString$) Then
        tString$ = Left$(tString$, Len(tString$) - 1)
        Call ParseString(tmpArray, tString$, Chr$(0))
        iCount% = UBound(tmpArray)
        ReDim guCGIData.FormSmallFields(iCount%)

        For i% = 1 To iCount%
            guCGIData.FormSmallFields(i%).key = tmpArray(i%)
```

continues

Listing 7.7. continued

```
            guCGIData.FormSmallFields(i%).value = GetKeyValue("Form Literal", _
                  tmpArray(i%), 255)
        Next
        guCGIData.FormFieldCount = iCount%
    End If

    'get the Form External section
    tString$ = GetKeyValue("Form External", "", 4096)
    If Len(tString$) Then
        tString$ = Left$(tString$, Len(tString$) - 1)
        Call ParseString(tmpArray, tString$, Chr$(0))
        iCount% = UBound(tmpArray)
        With guCGIData
            ReDim Preserve.FormSmallFields(.FormFieldCount + iCount%)
            For i% = 1 To iCount%
                j% = .FormFieldCount + i%
                .FormSmallFields(j%).key = tmpArray(i%)
                'get the value of the field
                buf$ = GetKeyValue("Form External", tmpArray(i%), 255)
                'the format of byf$ is:
                ' <pathname> SP <length>
                pos% = InStr(buf$, " ")
                pathname$ = Left$(buf$, pos% - 1)
                contentlen& = CLng(Mid$(buf$, pos% + 1))
                filenum% = FreeFile
                Open pathname$ For Binary Access Read As #filenum%
                .FormSmallFields(j%).value = Space$(contentlen&)
                Get #filenum%, ,.FormSmallFields(j%).value
            Next
           .FormFieldCount =.FormFieldCount + iCount%
        End With
    End If

End Sub
```

The GetFieldValue() Function

The `GetFieldValue()` function (see Listing 7.8) is used to retrieve the field values from the `guCGIData.FormSmallFields` array. Its sole parameter is the name of the field you'd like to retrieve. The `guCGIData.FormSmallFields` array must be filled before `GetFieldValue()` is called.

As an example, suppose the HTML form that launches the application contains a textbox input called `"LastName"`. You can retrieve the data entered into it by using this line:

```
GetFieldValue("LastName")
```

Listing 7.8. The `GetFieldValue()` function.

```
Public Function GetFieldValue(tFieldName As String) As String

    GetFieldValue = ""  'default to an empty string
```

```
    If Not (FieldPresent(tFieldName)) Then Exit Function
    For i% = 1 To guCGIData.FormFieldCount
        If guCGIData.FormSmallFields(i%).key = tFieldName Then
            GetFieldValue = guCGIData.FormSmallFields(i%).value
            Exit Function
        End If
    Next

End Function
```

The function defaults to an empty string if the value is not overridden. The function checks to see if the field specified by `tFieldName` is present in the `guCGIData.FormSmallFields` array by calling `FieldPresent()`. If it's not present, the function exits with the empty string as its return value. If the field is present, the function iterates through the array until it locates the field being retrieved. After locating the field, the function assigns its return value to the `.value` element for that item in the array.

The **OutputString** Procedure

The final procedure we'll examine before moving on to an actual application is `OutputString`. This procedure simply writes the string passed to it to the output file opened in `LoadCGIData()`. Listing 7.9 contains the code. Note that no error handling code is present. So that the error handling can be centralized, it is done by the `Sub Main` routine.

Listing 7.9. The **OutputString** procedure.

```
Public Sub OutputString(ptOutputString As String)

    Print #guCGIData.OutputFileHandle, ptOutputString

End Sub
```

Creating the HTML Form

You're getting closer to actually writing your first CGI applications. However, there's one more step to cover before you can move on. You first must create an HTML document (also known as a Web page). This Web page (shown in Figure 7.1) contains the data input controls in which the user can enter information to be passed to the CGI application. It also has a Submit button and a Reset button. When the user clicks the Submit button, the Web browser sends a request message to the server, which includes the name of the CGI application to launch. The Reset button is a special HTML control that clears out all the input boxes on that form.

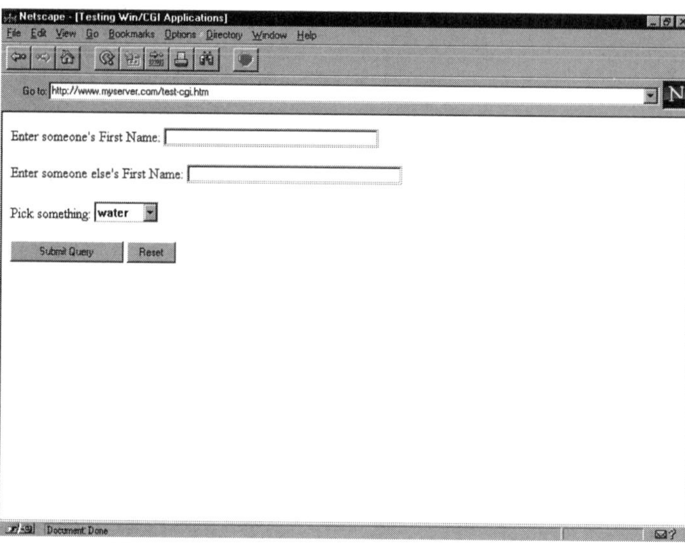

Figure 7.1.
The simple Web page for this chapter.

This Web page is created using the HTML code in Listing 7.10. Create this Web page on your server so that it is accessible to your Web browser.

While a complete explanation of the HTML contained in Listing 7.10 is beyond the scope of this chapter, a little explanation is in order. Appendix A, "Basic HTML Tags," contains more detailed explanations of the HTML coding used here.

Listing 7.10. The HTML for the simple Web page.

```
<HTML>
<HEAD><TITLE>Testing Win/CGI Applications</TITLE></HEAD><BODY>
<FORM METHOD=POST ACTION="/cgi-win/test-cgi.dll">
Enter someone's First Name: <INPUT NAME="Name1" TYPE="TEXT" SIZE="30"><p>
Enter someone else's First Name: <INPUT NAME="Name2" TYPE="TEXT" SIZE="30"><p>
Pick something: <SELECT Name ="Fetch" VALUE="water">
<OPTION>water</OPTION><OPTION>soda</OPTION><OPTION>worms</OPTION></SELECT><p>
<INPUT TYPE="SUBMIT">   <INPUT TYPE="RESET">
</FORM>
</BODY>
</HTML>
```

On the third line of Listing 7.10, you see the definition of an HTML `FORM` element. This element has several *tags* that define how the form operates. The first tag is `METHOD`. This defines the request method that the browser should use when sending the request message to the server after the Submit button is pressed. The choices are `GET` and `POST`. This simple Web page uses `POST`. The second tag (`ACTION`) specifies the application to be executed when the user clicks the form's Submit button. This is a URI, which can be either an absolute address or a relative address. Here, you're specifying

a relative address because the application to be executed (`test-cgi.dll`) resides on the same server as the Web page. Replace the text in quotes following the `ACTION` element with the URI for the application on your server.

NOTE:

The server used in this example is the Microsoft Internet Information Server (IIS). The Microsoft server doesn't directly support the Win/CGI specification. Appendix C, "Win/CGI on the Microsoft Internet Information Server," discusses the IIS and explains why the form is calling a `DLL` instead of an executable. For now, it's important only to know that the `DLL` specified creates the CGI data file and then launches the Visual Basic Win/CGI executable you'll create in the following sections.

The four lines following the `<FORM ...>` line specify the input controls being used. The first two lines define textboxes that have field names of `"Name1"` and `"Name2"` respectively. The third and fourth lines specify a single-select drop-down list box. The items that appear in the list are `"water"`, `"soda"`, and `"worms"`, with `"water"` being the default value. The field name for the listbox is `"Fetch"`.

The fifth line specifies the two buttons, `"Submit"` and `"Reset"`. Finally, the sixth line after the `<FORM ...>` line ends the form definition with the closing `</FORM>` tag.

Installing the Application on Your Web Server

This book assumes that you have Visual Basic installed on the machine that your Web server is running. This simplifies installation of the CGI applications you'll develop because all the system files required were loaded when Visual Basic was installed.

The first step is determining whether or not your server is set up to execute applications, and, if so, where those applications should reside. All Web servers should have some sort of directory setup mechanism. For the Microsoft Internet Information Server (IIS), you can find this by double-clicking the WWW service entry in the Internet Service Manager application and selecting the Directories tab. For the WebSite server, the Server Admin application has a tab called Mapping. By selecting the Windows CGI radio button in the List Selector frame on this tab, you can get a list of all the directories that can house Win/CGI applications.

While you're in the Web server's setup application, turn on CGI tracing or CGI debug mode, if available. With debugging on, the server does not delete the files created during the CGI process. This is useful for examining what data has been passed to the application and what the output file really looks like.

In WebSite, the debugging option is turned on using the Logging tab's CGI Execution checkbox in the Tracing Options frame. For the Microsoft IIS, this feature is unavailable "out of the box." Appendix C discusses how to turn on debug mode.

After the proper directory is set up, code the application and create an executable. Then, simply copy the executable to the Win/CGI directory specified on the WebSite server admin's Mapping tab or on the IIS's Directories tab. It can now be executed from a Web browser's URL entry box, a Web page, or by using the HTTP application created in Chapter 5, "Retrieving Information from the Web."

Win/CGI's Version of **Hello World**

The classic example used as the first application in many programming texts is a program called `Hello World`. This application simply displays the text `Hello World` on the system's output. For CGI applications, however, the classic application seems to be one that returns all the data contained in the CGI data file. That's what you'll code in this section.

The code you create here won't rely on `CGI32.BAS` for any of its routines. If you don't include `CGI32.BAS` in the project, you will need to declare the Windows API `GetPrivateProfileString()` function in the `Declarations` section of the code module. The code does rely on `FUNCS.BAS` for the `ParseString` procedure; so be sure to include that in your project or copy the procedure's code into your module.

Listing 7.11 contains the code for a `Sub Main` procedure. Place this code in a new module (you can either type it in or retrieve it from the CD-ROM included with the book). Select File | Make Exe File from the Visual Basic menu. On the Make EXE dialog box, enter **`test-cgi.exe`** as your executable name and make sure the path points to your `cgi-win` directory identified in the previous section. Once the executable is created, launch your Web browser and enter the URL for the page created in the section "Creating the HTML Form" earlier. Enter some information in the text boxes and click OK. You should see a page similar to Figure 7.2.

Listing 7.11. `Hello World` code.

```
Public Sub main()
    On Error GoTo FormError
    Dim ProfileFile$, buffer$
    Dim OutputFileHandle As Integer
    Dim KeyArray() As String

    'get the CGI data file/path
    If InStr(Command$, " ") Then
        ProfileFile$ = Left$(Command$, InStr(Command$, " ") - 1)
    Else
        ProfileFile$ = Command$
```

```
End If

'get the output path
buffer$ = Space$(256)
res& = GetPrivateProfileString("System", "Output File", _
       "", buffer$, 255, ProfileFile$)
buffer$ = Left$(buffer$, res&)
'get the next available file handle
OutputFileHandle = FreeFile
'open the file
Open buffer$ For Output Access Write As #OutputFileHandle

'write some header stuff to the file
Print #OutputFileHandle, "Content-Type: text/html"
Print #OutputFileHandle, ""
Print #OutputFileHandle, "<html><body>"

'define an array with all the section names
Dim Sections(7) As String
Sections(0) = "CGI"
Sections(1) = "Accept"
Sections(2) = "System"
Sections(3) = "Extra Headers"
Sections(4) = "Form Literal"
Sections(5) = "Form External"
Sections(6) = "Form Huge"
Sections(7) = "Form File"

For j% = 0 To 7
    tSection$ = Sections(j%)
    'get all of the fields in the section
    buffer$ = Space$(4096)
    res& = GetPrivateProfileString(tSection$, 0&, _
           "", buffer$, 4095, ProfileFile$)
    If res& > 1 Then
        'strip off the last chr$(0)
        buffer$ = Left$(buffer$, res& - 1)
        'put the field names into an array
        Call ParseString(KeyArray(), buffer$, Chr$(0))

        Print #OutputFileHandle, "[" & tSection$ & "]<br>"
        'write all of the keys
        For i% = 1 To UBound(KeyArray)
            'print the key name and stay on the same line
            Print #OutputFileHandle, KeyArray(i%) & "=";
            'get the value of the field
            buffer$ = Space$(255)
            res& = GetPrivateProfileString(tSection$, KeyArray(i%), _
                       "", buffer$, 255, ProfileFile$)
            buffer$ = Left$(buffer$, res&)
            'print it to the output file
            Print #OutputFileHandle, buffer$ & "<br>"
        Next i%
    End If
Next j%
```

continues

Listing 7.11. continued

```
    Print #OutputFileHandle, "</body></html>"

    'close the output file
    Close #OutputFileHandle
    End

FormError:
    If OutputFileHandle <> 0 then
        Seek #OutputFileHandle, 1
        Print #OutputFileHandle, "Content-Type: text/html"
        Print #OutputFileHandle, ""
        Print #OutputFileHandle, "<html><body>"
        Print #OutputFileHandle, "Error: " & Err & "<p>"
        Print #OutputFileHandle, Error$ & "<p></body></html>"
        Close #OutputFileHandle
    End If
    End
End Sub
```

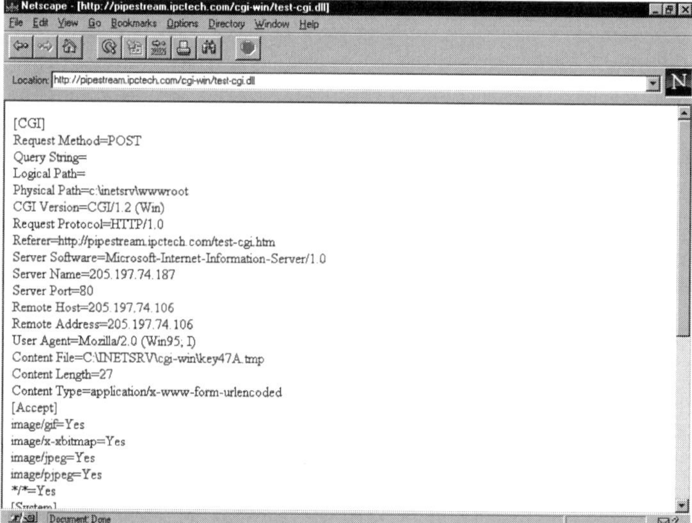

Figure 7.2.
The output of the `Hello World` application.

The code is fairly simple to understand. The first step is to obtain the path to the CGI data file from the command line. Then, retrieve the name of the output file from the CGI data file by using `GetPrivateProfileString()`. A new file handle is obtained, and the file is opened for output. The header lines are written to the file. These instruct the server that you're sending HTML formatted text.

An array is created to hold the names of the eight possible sections of the CGI data file. You then start a loop that loops through this array and extracts the information from the section if it exists. By calling `GetPrivateProfileString()` with a zero of the `LONG` data type (`0&`) as the second parameter, you can retrieve all the available items in the section specified by the first parameter. If the

section does not exist or contains no items, an empty string is returned. After calling `GetPrivateProfileString()` in this manner, you check to see if it returns a value greater than zero (remember that this function returns the length of the string it retrieves from the CGI data file). If it did indeed return a string, that string contains all the items in the current section you're iterating.

The items are separated by a `NULL` character (`CHR$(0)`) and end with two `NULL` characters. The code strips this last `NULL` before passing the string to `ParseString`, which fills `KeyArray` with all the item keys found for this section. Next, the code iterates through `KeyArray` and, using `GetPrivateProfileString()`, gets the value specified with each key.

Throughout the code several lines start with "`Print #OutputFileHandle,`". This is where the code writes information to the output file. In this case, the information is HTML formatted text. However, it could be any data you wish to send back to the client.

The error trapping is pretty basic in this program. Any error sends the program to the `FormError:` label. The code then checks to see if you have a file handle. If one is available, you'll write some information about the error to an HTML output file and exit. If the program had not yet obtained a file handle when the error occurred, the code simply ends, usually causing the Web browser to display a message to the user to the effect of `Server returned no data`.

The CGI StoryTeller

"Why did I create a nice form if all I'm going to do is look at the CGI data file?" you may be asking. Well, in this section, you're going to create an application that actually uses the information entered on the form. The application is still very basic, but it demonstrates the use of many of the functions contained in `CGI32.BAS`.

Start a new project in Visual Basic. Add `CGI32.BAS` and `FUNCS.BAS` as well as a new code module. This new module is where you'll place `Sub Main` and a procedure called `StoryTeller`. These two routines are shown in Listing 7.12.

Listing 7.12. `Sub Main` and `StoryTeller` code.

```
Public Sub main()
    On Error GoTo FormError

    If InStr(Command$, " ") Then
        guCGIData.ProfileFile = Left$(Command$, InStr(Command$, " ") - 1)
    Else
        guCGIData.ProfileFile = Command$
    End If

    If LoadCGIData() = 0 Then
        'if we couldn't load all the CGI data,
        'could we at least open the Output File?
        If guCGIData.OutputFileHandle <> 0 Then
```

continues

Listing 7.12. continued

```
            'yes - call ErrorHandler to handle this
            Call ErrorHandler(-1, "Error loading CGI Data File")
        Else
            'no - forget about anything else!
            End
        End If
    End If


    'let's tell a story!
    Call StoryTeller

FormError:
    Call ErrorHandler(Err, Error$)

End Sub

Public Sub StoryTeller()

    OutputString "Content-Type: text/html"
    OutputString ""
    OutputString "<html><head><title>CGI Story Teller!</title></head><body>"
    If Len(GetKeyValue("Name1")) And Len(GetKeyValue(("Name2")) Then
        OutputString "<h1>The Story of " & GetKeyValue("Name1")
        OutputString " and " & GetKeyValue("Name2") & "</h1>"
        OutputString "<p>"
        OutputString GetFieldValue("Name1") & " and " & GetFieldValue("Name2")
        OutputString " went up a hill to fetch a pail of "
        OutputString GetFieldValue("Fetch") & ".<p>"
        OutputString "<h2>Thank You for Reading!</h2>"
    Else
        OutputString "<h1>Hey! You have to enter both names "
        OutputString "or the story is meaningless!</h1>"
    End If
    OutputString "</body></html>"

    'close the output file
    Close #guCGIData.OutputFileHandle
    End

End Sub
```

As you can see, the use of routines from `CGI32.BAS` has greatly simplified the code. In `Sub Main`, the program starts in the same way as the previous program: It obtains the path to the CGI data file. Since you're using `CGI32.BAS`, however, assign the path of the data file to `guCGIData.ProfileFile`. Recall that `LoadCGIData()` uses this variable when retrieving the CGI data.

After the profile file is identified, the code calls `LoadCGIData()` and checks the return value. If the function returns zero (meaning some problem occurred loading the CGI data), it then checks to see whether a file handle has been assigned. If a file handle exists, a call is made to the `Errorhandler` routine in `CGI32.BAS`; if one doesn't exist, the program simply exits because it has no valid file to which it can write any output.

If you got past `LoadCGIData()`, it's time to move on to `StoryTeller`. This procedure is where all the output is created.

You first inform the server that you're sending HTML formatted text by using the `Content-Type` header field. This is followed by a blank line. Then you check to make sure the user has entered some text in both name fields on the HTML form. If the user hasn't, you return a nasty response message informing your user of the need to do so. If there are names, you create a small story by combining static HTML with the values entered in the form's fields (by using the `GetKeyValue()` function).

Finally, the procedure finishes off the HTML file, closes the output file, and ends.

Create the executable file as in the previous section. Use `test-cgi.exe` as the filename, so you can use the same HTML file as the input form. Rename the previous `test-cgi.exe` file if you want to keep a copy.

Using your Web browser, open the HTML file created earlier in this chapter. Enter some names, select an item from the list, and click Submit. You should see a page similar to Figure 7.3. Return to the form and click Reset. Then click Submit again to see a nasty response about leaving the names blank.

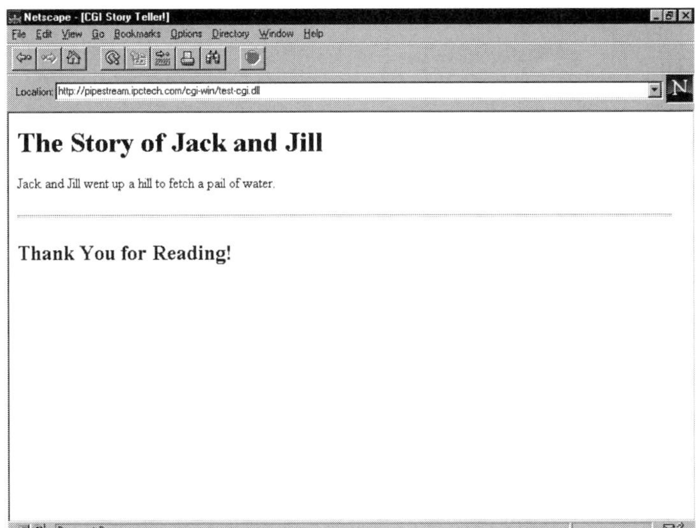

Figure 7.3.

Output of the `StoryTeller` application.

Summary

We've covered a lot of ground in this chapter. Most of the code samples are pretty basic and don't do a great deal. Still, you now have a good background with which to build real CGI applications.

If you're itching to create a useful CGI application to install on your Web server, Part II of the book presents several real-world applications you can adapt to meet your specific needs.

Chapter 8

Database Connectivity: The WebGuest Application

- Deciding What Data to Track
- Designing the WebGuest Site
- Creating the Database
- Coding the Applications
- Installing and Testing the Applications

So far, this book has covered the basics of programming for Web server applications. This chapter presents a complete server-side application that uses the Win/CGI interface. The WebGuest site actually consists of a suite of programs that each perform different functions. There are two applications that generate dynamic HTML pages, an application for recording registration information, one for searching the database, one for creating various lists from the database, and of course, one that displays the registered information.

The WebGuest site is an example of using CGI applications for guest book registration. This is probably the most popular use of CGI applications on the Web today. Just about every Web site that is capable of running CGI applications uses a guest book of some sort. The guest book is used to collect information about who is viewing the Web site, what equipment and Web browser the visitor are using, and what their interests in the site might be. Other sites employ CGI registration applications for gathering information from potential subscribers and for customer feedback and product support.

This chapter covers the design of the WebGuest site, the design of the database that stores the information gathered, and how to code and test the WebGuest site.

Deciding What Data to Track

Before you decide how your Web site should look or how you will program the applications that control the entry and display of guest book information, you must decide what information to collect. The type of data you'll track depends primarily on what you want to do with the information. If your site is used for software support, you'll need to know the specifics of the user's hardware and operating system. If your site enables the user to request additional information be sent to them, you'll need to collect input about how to send the information and what information to send.

Obviously, you can ask the user any question you wish. However, don't count on having too many people answer many questions about personal matters. Most users are happy to enter contact information and information about the software and hardware they're using. In addition, if you're marketing a product or service, the user will probably be willing to let you know his or her interest in your product or service. Also, demographic information such as age range, household makeup, gender, and so on, are frequently used to tailor a Web site to match the user's assumed interests. Most visitors to a site providing such customization won't mind providing this information, either.

The other consideration is the number of fields on the data entry form that the user must complete. If it contains too many questions or the form appears overwhelming, the user may choose to skip the form altogether. You must balance the information you require with the user's

willingness to provide that information. The key is to make sure the user perceives that he or she will receive some benefit from providing the requested information. If your Web site is used for marketing purposes, I'd recommend obtaining one of the many books that discuss Internet marketing strategies. My favorite is *Guerilla Marketing Online* by Jay Conrad Levinson and Charles Rubin.

For the WebGuest site, I've chosen to collect basic contact information. This includes name, address, work phone, e-mail address, and Web page URL. Users will also be able to choose an icon to represent their entry in the guest book. WebGuest will also track information provided by the CGI interface—the user's browser, the user's IP address, and the user's host name.

In addition to being able to enter information into the WebGuest database, users can also conduct searches on information entered by others. The search form is identical to the data entry form. The user can also list information, such as the type of Web browser being used. Using this feature, the user would be presented with a list of the Web browsers that have been used to access the WebGuest site. The list would include the name of the Web browser application and a count of the number of times that browser has been used at the WebGuest site. Beneath each entry in this list is a list of all the users who registered using that user agent. This list contains a hyperlink to a page providing the WebGuest entries for each of these users. As you'll see in the section titled "Designing The WebGuest Site," there are many other methods of searching and listing the data contained in the WebGuest database.

Obviously, when developing a Web site such as the WebGuest site you want to keep privacy in mind. If you collect any personal information such as gender, makeup of the household, income range, and so on, you probably don't want to make such information available to the public. You could provide summary data, such as what percentage of registered users are within a certain age range, as long as there is no way of connecting such information back to individual registrants.

Designing the WebGuest Site

With the considerations of the previous section clearly in mind, it's time to design the WebGuest site. The site starts at an entry page that provides links to the rest of the site. The structure of the WebGuest site is shown in Figure 8.1. The page at the top center of Figure 8.1 is the entry page. It serves as the launching pad for the journey through the WebGuest site.

The entry page, shown in Figure 8.2, is dynamically generated by one of the WebGuest applications. It provides a count of the number of records in the registration database as well as links to the registration page, the list page, and the search page. The application that generates the page is created from the `entry.vbp` project presented in the "Coding the Applications" section later in this chapter. The page is dynamically generated in order to provide the record count.

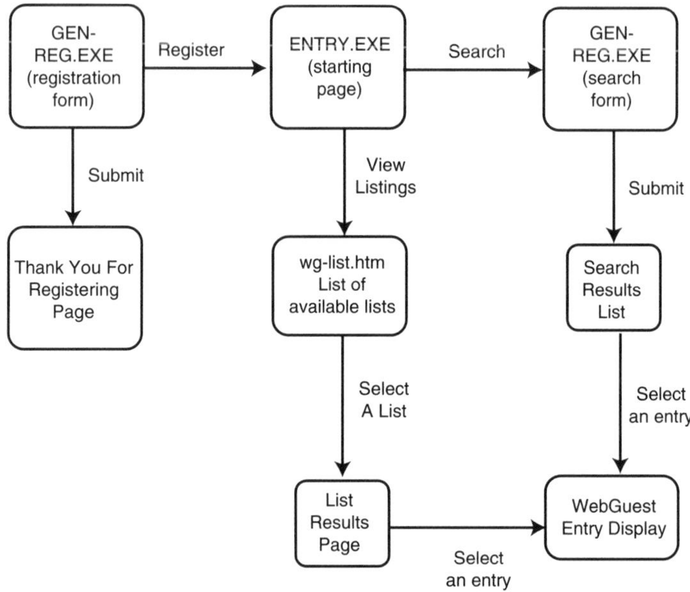

Figure 8.1.
The structure of the WebGuest site.

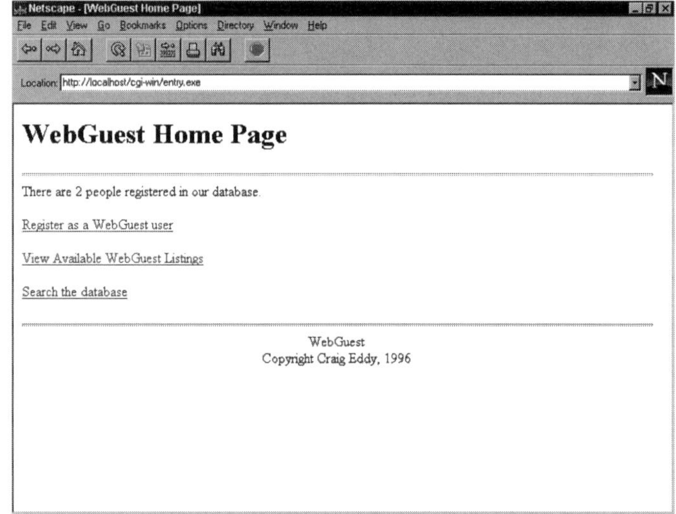

Figure 8.2.
The WebGuest entry page.

The first link on the entry page takes the user to the registration page, shown in Figure 8.3. The second link shown takes the user to the search page. The searching and registration pages are generated by the `gen-reg.exe` application, which the links on the entry page execute. The application is passed different query strings based on whether the search or register link is selected. The pages created are identical except for the action taken when the HTML Submit button is clicked and some of the text on the page. The registration page's form `POST`s the data to an application named `register.exe`. The search page's form `POST`s the form data to an application named `search.exe`.

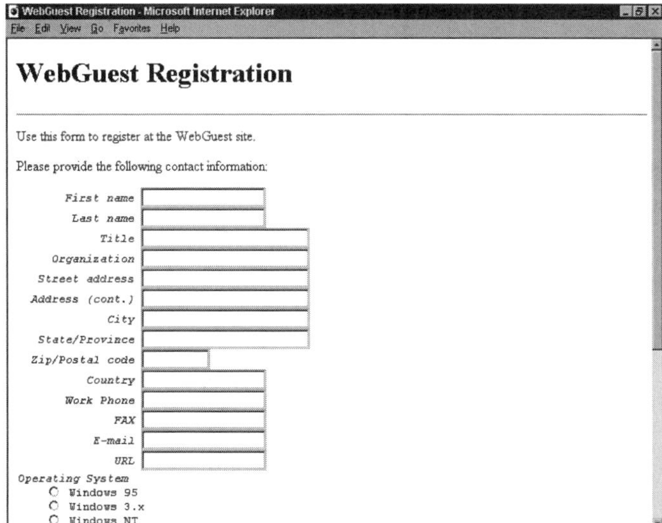

Figure 8.3.
The WebGuest registration form.

A CGI application is used to generate these pages in order to retrieve the paths to the available pictures from a table in the database. Although this is not required to make the application operate, it does allow the pictures used at the site to be changed without changing any HTML forms or the CGI applications.

The list page, shown in Figure 8.4, provides links to the available methods of listing the WebGuest data. This page is static—it is resident on the server, not generated by a CGI application. The HTML for the page, provided in Listing 8.1, should be placed in a file named `wg-list.htm`. The file should reside in the Web server's logical root directory. All the links execute the same CGI application, but with different query strings. This application, `gen-list.exe`, checks the provided query string and creates a list based on its value. In this chapter, I've provided four options: `List by Last Name`, `List by State`, `List by Remote Host`, and `List by User Agent`. It is quite simple to extend or modify the available lists, as you'll see in the code for `gen-list.exe`.

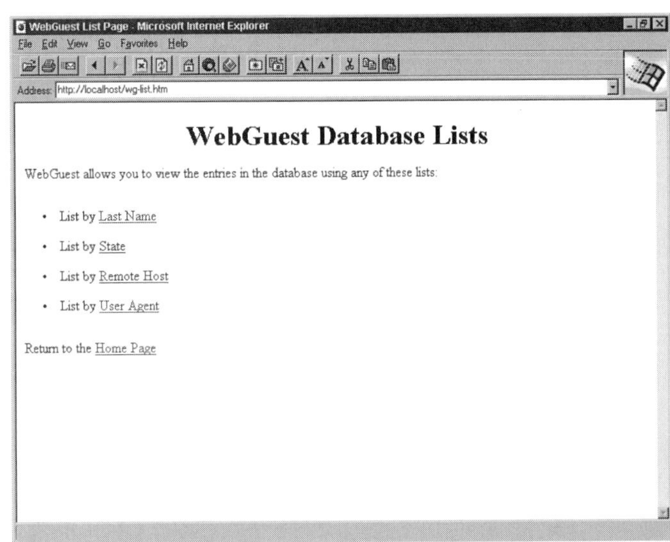

Figure 8.4.
The WebGuest list page.

Listing 8.1. The List page HTML.

```
<HTML><HEAD><TITLE>WebGuest List Page</TITLE></HEAD>

<BODY BGCOLOR="#FFFFFF">
<H1 ALIGN=CENTER>WebGuest Database Lists</H1>
<P ALIGN=LEFT>WebGuest allows you to view the entries in the database
using any of these lists:</P>
<UL>
<LI><P ALIGN=LEFT>List by <A HREF="/cgi-win/gen-list.exe?NAME">Last Name</A></P>
</LI>
<LI><P ALIGN=LEFT>List by <a href="/cgi-win/gen-list.exe?STATE">State</A></P>
</LI>
<LI><P ALIGN=LEFT>List by
<A HREF="/cgi-win/gen-list.exe?HOST">Remote Host</A></P>
</LI>
<LI><P ALIGN=LEFT>List by
<A HREF="/cgi-win/gen-list.exe?AGENT">User Agent</A></P>
</LI>
</UL>
<P>Return to the <A HREF="/cgi-win/entry.exe">Home Page</A></P>
</BODY>

</HTML>
```

The HTML pages created by `gen-list.exe` and `search.exe` provide links to the WebGuest entries for the items found. Figure 8.5 shows an example of the page produced when the `List by Last Name` link is clicked. These links create pages that provide all the information the users entered when they registered at the WebGuest site. They also provide the user's IP address, host name, and the browser used when registering. An example is shown in Figure 8.6.

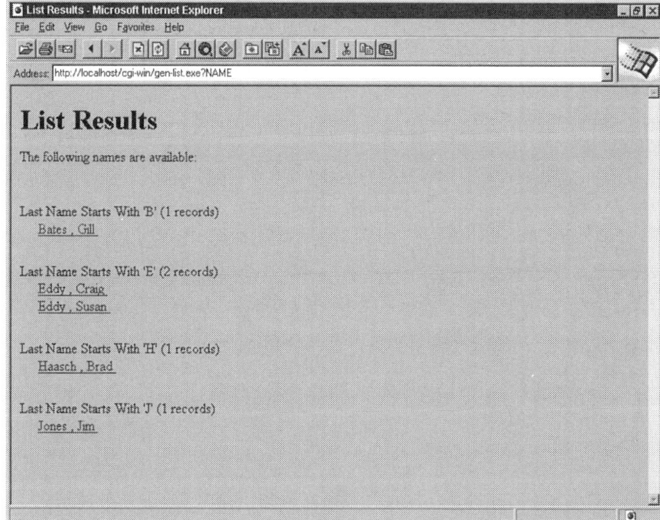

Figure 8.5.

A sample page from the `List by Last Name` link.

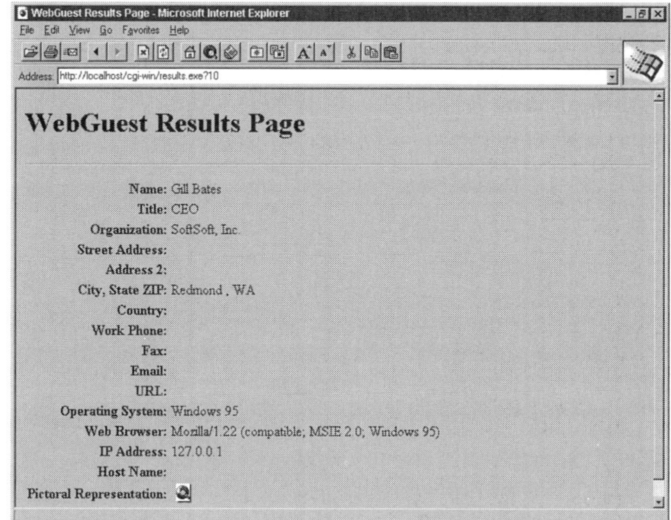

Figure 8.6.

The WebGuest Results page.

If this were a published site on the Internet, you might want to limit which data other people could view. For instance, some users may not want their e-mail address made public without their permission. A checkbox on the form next to possibly sensitive fields could be used to allow the registering user to mark those fields as private data. The CGI application that generates the results page would then exclude those fields from its output page for that registered user.

Creating the Database

The WebGuest database is a very simple one. It consists of two tables: one for the registration information provided by the user and one for the filenames of the pictures to be displayed on the registration and search pages. The applications presented in this chapter assume the data is stored in a Microsoft Access database, but this is not a necessity.

You can create the WebGuest database in any directory on your HTTP server machine, or in any directory which the JET engine or an ODBC driver can access. The WebGuest applications, as presented in this chapter, use a hard-coded path to the database file. This path could be stored in the registry and then retrieved when the application executes, but for simplicity I just hard-coded it.

NOTE:

The database can be created using either Jet 2.5 or Jet 3.0 tools. However, it is recommended that you use the Jet 3.0 database tools because performance is greatly improved with Jet 3.0.

After the database is created, you can proceed to the next major section, "Coding the Applications," and get into the real meat of this chapter.

The **Guests** Table

The main table, named `Guests`, contains all the fields that the user fills in on the registration page. It also has fields for some of the information provided by the user's Web browser and the HTTP server. This includes the Web browser's user agent designation and the user's IP address and host name.

Also included is an `AutoNumber` field (`GuestID`) which helps provide the registered user with a user identification number. This is useful for sites that provide service to the registered users on an ongoing basis.

The format of the `Guests` table is shown in Table 8.1. The table provides the field name, data type, and size for each field in the table. In this chapter's applications, none of the fields are required. The text fields should all allow zero-length strings to accommodate the fact that the user may not provide data for the field.

Table 8.1. The **Guests** table.

Field Name	*Data Type*	*Size*
`GuestID`	`AutoNumber`	Long Integer
`FirstName`	`Text`	255

Field Name	*Data Type*	*Size*
LastName	Text	255
Title	Text	255
Organization	Text	255
StreetAddress	Text	255
Address2	Text	255
City	Text	255
State	Text	255
ZipCode	Text	255
Country	Text	255
WorkPhone	Text	25
Fax	Text	25
Email	Text	255
URL	Text	50
OS	Text	25
PictureID	Text	10
UserAgent	Text	255
RemoteIP	Text	50
RemoteHost	Text	255

The **Pictures** Table

The other table in the database is called `Pictures`. This is where the names of the pictures displayed in the WebGuest site are stored. The registration page allows the user to choose a picture from the ones specified in this table. The selected picture is then displayed with that entry on the WebGuest results page.

The `Pictures` table consists of two fields: `PictureID` and `PathName`. The `PictureID` field is the primary key field that matches the `PictureID` foreign key field in the `Guests` table. As in the `Guests` table it is a 10 character `Text` field.

The `PathName` field is a 255 character `Text` field. This field is where you specify the *HTTP server-based* paths for the pictures to be displayed on the registration and search pages. The paths are relative to your HTTP server's *path space*. In other words, the `PathName` field for a picture should match the URI that would be used to retrieve the file from your HTTP server. If, for example, all the pictures reside in a directory named `IMAGES`, which is below your HTTP root directory, the `PathName` for a picture named `FACE.GIF` would be `/IMAGES/FACE.GIF`.

Coding The Applications

The WebGuest site utilizes several different CGI applications. These applications are built around the concepts discussed in Chapter 6, "The Win/CGI Interface," and the code presented in Chapter 7, "Creating CGI Applications in Visual Basic." If you have not reviewed these chapters, now is a good time to do so.

The Visual Basic projects in this chapter use the code modules discussed in Chapter 7, in addition to a module specific to each application. There is also a new module named `database.bas`. The code from the modules presented in Chapter 7 are not discussed or presented in this chapter. However, these modules are provided in the directory for this chapter on the CD-ROM accompanying the book.

This section presents the code for each application used in the WebGuest site. The first application, `entry.exe`, is by far the simplest. The most complicated is `search.exe`, which is where the data provided on the search page is parsed into a SQL statement that is used to produce a results page. The other applications, `gen-reg.exe` and `gen-list.exe`, are middle-of-the-road and don't require a lot of explanation if you understand the concepts presented in Chapters 6 and 7.

NOTE:

You must add a reference to the "Data Access Objects" library to all the Visual Basic projects created in this chapter. If the WebGuest database is created using the tools that came with Visual Basic 4 or with Access 95, add the "Microsoft DAO 3.0 Object Library" entry on the VB References dialog. If the database was created using Access 2.*x* or any of the tools that came with VB3, add the "Microsoft DAO 2.5/3.0 Compatibility Library" reference.

Coding `database.bas`

The `database.bas` module that is added to each of the projects in the WebGuest site contains a couple of basic database functions. These functions are `chknull()` and `tExecAndAnswer()`. The code for `database.bas` is presented in Listing 8.2. Either copy this module from the CD-ROM or create it using a text editor or Visual Basic. Save it in the directory you'll be using for the code of this chapter.

The function `chknull()` is used to allow direct string manipulations on database fields that may return `NULL` values. Because none of the fields in the `Guests` table are required, it is quite likely that some will return `NULL`. If you try to use a `NULL` value as a parameter for some of the Visual Basic functions, a runtime error occurs (Invalid use of `NULL`). The `chknull()` function provides a way to avoid checking the state (that is, whether or not it contains `NULL`) of the field every time you need to use the field.

`chknull()` has two parameters: a database `field` and a string. The string parameter is returned as the function result if the field passed to the function evaluates to a `NULL` value. Otherwise, the field's value is returned. As you can see from Listing 8.2, the code is not complicated. The `IsNull()` function is used in an `If...Then...Else` construct to check whether or not the field is `NULL`. If it is `NULL`, the string parameter is returned. If it's not `NULL`, the field is returned. Because the returned value is a string, you must use `Val()` or some other numeric conversion function if the field is a numeric type field.

The second function presented in Listing 8.2 is `tExecAndAnswer()`. This function takes a SQL statement and an open database variable as its parameters. The `pStatus` parameter is used as an output parameter. It returns the status of the result set. The SQL statement should be written so that it produces a single row, single column result set. An example of such a SQL statement is

```
Select Count(*) from Guests where State = 'VA'
```

This returns a count of the number of records in the `Guests` table that have `VA` as the value of their `State` field. The value of the first field of the first row of the result set is returned as a string to the code that called `tExecAndAnswer()`.

The `tExecAndAnswer()` function saves you the trouble of creating a recordset from the SQL statement. The function defines a local recordset variable named `sn`. The `pStatus` parameter is set to `DB_STATUS_OK`. Then the snapshot created by the `lsql$` parameter is opened using `OpenRecordset()`.

If an error occurs opening the snapshot or if snapshot contains no records, the `pStatus` return parameter is set to `DB_STATUS_NORESULTS`, and the function returns an empty string. Otherwise, the value of the first field is passed along with an empty string to `chknull()`. The return value from `chknull()` is used as the return value, and the function exits.

Listing 8.2. The code for `database.bas`.

```
Attribute VB_Name = "DBRoutines"
Global Const DB_STATUS_OK = 0
Global Const DB_STATUS_NORESULTS = 1

Public Function tExecAndAnswer(lsql$, db As Database, _
       pStatus As Integer) As String

    Dim sn As Recordset

    pStatus = DB_STATUS_OK
    on error resume next
    Set sn = db.OpenRecordset(lsql$, dbOpenSnapshot)
    if err then
    pStatus = DB_STATUS_NORESULTS
        tExecAndAnswer = ""
        exit function
    end if
```

continues

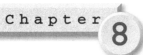

Listing 8.2. continued

```
    If sn.RecordCount = 0 Then
        pStatus = DB_STATUS_NORESULTS
        tExecAndAnswer = ""
    Else
        tExecAndAnswer = chknull(sn(0), "")
    End If

End Function

Public Function chknull (pfld as Field, ptNullDef as String) as String

    If IsNull(pfld) Then
        chknull = ptNullDef
    Else
        chknull = pfld
    endif

End Function
```

Generating the Entry Page

The initial page of the WebGuest site is generated by an application named `entry.exe`. This section covers the code used to create this page. The code that is added to the existing code base is minimal. Most of the grunt work is done by the routines developed in Chapter 7 that are contained in `cgi32.bas`.

Create a new project in Visual Basic. Add the `funcs.bas` and `cgi32.bas` modules from Chapter 7, the `database.bas` module developed in Listing 8.2, and a new module. Save this new module as `entry.bas`. Next, create a new procedure named `main` within `entry.bas`. This should be assigned as the project's Startup Form. The code for `Sub Main` is provided in Listing 8.3.

Listing 8.3. The code of `Sub Main` in `entry.bas`.

```
Public Sub main()
    On Error GoTo FormError
    Dim lsql$

    If InStr(Command$, " ") Then
        guCGIData.ProfileFile = Left$(Command$, InStr(Command$, " ") - 1)
    Else
        guCGIData.ProfileFile = Command$
    End If

    If LoadCGIData() = 0 Then
        'if we couldn't load all the CGI data,
        'could we at least open the Output File?
        If guCGIData.OutputFileHandle <> 0 Then
            'yes - call ErrorHandler to handle this
            Call ErrorHandler(-1, "Error loading CGI Data File")
        Else
```

```
            'no - forget about anything else!
            End
        End If
    End If

    'open the database
    Dim db As Database
    Set db = OpenDatabase("d:\website\cgi-win\webguest.mdb")

    OutputString "Content-Type: text/html"
    OutputString ""
    OutputString "<html><head><title>WebGuest Home Page</title>"
    OutputString "</head><body><H1>WebGuest Home Page</H1>"
    OutputString "<HR ALIGN=""CENTER"">"
    'now output the record count from the database:
    lsql$ = "Select Count(*) from Guests"
    OutputString "There are " & Trim$(tExecAndAnswer(lsql$, db, lStatus%))
    OutputString " people registered in our database.<P>"
    'set up the links to the other WebGuest pages:
    OutputString "<A HREF=""/cgi-win/gen-reg.exe?Register"">Register as "
    OutputString "a WebGuest user</A><p>"
    OutputString "<A HREF=""/wg-list.htm"">View Available WebGuest "
    OutputString "Listings</A><p>"
    OutputString "<A HREF=""/cgi-win/gen-reg.exe?Search"">Search the "
    OutputString " database</A><p><HR ALIGN=""CENTER"">"
    OutputString "<CENTER>WebGuest<br>Copyright Craig Eddy, 1996</CENTER>"
    OutputString "</body></html>"
    Close #guCGIData.OutputFileHandle
    db.Close
    End

FormError:
    Call ErrorHandler(Err, Error$)

End Sub
```

The first part of this procedure is the standard Win/CGI startup code that was developed in Chapter 7. The code first obtains the name of the CGI data file, then attempts to load the data that the server placed there. If the attempt to load the data fails (`LoadCGIData() = 0`), the procedure attempts to create some sort of output file to be returned to the user. This section of code is repeated in all the applications for the WebGuest site.

If the CGI data is successfully read from the data file, `Sub Main` continues by creating a database variable. The database is then opened, using the location of the `Guests` database created earlier in this chapter. As I stated earlier, I have hard-coded the path to the database for simplicity. The path could be stored in the system registry or you could use an ODBC data set name that points to the database.

The remainder of the procedure creates the HTML that will become the entry page. The `OutputString` procedure from `cgi32.bas` is used to write the HTML to the output file that the server returns to the user's Web browser.

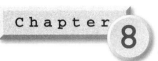

The first use of OutputString informs the HTTP server that the application is returning HTML formatted text. The next four calls to OutputString produce the beginnings of the HTML page. The following two calls to OutputString are where the record count is displayed. The tExecAndAnswer() function is used to return this record count.

The next three OutputString calls set up the links to the other pages in the WebGuest site. The first creates a link to the Registration page. This page is created by the gen-reg.exe application when the query string passed in the URL is "Register". The link's HREF element specifies the location of this application within the server's path space. For my server, the Win/CGI applications are located in the /cgi-win path. The physical location of this directory is set up using the server's administration tools.

Note the use of a pair of quote characters. It is good practice to enclose the textual elements of an HTML tag (such as the text after the equal sign in the HREF element) within double quotes. Because VB uses the double quote as the string delimiter, you must use a pair of double quotes to output a single double quote character. This will appear quite often within your CGI applications that output HTML formatted text.

The next OutputString call creates the link to the static WebGuest listing page, wg-list.htm. The last of these three calls to OutputString creates the link to the Search WebGuest page. This page is also created by gen-reg.exe, but the query string used is "Search".

Finally, the footer information for the page is written to the output file. Then the output file and the database are closed and the application ends. When a CGI application ends, control is returned to the HTTP server, which examines the output file and returns an HTTP response message to the user's Web browser, completing the HTTP transaction.

Now that the code has been entered, save the project and compile it into executable format. Name the executable file entry.exe. Save it in the project directory for now.

Generating the Search and Registration Pages

The WebGuest site uses a CGI program to create the HTML pages used to register at and search the WebGuest site. This program, gen-reg.exe, is very similar to the previous application. It produces an HTML page that contains an HTML form. The form is where data is entered by the user, either for registering information or for specifying search criteria.

To get started with gen-reg.exe, create a new project in Visual Basic. Add the funcs.bas, cgi32.bas, and database.bas modules and a new module. Save this new module as gen-reg.bas. Next, create a new procedure named main within gen-reg.bas. This should be assigned as the project's Startup Form. The code for Sub Main is shown in Listing 8.4.

Listing 8.4. The code of `Sub Main` in `gen-reg.bas`.

```
Public Sub main()
    On Error GoTo FormError

    If InStr(Command$, " ") Then
        guCGIData.ProfileFile = Left$(Command$, InStr(Command$, " ") - 1)
    Else
        guCGIData.ProfileFile = Command$
    End If

    If LoadCGIData() = 0 Then
        'if we couldn't load all the CGI data,
        'could we at least open the Output File?
        If guCGIData.OutputFileHandle <> 0 Then
            'yes - call ErrorHandler to handle this
            Call ErrorHandler(-1, "Error loading CGI Data File")
        Else
            'no - forget about anything else!
            End
        End If
    End If

    'open the database
    Dim db As Database
    Dim picturesDS As Recordset
    Set db = OpenDatabase("d:\website\cgi-win\webguest.mdb")
    Set picturesDS = db.OpenRecordset("Pictures", dbOpenSnapshot)

    'open the static text file
    Dim f%
    f% = FreeFile
    Open "d:\website\cgi-win\gen-reg.txt" For Binary Access Read As #f%
    fstr$ = Space$(FileLen("d:\website\cgi-win\gen-reg.txt"))
    'read the text into the fstr$ variable
    Get #f%, , fstr$

    'if this is a search, fix some of the default HTML
    If UCase$(guCGIData.QueryString) = "SEARCH" Then
        'the form should launch search.exe
        fstr$ = tReplaceChars(fstr$, "register.exe", "search.exe")
        'fix some text to make sense for a search form
        fstr$ = tReplaceChars(fstr$, "WebGuest Registration", "WebGuest Search")
        fstr$ = tReplaceChars(fstr$, "register at", "search")
    End If

    OutputString "Content-Type: text/html"
    OutputString ""

    'output the contents of the file:
    OutputString fstr$

    'if there are pictures, add them to the form:
    If picturesDS.RecordCount Then
        ' make a label depending on the mode we're in
        If UCase$(guCGIData.QueryString) = "SEARCH" Then
            OutputString "<pre>Select a picture to search for:</pre>"
        Else
```

continues

Listing 8.4. continued

```
            OutputString "<pre>Select a picture to represent yourself "
            OutputString "in our directory:</pre>"
        End If
        OutputString "<table>"
        'Output the first row
        OutputString "<tr><td align=right><input type=radio "
        'it defaults to checked if this is to be a registration page
        If UCase$(guCGIData.QueryString) <> "SEARCH" Then
            'use the "checked" element to select the radio button
            OutputString "checked "
        End If
        'the group name for these buttons is "Picture"
        ' the value for each button is the PictureID field
        OutputString "name=""Picture"" "
        OutputString "value=""" & picturesDS!PictureID & """></td>"
        'display the specified picture
        OutputString "<td width=50%><img src=""" & picturesDS!pathname
        OutputString """ align=middle width=40 height=38> </td></tr>"
        picturesDS.MoveNext
        While Not picturesDS.EOF
            ' repeat for each additional picture
            OutputString "<tr><td align=right><input type=radio "
            OutputString "name=""Picture"" "
            OutputString "value=""" & picturesDS!PictureID & """></td>"
            OutputString "<td width=50%><img src=""" & picturesDS!pathname
            OutputString """ align=middle width=40 height=38> </td></tr>"
            picturesDS.MoveNext
        Wend
        OutputString "</table>"
    End If

    'create and label the form's Submit button
    If UCase$(guCGIData.QueryString) = "SEARCH" Then
        OutputString "<p><input type=submit value=""Search"">"
    Else
        OutputString "<p><input type=submit value=""Register""> "
    End If
    'create and label the form's Reset button
    OutputString "<input type=reset value=""Reset Form""> </p>"

    'finish up
    OutputString "</form><hr></h5>Last revised: 4/20/96</h5>"
    OutputString "</body></html>"
    OutputString ""
    Close #guCGIData.OutputFileHandle
    picturesDS.Close
    db.Close
    End

FormError:
    Call ErrorHandler(Err, Error$)

End Sub
```

The procedure begins just like the `Sub Main` for `entry.exe`, with the loading of the CGI data file. After the CGI data is successfully loaded, the code opens the WebGuest database and creates a snapshot recordset. The `Pictures` table is the source for the recordset. If an error occurs while trying to open the database or recordset, the `On Error Goto FormError` at the start of the procedure causes a jump to the `FormError` label. This calls a routine in `cgi32.bas` that attempts to output the error message to the user's Web browser.

After the database has been successfully opened, the procedure retrieves some text from a static file located in the `cgi-win` directory. This file, named `gen-reg.txt`, contains most of the HTML that creates the search and registration forms. The contents of this file are shown in Listing 8.5.

Listing 8.5. The HTML contents of `gen-reg.txt`.

```
<html>
<head>
<title>WebGuest Registration</title>
</head>

<body bgcolor="#FFFFFF">
<h1>WebGuest Registration</h1>
<hr>
<p>Use this form to register at the WebGuest site.</p>
<form action="/cgi-win/register.exe" method="POST">
<p>Please provide the following contact information: </p>
<pre><em>       First name </em><input type=text
   size=25 maxlength=256 name="FirstName">
<em>        Last name </em><input type=text
   size=25 maxlength=256 name="LastName">
<em>            Title </em><input type=text size=35 maxlength=256 name="Title">
<em>     Organization </em><input type=text
   size=35 maxlength=256 name="Organization">
<em>   Street address </em><input type=text size=35
   maxlength=256 name="StreetAddress">
<em>  Address (cont.) </em><input type=text size=35
   maxlength=256 name="Address2">
<em>             City </em><input type=text size=35 maxlength=256 name="City">
<em>   State/Province </em><input type=text size=35 maxlength=256 name="State">
<em>  Zip/Postal code </em><input type=text size=12 maxlength=12 name="ZipCode">
<em>          Country </em><input type=text size=25
   maxlength=256 name="Country">
<em>       Work Phone </em><input type=text size=25
   maxlength=25 name="WorkPhone">
<em>              FAX </em><input type=text size=25 maxlength=25 name="FAX">
<em>           E-mail </em><input type=text size=25 maxlength=256 name="Email">
<em>              URL </em><input type=text size=25 maxlength=50 name="URL">
<em>Operating System </em>
    <input type="radio" name="OS" value="Windows 95">Windows 95
    <input type="radio" name="OS" value="Windows 3.x">Windows 3.x
    <input type="radio" name="OS" value="Windows NT">Windows NT
    <input type="radio" name="OS" value="Unix">Unix
    <input type="radio" name="OS" value="Macintosh">Macintosh
    <input type="radio" name="OS" value="Other">Other
</pre>
```

This file is read into a string variable named `fstr$`. As you can see from Listing 8.5, the HTML form contains an entry for just about every field in the `Guests` table. The other fields are filled in with data received from the CGI data file when the registration program is executed. The HTML in Listing 8.5 is set up to produce the registration page, not the search page. The `gen-reg` application will fix that in the next section of the code.

NOTE:

Appendix A contains an HTML reference guide. You may wish to refer to the section in that appendix that covers HTML forms.

After the file is read into `fstr$`, the procedure checks the CGI `Query String` parameter (`guCGIData.QueryString`) to determine whether it is producing a registration page or a search page. If it is producing a search page, the `tReplaceChars()` function (contained in `funcs.bas`) is called to replace the application to be executed with `search.exe` and to replace some of the existing text with text that is more meaningful for a search page.

Next, it's time to start writing the HTML output page. The procedure starts as `entry.exe` did, informing the server that it's returning HTML formatted text. Then, in one fell swoop, the entire contents of `fstr$` are written to the output file (`OutputString fstr$`).

The procedure finishes its output by cycling through the available records in the `Pictures` table. If there are some records in the table (`picturesDS.RecordCount > 0`), the procedure outputs them into an HTML table. The table contains two columns: one for a radio button which specifies which picture to use and one to display the picture. There is one row in the HTML table for each row in the recordset table.

CAUTION

When using the `value` element of an HTML form's input tag (as was done for the picture radio buttons), make sure the data entered as the value is contained on a single line in the output file. The HTML form submits the value as is. This means that if a carriage return exists within the `value` element's specified value, that carriage return is sent as part of the form data. This causes the application that reads the data to incorrectly interpret the data.

If the program is producing a registration page, the first picture found in the recordset is selected by default. This is done by using the `checked` element within an HTML radio button input type. The remainder of the code finishes the HTML for the current row and then cycles to the next record in the `pictureDS` recordset, producing an unselected radio button/picture row for each record in the recordset. When all the records have been processed, the `</TABLE>` tag is output to end the table definition.

The procedure then creates the two buttons on the form. One button is a Submit button that causes the user's Web browser to `POST` the data entered to the appropriate CGI application. The other button is a Reset button which, when clicked, clears the HTML form and restores any default settings specified in the HTML document (such as the default selected picture).

Finally, the procedure outputs the last of the HTML and closes the recordset, database, and output file. It then ends the application, returning control to the Web server. The server passes the HTML document just produced by the application back to the user's Web browser. If the user's browser is not capable of displaying HTML forms, the text will seem meaningless. However, most browsers, especially Windows-based browsers, are capable of displaying forms.

After the code is entered, save the project and compile the executable. Name the executable `gen-reg.exe` and leave it in the project directory for now.

The WebGuest Registration Application

The registration application takes the data that the user enters into the HTML form created by `gen-reg.exe` and stores it in the WebGuest database. The program then produces an output page that thanks the user for registering and provides them with a registration number.

This registration number could be used for any number of purposes. At my company we have an HTML form that people who want demo copies of our programs must fill out. When they have supplied the required information and successfully registered in our demo request database, they are provided a registration number. This number can be used to later return to the site to download the demos again without having to enter data again. It is also used for customer support purposes. Because the customers have entered information into our database that is useful in the customer support world, the customer support team has access to the data. It's all tied together using the assigned registration number.

Start a new project, adding the `funcs.bas`, `cgi32.bas`, and `database.bas` modules. Insert a new module and save it as `register.bas`. Insert a procedure named `main` into the new module. The code for `Sub Main` is given in Listing 8.6.

Listing 8.6. The code of `register.bas's Sub Main`.

```
Public Sub main()
    On Error GoTo FormError

    If InStr(Command$, " ") Then
        guCGIData.ProfileFile = Left$(Command$, InStr(Command$, " ") - 1)
    Else
        guCGIData.ProfileFile = Command$
    End If

    If LoadCGIData() = 0 Then
        'if we couldn't load all the CGI data,
        'could we at least open the Output File?
```

continues

Listing 8.6. continued

```
        If guCGIData.OutputFileHandle <> 0 Then
            'yes - call ErrorHandler to handle this
            Call ErrorHandler(-1, "Error loading CGI Data File")
        Else
            'no - forget about anything else!
            End
        End If
    End If

    'open the database
    Dim db As Database
    Dim guestDS As Recordset
    Set db = OpenDatabase("d:\website\cgi-win\webguest.mdb")
    'open a dynaset to add the information to
    Set guestDS = db.OpenRecordset("guests", dbOpenDynaset)
    'add a new record
    guestDS.AddNew

    'fill the data using the CGI function GetFieldValue()
    guestDS!FirstName = GetFieldValue("FirstName")
    guestDS!LastName = GetFieldValue("LastName")
    guestDS!Title = GetFieldValue("Title")
    guestDS!Organization = GetFieldValue("Organization")
    guestDS!StreetAddress = GetFieldValue("StreetAddress")
    guestDS!Address2 = GetFieldValue("Address2")
    guestDS!City = GetFieldValue("City")
    guestDS!State = GetFieldValue("State")
    guestDS!ZipCode = GetFieldValue("ZipCode")
    guestDS!Country = GetFieldValue("Country")
    guestDS!WorkPhone = GetFieldValue("WorkPhone")
    guestDS!Fax = GetFieldValue("Fax")
    guestDS!Email = GetFieldValue("Email")
    guestDS!URL = GetFieldValue("URL")
    guestDS!OS = GetFieldValue("OS")

    'verify the PictureID provided by the form:
    lsql$ = "Select Count(*) from Pictures where PictureID = '"
    lsql$ = lsql$ & GetFieldValue("Picture") & "'"
    If Val(tExecAndAnswer(lsql$, db, lStatus%)) = 0 Then
        'the PictureID specified does not exist!
        lStatus% = 1
    Else
        'the PictureID is valid, save to the dynaset
        guestDS!PictureID = GetFieldValue("Picture")
        lStatus% = 0
    End If

    'save the CGI data not provided on the form
    With guCGIData
        guestDS!UserAgent = .UserAgent
        guestDS!RemoteIP = .RemoteAddress
        guestDS!RemoteHost = .RemoteHost
    End With

    'update the record
    guestDS.Update
```

```
    'return to the record just added
    guestDS.Bookmark = guestDS.LastModified

    'produce the output page
    OutputString "Content-Type: text/html"
    OutputString ""
    OutputString "<html><head><title>Thanks for Registering</title>"
    OutputString "</head><body><H1>Thanks for Registering</H1>"
    OutputString "Your registration number is "
    OutputString Trim$(Str$(guestDS!GuestID))
    'was the PictureID valid?
    If lStatus% = 1 Then
        'No, inform the user
        OutputString "<br><hr ALIGN=""CENTER"">The selected picture "
        OutputString "was not found in the database!"
    End If
    'provide a link back to the entry page
    OutputString "<hr><A HREF=""/cgi-win/entry.exe"">WebGuest Home</A>"
    OutputString "</body></html>"
    'close down:
    Close #guCGIData.OutputFileHandle
    guestDS.Close
    db.Close
    End

FormError:
    Call ErrorHandler(Err, Error$)

End Sub
```

It should come as no surprise by now that the procedure begins exactly like the other two `Sub Mains` I've presented. The CGI data file is read, and the WebGuest database is opened. The procedure then opens a dynaset on the `Guests` table. This dynaset is where a new WebGuest entry is created and the form data is written.

After the dynaset is opened, a new record is added using the `AddNew` data access method. Then each field in the table that has a corresponding field on the registration form is filled in with data from the HTML form. The `GetFieldValue()` function from `cgi32.bas` is used to retrieve the values entered by the user. If the user left the form field empty, `GetFieldValue()` returns an empty string.

After all the form's textbox fields are processed, it's time to verify the chosen picture. Although the registration form is generated using the `Pictures` table to supply the `PictureIDs` used, there is no way of knowing if the user is filling in a valid form. The registration form could have been generated two months ago, left sitting in the user's Web browser, and the user is just now filling in the data. Perhaps the picture database has changed in that time. It's a far-fetched scenario, but it certainly can happen. So, `register.exe` plays it safe and verifies the supplied `PictureID` by performing a `SELECT Count(*) from Pictures where PictureID =` query, using the `Picture` field the HTML form supplied as the criteria for the `WHERE` clause. If a count of zero is returned, the `PictureID` supplied is invalid. Otherwise, the `PictureID` is good, so the data is placed in the dynaset's `PictureID` field.

Next, some of the information supplied by the Win/CGI interface is added to the record. These fields include `UserAgent`, `RemoteIP`, and `RemoteHost`. All these are supplied as elements of the `guCGIData` global variable that contains the data read from the CGI data file. The fields are useful to the WebGuest database because they provide some demographic information about the user's location (thanks to `RemoteIP` and `RemoteHost`) and his or her Web browser (via the UserAgent element).

After the data is appended to the dynaset, the `Update` method is invoked to save the new record. Because `Update` moves the dynaset's record pointer and you need to access the `GuestID` field of the record just added, it is necessary to move the record pointer back to the record just added. Fortunately, the Data Access Objects provide a recordset property named `LastModified` which contains a bookmark to the last record modified. By setting the `Bookmark` property of a recordset to `LastModified`, you'll return to the record just added or modified. That's how `register.exe` gets back to the record.

Finally, it's time to produce the HTML output. A nice "Thank You" message is printed for the user. Then the `GuestID` field of the dynaset is displayed as the user's registration number. If the `PictureID` supplied is invalid, a message to that effect is printed next. A link back to the entry page is provided next, then the last of the HTML is output, and the application closes down in the normal Win/CGI fashion.

After you enter the code, save the project and compile the executable. Name the executable `register.exe` and leave it in the project directory for now.

The WebGuest Search Application

The search application takes data generated by the HTML search form and performs a search on the `Guests` table. Any matching records found are displayed in a list formatted as Last Name, First Name. The items in the list are hyperlinks that cause WebGuest to display the complete entry for that record. A sample page showing the results of a search is shown in Figure 8.7.

To start the project, open a new project in VB. Add the `funcs.bas`, `cgi32.bas`, and `database.bas` modules. Insert a new module and save it as `search.bas`. Insert a procedure named `main` into the new module. The code for `Sub Main` is given in Listing 8.7.

The procedure has the same beginnings as the rest of the applications. After the CGI data is successfully obtained, the code outputs the start of the HTML output page.

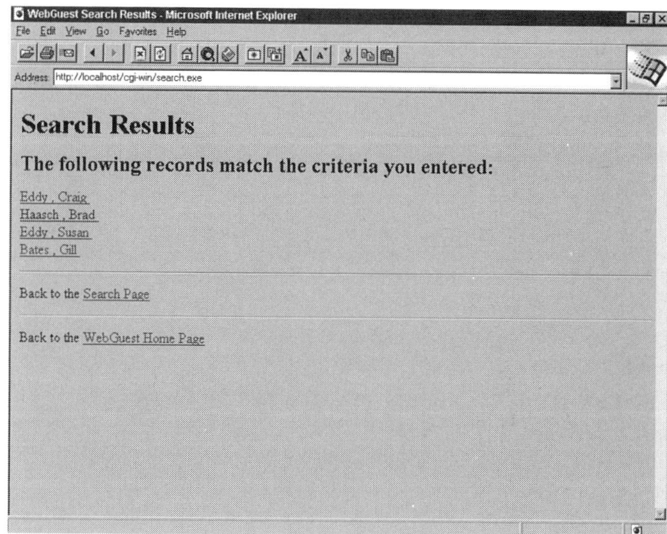

Figure 8.7.
A sample search results page.

Listing 8.7. The code of `Sub Main` from `search.bas`.

```
Public Sub main()
    On Error GoTo FormError

    If InStr(Command$, " ") Then
        guCGIData.ProfileFile = Left$(Command$, InStr(Command$, " ") - 1)
    Else
        guCGIData.ProfileFile = Command$
    End If

    If LoadCGIData() = 0 Then
        'if we couldn't load all the CGI data,
        'could we at least open the Output File?
        If guCGIData.OutputFileHandle <> 0 Then
            'yes - call ErrorHandler to handle this
            Call ErrorHandler(-1, "Error loading CGI Data File")
        Else
            'no - forget about anything else!
            End
        End If
    End If

    'start the output
    OutputString "Content-Type: text/html"
    OutputString ""
    OutputString "<html><head><title>WebGuest Search Results</title>"
    OutputString "</head><body><H1>Search Results</H1>"

    'check to see if the user filled in anything:
    If guCGIData.FormFieldCount = 0 Then
        'no fields were filled in:
        OutputString "<h2>No search fields were found!</h2>"
```

continues

Listing 8.7. continued

```
        OutputString "</body></html>"
        Close #guCGIData.OutputFileHandle
        End
    End If

    'create the SQL statement:
    lsql$ = "Select LastName, FirstName, GuestID from Guests where "
    'create the WHERE clause:
    lwhere$ = ""
    For i% = 1 To guCGIData.FormFieldCount
        'the form field corresponding to PictureID is named Picture:
        If guCGIData.FormSmallFields(i%).key = "Picture" Then
            lField$ = "PictureID"
        Else
            lField$ = guCGIData.FormSmallFields(i%).key
        End If

        'get the value entered on the form
        lValue$ = Trim$(guCGIData.FormSmallFields(i%).value)

        'make sure there is actually data in the field:
        If Len(lValue$) Then
            If Len(lwhere$) Then
                lwhere$ = lwhere$ & " and "
            End If
            lwhere$ = lwhere$ & lField$

            'replace any single quotes with double-quotes:
            lValue$ = tReplaceChars(lValue$, "'", "''")

            'check for a wildcard search
            If Right$(lValue$, 1) = "*" Then
                'wildcard searches use LIKE
                lwhere$ = lwhere$ & " LIKE "
            Else
                'standard search, use equality
                lwhere$ = lwhere$ & " = "
            End If
            'recall that all database fields are TEXT:
            lwhere$ = lwhere$ & "'" & lValue$ & "'"
        End If
    Next

    'check to see if lwhere$ is empty
    If Len(Trim$(lwhere$)) = 0 Then
        'no fields were filled in:
        OutputString "<h2>No search fields were found!</h2>"
        OutputString "</body></html>"
        Close #guCGIData.OutputFileHandle
        End
    End If

    'append the WHERE clause to the SQL statement:
    lsql$ = lsql$ & lwhere$
```

```
    'open the database
    Dim db As Database
    Dim guestDS As Recordset
    Set db = OpenDatabase("d:\website\cgi-win\webguest.mdb")
    'open a snapshot based on the SQL created above
    Set guestDS = db.OpenRecordset(lsql$, dbOpenSnapshot)

    'create the output
    If guestDS.RecordCount Then
        'there were records found!
        OutputString "<h2>The following records match the "
        OutputString "criteria you entered:</h2>"
        ' output in list format:
        While Not (guestDS.EOF)
            OutputString "<a HREF=""/cgi-win/results.exe?"
            OutputString guestDS!GuestID & """>"
            If Not (IsNull(guestDS!LastName)) Then
                OutputString guestDS!LastName
                If Not (IsNull(guestDS!FirstName)) Then OutputString ", "
            End If
            OutputString chknull(guestDS!FirstName, "")
            OutputString "</a><br>"
            guestDS.MoveNext
        Wend
    Else
        'no records found:
        OutputString "<h2>No records match the criteria you entered.</h2>"
        OutputString "The SQL string used was:<br>" & lsql$
    End If

    'provide links to search page and home page
    OutputString "<hr>Back to the <a HREF=""/cgi-win/gen-reg.exe?Search"">"
    OutputString "Search Page</a><br>"
    OutputString "<hr>Back to the <a HREF=""/cgi-win/entry.exe"">"
    OutputString "WebGuest Home Page</a><br>"
    OutputString "</body></html>"

    'close down:
    Close #guCGIData.OutputFileHandle
    guestDS.Close
    db.Close
    End

FormError:
    Call ErrorHandler(Err, Error$)

End Sub
```

The line `If guCGIData.FormFieldCount = 0 Then` tests to see whether the user left the search form blank. If the form has been left blank, there should be no fields in the CGI data file. However, some browsers will still send the empty fields anyway, so later the code will check each field to make sure it has data. If the `FormFieldCount` is zero, a suitable error message is output to the page and the program ends.

The next task is to create the SQL statement that actually performs the search. The WHERE clause of the SQL statement is generated separately so you can verify that there are really criteria to search for. The code loops through each of the CGI fields that it finds. The FormFieldCount element of the guCGIData variable provides a count of the number of fields that were found. The code loops once for each field (For i% = 1 to guCGIData.FormFieldCount).

Once inside the loop, the first order of business is to fix an anomaly of the HTML search form. The code that generates the where clause uses the HTML form's field names as the database field names. The radio buttons for the pictures are in a group named Picture. This means that the field name passed in the CGI data file will be Picture. The code checks to see if the field currently being processed is named Picture. If it is, the value of the lField$ variable is set to PictureID. Otherwise, lField$ is set to guCGIData.FormSmallFields(i%).key, which is the field name of the current form field.

Next, the value specified for the field is assigned to the variable lValue$. Then lValue$ is checked to make sure it contains actual text. If so, the code appends to the WHERE clause. Because there may be multiple fields filled in on the search form, the code appends an and to the WHERE clause if it already contains some criteria. The field name is then appended to the WHERE clause. If the criteria specified in the field value contains any single quote characters, they are replaced with double quotes. This is necessary because the SQL string being generated uses single quotes to delimit the values being searched.

The next statement, If **Right**$(lValue$, 1) = "*" Then, checks to see whether the user has specified a wildcard in the field's value. The wildcard is used to search on a field that *begins with* the text entered in the field. This uses the LIKE comparison operator instead of the equal sign to do the comparison. Finally, the field's value is appended to the WHERE clause and delimited with single quotes because all the Guests table's fields (except GuestID, which isn't searchable anyway) are text fields. The code then loops to the next available field.

After the WHERE clause is generated, it is checked to make sure it contains some characters. If it is empty, the user left the HTML form blank or filled with spaces. In these cases, the program prints an error message to the output page and ends.

If the WHERE clause contains text, it is appended to the SQL statement. The WebGuest database is opened and a snapshot is created from the SQL statement.

The procedure then checks the **RecordCount** property of the snapshot. If it is greater than zero, the records of the snapshot are output in a list. Each item in the list displays the name of the registered user and provides a link to that user's results page. This link uses the results.exe application discussed shortly.

If no records match the criteria specified, the program outputs a message to that effect and provides the SQL statement used in the query. Because most of the field names are easy to relate to the form, the user shouldn't have much trouble understanding the SQL statement. I put it in mainly for debugging purposes, so you can remove it if you wish.

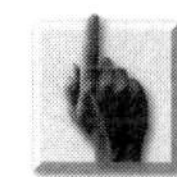

Finally, the program outputs links back to the search page and the WebGuest home page and closes the output file, the snapshot, and the database.

Save the project and compile the code into an executable named `search.exe`.

Generating the List Pages

The WebGuest List pages are used to list all the records registered in the database, grouped by a specific field. The HTML page `wg-list.htm` which is in the server's document root directory contains four links. These links all execute the `gen-list.exe` application, but with a different query string. The application then examines the query string to determine which field in the `Guests` table to use in grouping the records. The output page, an example of which is shown in Figure 8.5, contains each grouping with the available records in that group listed below the group's heading. Each record listing is a hyperlink to the record's full WebGuest entry.

To begin, open a new project in Visual Basic. Add our standard `funcs.bas`, `cgi32.bas`, and `database.bas` modules. Insert a new module and save it as `gen-list.bas`. Insert a procedure named `main` into the new module. The code for the `Sub Main` procedure is given in Listing 8.8.

Listing 8.8. The code of `Sub Main` from `gen-list.bas`.

```
Public Sub main()
    On Error GoTo FormError

    If InStr(Command$, " ") Then
        guCGIData.ProfileFile = Left$(Command$, InStr(Command$, " ") - 1)
    Else
        guCGIData.ProfileFile = Command$
    End If

    If LoadCGIData() = 0 Then
        'if we couldn't load all the CGI data,
        'could we at least open the Output File?
        If guCGIData.OutputFileHandle <> 0 Then
            'yes - call ErrorHandler to handle this
            Call ErrorHandler(-1, "Error loading CGI Data File")
        Else
            'no - forget about anything else!
            End
        End If
    End If

    'open the database
    Dim db As Database
    Dim listDS As Recordset
    Dim guestDS As Recordset

    Set db = OpenDatabase("d:\website\cgi-win\webguest.mdb")

    Select Case UCase$(guCGIData.QueryString)
    Case "NAME"
```

continues

Listing 8.8. continued

```
        ltType$ = "names"
        ltNice$ = "Last Name Starts With"
        lsql$ = "Select Count(*), Left(LastName,1) from Guests "
        lsql$ = lsq$ & "Group By Left(LastName,1) order by Left(LastName,1)"
        lsql2$ = "Select LastName, FirstName, GuestID from Guests "
        lsql2$ = lsql2$ & "where Left(LastName,1) = '"
    Case "STATE"
        ltType$ = "states"
        ltNice$ = "State is"
        lsql$ = "Select Count(*), State from Guests Group By State "
        lsql$ = lsql$ & "order by State"
        lsql2$ = "Select LastName, FirstName, GuestID from Guests "
        lsql2$ = lsql2$ & "where State = '"
    Case "HOST"
        ltType$ = "remote hosts"
        ltNice$ = "Remote Host is"
        lsql$ = "Select Count(*), RemoteHost from Guests Group By "
        lsql$ = lsql$ & "RemoteHost order by RemoteHost"
        lsql2$ = "Select LastName, FirstName, GuestID from Guests "
        lsql2$ = lsql2$ & "where RemoteHost = '"
    Case "AGENT"
        ltType$ = "user agents"
        ltNice$ = "User Agent is"
        lsql$ = "Select Count(*), UserAgent from Guests Group By "
        lsql$ = lsql$ & "UserAgent order by UserAgent"
        lsql2$ = "Select LastName, FirstName, GuestID from Guests "
        lsql2$ = lsql2$ & "where UserAgent = '"
    Case Else
        OutputString "Content-Type: text/html"
        OutputString ""
        OutputString "<html><head><title>Invalid Query String</title>"
        OutputString "</head><body><H1>Invalid Query String</H1>"
        OutputString "An invalid query string was passed to gen-list.exe"
        OutputString "</body></html>"
        OutputString ""
        Close #guCGIData.OutputFileHandle
        End

    End Select
    Set listDS = db.OpenRecordset(lsql$, dbOpenSnapshot)

    OutputString "Content-Type: text/html"
    OutputString ""
    OutputString "<html><head><title>List Results</title>"
    OutputString "</head><body><H1>List Results</H1>"
    If listDS.RecordCount Then
        OutputString "The following " & ltType$ & " are available:<p><DL>"
        While Not (listDS.EOF)
            OutputString "<DT>"
            OutputString ltNice$ & " '" & chknull(listDS(1), "?") & "'"
            OutputString " (" & Trim$(chknull(listDS(0), "?"))
            OutputString " records)</DT>"
            'get each of the records that match the GROUP BY
            On Error Resume Next
            Set guestDS = db.OpenRecordset(lsql2$ & listDS(1) & "'", _
                                dbOpenSnapshot)
```

```
            If Err = 0 Then
                While Not (guestDS.EOF)
                    OutputString "<DD><a HREF=""/cgi-win/results.exe?"
                    OutputString guestDS!GuestID & """>"
                    If Not (IsNull(guestDS!LastName)) Then
                        OutputString guestDS!LastName
                        If Not (IsNull(guestDS!FirstName)) Then
                            OutputString ", "
                        End If
                    End If
                    OutputString chknull(guestDS!FirstName, "")
                    OutputString "</a></DD>"
                    guestDS.MoveNext
                Wend
            Else
                OutputString "<DD>Error retrieving the records "
                OutputString "for this item!</DD>"
            End If
            OutputString "<p>"
            listDS.MoveNext
        Wend
        OutputString "</DL>"
    Else
        OutputString "No " & ltType$ & " available to list"
    End If
    OutputString "</body></html>"
    guestDS.Close
    listDS.Close
    db.CloseClose #guCGIData.OutputFileHandle
    End

FormError:
    Call ErrorHandler(Err, Error$)

End Sub
```

After the standard CGI application code, the program defines two recordset variables and opens the database. The `Select Case Ucase$(guCGIData.QueryString)` code utilizes the CGI `Query String` parameter to decide where to go next. The CGI `Query String` parameter is the portion of the URL that appears after the question mark. If the user clicks on the `List by Last Name` link shown in Figure 8.5, the user's Web browser attempts to retrieve the URI `/cgi-win/gen-list.exe?NAME`. The `Query String` in this case will be `NAME`.

The program generates several string variables whose value depends on the CGI `Query String` parameter. The strings are used when opening the snapshots and for labels. If an invalid `Query String` parameter has been found, the program falls into the `Case Else` portion of the `Select Case`, displays an appropriate error message, and exits.

After the string variables are defined, the first snapshot is opened. This snapshot, `listDS`, contains the data for the group headers. If the snapshot contains no records, a suitable message is output to the HTML page. If there are records, the program loops through each record in the snapshot. It first outputs a line of HTML that displays the group headers. This is done starting with the line of code that reads `OutputString "<DT>"` and continuing for two more lines. The `"<DT>"` tag begins a special type of HTML tag known as a definition. The `"<DT>"` tag surrounds the term to be defined. The `"<DD>"` tag surrounds the definition of the term. Web browsers display the definition slightly indented on the next line after the term. Although the application is not using this to display a definition, the format is perfect for displaying grouped information.

After the group header is written, a snapshot containing all the WebGuest entries that belong to the current group is opened. Each resulting record is output using the same format as the search results page: The name is listed and is a hyperlink to the full entry for that record.

After all the records for the current group are output, the program moves the grouping snapshot to its next record and repeats the process. After all groups have been handled, the program finishes the HTML output, closes the database, the snapshots, and the output file, and ends.

Save the project and compile the executable as `gen-list.exe`.

Generating the Results Page

The last piece of the WebGuest site is where the final results of any searching and listing are displayed. The results.exe application creates an HTML file for a specific record in the `Guests` table. The query string provided in the URI for this application specifies the `GuestID` of the record to be displayed. The record is displayed in an HTML table in order to provide some measure of formatting. An example of the results page is shown in Figure 8.6.

To begin, start a new project. Add `funcs.bas`, `cgi32.bas`, and `database.bas` to the project. Insert a new module and save it as `results.bas`. Insert a procedure named `main` into the new module. The code for the `Sub Main` procedure is given in Listing 8.9.

Listing 8.9. The code of `Sub Main` from `results.bas`.

```
Public Sub main()
    On Error GoTo FormError

    If InStr(Command$, " ") Then
        guCGIData.ProfileFile = Left$(Command$, InStr(Command$, " ") - 1)
    Else
        guCGIData.ProfileFile = Command$
    End If

    If LoadCGIData() = 0 Then
        'if we couldn't load all the CGI data,
        'could we at least open the Output File?
        If guCGIData.OutputFileHandle <> 0 Then
            'yes - call ErrorHandler to handle this
            Call ErrorHandler(-1, "Error loading CGI Data File")
        Else
            'no - forget about anything else!
            End
        End If
    End If
```

```
'open the database
Dim db As Database
Dim guestDS As Recordset
Set db = OpenDatabase("d:\website\cgi-win\webguest.mdb")

OutputString "Content-Type: text/html"
OutputString ""
OutputString "<html><head><title>WebGuest Results Page</title>"
OutputString "</head><body><H1>WebGuest Results Page</H1>"
OutputString "<HR ALIGN=""CENTER"">"

lsql$ = "Select * from Guests left join Pictures on Guests.PictureID "
lsql$ = lsql$ & "= Pictures.PictureID where GuestID = "
lsql$ = lsql$ & Val(guCGIData.QueryString)
Set guestDS = db.OpenRecordset(lsql$, dbOpenSnapshot)

'if there is a matching registered user:
If guestDS.RecordCount Then
    'output the data
    OutputString "<table>"
    OutputString "<tr><td ALIGN=""right""><b>Name:</b></td>"
    OutputString "<td>" & chknull(guestDS!FirstName, "") & " "
    OutputString chknull(guestDS!LastName, "") & "</td></tr>"
    OutputString "<tr><td ALIGN=""right""><b>Title:</b></td>"
    OutputString "<td>" & chknull(guestDS!Title, "") & "</td></tr>"
    OutputString "<tr><td ALIGN=""right""><b>Organization:</b></td>"
    OutputString "<td>" & chknull(guestDS!Organization, "") & "</td></tr>"
    OutputString "<tr><td ALIGN=""right""><b>Street Address:</b></td>"
    OutputString "<td>" & chknull(guestDS!StreetAddress, "") & "</td></tr>"
    OutputString "<tr><td ALIGN=""right""><b>Address 2:</b></td>"
    OutputString "<td>" & chknull(guestDS!Address2, "") & "</td></tr>"
    OutputString "<tr><td ALIGN=""right"">"
    OutputString "<b>City, State ZIP:</b></td><td>"
    If Len(chknull(guestDS!City, "")) Then
        OutputString chknull(guestDS!City, "")
        If Len(chknull(guestDS!State, "")) Then OutputString ", "
    End If
    OutputString chknull(guestDS!State, "") & " "
    OutputString chknull(guestDS!ZipCode, "") & "</td></tr>"
    OutputString "<tr><td ALIGN=""right""><b>Country:</b></td> "
    OutputString "<td>" & chknull(guestDS!Country, "") & "</td></tr>"
    OutputString "<tr><td ALIGN=""right""><b>Work Phone:</b></td>"
    OutputString "<td>" & chknull(guestDS!WorkPhone, "") & "</td></tr>"
    OutputString "<tr><td ALIGN=""right""><b>Fax:</b></td> "
    OutputString "<td>" & chknull(guestDS!Fax, "") & "</td></tr>"

    'output the EMail address w/ a mailto: directive
    OutputString "<tr><td ALIGN=""right""><b>Email:</b></td><td> "
    If Len(chknull(guestDS!Email, "")) Then
        OutputString "<A HREF=""mailto:"
        OutputString chknull(guestDS!Email, "") & """>"
        OutputString chknull(guestDS!Email, "") & "</A><br>"
    End If
    OutputString "</td></tr>"
```

continues

Listing 8.9. continued

```
        'output the URL as a hyperlink if it exists
        OutputString "<tr><td ALIGN=""right""><b>URL:</b></td><td> "
        If Len(chknull(guestDS!URL, "")) Then
            OutputString "<A HREF=""" & chknull(guestDS!URL, "")
            OutputString """>" & chknull(guestDS!URL, "") & "</A><br>"
        End If
        OutputString "</td></tr>"

        OutputString "<tr><td ALIGN=""right""><b>Operating System:</b></td> "
        OutputString "<td>" & chknull(guestDS!OS, "") & "</td></tr>"
        OutputString "<tr><td ALIGN=""right""><b>Web Browser:</b></td>"
        OutputString "<td>" & chknull(guestDS!UserAgent, "") & "</td></tr>"
        OutputString "<tr><td ALIGN=""right""><b>IP Address:</b></td> "
        OutputString "<td>" & chknull(guestDS!RemoteIP, "") & "</td></tr>"
        OutputString "<tr><td ALIGN=""right""><b>Host Name:</b></td>"
        OutputString "<td>" & chknull(guestDS!RemoteHost, "") & "</td></tr>"

        'if there is a valid picture, display it:
        If Len(chknull(guestDS!pathname, "")) Then
            OutputString "<tr><td ALIGN=""right""><b>Pictoral "
            OutputString "Representation:</b></td>"
            OutputString "<td><img align=""absmiddle"" src="""
            OutputString guestDS!pathname & """ alt=""WebGuest "
            OutputString "Picture""></td></tr>"
        End If
        OutputString "</table>"
    Else
        'no matching entry, print message
        OutputString "<H2>No entries matched the GuestID provided!</H2>"
    End If
    OutputString "</body></html>"

    'close everything
    guestDS.Close
    db.Close
    Close #guCGIData.OutputFileHandle
    End

FormError:
    Call ErrorHandler(Err, Error$)

End Sub
```

After the CGI data is read and some header information is output to the HTML output file, the SQL statement that retrieves the record is created. The SQL statement is

```
SELECT * FROM Guests LEFT JOIN Pictures on Guest.PictureID =
      Pictures.PictureID WHERE GuestID = x
```

The SQL statement uses a `LEFT JOIN` on the `Guests` and `Pictures` tables to produce the recordset. The `LEFT JOIN` ensures that a record will be returned, even if there is no `PictureID` for the record specified by `GuestID`. The `x` is replaced with the `GuestID` specified in the `Query String` parameter. The recordset is then opened.

If the recordset contains a record, its fields are output in an HTML table format. The table defined in the output consists of two columns and multiple rows. The left column displays a label for the field. It is right-justified. The right column displays the data from the recordset. The `Email` field is output using a `mailto:` hyperlink. Clicking on such a link in an e-mail-aware Web browser causes the browser to create a new e-mail message addressed to the mailbox specified in the link. The URL field is also output as a hyperlink, and clicking it causes the Web browser to load the resource specified by the URL. Finally, if a picture is specified for the record, it is displayed using the `<IMG>` tag.

If no records are found, the application outputs a message to that effect.

After all the HTML has been output, the application closes the snapshot, the database, and the output file, and ends.

Save the project and compile it into an executable named `results.exe`.

Installing and Testing the Applications

Now that the WebGuest database and applications have been created, it's time to install and test them on your HTTP server. If you haven't already done so, compile each project into executable form, naming them `entry.exe`, `gen-reg.exe`, `register.exe`, `search.exe`, `gen-list.exe`, and `results.exe`. Also, if you haven't created `wg-list.htm` and `gen-reg.txt` and placed them in your server's root document directory and Win/CGI directory, respectively, do so now (see Listing 8.1 and Listing 8.5 for the HTML to create these files).

Installing the Applications

The executable files should be copied into the Windows CGI or executable application directory as set up for your HTTP server.

For the WebSite server (which I used in developing these applications; a demo version is provided on the CD-ROM), the directories for Windows CGI applications are specified on the Mapping tab of the WebSite Server Admin application (see Figure 8.8). The Win/CGI URL Path element should be specified when creating links to these applications either in an HTML page or another CGI application.

For testing purposes, you should also enable CGI's Debug mode. With the WebSite Server Admin tool, this is done by enabling the CGI Execution tracing option on the Logging tab. This causes WebSite to leave the temporary files created during the CGI execution process in the CGI temporary storage directory. If this option is not enabled, the server will delete all these files after returning control to the user's Web browser.

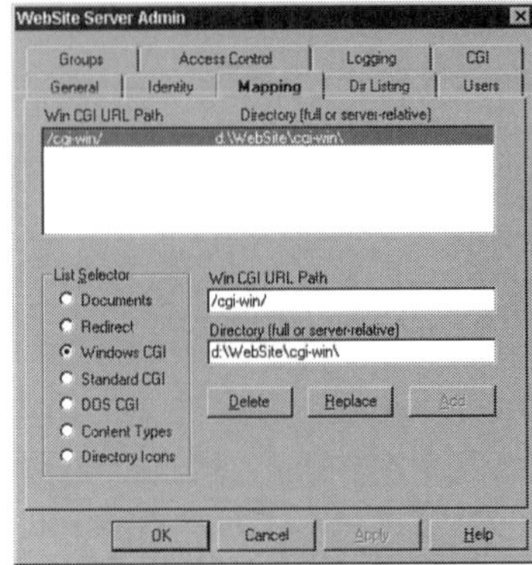

Figure 8.8.
The WebSite Server Admin's Mapping tab.

Testing the Applications

Fortunately, testing the WebGuest application is much easier than coding it. Before you begin to test the WebGuest site, check the following:

- You have created the WebGuest database and properly referenced it in all the `OpenDatabase()` method invocations.
- You have created the file `wg-list.htm` (see Listing 8.1) and placed it in your Web server's document root directory.
- You have created the file `gen-reg.txt` (see Listing 8.5) and placed it in your Web server's Win/CGI directory.
- You have compiled all the projects into executable form and copied them to the Win/CGI directory.
- Your Web server is running and accepting connections. If you wish to trace through the applications, enable the CGI tracing feature if available (see the "Installing the Applications" section above for a how-to for the WebSite server).
- Your Web browser is capable of using HTML forms.

After you've checked all these points, launch your Web browser. Enter a URL that points to the `entry.exe` application. For example, on my local server I have the Win/CGI programs in a logical directory named `cgi-win`. The URL for `entry.exe` on my server (if I'm running my Web browser on the same machine) is `http://localhost/cgi-win/entry.exe`.

NOTE:

The reference to `localhost` refers to the local machine and is assigned to the loopback IP address (`127.0.0.1`).

The page should load and display a message saying that there are zero people registered in the database. The page should look like Figure 8.2. If not, return to the `entry.vbp` project, review the code, and try to determine the problem.

If you have CGI tracing enabled, locate the directory that your server uses to store temporary CGI files (for WebSite, this defaults to a directory named `cgi-temp` which is a subdirectory of the WebSite `install` directory). Change the Visual Basic command-line arguments option to point to the newest `.INI` file in the temporary directory. This will be the file the server created before launching the application. You can view its contents using Notepad. By setting the command-line argument to point to this file, you can step through the application to see just what occurred.

If a run-time error occurs while the CGI program is executing, a special page returns and specifies the error description, error number, and specifics about the execution. This can be handy for tracking down coding errors or database problems.

The troubleshooting tips apply to any CGI program you write. Although the application will eventually run without any human interaction at the server, that doesn't have to be the case while you're writing the application.

From the entry page, click on the `Register` link. The registration page shown in Figure 8.3 should appear. Enter some information for yourself and click the Submit button. After the application executes, you should see a page thanking you for registering and providing a registration number. This number is the `GuestID` field assigned to the record you just entered. Return to the registration page (you can use the Back feature of your Web browser to avoid waiting for the `gen-reg.exe` application to execute again) and enter the information for a few of your friends. Try to enter a variety of data in the Last Name and State fields. Also, if you have several Web browsers on your machine, try using different ones each time. This will give you more varied lists when you list by user agent.

If an error occurs, follow the troubleshooting tips provided in the preceding paragraphs.

After you've entered enough data to satisfy your future curiosity, return to the Entry page. Click on the `View Available WebGuest Listings` link. The page from Figure 8.4 should appear. If you get a message saying that the resource could not be located, check that the file `wg-list.htm` exists in the Web server's document root. If the file exists there, check to make sure the link that was clicked on the entry page points to `/wg-list.htm`. If it doesn't, the problem lies in `entry.exe`. If the file was found but doesn't appear correctly, check the HTML coding within the file. In particular, look for unmatched quotes and angled brackets. Each < must have a corresponding > in the proper place, or the Web browser will be unable to interpret the document correctly.

After the page loads correctly, click any of the links to see the listing. The page should appear similar to Figure 8.5, depending on the list you chose. Select one of the WebGuest entry links, and the information you entered for that person should appear as in Figure 8.6.

After you've listed to your heart's content, return to the Entry page. Click the `Search the Database` link. The `gen-reg.exe` program produces a search page that should look like Figure 8.9. Enter some text to search for. Use the wildcard character also (the asterisk at the end of a piece of text). Select an operating system if you entered some when creating the entries. Click the Search button. If all goes as planned, a Search Results page similar to Figure 8.7 appears. Select any of the entries on the list to see the full entry.

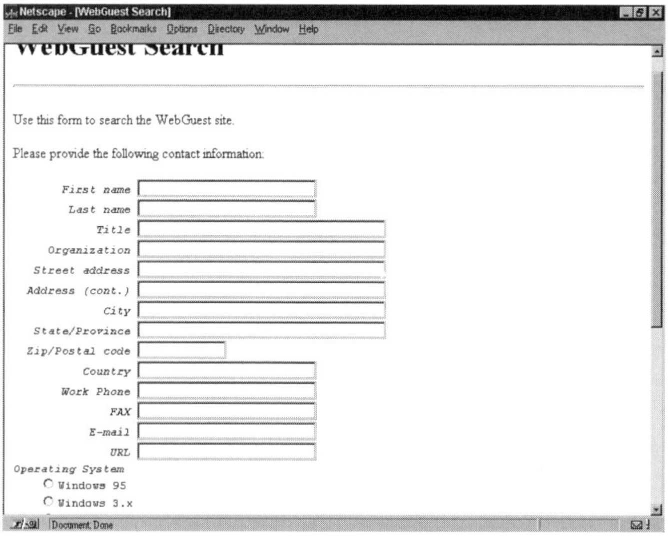

Figure 8.9.
The WebGuest Search Form page.

Summary

I hope you survived the testing process without having to revisit the Visual Basic projects too frequently. Debugging CGI applications is a looping process: load the page, click the link that causes the app to launch, interpret the resulting page, return to the VB project and run interactively using the CGI temporary data files, recompile the executable, and return to the first step. It's a tedious process but if you enjoy programming it can become addictive!

The WebGuest project is just the tip of the iceberg when it comes to Web-based customer information gathering and dissemination. You can take the concepts you learned in this chapter and apply them to just about any application where you'd like to connect a database to your Web server. That is, indeed, the beauty of the Win/CGI interface and the reason that the interface is called a gateway—these applications truly serve as gateways between your Web server and any system accessible to the machine the Web server runs on.

9

Connecting to OLE Servers: Using the Web as a Front-End to Schedule Plus

- Designing the Application
- Setting Up SPlus Resources
- The Basics of the SPlus OLE Model
- Designing the Input Forms
- Coding the Applications
- Installing and Testing the Applications
- Extending the Application

As I'm fond of mentioning, CGI applications are the ultimate gateway between a Web server and any other system to which the Web server machine has access. This point cannot be overstated to the programmer who is trying to hang on to legacy data or existing systems, yet wishes to integrate the Web into the IS environment. This chapter serves as one more basic example of connecting an existing system, Microsoft's Schedule Plus, to the Web.

NOTE:

The application in this chapter requires that Microsoft Schedule Plus Version 7 be installed on the machine running the Web server. Also, a valid Schedule Plus schedule must be accessible, whether it is for a Microsoft Exchange Server mailbox or simply a schedule file residing on the Web server machine. The example provided in this chapter assumes you have Microsoft Exchange Server installed. It uses an Exchange mailbox as the resource for the Schedule Plus schedule it accesses. The code can be modified, however, to open a local schedule file.

The purpose of Schedule Plus, as you can probably guess, is to manage a schedule or a group of schedules. In the typical LAN environment, an e-mail system such as Microsoft Exchange is already in place. Adding Microsoft Schedule Plus enables the enterprise to extend its e-mail system into the realm of time and contact management. The example presented in this chapter demonstrates the setting of a doctor's appointment using a CGI application. The CGI application connects an HTML form to a Schedule Plus database. The application examines a predetermined Schedule Plus schedule for available appointment times on a date that the Web page user enters. The user is then able to pick one of the available times and book an appointment. The CGI application then creates the new appointment on the Schedule Plus database. Now, anyone in the office that has access to that schedule by way of the local LAN can see that an appointment has been created, who created it, and the reason for the appointment.

Schedule Plus (hereafter called "SPlus") operates alongside Microsoft Exchange Server and uses the same mailboxes and logins as Exchange. Although it has just recently been released, the two applications developed in this chapter work only with the released versions of Exchange Server and SPlus version 7. The reason for this is quite simple: SPlus version 7 can operate as an OLE automation server. Previous versions of SPlus require calls to the SPlus DLL and are cumbersome, at best, to program. Also, version 7 introduces a small contact-management module into the product. The example in this chapter assumes all the patients have been entered into the `Contacts` table. This enables the application to work off a single key field, which the user enters (the Patient ID), and to set up the appointment with information taken from the patient's contact record. This saves users from having to enter personal information every time they wish to make an appointment.

The SPlus OLE interface, documented in Microsoft's BackOffice Software Developer's Kit (SDK), is slick and easy to use. It provides access to all the details within an SPlus database, including the appointments, contacts, tasks, and projects. There is a small section in this chapter, "The Basics of the SPlus OLE Model," which briefly describes the object model for SPlus. Microsoft has published several fair pieces on controlling the SPlus OLE automation server with VB. These are listed in the bibliography (Appendix D).

Designing the Application

The appointment setting site and accompanying applications are very basic. The main purpose of this chapter is to illustrate how to connect a Web site to an OLE automation server that is accessible by the server machine. The schedule that is used in this chapter's examples is for a resource. A resource is a special type of SPlus schedule that represents any entity shared among the users of the system. Resources can include conference rooms, audio-visual equipment, computers, and any other item (or even a person such as an audio/visual technician) that can be shared. Resources can be invited to meetings and have appointments scheduled for them, which is how the applications in this chapter operate.

The resource used in this chapter is named "Exam Room A" and represents an examination room in a doctor's office. In this simple example, the doctor has a small practice with only one examination room. The application could easily be expanded to handle multiple examination rooms if necessary. The applications use the exam room schedule instead of the doctor's personal schedule because the exam room is the actual resource being reserved. For example, the doctor may be out sick that day and another doctor may be covering the patients.

When patients wish to set up an appointment, they point their Web browser to the Appointment Request page shown in Figure 9.1. The user then enters the desired date, their Patient ID, and the reason they are requesting the appointment. When the Submit button is clicked, the first of the Win/CGI applications developed in this chapter is implemented.

This application, `checkscd.exe`, first verifies the date entered. The date must be a valid date, must not be before the current date, and must not fall on a Saturday or Sunday. The other fields are checked to make sure something has been entered. The application then opens the schedule for Exam Room A and verifies that the supplied Patient ID identifies an existing contact. The `Contacts` table in SPlus has a number of fields labeled `Userx`. The application uses `User1` to store the Patient ID data.

If a valid Patient ID has been entered, the application next checks the Free/Busy indicators for the date requested, and, if there are any available times on the day selected, it outputs an HTML form that has a radio button for each available time slot on the date requested. All appointments are 30 minutes long and begin on the half-hour. If there are no available times, the HTML page returned notifies the user of that fact. An example HTML output page is shown in Figure 9.2.

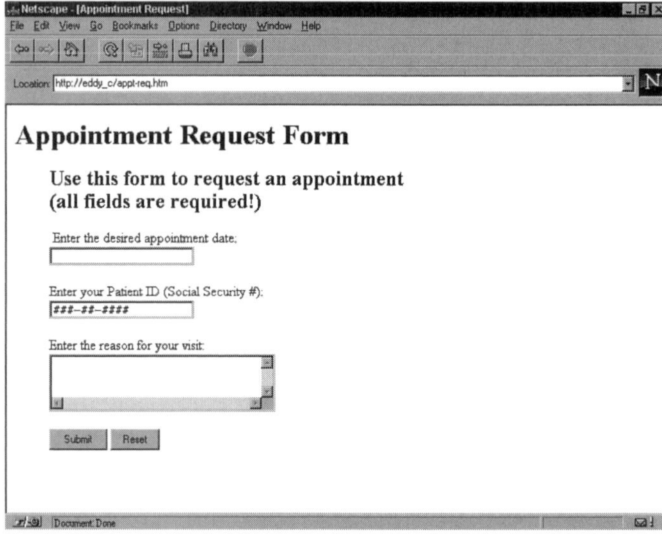

Figure 9.1.
The Appointment Request page.

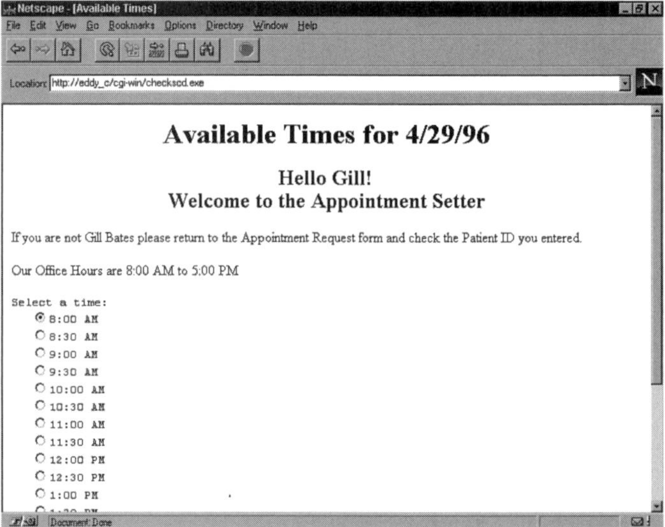

Figure 9.2.
The Available Times page.

The form has a button labeled Book Appointment, which the user clicks after selecting an appointment time. This launches the CGI application named `makeappt.exe`. This application creates the new appointment on Exam Room A's schedule and outputs a verification page to the user, confirming the appointment as well as the user's phone number. The phone number is retrieved from the SPlus `Contacts` table.

At this point, a new appointment has been entered into the SPlus database for Exam Room A. Anyone in the doctor's office who can connect to the Exchange Server can open Exam Room A's schedule and see the appointments that have been booked. The `makeappt` application places the patient's name and the reason for the appointment in the SPlus appointment description. A sentence indicating that the appointment was booked using the Web is placed in the SPlus appointment's `Notes` field. The appointment record is linked to the contact record using the SPlus internal `ItemID` for the patient's contact record.

Anyone using the SPlus front end can then print a daily, weekly, or monthly view for the exam room. The daily printout can be placed at the receptionist's desk so patients can be checked off as they show up for their appointments. The doctor could use the weekly printout to schedule his next golf outing. The monthly printout could be used to see if additional staff needs to be brought on for the month in the case of a run on the office. The possibilities are endless!

Setting Up SPlus Resources

The first step in this chapter's journey is to create the schedule for Exam Room A. As mentioned in the introduction, SPlus schedules that are used in group scheduling settings are always tied to an Exchange mailbox. This section covers creating the mailbox and setting the schedule for the mailbox to represent a resource.

Create the Exam Room A mailbox by using the following steps:

1. Log on to a Windows-NT machine as a user that has Exchange administrator privileges.
2. In the Program Manager's Microsoft Exchange group, double-click the Microsoft Exchange Administrator icon.
3. If you are prompted to enter a server name, enter the name of your Exchange server machine. If you are not prompted for a name, but the application doesn't connect to the server you want to use for this chapter, use the File | Connect to Server menu to connect to the correct server. The Microsoft Exchange Administrator application should now be loaded and displaying the configuration screen for your server. Figure 9.3 shows an example of how this screen looks.

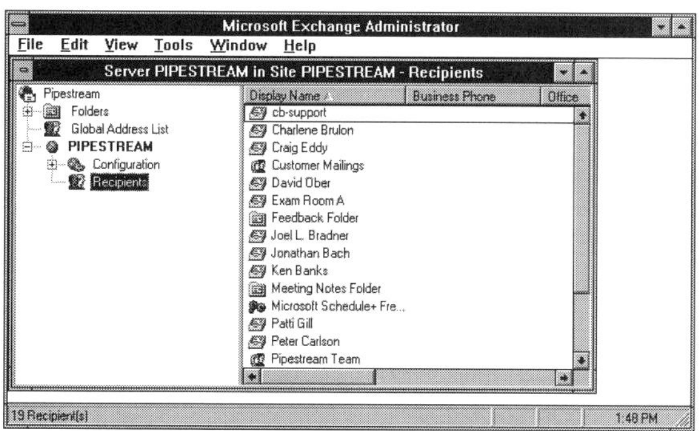

Figure 9.3.
The Microsoft Exchange Administrator.

4. Select the Recipients container in the left pane of the server window. Use the File | New Mailbox menu to create a new mailbox.
5. The Mailbox Properties page appears. Enter the information as shown in Figure 9.4. For the Primary Windows NT Account field, select any account that can log on to the network. I usually use my own account for these types of mailboxes. This makes accessing the mailbox a little easier.

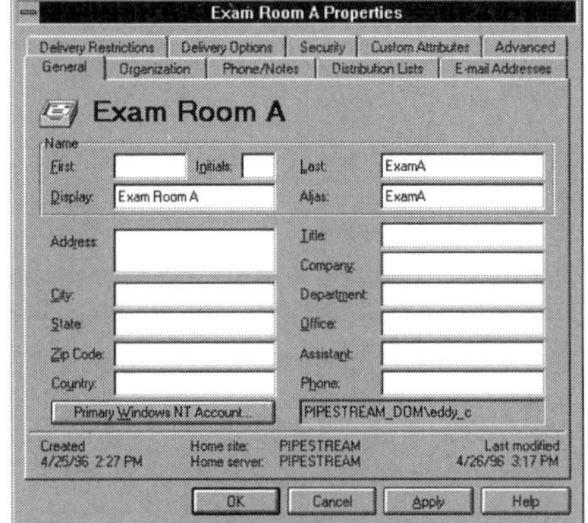

Figure 9.4.
The Exam Room A Exchange mailbox property sheet.

6. Adjust any of the properties on the other property tabs as you see fit. The Exchange site I administer has very few users, so I typically don't have to concern myself with many of the issues facing administrators of larger Exchange sites, such as mailbox visibility, permissions, and directory replication.
7. When you've finished creating the mailbox, click the OK button.

Now that the mailbox has been created, it's time to open it with SPlus. In SPlus, you'll specify that the schedule is for a resource, set some options, add some dummy appointments, and create a few patients in the SPlus `Contacts` table.

NOTE:

I use the Windows 95 Exchange client applications so these instructions are specific to Windows 95. The NT Exchange clients may require different steps to accomplish the same tasks.

The first step is to create an Exchange profile that opens the Exam Room A mailbox as follows:

1. From the Windows 95 Start menu, select Settings | Control Panel. Double-click the Mail and Fax icon or list entry (depending on your list view).
2. On the Microsoft Exchange Settings Properties dialog, click the Show Profiles button. The dialog changes to the Mail and Fax dialog, containing a list of the currently defined Exchange profiles.

3. Click the Add button. The Inbox Setup Wizard appears, similar to Figure 9.5.

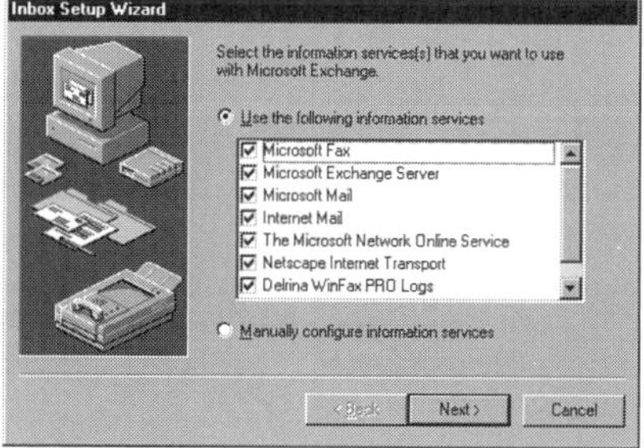

Figure 9.5.
The Inbox Setup Wizard.

4. Deselect all the selected information services except for the entry for Microsoft Exchange Server. Click the Next button.
5. The next dialog is where you enter the profile name to be used for this profile. Enter **`Exam Room A`** and click the Next button.
6. The next dialog is where the Exchange server name and mailbox are entered. Enter the name of your Exchange server in the top textbox. Enter **`Exam Room A`** in the Mailbox field. Click the Next button.
7. The answers entered on the three dialogs that follow can be left at their respective default values. Click Next on each dialog until you reach a dialog that has the Finish button. Click Finish.
8. You will be returned to the Mail and Fax dialog. Click the Close button to finish the profile setup process.

The next step is to open the Exam Room A schedule in SPlus. An intermediate step may be necessary, however. Your Exchange settings must enable you to select a profile to be used when you log on using an Exchange Server client application. If you don't see the Choose Profile dialog (Figure 9.6) when you start Exchange or SPlus, you need to follow these steps to enable this feature:

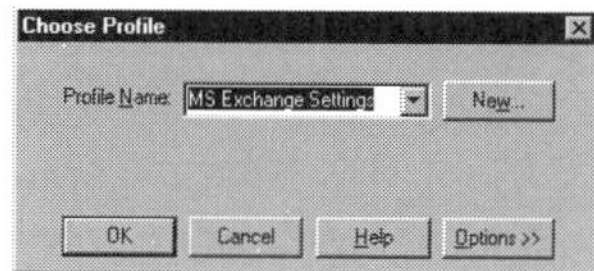

Figure 9.6.
The Exchange Choose Profile dialog.

1. Start Microsoft Exchange.
2. Select the Tools | Options menu.
3. On the General tab of the Options dialog, select the radio button labeled Prompt for a profile to be used. This radio button is in the frame titled When starting Microsoft Exchange.

4. Click OK.
5. Exit Exchange by using the File | Exit and Log Off menu. You must use the Exit and Log Off menu, not the Exit menu.

Now that you can select the profile that will be used, continue with these steps:

1. Launch Microsoft SPlus. When the Choose Profile dialog appears, select the Exam Room A profile from the drop-down list. Click OK.
2. The SPlus application loads and opens the schedule for Exam Room A. Figure 9.7 shows the initial screen of SPlus.

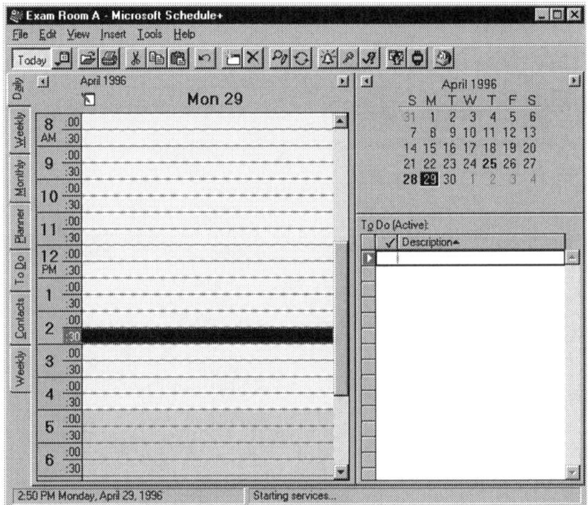

Figure 9.7.
SPlus with Exam Room A loaded.

3. Open the Options dialog by selecting the Tools | Options menu.
4. Check the boxes labeled This account is for a resource and Automatically accept meeting requests.
5. If you want to change the office hours from the defaults (8 AM to 5 PM), do so by using the Day Starts At and Day Ends At spin boxes. The dialog should appear similar to Figure 9.8. Click the OK button.
6. Back on the SPlus main screen, use the Insert | Appointment menu to add some appointments to the schedule. Make sure the appointments occur on Monday through Friday between the start and end hours specified. These will be used to test the available times feature of the CGI applications.

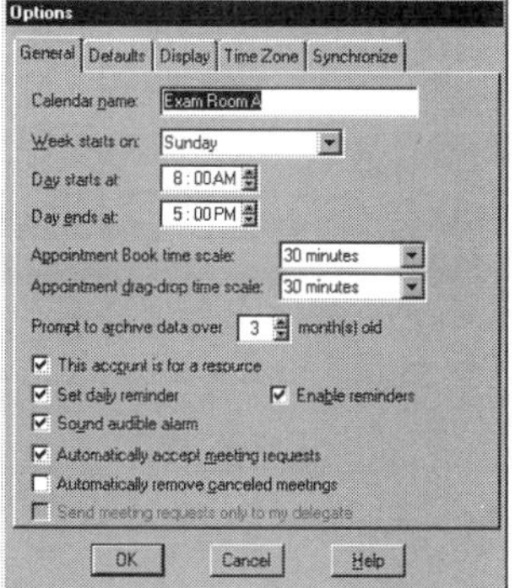

Figure 9.8.

The SPlus Options dialog for Exam Room A.

7. After you've created some appointments, create some contacts to serve as patients. The Insert | Contact menu adds a new contact. You must enter a first name, last name, home phone, and `User 1` field for each contact. The `User 1` field should be formatted as a Social Security number (###-##-####). Make a note of the numbers you use here. They'll be entered on the Request Appointment Web page as the Patient ID. Only one contact record is required, but to fully test the applications you should enter at least two contacts.
8. Exit SPlus using the File | Exit and Log Off menu.

Now that the Exam Room A resource has been created and loaded with some data, you can move on to the next section. It provides a very basic discussion of SPlus OLE automation programming. If you are already familiar with controlling OLE automation servers in general or SPlus in particular, feel free to skip the next section and proceed to the section titled "Designing the Input Forms."

The Basics of the SPlus OLE Model

First the bad news—the SPlus OLE automation object model is by far the most complicated OLE model I've seen. Now, for the good news—to effectively control the SPlus OLE automation server from Visual Basic you only need to learn a few basic concepts.

SPlus uses a concept known as *object overloading* to expose most of the data contained in a schedule. This means that one class is used for many named objects. The SPlus type library exposes only five objects: `Application`, `Schedule`, `Table`, `Item`, and `Property`. The objects are hierarchical in nature, with the `Application` object being topmost and the `Property` object at the bottom. In this section I'll take you through to the Item level. A serious discussion of using the `Property` object is beyond the scope and needs of this chapter. See the Bibliography in Appendix D for further resources covering the `Property` object.

The Application Object

The Application object is the only one that can be created at runtime. All the other objects are derived from the Application object. Although I've seen the code to create a SPlus application object written many ways, the only code I've been able to make work is

```
Dim objSPlusApplication as Object
Set SPlusApplication = CreateObject("SchedulePlus.Application.7")
```

so that's the code I've used in this chapter's examples.

The Application object has many useful properties and three very useful methods. The more interesting and useful properties are presented in Table 9.1. The only property of the Application object used in this chapter is ScheduleLogged.

Table 9.1. The Application object's properties.

Property	*Data Type*	*Description*
ScheduleLogged	Object	Returns a schedule object for the currently logged in mailbox.
IsMailEnabled	Long	Boolean that indicates whether mail is enabled.
UserName	String	The display name of the logged in mailbox.
UserAddress	String	The e-mail address for the logged in mailbox.
LoggedOn	Long	Boolean that indicates whether or not the Application object is logged on to the mail system.

The three methods are Logon, ScheduleForUser, and ScheduleForFile. The examples in this chapter use the Logon method, but not the other two. The Logon method is used to log on to the mail system. The method is defined by

```
object.Logon [profile name], [profile password], [show dialog], [parent window]
```

where *profile name* is the name of an Exchange profile to be used, such as Exam Room A, for the profile created when the Exam Room A resource was created. The *profile password* is the password for the named profile. The *show dialog* flag is used to instruct SPlus to display the Choose Profile dialog. The *parent window* parameter specifies the handle to the window that will be the parent window for the dialog box, if displayed.

Two examples should clarify the Logon method. The first,

```
objSPlusApplication.Logon "", "", 1
```

causes the SPlus OLE automation server to display the Choose Profile dialog. The method does not return until the user either selects a profile to use or clicks the dialog's Cancel button. The Cancel button causes a trappable runtime error to occur.

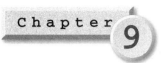

The second example,

```
objSPlusApplication.Logon "Exam Room A"
```

is the code used in the applications in this chapter. Because the profile was created on the Web server machine, there is no problem with hard-coding the profile name. Also, because the applications run as Win/CGI applications, using the first example would be futile because there would likely be no one seated at the machine to select the proper Exchange profile. The application would be stuck on that line of code, probably until the server was rebooted.

The other two methods, `ScheduleForUser` and `ScheduleForFile` are used to open other schedules. The `ScheduleForUser` method is incorrectly documented in the most recent version of the SPlus Programmer's Reference. The only way I have been able to open another user's schedule with this method is

```
Set objSched = objSPlusApplication.ScheduleForUser(tEMailAddress$, "", 1, 1)
```

where the `tEMailAddress$` is the fully-qualified Exchange e-mail address for the mailbox of interest and the `1, 1` has something to do with the mode in which the schedule is to be opened. Unfortunately, I am unable to explain why this code works, but it does for now!

The `Schedule` Object

The `Schedule` object provides a gateway to all the `Table` objects that actually contain the schedule's information. The `Schedule` object also provides properties to access the user options for the schedule, such as Start of Day and End of Day. Table 9.2 lists the more interesting properties of the `Schedule` object.

Table 9.2. The `Schedule` object's properties.

Property	*Data Type*	*Description*
`DayEndsAt`	Long	Number of half hours from midnight until the end of the day.
`DayStartsAt`	Long	Number of half hours from midnight until the start of the day.
`DayOfWeekStart`	Long	Indicates the day the week starts on.
`UserName`	String	The display name of the logged in mailbox.
`UserAddress`	String	The e-mail address for the logged in mailbox.

continues

Table 9.2. continued

Property	*Data Type*	*Description*
`DisallowAppointmentOverlap`	Long	Boolean value that indicates whether or not to allow overlapping appointments to be scheduled; used mostly for resources.
`DisallowRecurringItems`	Long	Boolean value that indicates whether or not to allow recurring items to be scheduled.

All the `Table` objects listed in the following section are accessed using the `Schedule` object. For example,

```
set objContacts = objCurrSched.Contacts
```

sets the object `objContacts` to the `Contacts` table contained within the schedule represented by `objCurrSched`.

There are two methods worth mentioning here. The first, `Activate`, is used to activate the SPlus application and load the schedule referenced by the `Schedule` object just as though you had launched SPlus from Windows 95. This method isn't used in this chapter, but I use it a lot when debugging SPlus controllers.

The second method, `FreeBusy`, is one of the keys to making the applications in this chapter work. It takes a date as one of its parameters and returns the free/busy information for the month that the supplied date falls in. The return value is a string of zeros and ones, where a zero means that there are no appointments scheduled during that interval, and a one means that there are. The second parameter is optional. If specified, it sets the interval in minutes that each zero or one represents. If not specified, the interval defaults to 30 minutes. The return string contains free/busy information for each interval from midnight (AM) on the first of the month, up until midnight (PM) on the last day of the month.

The `Table` Object

The `Table` object is the first of the overloaded objects. Therefore, you probably will never use the word "Table" anywhere in your SPlus code. Instead, you will refer to one of the many data tables within the `Schedule` object (`Appointments`, `Contacts`, `Tasks`, `Events`, and so forth).

Each `Table` object has the same properties and methods, which are listed in Table 9.3 and Table 9.4.

Table 9.3. The `Table` object's properties.

Property	*Data Type*	*Description*
`IsEndOfTable`	Long	Indicates whether the cursor position is at the end of the table.
`Position`	Long	The current position of the cursor in the table.
`Rows`	Long	The number of items currently in the table.

Table 9.4. The `Table` object's methods.

Methods	*Description*
`New`	Creates a new object in the table.
`Item`	Returns an `Item` object for the table.
`DeleteItem`	Deletes an `Item` object in the table.
`Skip`	Skips a specified number of rows forward or back in the table.
`Reset`	Sets the current item to the first item in the table.
`SetRange`	Restricts the table to a specified date range.
`SetRestriction`	Sets a simple restriction on a simple table.

You operate on a `Table` object in a manner similar to using the `Data Access` objects. Think of the table as a linked list of items (which is what it really is). When a table is first opened, the record pointer (if you will) is pointing at the first item in the list. By using the `Skip` method, you move the record pointer to the next item in the list. This continues until you reach the last item in the list. At this time, the `IsEndOfTable` property for the table is set to `True`.

To access a particular property of the current item, you must use the `Item` method. For example,

```
Debug.Print objContacts.Item.FirstName
```

prints the first name of the current contact (if there is a current contact) to the Debug window. The `Item` method also accepts a string parameter that specifies the `ItemID` of an item in the referenced table. This is useful for pinpointing an item in a table *if you know its* `ItemID`.

The `New` method creates a new item in the table, and the `DeleteItem` method deletes either the current item or the item matching the method's `ItemID` parameter if specified. The `Reset` method moves the record pointer to the first item in the table, and the `Skip` method skips to the next record. You can also skip over multiple records or skip backward by specifying a number as a parameter to the `Skip` method.

Finally, the `SetRange` method is used to limit the records returned by the `Table` object to the ones that fall within the date range specified. This is useful for `Appointments`, for example. The more powerful `SetRestriction` method enables you to restrict the items available to those matching the criteria specified by the method's parameters. This method is used in the applications in this chapter to pinpoint the `Contacts` table item for the patient who is setting the appointment.

The `Item` Object

The `Item` object is used to access the properties of a given Table object. The `Table` object may be an appointment, task, alarm, attendee, event, project, or contact. Each `Table` object's `Item` object has its own specific set of properties, but any property can be set on any item. SPlus simply ignores you when you attempt to set a property that is not valid for the `Item` object referenced. For example, you can set the `FirstName` property on an `Appointment` item, but Splus will simply ignore you.

The only property or method that I'll discuss here is the `Flush` method. This method is invoked whenever you want to save changes you've made to an `Item`'s properties or when you have created a new item by using the `Table` object's `New` method. The `makeappt` application demonstrates the use of `New` and `Flush` when it adds the patient's appointment to the SPlus `Appointments` table.

Summarizing the SPlus Object Model

I realize that the material I've covered may seem either overwhelming or may be completely inadequate. This section has only covered the basics of the SPlus OLE model. A more complete accounting can be found in the *Schedule Plus Programmer's Guide and Reference* available on the Microsoft Developer's Network CD or through the BackOffice SDK, also available from Microsoft. I have tried to cover, though, the solutions to all the problems I encountered in attempting to control the SPlus OLE automation server.

The method I finally resorted to when learning the programming model was to declare a bunch of global `object` variables, start an empty application, break execution, and then write code in the Debug window. I hope the preceding information, the examples to follow, and the reference material referred to in the Bibliography provides you with enough information to effectively utilize the SPlus OLE automation server. If all else fails, simply copy the code I've provided and use it anywhere you need to.

Designing the Input Forms

The Web site for this chapter consists of three HTML pages. The initial page (the Appointment Request page) is a static page that you should create in a suitable document directory on your Web server. The other two pages are created by the two CGI applications developed in this chapter. This section presents the full HTML of the Appointment Request page and simply discusses

    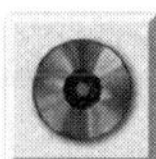

the other two pages. The HTML for the other two pages is generated by the applications developed in the next section.

The Appointment Request page (see Listing 9.1) is a simple HTML form page. The user enters the date of the preferred appointment, the Patient ID, and the reason for requesting an appointment. The names for the fields are `Date`, `PatientID`, and `Reason`, respectively. The first two fields are single-line textboxes. The reason field is a multiline textbox in case the user wishes to provide details of the problem. Because the Patient ID is the patient's Social Security number, the default text for that field is `"###-##-####"` to help remind the user to enter an SSN.

The `FORM` tag defines how the form operates when its Submit button is clicked. For the Appointment Request form, the browser issues a `POST` request to a resource whose URI is `/cgi-win/checkscd.exe`. The `POST` request message passes the data entered on the form to the first application developed in this chapter (`checkscd`). The data is passed using the three CGI parameters (`Date`, `PatientID`, and `Reason`) defined within the form. The form also has a Reset button, which returns the fields to their default state.

Listing 9.1. The Appointment Request page.

```
<html><head><title>Appointment Request</title></head>
<body>
<h1 align=left>Appointment Request Form</h1>
<blockquote>
<h2 align=left>Use this form to request an appointment<br>
(all fields are required!)</h2>
</blockquote>
<form action="/cgi-win/checkscd.exe" method="POST">
<blockquote>
<p> Enter the desired appointment date:<br>
<input type=text size=20 maxlength=256 name="Date"> </p>
</blockquote>
<blockquote>
<p>Enter your Patient ID (Social Security #):<br>
<input type=text size=20 maxlength=256 name="PatientID" value="###-##-####"></p>
</blockquote>
<blockquote>
<p>Enter the reason for your visit: <br>
<textarea name="Reason" rows=3 cols=30></textarea></p>
</blockquote>
<blockquote>
<p><input type=submit value="Submit"> <input type=reset value="Reset"></p>
</blockquote>
</form>
</body></html>
```

The HTML form produced by the `checkscd` application is the Available Times page. It contains a radio button for each available appointment slot, a Submit button (labeled Book Appointment), and a Reset button. The HTML definition for a radio button is

```
<input type=radio name=group_name value=individual_value [checked] >
```

The `type` element defines the input as a radio button. The `name` element defines the group to which the radio button belongs. This element must be the same for each radio button in the group. The `value` element defines the value that will be passed to the server by the Web browser application if this particular radio button is selected when the Submit button is clicked. The optional `checked` element specifies that this particular radio button should be selected by default. Note that the text that appears to the right of the radio button is not specified within the `<INPUT>` tag. Instead, you can place any valid HTML elements after the radio button. The Web browser renders the radio button similar to a VB radio button that has an empty string as its `Caption` property.

The Available Times form also has two hidden fields. These fields contain the Patient ID field and the Reason field that the user entered on the Appointment Request form. These fields are needed to complete the appointment setup and must be passed to the next application when the form's Book Appointment button is clicked. The form's action specifies a `POST` request to a resource located at `/cgi-win/makeappt.exe`. This is the `makeappt` application developed later in the chapter.

The final page is generated by `makeappt`. It provides a verification notice to the user that the appointment has indeed been created. It also informs the user that someone from the office will call 24 hours in advance of the appointment to follow up. The patient's phone number is also listed so the user can verify that it is correct.

This page is a simple HTML output page. No form is present and nothing fancy takes place.

All the HTML for these last two pages is generated by the two applications that are discussed in the next section. This section was intended to explain the design behind the HTML generated by the applications.

Coding the Applications

Two applications are used in the Web site described at the beginning of this chapter. The first, `checkscd`, takes the data the user has entered on the Appointment Request form and creates a page with some header information and an HTML form. If valid data has been entered on the Appointment Request form, the HTML form contains a radio button for each appointment time available on the date the user entered.

Clicking the Book Appointment button on this form causes the other application for this chapter, `makeappt`, to execute. This application takes the data entered on the previous two forms and creates an appointment on Exam Room A's SPlus schedule. The application then creates a confirmation page to display to the user.

This section discusses the code for these two applications. As you are aware if you've read the other chapters discussing Win/CGI applications, both projects contain a module named `CGI32.BAS`. This module is where the functions, user-defined data types, and global variables that I use in CGI applications are stored. The module `FUNCS.BAS` is also required in the project because `CGI32.BAS` calls some of its procedures. The code for these two modules is in Chapter 7, "Creating CGI

Applications in Visual Basic." It is also available in the same directory on the CD-ROM as the code for this chapter.

The two applications have a function named `IsTimeAvailable()` in common. Rather than creating a separate module just to store this function, I simply copied the code for it into the main module for both projects. The code for `IsTimeAvailable()` is discussed in the following section.

The **checkscd** Application

To create the `checkscd` application, start a new Visual Basic project. Add the `CGI32.BAS` and `FUNCS.BAS` modules to the project. Insert a new module and save it as `CHECKSCD.BAS`. This module will contain two procedures: `Main` and `IsTimeAvailable()`. The code for both procedures appears in full in Listing 9.2, which is at the end of this section. You must also add a reference to the SPlus object library using Visual Basic's Tools | References menu. On the References dialog, click the Browse button and locate the file `SP7EN32.OLB`. It is most likely located in the directory where SPlus has been installed.

The **IsTimeAvailable** Function

The `IsTimeAvailable` function, defined by this line

```
Public Function IsTimeAvailable(ptFreeBusy As String, _
         pvStart As Variant, pvEnd As Variant) As Integer
```

takes a string and two date/times as parameters and returns a Boolean result. The string parameter is a free/busy string which should be obtained by using the SPlus Schedule object's `FreeBusy` method. The date/times specify the start and end of the time period of interest.

The function examines the substring of the free/busy string that corresponds to the time period of interest. If that substring contains at least one `"1"`, the function returns `False` because this indicates that the schedule is busy at some point during the interval. The schedule must be free for the *entire* interval in order for this function to return `True`.

The function starts by first checking to see if there are any ones at all in the string. If there aren't, then the schedule is free for the entire month represented by the free/busy string, and the function returns `True` without any further processing required.

If there is at least one `"1"` in the string, the function must determine which characters in the string represent the free/busy information for the time period provided by the two date/time parameters. The first step is to determine the number of intervals that have occurred between midnight (AM) on the first day of the month and the times specified for the `pvStart` and the `pvEnd` parameters. The function then gets the substring from the string parameter that represents this interval. If there are any ones in this substring, the schedule is considered busy for the time period specified by the `pvStart` and the `pvEnd` parameters, and the function returns `False`. Otherwise, the function returns `True`.

The Sub Main Procedure

As in the other Win/CGI applications presented in this book, the `Main` procedure is where all the execution takes place. When the procedure ends, so does the CGI application.

The first section of code contains the typical Win/CGI startup code. This code has been discussed in previous chapters (Chapter 7 and Chapter 8, "Database Connectivity: The WebGuest Application") and won't be rehashed here.

After the startup code, the application validates the data entered on the Appointment Request form. The following validation rules are applied:

- The appointment date must be a valid date, must be on or after the current date, and must not fall on a Saturday or Sunday.
- The reason textbox must be filled in.
- The Patient ID must be filled in with a valid Patient ID (the check for validity is done in the next section of code, after the SPlus objects are created).

If the data fails any of the validation tests, the application returns a page to the user indicating the error.

After the basic validation has been passed, the application moves on to some SPlus code. The first step is to dimension object variables for each SPlus object that will be accessed. This application uses the `Application` object (`objSplusApp`), a `Schedule` object (`objCurrScd`), and the `Contacts Table` object (`objContacts`).

Next, the `Application` object is created with this line:

```
Set objSPlusApp = CreateObject("SchedulePlus.Application.7")
```

The code assumes that the shell the application is currently running under does not have a logged on mail session, so the `LoggedIn` property is not checked. Instead, a login to SPlus is accomplished using

```
objSPlusApp.Logon "Exam Room A"
```

This line uses the Exam Room A profile to log on to the SPlus and Exchange systems. After the successful logon, a reference to Exam Room A's schedule is created by executing

```
Set objCurrScd = objSPlusApp.ScheduleLogged
```

which returns the schedule for the logged in mailbox. Next,

```
Set objContacts = objCurrScd.Contacts
```

grabs a reference to the `Contacts` table for the schedule. The `Contacts` table is where all the office's patients are stored. The `Contacts` table is used to validate the Patient ID entered on the Appointment Request form and to provide some user-friendly text (in this application, the patient's name).

  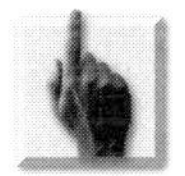  

The Patient ID is stored as a Social Security number and is, therefore, formatted as "###-##-####". The form field is retrieved from the CGI data, formatted as a SSN, and stored in a local variable by executing

```
ltFormattedID$ = Format$(GetFieldValue("PatientID"), "###-##-####")
```

The next step is to validate that the ID entered exists in the Contacts table. The Patient ID is stored in the Contacts table's User1 field. The SetRestriction method of the objContacts Table object is invoked to restrict the table to only those records that have a User1 field equal to the formatted Patient ID with this line:

```
objContacts.SetRestriction "User1", ltFormattedID$, "=="
```

The application assumes that a given Patient ID/SSN is used only once in the Contacts table. If the value of the objContacts.IsEndOftable property is True, then the Contacts table does not contain any records having the Patient ID entered on the Appointment Request form. In this case, the application outputs an HTML page to the user informing him or her of the fact that the ID entered is invalid. The program then logs off the SPlus Application object (using the Logoff method) and sets the object to Nothing.

NOTE:

Whenever you close an application that has logged on using an SPlus Application object, you *must* perform the Logoff and set the Application object to Nothing or you will leave the SPlus OLE automation server running. When this has happened, I have been unable to perform a Logon method without first manually shutting down the SPlus server.

After the Patient ID is validated, the application retrieves the patient's name using the Item method and the FirstName and LastName properties of the Contacts table:

```
ltFirstName$ = objContacts.Item.FirstName
ltLastName$ = objContacts.Item.LastName
```

Recall that the SetRestriction method has placed the Contacts table record pointer at the record for the contact whose User1 field equals the Patient ID entered on the Appointment Request form.

Now that the patient information is out of the way, the application concentrates on determining which appointment times are available on the date requested. The start and end times of the office's hours are retrieved from the Schedule object with

```
liDayStart = objCurrScd.DayStartsAt
liDayEnd = objCurrScd.DayEndsAt
```

The DayStartsAt and DayEndsAt properties return an integer representing the number of half hours that occur between midnight (AM) and the start and end times specified in the schedule's preferences. These integers are converted to actual time values using

```
lvStartTime = TimeValue(DateAdd("n", liDayStart * 30, "12:00:00 AM"))
lvEndTime = TimeValue(DateAdd("n", liDayEnd * 30, "12:00:00 AM"))
```

Next, the FreeBusy method is invoked to obtain the free/busy string for the month in which the requested date falls:

```
ltFreeBusy$ = objCurrScd.FreeBusy(ltDate$)
```

And, finally, the SPlus object is logged off and closed down using

```
objSPlusApp.Logoff
Set objSPlusApp = Nothing
```

The logoff is done before the actual end of the code in order to free the memory and resources used by the SPlus server for any other concurrent connections to use. Because the objects won't be used again by the application, there's no need to keep them around.

After the SPlus code, the application begins to build the HTML output page. The OutputString procedure is called several times to produce HTML that appears at the top of the page. Then, a variable named ltForm$ is created to store the HTML for the form, which contains the radio buttons for the available appointment times. The HTML is stored to a variable instead of being placed directly into the output file because of the chance that no times may be available on the date requested. In this case, the HTML form will not be created on the output page.

The code that creates the form starts with the form's <FORM> tag and specifies the HTTP method to be used (POST) as well as the action to be taken (/cgi-win/makeappt.exe). Then, several hidden fields are placed on the form. These fields contain the Patient ID and the text of the Reason field. This data is needed by makeappt in order to properly create the SPlus appointment for the patient.

A flag named liTimeAvailable% is used to keep track of whether or not any available times have been found. The code loops from the beginning to the end of office hours, checking each half-hour interval for an available time. If an interval is available, a radio button is created on the HTML form to represent that time period and the liTimeAvailable% flag is set to True. If this is the first available time that has been identified, the radio button's checked element is used to select the time by default on the form.

The form ends with the Submit button (labeled Book Appointment) and the Reset button.

If the liTimeAvailable% flag is set to True, the contents of ltForm$ are written to the output page. Otherwise, a message informing the user that no times are available is output.

The application ends by finishing off the HTML and closing the output file.

Take note, also, of the code in Listing 9.2 that occurs after the FormError label. As I stated earlier, you must close any logged-on SPlus Application objects. This is true even in an error condition, so the Logoff and Nothing code are copied here as well.

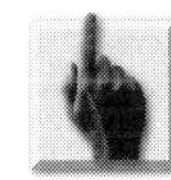

Listing 9.2. The `checkscd` module.

```
Public Sub Main()

'=================================
' Typical Win/CGI startup code
'

    On Error GoTo FormError

    If InStr(Command$, " ") Then

guCGIData.ProfileFile = Left$(Command$, InStr(Command$, " ") - 1)
    Else
        guCGIData.ProfileFile = Command$
    End If

    If LoadCGIData() = 0 Then
        'if we couldn't load all the CGI data,
        'could we at least open the Output File?
        If guCGIData.OutputFileHandle <> 0 Then
            'yes - call ErrorHandler to handle this
            Call ErrorHandler(-1, "Error loading CGI Data File")
        Else
            'no - forget about anything else!
            End
        End If
    End If

    OutputString "Content-Type: text/html"
    OutputString ""
'
' End of Win/CGI startup code
'=================================

'=================================
' Validate form data
'

    'validate the date entered on the form:
    ltDate$ = Trim$(GetFieldValue("Date"))
    If Not (IsDate(ltDate$)) Then
        'an invalid date was entered
        OutputString "<h2>You entered an invalid date</h2>"
        OutputString "The date you entered was: " & ltDate$
        OutputString "</body></html>"
        Close #guCGIData.OutputFileHandle
        End
    End If
    If DateValue(ltDate$) < DateValue(Now) Then
        'the date was prior to today
        OutputString "<h2>You entered a date that has passed</h2>"
        OutputString "The date you entered was: " & ltDate$
        OutputString "</body></html>"
        Close #guCGIData.OutputFileHandle
        End
    End If
```

continues

Listing 9.2. continued

```
    If WeekDay(ltDate$) = vbSunday Or WeekDay(ltDate$) = vbSaturday Then
        'the date was for a Saturday or Sunday
        OutputString "<h2>You entered a date that is a Saturday or Sunday</h2>"
        OutputString "Our offices are opened Monday thru Friday.<p>"
        OutputString "The date you entered was: " & ltDate$
        OutputString "</body></html>"
        Close #guCGIData.OutputFileHandle
        End
    End If

    'make sure the user entered a reason
    If Len(Trim$(GetFieldValue("Reason"))) = 0 Then
        OutputString "<h2>You Forgot to Enter a Reason</h2>"
        OutputString "You must enter a reason for the appointment!"
        OutputString "</body></html>"
        Close #guCGIData.OutputFileHandle
        End
    End If

    'make sure the user entered a patient ID
    If Len(Trim$(GetFieldValue("PatientID"))) = 0 Then
        OutputString "<h2>There is no Patient ID</h2>"
        OutputString "</body></html>"
        Close #guCGIData.OutputFileHandle
        End
    End If
'
' End of form data validation
'===================================

'===================================
' Schedule+ Code
'
    'Dimension some objects
    Dim objSPlusApp As Object
    Dim objCurrScd As Object
    Dim objContacts As Object

    'create the Schedule Plus (S+) object
    Set objSPlusApp = CreateObject("SchedulePlus.Application.7")

    'log on using the "Exam Room A" Exchange profile
    ' this profile logs on to the Exam Room A mailbox & schedule
    objSPlusApp.Logon "Exam Room A"

    'get the schedule for the logged-on user (Exam Room A)
    Set objCurrScd = objSPlusApp.ScheduleLogged

    'validate the Patient ID entered
    'Patients are stored in the schedule's Contacts table
    Set objContacts = objCurrScd.Contacts

    'User1 is the Patient ID, set a restriction
    ltFormattedID$ = Format$(GetFieldValue("PatientID"), "###-##-####")
    objContacts.SetRestriction "User1", ltFormattedID$, "=="
```

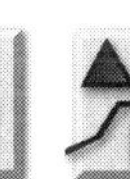

```
    'if we're at the end of the Contacts table, no such Patient ID
    If objContacts.IsEndOfTable Then
        OutputString "<h2>Your Patient ID Is Invalid!</h2>"
        OutputString "The ID you entered was: " & ltFormattedID$
        OutputString "<p>Your Patient ID is your Social Security Number"
        OutputString "</body></html>"
        Close #guCGIData.OutputFileHandle
        'close the S+ objects (VERY IMPORTANT!!!!)
        objSPlusApp.Logoff
        Set objSPlusApp = Nothing
        End
    End If

    'get the patient's first name from the Contacts table:
    ltFirstName$ = objContacts.Item.FirstName
    ltLastName$ = objContacts.Item.LastName

    'get the day starting and ending times for the schedule
    ' these values are the number of 1/2 hours between midnight
    ' and the Day Starts and Day Ends settings for the schedule
    liDayStart = objCurrScd.DayStartsAt
    liDayEnd = objCurrScd.DayEndsAt
    lvStartTime = TimeValue(DateAdd("n", liDayStart * 30, "12:00:00 AM"))
    lvEndTime = TimeValue(DateAdd("n", liDayEnd * 30, "12:00:00 AM"))

    'get the FreeBusy string for the date entered
    ' NOTE: S+ returns a string for the ENTIRE month starting at day 1
    ltFreeBusy$ = objCurrScd.FreeBusy(ltDate$)

    'close the S+ objects (VERY IMPORTANT!!!!)
    objSPlusApp.Logoff
    Set objSPlusApp = Nothing
'
' End of Schedule+ Code
'=====================================

    OutputString "<html><head><title>Available Times</title></head>"
    OutputString "<center><h1>Available Times for " & ltDate$ & "</h1>"
    OutputString "<h2>Hello " & ltFirstName$ & "! <br>"
    OutputString "Welcome to the Appointment Setter</h2></center>"
    OutputString "If you are not " & ltFirstName$ & " " & ltLastName$
    OutputString " please return to the Appointment Request form and check "
    OutputString "the Patient ID you entered.<p>"
    OutputString "Our Office Hours are " & Format$(lvStartTime, "H:NN AM/PM")
    OutputString " to " & Format$(lvEndTime, "H:NN AM/PM")

    'create a string to hold the form definition
    ' (if there are no available times for the chosen date, the
    '  form won't be output to the return page)
    ltForm$ = "<form method=""post"" action=""/cgi-win/makeappt.exe"">"
    'hidden field to pass the Patient ID to makeappt
    ltForm$ = ltForm$ & "<input type=hidden name=""PatientID"""
    ltForm$ = ltForm$ & " value=""" & ltFormattedID$ & """>"
    'hidden field to pass the reason to makeappt
    ltForm$ = ltForm$ & "<input type=hidden name=""Reason"""
    ltForm$ = ltForm$ & " value=""" & GetFieldValue("Reason") & """>"
```

continues

Listing 9.2. continued

```
    ltForm$ = ltForm$ & "<pre>Select a time:" & Chr$(13)
    liTimesAvailable% = False   'flag for existence of avail. times
    For i% = 1 To liDayEnd - liDayStart
        'appts are every half hour on the half hour
        ltLoopStart$ = DateAdd("n", 30 * (i% - 1), ltDate$ & " " & lvStartTime)
        ltLoopEnd$ = DateAdd("n", 30, ltLoopStart$)
        'check the FreeBusy string to see if this time is avail.
        If IsTimeAvailable(ltFreeBusy$, Trim$(ltLoopStart$), _
           Trim$(ltLoopEnd$)) Then
'this time is available, output to the form
            ltForm$ = ltForm$ & "   <input type=radio name=""Time"" "
            'If liTimesAvailable% is False, this is the first available
            '  time, so make this radio button selected
            If Not (liTimesAvailable%) Then
                ltForm$ = ltForm$ & "checked "
            End If
            'finish creating the radio button,
            ' the value is the start date/time of the appt.
            ltForm$ = ltForm$ & "value=""" & ltLoopStart$ & """>" & _
                Format$(TimeValue(ltLoopStart$), "H:NN AM/PM") & Chr$(13)
            'turn the flag to True
            liTimesAvailable% = True
        End If
    Next
    'finish up the form
    ltForm$ = ltForm$ & Chr$(13)
    ltForm$ = ltForm$ & "<input type=submit value=""Book Appointment"">"
    ltForm$ = ltForm$ & "     <input type=reset></pre></form>"

    'if there are available times, output the form variable
    If liTimesAvailable% Then
        OutputString ltForm$
    'otherwise output an apology
    Else
        OutputString "<h2>Sorry, nothing available on "
        OutputString "the date you selected.</h2>"
End If

    'finish up
    OutputString "</body></html>"
    Close #guCGIData.OutputFileHandle
    End

'=====================================
' Handler for all run-time errors
'
FormError:

    'close the S+ objects (VERY IMPORTANT!!!!)
    If Not (objSPlusApp Is Nothing) Then
        objSPlusApp.Logoff
        Set objSPlusApp = Nothing
    End If
```

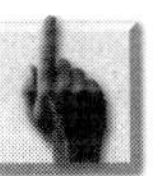

```
    'call the standard Win/CGI error handler:
    Call ErrorHandler(Err, Error$)

End Sub

Public Function IsTimeAvailable(ptFreeBusy As String, _
      pvStart As Variant, pvEnd As Variant) As Integer
'given a FreeBusy string from a Schedule+ schedule,
    ' and start and end times, determine the FreeBusy status
    ' for the given time period (a status of busy for any part
    ' of the interval returns False)

    'some constants used
    Const FREE_BUSY_INTERVAL = 30
    Const MINUTES_PER_DAY = 24 * 60

    Dim lvStartOfMonth As Variant
    Dim llMinutes As Long
    Dim liStart As Integer
    Dim liEnd As Integer
    Dim ltFreeBusyOfInterest$

    IsTimeAvailable = True

    'if the FreeBusy string contains no "1"s, all times are available
    If InStr(ptFreeBusy, "1") = 0 Then Exit Function

    'get the start of the month
    lvStartOfMonth = DateValue(DateAdd("d", 1 - Day(pvStart), (pvStart)))

    'get the number of intervals between the start of the month
    ' and pvStart
    llMinutes = DateDiff("n", lvStartOfMonth, pvStart)
    ' use the DIV operator to return an integer
    liStart = (llMinutes \ FREE_BUSY_INTERVAL) + 1
    ' if there was a remainder, add 1 to the interval number
    If llMinutes Mod FREE_BUSY_INTERVAL > 0 Then liStart = liStart + 1

    'get the number of intervals between the start of the month
    ' and pvEnd
    llMinutes = DateDiff("n", lvStartOfMonth, pvEnd)
    ' use the DIV operator to return an integer
    liEnd = (llMinutes \ FREE_BUSY_INTERVAL) + 1
    ' if there was a remainder, add 1 to the interval number
    If llMinutes Mod FREE_BUSY_INTERVAL > 0 Then liEnd = liEnd + 1

    'get the free/busy string for the time interval we're interested in
    ltFreeBusyOfInterest$ = Mid$(ptFreeBusy, liStart, liEnd - liStart)

    'return the result based on whether or not a "1" is in the interval
    If InStr(ltFreeBusyOfInterest$, "1") Then
        IsTimeAvailable = False
    Else
        IsTimeAvailable = True
    End If

End Function
```

The makeappt Application

The makeappt application takes the selected appointment time and the hidden fields from the HTML form generated by checkscd and creates a new SPlus appointment item on the Exam Room A schedule. To create the application, start a new project. Add the CGI32.BAS and FUNCS.BAS modules and insert a new module. Copy the IsTimeAvailable() function from CHECKSCD.BAS into the new module and save the new module as MAKEAPPT.BAS. Insert a new procedure named Main and copy the code from Listing 9.3 into this new procedure.

The code at the beginning of Sub Main is virtually identical to the Sub Main code of CHECKSCD.BAS, so I won't bother repeating the details. The discussion in this section starts at the line of code following the comment Start of new code!! about three-quarters down Listing 9.3.

The first line,

```
Set objNewAppointment = objCurrScd.Appointments.New
```

creates a new Item object in the schedule's Appointments table. This is filled with the properties that are necessary to define the appointment that the patient has requested. To simplify the typing necessary,

```
With objNewAppointment
```

causes all property assignments to refer to the new appointment item. The lines of code following the With are where the appointment's properties are specified. These properties are the starting date/time, the ending date/time, the tentative flag (BusyType), the Notes, the alarm flag (Ring), and the actual text of the appointment (Text). Note also that the appointment's ContactItemID is set by

```
.ContactItemId = objContacts.Item.ItemID
```

This assigns the ContactItemID to the ItemID for the current contact referred to by objContacts.Item. This, because of code executed earlier, points to the Contacts table record for the Patient ID specified in the CGI data.

After all the properties are assigned, the new appointment item's Flush method is invoked, and the Item object is set to Nothing in order to actually save the property assignments:

```
objNewAppointment.Flush
Set objNewAppointment = Nothing
```

The remainder of the code simply outputs an HTML verification page to the user and closes down using the standard CGI close code.

Listing 9.3. `Sub Main` of the `makeappt` module.

```
Public Sub Main()

'================================
' Typical Win/CGI startup code
'
    On Error GoTo FormError

    If InStr(Command$, " ") Then
guCGIData.ProfileFile = Left$(Command$, InStr(Command$, " ") - 1)
    Else
        guCGIData.ProfileFile = Command$
    End If

    If LoadCGIData() = 0 Then
        'if we couldn't load all the CGI data,
        'could we at least open the Output File?
        If guCGIData.OutputFileHandle <> 0 Then
            'yes - call ErrorHandler to handle this
            Call ErrorHandler(-1, "Error loading CGI Data File")
        Else
            'no - forget about anything else!
            End
        End If
    End If

    OutputString "Content-Type: text/html"
    OutputString ""
'
' End of Win/CGI startup code
'================================

'================================
' Validate form data
'
    'check the date/time selected on the form:
    ltDate$ = Trim$(GetFieldValue("Time"))
    If Not (IsDate(ltDate$)) Then
        OutputString "<h2>An invalid date was sent to MakeAppt.exe</h2>"
        OutputString "The date sent was: " & ltDate$
        OutputString "</body></html>"
        Close #guCGIData.OutputFileHandle
        End
    End If

    If Len(Trim$(GetFieldValue("Reason"))) = 0 Then
        OutputString "<h2>You Forgot to Enter a Reason</h2>"
        OutputString "You must enter a reason for the appointment!"
        OutputString "</body></html>"
        Close #guCGIData.OutputFileHandle
        End
    End If

    If Len(Trim$(GetFieldValue("PatientID"))) = 0 Then
        OutputString "<h2>There is no Patient ID</h2>"
        OutputString "</body></html>"
```

continues

Listing 9.3. continued

```
        Close #guCGIData.OutputFileHandle
        End
    End If
'
' End of form data validation
'===================================

'===================================
' Schedule+ Code
'
    Dim objSPlusApp As Object
    Dim objCurrScd As Object
    Dim objContacts As Object
    Dim objAppointments As Object

    'create the Schedule Plus (S+) object
    Set objSPlusApp = CreateObject("SchedulePlus.Application.7")

    'log on using the "Exam Room A" Exchange profile
    ' this profile logs on to the Exam Room A mailbox & schedule
    objSPlusApp.Logon "Exam Room A"
    'get the schedule for the logged-on user (Exam Room A)
    Set objCurrScd = objSPlusApp.ScheduleLogged

    'validate the Patient ID entered
    'Patients are stored in the Exam Room A contact list
    Set objContacts = objCurrScd.Contacts
    'User1 is the Patient ID, set a restriction
    ltFormattedID$ = Format$(GetFieldValue("PatientID"), "###-##-####")
    objContacts.SetRestriction "User1", ltFormattedID$, "=="

    'if we're at the end of the Contacts table, no such Patient ID
    If objContacts.IsEndOfTable Then
        OutputString "<h2>Your Patient ID Is Invalid!</h2>"
        OutputString "The ID you entered was: " & ltFormattedID$
        OutputString "<p>Your Patient ID is your Social Security Number"
        OutputString "</body></html>"
        Close #guCGIData.OutputFileHandle
        'close the S+ objects (VERY IMPORTANT!!!!)
        objSPlusApp.Logoff
        Set objSPlusApp = Nothing
        End
    End If
    'get the patient's first name from the Contacts table:
    ltFirstName$ = objContacts.Item.FirstName
    ltLastName$ = objContacts.Item.LastName
    ltPhone$ = objContacts.Item.PhoneHome

    'get the FreeBusy string for the date entered
    ' NOTE: S+ returns a string for the ENTIRE month starting at day 1
    ltFreeBusy$ = objCurrScd.FreeBusy(ltDate$)

    'the end date/time will be 30 minutes after the start date/time
    ltEnd$ = DateAdd("n", 30, ltDate$)

    'check the FreeBusy string to see if this time is avail.
```

```
    If IsTimeAvailable(ltFreeBusy$, Trim$(ltDate$), Trim$(ltEnd$)) = 0 Then
        'time is not available
        OutputString "<head><title>Conflicting Appointment</title></head>"
        OutputString "<h2>The Selected Time Is Unavailable!</h2>"
        OutputString "The time you selected has likely been taken "
        OutputString "after you loaded the previous form. Please "
        OutputString "use your browser's Back feature to return to "
        OutputString "the Appointment Request page and click Submit"
        OutputString "again."
        OutputString "</body></html>"
        Close #guCGIData.OutputFileHandle
        'close the S+ objects (VERY IMPORTANT!!!!)
        objSPlusApp.Logoff
        Set objSPlusApp = Nothing
        End
    End If

'================================
' Start of new code!!
'================================
    'everything is a GO, create the new appointment
    Set objNewAppointment = objCurrScd.Appointments.New
    With objNewAppointment
        .Start = ltDate$
        .End = ltEnd$
        .BusyType = 1        'Non-tentative
        .Notes = "Requested via the Web on " & Format$(Now, "short date")
        .Ring = 0            'No alarm
        .ContactItemId = objContacts.Item.ItemID
        ltText$ = ltFirstName$ & " " & ltLastName$ & Chr$(13) & Chr$(10)
        ltText$ = ltText$ & Trim$(GetFieldValue("Reason"))
        .Text = ltText$
    End With
    'save the appointment
    objNewAppointment.Flush

    'close the S+ objects (VERY IMPORTANT!!!!)
    Set objNewAppointment = Nothing
    objSPlusApp.Logoff
    Set objSPlusApp = Nothing
'
' End of Schedule+ Code
'=====================================

    OutputString "<html><head><title>Appointment Booked</title></head>"
    OutputString "<center><h1>Appointment Booked</h1></center>"
    OutputString "Your appointment time, " & Format$(ltDate$, "H:NN AM/PM")
    OutputString " on " & Format$(ltDate$, "short date")
    OutputString ", has been verified. <br>Our office will call within "
    OutputString "24 hours of the appointment to verify. <br>"
    OutputString "We will call you at "
    OutputString ltPhone$ & ". If this number is not correct, please contact "
    OutputString "our office right away!"

    'finish up
    OutputString "</body></html>"
    Close #guCGIData.OutputFileHandle
    End
```

continues

Listing 9.3. continued

```
FormError:
    'close the S+ objects (VERY IMPORTANT!!!!)
    If Not (objSPlusApp Is Nothing) Then
        objSPlusApp.Logoff
        Set objSPlusApp = Nothing
    End If
    Call ErrorHandler(Err, Error$)
End Sub
```

Installing and Testing the Applications

Now that you've entered the code, it's time to install and test the applications. Fortunately, this is a simple Web site to test. There are only two forms requiring user input and only two applications.

Installing the Applications

Possibly the trickiest part is getting the path to the SPlus server working properly. If your Web server is running on a machine that can run Microsoft Exchange or Schedule Plus and successfully connect to an Exchange server, then you should have no problems with the code. If the Web server is not running on such a machine, you need to make it do so. Install the Microsoft Exchange client on the Web server machine. Then follow the instructions in this chapter's section titled "Setting Up SPlus Resources" to set up the Exam Room A mailbox and schedule.

If you haven't yet created any contacts or appointments on the Exam Room A schedule, do so now. Follow the instructions given in the "Setting Up SPlus Resources" section.

If all is a go on connecting to the Exchange server from your Web server machine, it's time to install the applications. Compile the applications into executable form, using the names `checkscd.exe` and `makeappt.exe`. Copy these files into your Web server's Win/CGI application directory.

Create the Appointment Request page given in Listing 9.1. You can give it any name you wish, but it must be saved into a directory that is a valid document directory for your Web server. Otherwise, it won't be accessible to a Web browser.

Testing the Applications

Start your Web server if it's not already running. Load the Appointment Request page. Enter a date that corresponds to a day on which you created an appointment on the schedule. Enter the Patient ID for one of the contacts you entered. Enter some text in the Reason field, and click the Submit button.

After the CGI application churns for a while (the SPlus OLE automation server can be *very* slow at creating the `Application` object and at performing the `Logon` method), you see a page that contains radio buttons for each of the available times on the date specified. The times for which you have already created appointments on the schedule should not be listed. If some of these times are listed, check the code in the `IsTimeAvailable()` function. The code for this function is in Listing 9.2.

If the page has loaded successfully, view the HTML source for this document. You should see the HTML for the form, and it should include hidden fields containing the data you entered for Patient ID and Reason on the Request Appointment form. If not, check and correct the code that creates `ltForm$` in `Sub Main` of `CHECKSCD.BAS`.

If the page displays some available times, select a time using the radio buttons provided. For this test, don't click the Book Appointment button yet. Instead, launch SPlus and open the schedule for Exam Room A. Move to the date you specified for the appointment and create an appointment at the same time as the radio button you selected. Close SPlus. Now click the Book Appointment button. This action should create a conflicting appointment on the schedule. The `makeappt` application should return a page resembling Figure 9.9. If the Appointment Booked page is returned and you're sure your dates and times will cause a conflict, check the code in `MAKEAPPT.BAS` that appears immediately before the new code comment label. This is how the `makeappt` application ensures that user A's time has not been chosen simultaneously by another user during the lapse between creating the page, selecting a time, and clicking the Book Appointment button.

Use the Back command in your Web browser to return to the Available Times page. Choose a time that will not cause a conflict and click the Book Appointment button. You could also use Back one more time to return to the Request Appointment page and click the Submit button there. This would create a new Available Times page that no longer includes the conflicting times. Either way, clicking the Book Appointment button should now produce the Appointment Booked page shown in Figure 9.10.

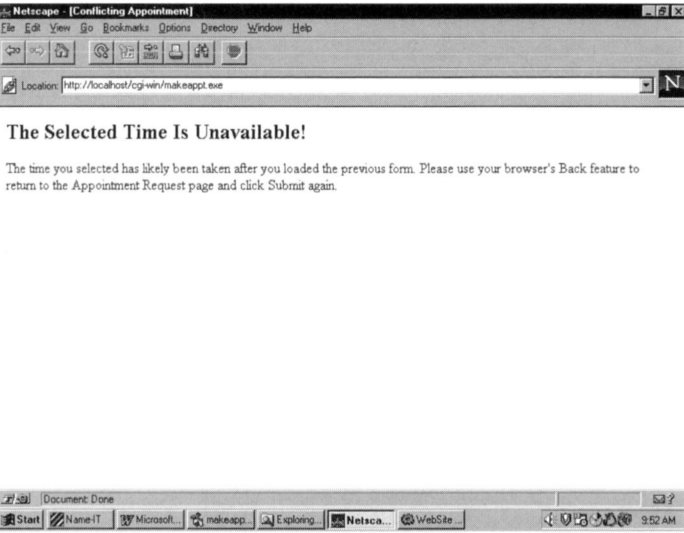

Figure 9.9.
The Conflicting Appointment page.

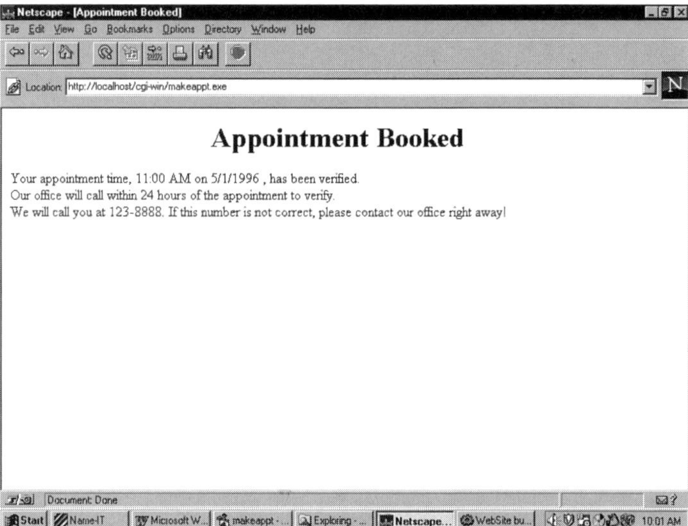

Figure 9.10.
The Appointment Booked page.

To verify that the appointment has indeed been created, launch SPlus and open the schedule for Exam Room A. Open the date for which you created the appointment from the Web page. The screen should look similar to Figure 9.11. Don't be alarmed that only the patient name is shown on the line for the appointment. The `Text` property of the appointment is assigned with a carriage-return/line-feed character separating the patient's name from the reason for the appointment.

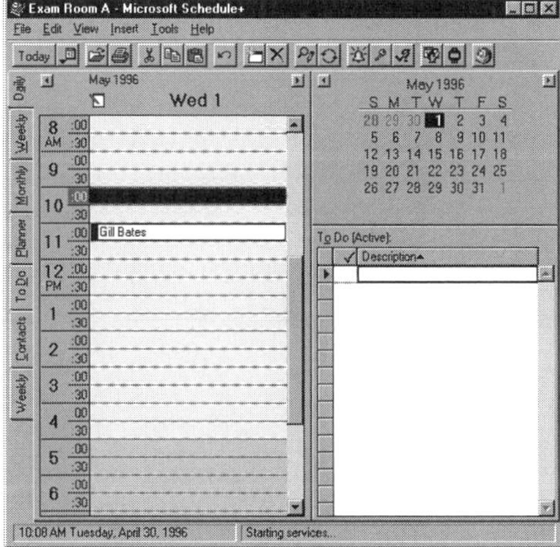

Figure 9.11.
SPlus displaying the appointment just created.

If you use the Edit | Edit Item menu while the appointment is selected, you can see where the properties assigned in the `makeappt` code are displayed within SPlus, including the full text of the `Text` property. For example, the Notes tab shown in Figure 9.12 illustrates how SPlus displays an appointment's `Notes` property.

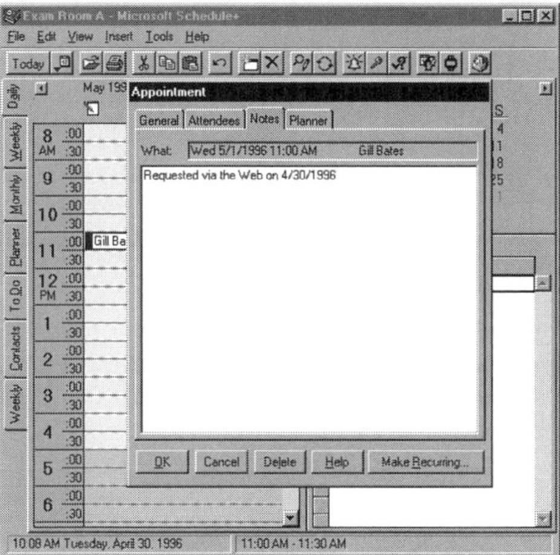

Figure 9.12.
The Notes tab for the appointment just created.

Extending The Application

There are many ways you can extend this application to provide greater functionality. I'll leave the coding up to you, but here are a few possible ideas:

- Add e-mail functionality to provide the ability to send a confirmation message to the patient.

- Extend the e-mail functionality to send a reminder message a few days before the actual appointment. This would save the receptionist from having to make a reminder phone call.
- Add some restrictions on how many appointments can be created on a given day. This would allow the office to accept emergency appointments by leaving slots open.
- Add links to some patient information that would let the patient review what procedures have been performed in the past, what procedures will be performed at the upcoming appointment, and any other pertinent information.

Summary

This chapter demonstrated how to connect your Web pages to any OLE automation server accessible to the machine running your Web server. This topic will become increasingly more important as VB4 advances the creation of OLE servers. VB4 has made it possible and, in fact, simple to create an OLE automation server using Visual Basic. This means that any existing application, or at least some pieces of it, can easily be converted to server as an OLE automation server. I hope this chapter has shown you how easy it is to use the Win/CGI interface to access such servers.

The chapter also should have whetted your appetite to explore the SPlus OLE automation server in more detail. Although the SPlus OLE object is complicated and can be cumbersome to use it is a fun server to control, once you get past the few pitfalls. I'm sure any programmer who is responsible for applications used in a workgroup or enterprise environment can think of myriad ways to use the SPlus OLE server to their benefit.

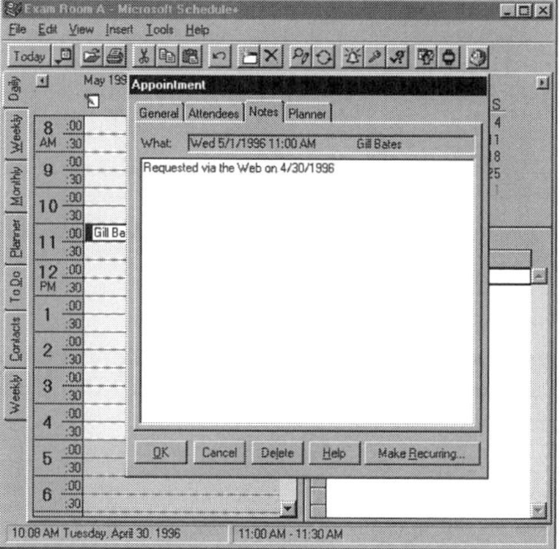

Chapter 10

Using OLEISAPI with the Microsoft Internet Information Server

http://www.microsoft.com

Microsoft has finally jumped head-first into the world of the Internet. One of its first entries into the mainstream Internet product area was the Internet Explorer, a Web browser that originally shipped with the Microsoft Plus! product but which you can now freely download from the Microsoft Web site (http://www.microsoft.com). After the Internet Explorer, the buzz about Microsoft was that it would finally release a Web server that was integrated with Windows NT. An FTP service was already built into NT, but it wasn't the friendliest FTP server you could use.

In early 1996, Microsoft did release its NT Web server and even announced that it would be bundled free of charge in future versions of Windows NT Server. The Microsoft Web server is more than just a Web server, as the name of the product suggests. Microsoft named the product the Internet Information Server (IIS) because it includes not only a Web server, but also a Gopher server and an FTP server. In releasing a Gopher and FTP server as well, Microsoft recognized that not all information on the Internet is stored on Web sites. However, the topic of this book is Web programming, so that's where I'll focus this chapter.

http://www.process.com

As is typical of Microsoft, a product is not complete until it has an API that programmers can use to extend or control the product. The same holds true for the IIS. You can extend the services available on your IIS-based Web site by using the IIS API (known as the Internet Server API, or ISAPI for the acronym-inclined). The ISAPI spec was written with the help of Process Software (http://www.process.com) and provides the interface between the IIS and the DLL extensions that you write. DLL is an acronym for *Dynamic Link Library*, a fact that is important to keep in mind for this discussion.

"That all sounds wonderful," you're probably thinking. "But I can't write a DLL with Visual Basic." So what's the point? Every time I think Microsoft has forgotten the VB programmer when introducing a new product, I'm proven incorrect. The ISAPI spec is no exception.

Microsoft provides several examples with the IIS that allow VB programs to run on the IIS. These examples, the ISAPI spec, and several other examples are also provided with the ActiveX Software Development Kit (SDK), which is currently available in beta form at the Microsoft Web site.

The first example is IS2WCGI which provides an interface between the IIS and existing CGI applications. This is useful when attempting to run the programs from previous chapters on your IIS. This example and its usage are discussed in Appendix C, "Win/CGI on the Microsoft Internet Information Server."

The second example is the OLEISAPI sample which is the topic of this chapter. OLEISAPI is an ISAPI-compliant DLL that activates OLE Automation servers. These servers can be written with any tool capable of creating OLE Automation servers. This includes, of course, Visual Basic 4.

The first half of this chapter provides an introduction to the ISAPI specification. The second half of the chapter provides a working example of an OLEISAPI application that you can modify to use on your own site. The example is a bare-bones online catalog browser and ordering site. It's far from being a complete system, but it does provide enough examples to allow you to take what's presented and use it on your own server.

NOTE:

This chapter will be of little use to any programmer who is not using an ISAPI-compliant Web server. If your Web server is not ISAPI-compliant, you may wish to skip this chapter.

The Advantages of OLEISAPI over Win/CGI

There are several advantages of using an ISAPI-compliant application instead of a CGI application. The most significant to the users of your Web site is performance. Although I haven't seen any benchmarks, personal experience has shown me that an ISAPI application (even the ones using the OLEISAPI interface described in this chapter) are at least twice as fast at returning their results than CGI applications. The reasons for this are discussed in this section.

The IIS is able to run ISAPI-compliant DLLs as extensions, meaning the DLL is loaded into the same address space that the server is using. This allows the DLL access to all the resources that are available to the IIS server. The DLL is also left in memory until the server decides it can be unloaded, meaning that minimal overhead is required the next time the ISAPI DLL is called. Both of these facts significantly improve the performance of Web-based applications.

A huge performance killer for CGI applications is the fact that the server must create a separate process for that application to run in. This is a time-consuming and RAM-consuming endeavor. The ISAPI interface overcomes this by using a DLL. The server can then use the Win32 API to provide *run-time* dynamic linking to an ISAPI-compliant DLL. The server uses `LoadLibrary()` and `GetProcAddress()` to retrieve the starting address of specific functions in the DLL. The server uses these functions, or *entry-points*, as defined by the ISAPI specification which is discussed in the next section.

The VB Programmer's Introduction to the ISAPI Spec

Although a knowledge of C++ is helpful to fully understand the ISAPI specification, the information required to use the OLEISAPI sample to access VB-written OLE Automation servers is not that difficult. This section provides a brief introduction to how ISAPI-compliant DLLs are written. The second half of the section discusses the OLE methods you must expose in order to use the OLEISAPI DLL.

ISAPI Basics

Most of the information in this section is taken from "A Specification for Writing Internet Server Applications" which is available as `ISAPI.HTM` in the ActiveX SDK. I've simplified and reorganized the information for use in understanding the example provided in this chapter.

An ISAPI-complaint DLL is must have two specific entry points. These are functions that the IIS calls when using the DLL. The first entry point is `GetExtensionVersion()`. This function is called by the server when the DLL is loaded by the server (recall that the DLL may not be unloaded when it has finished, meaning that this function is not called *every* time a client requests the DLL, only when the DLL is loaded). The second function is `HttpExtensionProc()`, which servers as the ISAPI equivalent to `Sub Main` in a VB program.

The `GetExtensionVersion()` function provides the server with the version number of the ISAPI specification on which the DLL is based and a short textual description of the extension, such as `"OLE Automation Gateway"`, which is the string returned by the OLEISAPI DLL. This function is called only once after the DLL is loaded.

The `HttpExtensionProc()` function is where all the interaction between the Web server and the DLL takes place. The server calls this function for each client request it receives. However, because the DLL is loaded only once, the server already has all the information it needs to call this function on each subsequent client request.

The server communicates with `HttpExtensionProc()` using a data structure called the `EXTENSION_CONTROL_BLOCK` (ECB). This structure contains information necessary to the DLL, including translated path information (that is, server-relative paths are translated to physical paths), the query string, and the request method. A pointer to an ECB is provided as a parameter to the function. The ISAPI specification provides the details of the ECB, which are beyond the scope of this introduction.

Although the ECB provides a wealth of information, not all the standard CGI variables are present. To provide the DLL with access to the remainder of the CGI data, the ECB provides a pointer to a function named `GetServerVariable().GetServerVariable()` retrieves information based on which server variable name is passed as its `lpszVariableName` parameter. The available variables include

`REMOTE_ADDR`, `REMOTE_HOST`, `SERVER_NAME`, `AUTH_TYPE`, and a special variable named `HTTP_ALL`. Calling `GetServerVariable()` with `HTTP_ALL` returns all the HTTP request message headers that aren't provided by one of the other variables. This includes the common CGI variables `User Agent` and `Accept`.

Using the OLEISAPI DLL

If you feel overwhelmed by the previous section, don't worry—you don't need to completely understand the ISAPI spec to use the OLEISAPI DLL. This section describes the OLEISAPI object model and discusses how to code the HTML documents that make requests using the OLEISAPI DLL.

The OLEISAPI DLL, once compiled, should be placed in a directory that the IIS recognizes as an executable directory. I've placed mine in the `/scripts` server-relative directory (`c:\inetsrv\scripts` is the physical path). You'll reference this server-relative directory in any URLs that are used to access OLEISAPI-compliant objects.

The OLEISAPI Object Model

The OLEISAPI DLL is used to invoke OLE Automation objects. These objects are invoked using the object method specified in the URL that requests the resource (see the next section for details). The OLEISAPI DLL invokes these methods using the same parameters each time, regardless of the method being invoked. This section describes that object model.

OLE methods that are accessed using OLEISAPI should have the following definition in a VB class module:

```
Sub MethodToBeCalled(ptRequest as String, ptResponse as String)
```

where `MethodToBeCalled` is the name of the method, `ptRequest` is an input containing the request data, and `ptResponse` is where the object places the method's output.

The `ptRequest` parameter contains the request data. If the request is a `GET` request, such as a hyperlink, the `ptRequest` parameter contains the query string provided in the URL. If the request is a `POST` request, the parameter contains the form data encoded as

```
Field1=Field1_Date&Field2=Field2_Data ...
```

If any of the data entered on the form contains spaces, they are replaced with plus signs. Therefore, if **`Jim Smith`** were entered in one of the form fields, it would be passed to the method as `"Jim+Smith"`. The OLE method must then convert this back to `"Jim Smith"`.

The response output is placed by the method into `ptResponse`. The data placed in this parameter must begin with `Content-Type:` followed by a valid MIME type (typically `text/html`). The OLEISAPI DLL returns this data to the Web server, which in turn sends it on to the requesting client.

Addressing OLEISAPI-Compliant Objects in HTML

When coding links to an object using the OLEISAPI DLL, you provide the OLEISAPI DLL with the server name, object's class name, and the name of the method to invoke. A sample HTML document, `default.htm`, is included with the OLEISAPI sample. It contains examples of the three possible HTML addressing mechanisms for accessing the object.

If the link is a `GET` link (such as a hyperlink within a Web document), you provide the query string within the link. The link consists of a path to the OLEISAPI DLL, followed by the OLE `PROGID` for the object, and the name of the method to be invoked. The query string is then provided following a question mark that follows the method name. For example,

```
<A HREF="/scripts/oleisapi.dll/MyObject.MyClass.MyMethod?field1=hello>
```

begins a link that invokes the `MyMethod` method of an object class called `MyClass`, which is contained in an OLE object named `MyObject`. If any of the data contains spaces, they must be encoded as plus signs within the URL.

If the object is being invoked from an HTML form, the `action` element of the `form` tag should resemble

```
action="/scripts/oleisapi.dll/MyObject.MyClass.MyMethod"
```

The data provided in the `ptRequest` parameter is created using the data entered on the HTML form. Note that any information passed as a query string in the `action` element is not passed to `MyMethod` and is wasted effort. Instead of using the query string, simply create hidden fields on the HTML form to pass the data.

You'll see more examples of OLEISAPI HTML coding when this chapter's examples are discussed.

Creating an Online Catalog with OLEISAPI

Now that the basics of using the OLEISAPI server extension have been covered, it's time to put the information to use. This section presents the online catalog system for Widgets Unlimited, a fictitious company that manufactures, you guessed it, widgets.

Widgets Unlimited has a Web server running on the IIS and wants to provide its current and prospective customers with a means of browsing the company's current catalog. In addition, the company wants to be able to sign up new customers and allow the customers to order while browsing the catalog. The benefits of this system to Widgets Unlimited is that a marketing presence is available 24 hours a day that, once it's set up, requires no additional sales staff. The benefit to customers is that they have the latest information from the company available at all times. They can shop when it's convenient, not when the Widgets Unlimited phone banks are staffed.

Designing the Application

For this chapter, the Widgets Unlimited (WU) site is very basic. You'll find room for improvement as well as additional features. However, the purpose of this chapter is to introduce you to programming OLEISAPI-compliant applications using Visual Basic. Therefore, I won't spend a lot of time developing an elaborate order entry and customer information management site. This could certainly be done but is beyond the needs of this chapter.

The WU site consists of two static Web pages, `catalog.htm` and `create.htm`, which reside in the document root directory of WU's IIS Web server. The `catalog.htm` page, shown in Figure 10.1, serves as the front door or entry to the online catalog. It provides a link to `create.htm` (where customer records are created) and a link to the dynamic catalog browsing page. The form shown is for current customers to use as a login form. A form at the bottom of the page (not shown in Figure 10.1) helps current customers who have forgotten their password to request that the system send the password via e-mail.

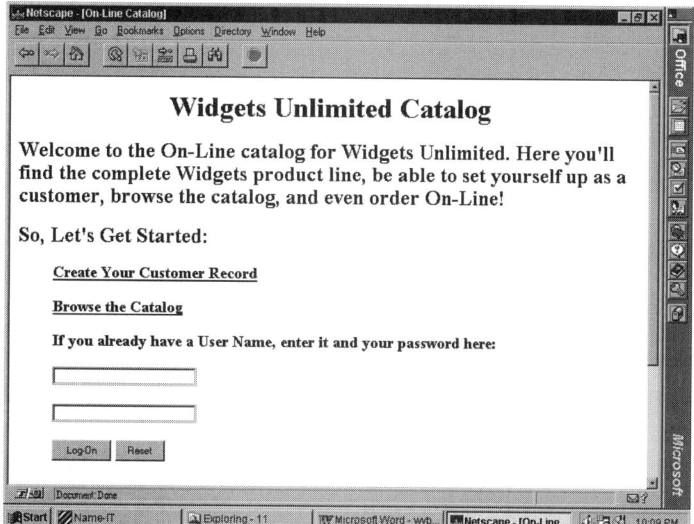

Figure 10.1.
The Online Catalog entry page.

The page where new customers can create a customer record is `create.htm`, shown in Figure 10.2. This page contains a form for the user to enter the information necessary to obtain a User Name. After someone has a User Name and password, he or she can place orders online while browsing the catalog. The only required fields on the form are User Name, e-mail address, and the password fields. However, the mailing address would be necessary before ordering anything. The user is required to enter the chosen password twice, a common practice to ensure that the user has typed the password correctly.

Netscape - [Create Your Customer Record]

File Edit View Go Bookmarks Options Directory Window Help

Create Your User Name

To create a User Name, you must enter some information about yourself (fields in BOLD are required):

User Name: (10 chars. max)
First Name:
Last Name:
Address:
City, State, ZIP:
Country:
Phone:
E-Mail:
Password: (8 chars. max)
Verify Password:

Submit Reset

Your User Name must be unique. If you receive a response saying that the User Name you chose was not unique, use the Back feature of your browser to return to this page and try again.

Document: Done

Start Name-IT Exploring - 11 Microsoft Word ... Netscape - [Cr... 10:16 PM

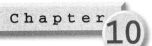

Figure 10.2.
The `create.htm` user creation page.

The `Browse The Catalog` link on the entry page takes the user to a dynamically generated listing of the current catalog contents. The link summons the OLEISAPI DLL and instructs it to invoke a method in the `CATALOG` OLE Automation object created later in this chapter. This OLE method produces an output page similar to Figure 10.3. The page is produced by querying the WU database's `Products` table for the current product list. The `Products` table provides product name, pricing, and even a server-relative path to a picture of the product. The picture is displayed alongside the product information.

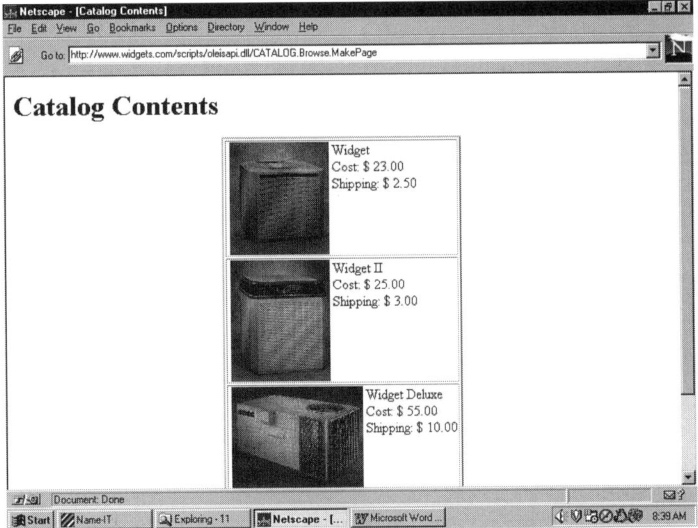

Figure 10.3.
A sample product listing page.

If users are current customers of WU, they can enter their user name and password in the boxes provided on the entry page. Clicking the Log-On button launches `OLEISAPI.DLL` and invokes another OLE method contained in the `CATALOG` object. This method verifies the entered user name and password and, if they're valid, produces the page shown in Figure 10.4. This page provides a link to the online catalog just described, as well as a link to a page where users can update their customer information (this page is not implemented in this chapter). The online catalog that the current user browses (see Figure 10.5) contains an `Order` link for each product. Clicking the `Order` link causes the system to place an order for that product for the current user.

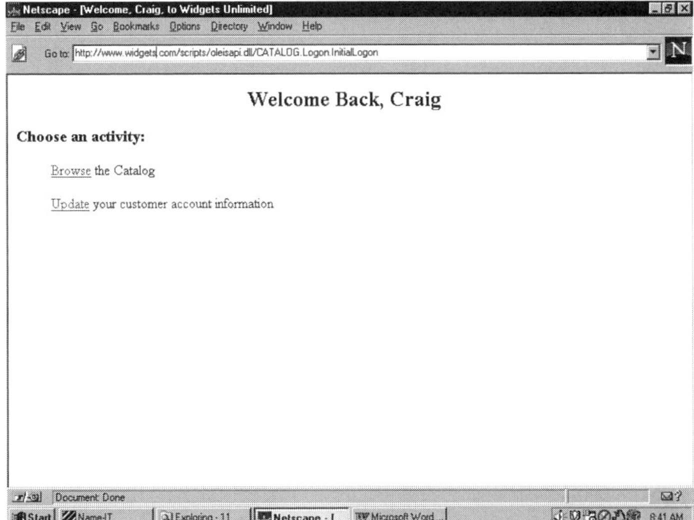

Figure 10.4.
The page for current customers.

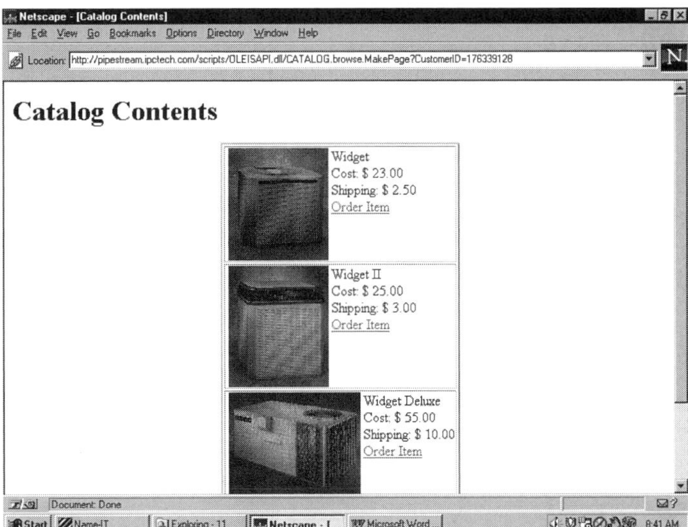

Figure 10.5.
The online catalog page for current customers.

Designing the Database

The database that powers the WU site as presented in this chapter is not very complex. It consists of only two tables: `Customers` and `Products`. The `Customers` table stores the customer information for each user who has created a user name using the form found on `create.htm`. The `Products` table is maintained by the WU Marketing department and consists of product information as well as a link to a picture of the product.

NOTE:

The application presented in this chapter uses Microsoft Access as the database engine. This was done only for convenience. In your applications you can use any database platform that the server machine has access to. I've also hard-coded a path to the database. You may wish to use ODBC to provide path-independence to your application.

You can use any tool you are comfortable with to create the database. I used Microsoft Access 95, but the Data Manager add-in application that ships with VB4 will work just as well for this simple database. Create the database and save it in any directory accessible to applications executing on your Web server machine.

Tables 10.1 and 10.2 list the fields in the two tables. All the text fields should allow zero-length strings for convenience Otherwise, you'd have to check each field from the HTML form to make sure it contains data. If it didn't contain data, you'd have to assign a string such as `" "` to the database fields. It's much simpler to just allow zero-length strings. Then you can simply assign the database field the value in the HTML form field.

Table 10.1. The `Customers` table.

Field Name	*Data Type*	*Size*
CustomerID	AutoNumber	Long integer
FirstName	Text	20
LastName	Text	20
Address	Text	50
City	Text	30
State	Text	20
ZIP	Text	10
Country	Text	20
EMail	Text	50
Password	Text	8

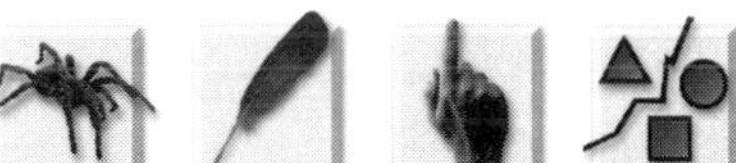

Field Name	Data Type	Size
Phone	Text	20
UserName	Text	10

The `Customers` table contains one field for each field shown in Figure 10.2 plus a `CustomerID` field. `CustomerID` is an AutoNumber field and serves as the primary key for the table. If the application were expanded to include order entry or a shopping cart system, the `CustomerID` would serve as a foreign key in the additional tables required to implement such systems. The `UserName` and `Password` fields are filled by users when they return to the site and wish to browse the catalog and place orders. The `UserName` must be unique and is not case-sensitive.

Table 10.2. The `Products` table.

Field Name	Data Type	Size/Default Value
ProductID	AutoNumber	Long integer
ProductName	Text	50
PictureURL	Text	50
Description	Memo	
Cost	Currency	0 (default)
Shipping	Currency	0 (default)

The `Products` table is where information about the various WU products is kept. The `ProductID` `AutoNumber` field is the table's primary key. The `PictureURL` field is used to store the URL that points to a picture of the product. This URL can be either an absolute path (such as `http://www.widgets.com/images/product1.jpg`) or a relative path (such as `/images/product1.jpg`). If a relative path is used, make sure it is one that will be correctly translated by the Web server. You can check this by appending the relative path to your server root directory's absolute URL and entering the resulting URL into a Web browser's URL input area. It is recommended that you use relative paths whenever possible. That way, if your server's root URL changes, you won't have to update every path in your site to match the new root URL.

Designing the HTML Pages

The two HTML pages, `catalog.htm` and `create.htm`, are simple HTML pages. You can use a text editor or any of the readily available HTML editors to create these pages.

The HTML for the two pages is provided in Listing 10.1 and Listing 10.2. The HTML files are also provided in the same directory as the sample code on the CD-ROM that accompanies the book. Create the two pages and save them in the document root directory of your Web server. After they're created, load them using a Web browser to make sure they match Figures 10.1 and 10.2.

Listing 10.1. The HTML for `catalog.htm`.

```
<html>
<head><title>Online Catalog</title></head>

<body>
<h1 align=center>Widgets Unlimited Catalog</h1>
<h2 align=left>Welcome to the On-Line catalog for Widgets Unlimited.
 Here you'll find the complete Widgets product line, be able
to set yourself up as a customer, browse the catalog, and even
order On-Line!</h2>
<h2 align=left>So, Let's Get Started:</h2>
<blockquote>
<h3 align=left><a href="/create.htm">Create Your Customer Record</a></h3>
<h3 align=left><a href="/scripts/oleisapi.dll/CATALOG.Browse.MakePage">
Browse the Catalog</a></h3>
<form action="/scripts/oleisapi.dll/CATALOG.Logon.InitialLogon" method="POST">
<h3>If you already have a User Name, enter it and your password here:</h3>
<h3><input type=text size=20 maxlength=256 name="UserName"> </h3>
<h3><input type=password size=20 maxlength=256 name="Password"></h3>
<h3 align=left><input type=submit value="Log-On">
<input type=reset value="Reset"></h3></form>
</blockquote>
<hr>
<blockquote>
<form action="/scripts/oleisapi.dll/CATALOG.Logon.ForgotPWD" method="POST">
<h3>If you forgot your password, enter your User Name here
and we'll e-mail your password to you:</h3>
<p><input type=text size=20 maxlength=256 name="UserName"></p>
<p><input type=submit value="Submit"> <input type=reset value="Reset"></p>
</form>
</blockquote>
</body></html>
```

Listing 10.2. The HTML for `create.htm`.

```
<html><head>
<title>Create Your Customer Record</title></head>

<body>
<h1 align=center>Create Your User Name</h1>
<h3 align=left>To create a User Name, you must enter some
information about yourself<br>(fields in BOLD are required):</h3>
```

```
<form action="/scripts/oleisapi.dll/CATALOG.Logon.Create" method="POST">
<pre><strong>User Name</strong>:        <input type=text size=20
maxlength=10 name="UserName"> (10 chars. max)
First Name:        <input type=text size=20 maxlength=20 name="FirstName">
Last Name:         <input type=text size=20 maxlength=20 name="Lastname">
Address:           <input type=text size=30 maxlength=50 name="Address">
City, State, ZIP: <input type=text size=20 maxlength=30 name="City">
<input type=text size=9 maxlength=20 name="State"><input type=text
size=10 maxlength=10 name="ZIP">
Country:           <input type=text size=20 maxlength=20 name="Country">
Phone:             <input type=text size=20 maxlength=20 name="Phone">
<strong>E-Mail</strong>:           <input type=text size=20
maxlength=50 name="EMail">
<strong>Password</strong>:         <input type=password size=20
maxlength=8 name="Password">(8 chars. max)
<strong>Verify Password</strong>:  <input type=password size=20
maxlength=8 name="Verify"></pre>
<div align=left>
<pre>      <input type=submit value="Submit">
        <input type=reset value="Reset"></pre>
</div>
</form>
<h3>Your User Name must be unique. If you receive a response
saying that the User Name you chose was not unique, use the
Back feature of your browser to return to this page and try again.</h3>
</body></html>
```

Coding the Application

All the objects that are used in the Widgets Unlimited OLEISAPI site are contained within a single OLE DLL. This DLL is named `CATALOG.DLL`. This will also be the name of the VB project (`CATALOG.VBP`) that creates the DLL. The DLL contains two object classes: `LOGON`, which contains the user-related OLE methods, and `Browse`, which contains the catalog-related OLE methods.

For each object class contained within a VB OLE object, there must be a class module in the VB project. The filename of the class module is irrelevant, but the module name assigned on the module's property sheet must match the class name you wish to use.

The easiest location to create and compile the object is on the machine on which your IIS is running. If you compile the object on another machine, you must ensure that it is set up properly on the server machine. This includes copying to the server machine all the Visual Basic DLLs needed to run the object and registering the object on the server machine using `REGSVR32.EXE`. If you run VB on the server machine, all these details are taken care of automatically.

To get started, run Visual Basic and create a new project. You should remove the default form from the project because there won't be a user-interface component to the OLE DLL. Also, remove all the custom controls because they won't be needed either. The References dialog should contain a reference to the Microsoft DAO 3.0 Object Library.

Next, add two class modules using Insert | Class Module. When the module appears, press F4 to open the Properties window for the module. One module should have its `Name` property set to `Browse`. The other should be set to `LOGON` (the all-caps is not significant, it's just a personal preference I have when dealing with logon objects). Both modules should be `Public` objects that have an `Instancing` property of `Creatable MultiUse`. The Properties window, with the exception of the `Name` property, should match Figure 10.6. Save these files as `BROWSE.CLS` and `LOGON.CLS`.

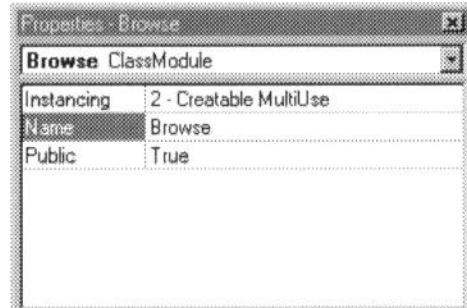

Figure 10.6.
The property sheet for an OLEISAPI object's class module.

After the two class modules have been added to the project, add the `DATABASE.BAS` module created in Chapter 8, "Database Connectivity: The WebGuest Application," and the `FUNCS.BAS` module created in Chapter 7, "Creating CGI Applications in Visual Basic." These files are also included in this chapter's directory on the CD-ROM.

Next, add a new module using Insert | Module. Save this module as `GENERAL.BAS`. It will be used to hold some routines that will be specific to the OLE object created in this chapter.

Add another new module and save it as `OLEISAPI.BAS`. This module will house some routines that can be used in any OLEISAPI objects you may write in the future. It provides functions similar to some of those found in `CGI32.BAS` that was developed in Chapter 7.

After all the modules have been set up, it's time to specify that this project will be used to create an OLE object. Open the project's properties dialog using Tools | Options. Select the Project tab. Set the Project Name to `Catalog`. In the Start Mode frame, select OLE Server. Then, enter some text in the Application Description such as **`Catalog Object for OLEISAPI`**. Leave the Compatible OLE Server textbox empty. The dialog should resemble Figure 10.7.

Finally, save the project as `CATALOG.VBP`.

If you've started from scratch as opposed to loading the project from the CD-ROM, you're now ready to enter the code. The following sections provide the listings and a short description for each module. Most of the code is far from rocket science and won't need much of an explanation. The purpose of this chapter is to demonstrate the building of an OLE object that is invoked from the OLEISAPI DLL. This is accomplished in the methods contained in the `Browse` and `LOGON` class modules.

Figure 10.7.

The Project's property sheet.

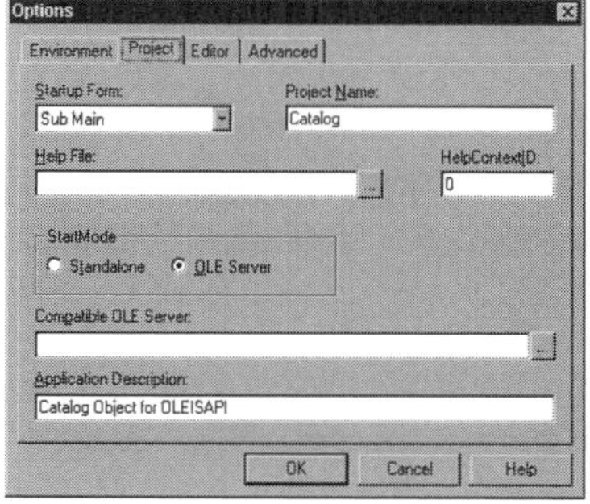

The **OLEISAPI.BAS** Module

The code for the `OLEISAPI.BAS` module is provided in Listing 10.3. It consists of three functions that are used to retrieve information from the query string provided as the `ptRequest` parameter to an OLEISAPI-compliant OLE object method.

The declarations section defines the `ParameterType` user-defined type and a global array named `Parameters()` that will be used to store the field values passed in the query string. Recall that the query string is formatted as

```
Field1=Value1&Field2=Value2&Field3=Value3 ...
```

where each field/value pair is separated by an ampersand, and the value is separated from the field name by an equal sign.

CAUTION:

A field may be passed on the query string with an empty value even if no data has been entered on the HTML form. This will be passed as `Field1=&Field2=Value2...` where `Field1` has no text entered on the form. Also, checkboxes on an HTML form are passed in this manner if they are checked. If the checkbox is not checked, the field name is not passed to the application.

The global variable `ParameterCount` contains the number of fields parsed from the query string.

The first procedure, `ParseQuery`, takes the delimited query string and places the field/value pairs into the `Parameters()` array. The `Key` element contains the field's name. The `Value` element contains the value assigned to the field.

The first step is to replace any plus signs found in the string with spaces (recall that any spaces contained in the query string are encoded using a plus sign). The next step is to call the `ParseString()` function contained in `FUNCS.BAS` to retrieve each field/value pair. The `ParseString()` function takes a delimited string and parses it into an array containing one element for each delimited occurrence in the string. Once that is accomplished, the `ParameterCount` variable is set to the upper bound of the array that `ParseString()` just loaded.

Finally, the array is iterated through and used to fill the `Parameters()` global array with the `Key` and `Value` elements taken from the parsed array.

The two functions found in the module, `ParamPresent()` and `GetParam()`, are used to determine whether a field specified is in the query string and to retrieve the value of a specific field, respectively.

The `Sub Main` procedure is present to satisfy VB's need for such a routine. It must be left empty or the object does not function properly when invoked by the OLEISAPI DLL. However, while you are debugging the project, this is where you should place any test code. For example, you may wish to invoke one of the OLE methods to see what value is returned. Simply declare a new object variable typed as the name of the object you're testing (`LOGON` or `Browse`), and invoke the method you're testing:

```
Dim objLogon as New LOGON
objLogon.InitialLogin "UserName=Foo&Password=Bar", ltReturnVAlue$
Debug.Print ltReturnValue$
```

This creates a new `LOGON` object and invokes the `InitialLogon` method. The `ptResult` method parameter is placed into `ltReturnValue$` and printed to the VB Debug window. Remember, when you're ready to compile your object, remove all the code from `Sub Main`.

Listing 10.3. The `OLEISAPI.BAS` code.

```
Type ParameterType
    Key As String
    Value As String
End Type

Global Parameters() As ParameterType
Global ParameterCount As Integer

Public Sub ParseQuery(ptQuery As String)

    Dim i%, nPos%
    Dim ltTemp      As String
    Dim lParamArray() As String

    'replace the plusses with spaces
    ltTemp = tReplaceChars(ptQuery, "+", " ")
    ParseString lParamArray, ltTemp, "&"
    ParameterCount = UBound(lParamArray)
    ReDim Parameters(ParameterCount)

    For i% = 1 To ParameterCount
        ltTemp = lParamArray(i%)
        nPos = InStr(ltTemp, "=")
        If nPos Then
            Parameters(i%).Key = Left$(ltTemp, nPos - 1)
            Parameters(i%).Value = Mid$(ltTemp, nPos + 1)
        End If
    Next i%

End Sub
```

```
Public Function GetParam(ByVal ptParam As String) As String

    ptParam = UCase$(ptParam)
    GetParam = ""

    For i% = 1 To ParameterCount
        If UCase$(Parameters(i%).Key) = ptParam Then
            GetParam = Parameters(i%).Value
            Exit Function
        End If
    Next

End Function

Public Function ParamPresent(ByVal ptParam As String) As Integer

    ptParam = UCase$(ptParam)
    ParamPresent = 0

    For i% = 1 To ParameterCount
        If UCase$(Parameters(i%).Key) = ptParam Then
            ParamPresent = i%
            Exit Function
        End If
    Next

End Function

Public Sub Main()

End Sub
```

The GENERAL.BAS Module

The module `GENERAL.BAS` contains code specific to the `Catalog` object. It contains functions used for validating form data and for producing an error report page. It also contains a standard routine for opening the database, `DBOpen`, which is called whenever a method needs to access the database. The code is presented in Listing 10.4.

The declarations section declares a global database variable. A global is used because the same database will be used for all the routines contained within the object, particularly the routines found in `GENERAL.BAS`. A constant is used for the database path and the server-relative path to OLEISAPI.DLL so that you have to modify the values to match your server setup in only one place.

The function `ValidateUserName()` first checks to make sure a non-empty user name has been entered by the user. If a user name is not entered, an error string is returned. If a user name has been entered, the value is checked against the `Customers` table to see if such a user name exists. If it does not exist (note that is not a case-sensitive search), an error message is returned. The error message contains links back to the home page and also to the `create.htm` page.

The function `ValidatePWD()` checks for the existence of the password field. If it's present, the function compares the value with the value stored in the database for the `UserName` provided. If the two passwords don't match, an error string is returned. The error string contains a link to the `ForgotPWD` method of the `LOGON` object. This method (though not fully implemented in this chapter) is used to e-mail a copy of the correct password to the e-mail address the user specified when creating the account.

The function `ValidateCustomerID()` is used to validate a `CustomerID`. After the user logs into the system through the `InitialLogon` method, the resulting HTML pages reference the customer's ID instead of the user name. This simplifies matters when the system is expanded and the `Customers` table is related to other tables through the `CustomerID` field.

The `ProduceError()` function is used by all the OLE methods to produce a standard error page should a runtime error occur. The procedure takes two parameters: the class name of the object (`pClass$`) and the method in which the error occurred (`pMethod$`). The function returns the complete HTML contents that are to be assigned to the OLE method's response parameter.

Listing 10.4. The code for `GENERAL.BAS`.

```
'database variable and path
Global db As Database
Global Const DB_PATH = "c:\inetsrv\scripts\catalog.mdb"

'server-relative path to oleisapi.dll:
Global Const OLEISAPI_PATH = "/scripts/OLEISAPI.dll"

Public Function ValidateUsername(pHTML$, db As Database) As Integer

    ValidateUsername = False

    If ParamPresent("UserName") = 0 Or Len(GetParam("UserName")) = 0 Then
        pHTML$ = pHTML$ & "Invalid Login</title></head><body>"
        pHTML$ = pHTML$ & "<H1>You did not enter a User Name</H1>"
        pHTML$ = pHTML$ & "<H3>Your User Name is required for logon</H3>"
        pHTML$ = pHTML$ & "<HR ALIGN=CENTER>Return to "
        pHTML$ = pHTML$ & "<A HREF=""/catalog.htm"">Home Page</a>"
        pHTML$ = pHTML$ & "</body></HTML>"
        Exit Function
    End If

    lsql$ = "Select Count(*) from Customers where UserName= '"
    lsql$ = lsql$ & GetParam("UserName") & "'"
    If Val(tExecAndAnswer(lsql$, db, lStatus%)) = 0 Then
        pHTML$ = pHTML$ & "Invalid Login</title></head><body>"
        pHTML$ = pHTML$ & "<H1>You Entered an invalid User Name</H1>"
        pHTML$ = pHTML$ & "<A HREF=""/create.htm"">Create One</a><p>"
        pHTML$ = pHTML$ & "<H3>The User Name was not found in the database</H3>"
        pHTML$ = pHTML$ & "<HR ALIGN=CENTER>Return to "
        pHTML$ = pHTML$ & "<A HREF=""/catalog.htm"">Home Page</a>"
        pHTML$ = pHTML$ & "</body></HTML>"
        Exit Function
    End If
```

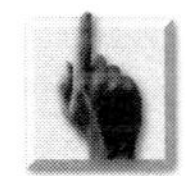

```
    ValidateUsername = True

End Function

Public Function ValidatePWD(pHTML$, db As Database) As Integer

    ValidatePWD = False

    If ParamPresent("Password") = 0 Or Len(GetParam("Password")) = 0 Then
        pHTML$ = pHTML$ & "Invalid Login</title></head><body>"
        pHTML$ = pHTML$ & "<H1>You did not enter a Password</H1>"
        pHTML$ = pHTML$ & "<H3>Your Password is required for logon</H3>"
        pHTML$ = pHTML$ & "<HR ALIGN=CENTER>Return to "
        pHTML$ = pHTML$ & "<A HREF=""/catalog.htm"">Home Page</a>"
        pHTML$ = pHTML$ & "</body></HTML>"
        Exit Function
    End If

    lsql$ = "Select Password from Customers where Username = '"
    lsql$ = lsql$ & GetParam("UserName") & "'"
    If UCase$(tExecAndAnswer(lsql$, db, lStatus%)) <> _
       UCase$(GetParam("Password")) Then
        pHTML$ = pHTML$ & "Invalid Password</title></head><body>"
        pHTML$ = pHTML$ & "<H1>You Entered an Invalid Password</H1>"
        pHTML$ = pHTML$ & "<H3>The Password you entered was "
        pHTML$ = pHTML$ & " incorrect.</H3>"
        pHTML$ = pHTML$ & "If you've forgotten your password, "
        pHTML$ = pHTML$ & "<A HREF=""" & OLEISAPI_PATH
        pHTML$ = pHTML$ & "/CATALOG.Logon.ForgotPWD"">"
        pHTML$ = pHTML$ & "click here</A> and we'll e-mail it to you."
        pHTML$ = pHTML$ & "<HR ALIGN=CENTER>Return to "
        pHTML$ = pHTML$ & "<A HREF=""/catalog.htm"">Home Page</a>"
        pHTML$ = pHTML$ & "</body></HTML>"
        Exit Function
    End If

    ValidatePWD = True

End Function

Public Function ValidateCustomerID(pHTML$, db As Database)

    ValidateCustomerID = False

    If ParamPresent("CustomerID") = 0 Or Len(GetParam("CustomerID")) = 0 Then
        pHTML$ = pHTML$ & "Invalid Login</title></head><body>"
        pHTML$ = pHTML$ & "<H1>You did not enter a Customer ID</H1>"
        pHTML$ = pHTML$ & "<H3>Your Customer ID is required for logon</H3>"
        pHTML$ = pHTML$ & "<HR ALIGN=CENTER>Return to "
        pHTML$ = pHTML$ & "<A HREF=""/catalog.htm"">Home Page</a>"
        pHTML$ = pHTML$ & "</body></HTML>"
        Exit Function
    End If

    lsql$ = "Select Count(*) from Customers where CustomerID= "
    lsql$ = lsql$ & GetParam("CustomerID")
```

continues

Listing 10.4. continued

```
    If Val(tExecAndAnswer(lsql$, db, lStatus%)) = 0 Then
        pHTML$ = pHTML$ & "Invalid Login</title></head><body>"
        pHTML$ = pHTML$ & "<H1>You Entered an Invalid Customer ID</H1>"
        pHTML$ = pHTML$ & "<H3>The Customer ID was not found in the "
        pHTML$ = pHTML$ & " database</H3><HR ALIGN=CENTER>Return to "
        pHTML$ = pHTML$ & "<A HREF=""/catalog.htm"">Home Page</a>"
        pHTML$ = pHTML$ & "</body></HTML>"
        Exit Function
    End If

    ValidateCustomerID = True

End Function

Public Sub DBOpen()

    Set db = OpenDatabase(DB_PATH)

End Sub

Public Function ProduceError(pClass$, pMethod$)
    Dim lHTML$

    lHTML$ = "Content-Type: text/html" & vbCrLf & vbCrLf
    lHTML$ = lHTML$ & "<html><head><title>Error Occurred</title>"
    lHTML$ = lHTML$ & "</head><body><H1>An Error Occurred During
    lHTML$ = lHTML$ & Login</H1>" & vbCrLf
    lHTML$ = lHTML$ & "Class: " & pClass$ & "<br>Method: "
    lHTML$ = lHTML$ & pMethod$ & "<p>Error Code: " & Err & "<br>"
    lHTML$ = lHTML$ & "Description: " & Error$ & "<p>"
    lHTML$ = lHTML$ & "Request: " & request & "<p>"
    lHTML$ = lHTML$ & "Please report this information to the "
    lHTML$ = lHTML$ & "system administrator</body></html>"
    ProduceError = lHTML$

End Function
```

The LOGON Class Module Code

The LOGON class module presented in Listing 10.5 contains all the code related to the Customers table in the database. The LOGON class provides four methods that may be called: InitialLogon, ForgotPWD, Maintain, and Create. All four are defined with the same two parameters, request as string, response as string, so that they may be called by the OLEISAPI DLL. This DLL requires that these two, and *only* these two, parameters be present in any methods that are accessed using OLEISAPI.

The ForgotPWD and Maintain methods don't really do anything except produce the same output page every time they're invoked. In a complete system, these methods would be used to help maintain the Customers table.

The `InitialLogon` method is the method that is invoked when the user clicks the Log-On button on the entry page. After the beginning of the HTML output starts, the method replaces any carriage returns or line-feed characters that may be in the query string with empty strings. Each field of form data on the Widgets Unlimited site is one line, so these characters are invalid anyway. The OLEISAPI DLL always seemed to pass the query string to the method with a CR/LF at the end. This caused validation functions to fail, so the method strips those characters out of the query string. The method then calls the `ParseQuery` procedure, opens the database, and validates the form data. If all the validation passes, the remainder of the output page is produced. For an existing customer, the output page (shown in Figure 10.4) contains links to browse the catalog or maintain customer information. After the HTML for the output page is produced, it is assigned to the `response` parameter, the database is closed, and the method exits.

If a runtime error occurs, it is trapped, and execution continues with the label `InitialLogonErr:`. The procedure assigns the `response` parameter the value of the `ProduceError()` function when called with `"Logon"` and `"InitialLogon"` as its parameters. The method then exits. Errors are handled in an identical way within each method in the `Catalog` object.

The `Create` method starts off in a manner similar to `InitialLogon`. After the database is opened and the form data validated, a recordset is created to hold the new customer record. The fields of the `Customers` table directly parallel those contained on the HTML form found in `create.htm`, with the exception of `CustomerID`. Because `CustomerID` is an `AutoNumber` field, it is assigned a value by the Jet Engine when the new record is added to the database using the Jet `Update` method.

After a new record is updated, the record pointer no longer points to the new record. However, a bookmark to the new record is contained in the `LastModified` property of the recordset. The method assigns this property to the recordset's `Bookmark` property to move the record pointer back to the newly added record. This occurs so the method can retrieve the assigned `CustomerID` value.

The `CustomerID` for the new record is used when producing the method's output page. The output page consists of the same links as the page produced by `InitialLogon`—a link to browse the catalog as a customer and a link to maintain the customer record.

Listing 10.5. The code for `LOGON.CLS`.

```
Public Sub InitialLogon(request As String, response As String)

    On Error GoTo InitialLogonErr

    Dim lHTML$      'local variable to hold the HTML
    Dim lsql$
    Dim lTxt$

    lHTML$ = "Content-Type: text/html" & vbCrLf & vbCrLf
    lHTML$ = lHTML$ & "<html><head><title>"

    'parse the parameters
    ' replace any CrLf characters w/ empty spaces (everything is one line)
    lTxt$ = tReplaceChars(request, Chr$(13), "")
```

continues

Listing 10.5. continued

```
    lTxt$ = tReplaceChars(lTxt$, Chr$(10), "")
    ParseQuery lTxt$

    'open the database
    DBOpen

    'validate the form data
    If (ValidateUsername(lHTML$, db) = False) Then
        response = lHTML$
        db.Close
        Exit Sub
    End If
    If (ValidatePWD(lHTML$, db) = False) Then
        response = lHTML$
        db.Close
        Exit Sub
    End If

    'get the UserName field
    UserName$ = GetParam("Username")

    'Produce the output page:

    'get some customer information
    Dim snap As Recordset
    lsql$ = "Select * from Customers where UserName = '" & UserName$ & "'"
    Set snap = db.OpenRecordset(lsql$, dbOpenSnapshot)
    CustID$ = snap("CustomerID")
    lName$ = chknull(snap("FirstName"), "Widgets Customer")
    lHTML$ = lHTML$ & "Welcome, " & snap("FirstName") & ", "
    snap.Close

    lHTML$ = lHTML$ & "to Widgets Unlimited</title></head><body>" & vbCrLf
    lHTML$ = lHTML$ & "<CENTER><H2>Welcome Back, " & lName$ & "</H2></CENTER>"
    lHTML$ = lHTML$ & "<H3>Choose an activity:</H3>" & vbCrLf
    lHTML$ = lHTML$ & "<blockquote>" & vbCrLf

    'link to browse the catalog as a customer
    lHTML$ = lHTML$ & "<a HREF=""" & OLEISAPI_PATH & "/CATALOG.browse.MakePage?"
    lHTML$ = lHTML$ & "CustomerID=" & CustID$ & """>Browse</a> "
    lHTML$ = lHTML$ & "the Catalog<p>"

    'link to the (unsupported) customer record maintenance page
    lHTML$ = lHTML$ & "<a HREF=""" & OLEISAPI_PATH & "/CATALOG.Logon.maintain?"
    lHTML$ = lHTML$ & "CustomerID=" & CustID$ & """>Update</a> "
    lHTML$ = lHTML$ & "your customer account information<p>"

    response = lHTML$
    db.Close
    Exit Sub

InitialLogonErr:
    response = ProduceError("Logon", "InitialLogon")
    Exit Sub

End Sub
```

```
Public Sub ForgotPWD(request As String, response As String)

    'customer forgot password, e-mail it to them
    response = "<html><head><title>Request Acknowledged</title></head><body>"
    response = "<H2>Your password will be sent to the e-mail "
    response = response & " address on file.</H2></body></html>"

End Sub

Public Sub Maintain(request As String, response As String)
    'not supported, just produce some output:
    response = "<html><head><title>Not Yet Supported</title></head><body>"
    response = response & "<H1>Customer Account Maintenance not yet "
    response = response & " supported</H1></body></html>"

End Sub


Public Sub Create(request As String, response As String)

    On Error GoTo CreateErr

    Dim lHTML$      'local variable to hold the HTML
    Dim lsql$
    Dim lTxt$

    lHTML$ = "Content-Type: text/html" & vbCrLf & vbCrLf
    lHTML$ = lHTML$ & "<html><head><title>"

    'parse the parameters
    ' replace any CrLf characters w/ empty spaces (everything is one line)
    lTxt$ = tReplaceChars(request, Chr$(13), "")
    lTxt$ = tReplaceChars(lTxt$, Chr$(10), "")
    ParseQuery lTxt$

    'validate required fields:
    If ParamPresent("UserName") = 0 Or ParamPresent("Email") = 0 Or _
      ParamPresent("Password") = 0 Or ParamPresent("Verify") = 0 Or _
      Len(GetParam("UserName")) = 0 Or Len(GetParam("Email")) = 0 Or _
      Len(GetParam("Password")) = 0 Or Len(GetParam("Verify")) = 0 Then
        lHTML$ = lHTML$ & "Validation Error</title></head><body>"
        lHTML$ = lHTML$ & "<H2>User Name, E-Mail, Password, and Verify "
        lHTML$ = lHTML$ & "fields must have data</H2>"
        lHTML$ = lHTML$ & "</body></html>"
        response = lHTML$
        Exit Sub
    End If

    'open the database
    DBOpen

    'validate uniqueness of UserName
    lsql$ = "Select count(*) from Customers where UserName = '"
    lsql$ = lsql$ & GetParam("UserName") & "'"
    If Val(tExecAndAnswer(lsql$, db, lStatus%)) Then
        lHTML$ = lHTML$ & "Validation Error</title></head><body>"
        lHTML$ = lHTML$ & "<H2>The User Name you chose has been taken.</H2>"
        lHTML$ = lHTML$ & "</body></html>"
```

continues

Listing 10.5. continued

```
        response = lHTML$
        Exit Sub
    End If

    'validate password
    If UCase$(GetParam("Password")) <> UCase$(GetParam("Verify")) Then
        lHTML$ = lHTML$ & "Validation Error</title></head><body>"
        lHTML$ = lHTML$ & "<H2>Passwords Did Not Match!</H2>"
        lHTML$ = lHTML$ & "</body></html>"
        response = lHTML$
        Exit Sub
    End If

    'create a recordset to hold the new customer record
    Dim ds As Recordset
    Set ds = db.OpenRecordset("Customers", dbOpenDynaset)
    'add the new record
    ds.AddNew
    'set the field data from the HTML form data
    ds!UserName = GetParam("UserName")
    ds!FirstName = GetParam("FirstName")
    ds!LastName = GetParam("LastName")
    ds!Address = GetParam("Address")
    ds!City = GetParam("City")
    ds!State = GetParam("State")
    ds!ZIP = GetParam("Zip")
    ds!Phone = GetParam("Phone")
    ds!EMail = GetParam("EMail")
    ds!Password = GetParam("Password")
    'update the reocrd
    ds.Update
    'move the record pointer BACK to the record just added
    ds.Bookmark = ds.LastModified
    'get the CustoemrID AutoNumber field
    CustID$ = Trim$(Str$(ds!CustomerID))

    'produce the HTML output page
    lHTML$ = lHTML$ & "Welcome Aboard!</title></head><body>"
    lHTML$ = lHTML$ & "<H1>User Name Created!</H1><p>"
    lHTML$ = lHTML$ & "<H3>Choose an activity:</H3>" & vbCrLf
    lHTML$ = lHTML$ & "<blockquote>" & vbCrLf
    'link to browse the catalog as a customer
    lHTML$ = lHTML$ & "<a HREF=""" & OLEISAPI_PATH & "/CATALOG.browse.MakePage?"
    lHTML$ = lHTML$ & "CustomerID=" & CustID$ & """>Browse</a> "
    lHTML$ = lHTML$ & "the Catalog<p>"
    'link to the (unsupported) customer record maintenance page
    lHTML$ = lHTML$ & "<a HREF=""" & OLEISAPI_PATH & "/CATALOG.Logon.maintain?"
    lHTML$ = lHTML$ & "CustomerID=" & CustID$ & """>Update</a> "
    lHTML$ = lHTML$ & "your customer account information<p>"

    'finish up and exit
    response = lHTML$ & "</body></html>"
    db.Close
    Exit Sub
```

```
CreateErr:
    response = ProduceError("Logon", "Create")
    Exit Sub

End Sub
```

The **Browse** Object's Code Module

The `Browse` object provides only two methods: `MakePage` and `Order`.

The `MakePage` method produces the catalog listing pages shown in Figures 10.3 and 10.5. If the method is passed a `CustomerID` field in the query string, the customer catalog page of Figure 10.5 is produced. Otherwise, the standard catalog page of Figure 10.3 is produced.

The method uses the same startup code as the methods discussed previously. After the database is opened, the code checks to see if a `CustomerID` field is present in the query string. The `CustomerID` field is present in the query string if a valid customer has requested to view the catalog. If `CustomerID` is present, it is validated using `ValidateCustomerID()`.

The `Products` table is then loaded into a recordset variable. If any records are in the table (it would be a pretty dull catalog without any), they are displayed within an HTML `<TABLE>` tag. Each record is checked to see whether a picture is specified. If so, an `<IMG>` tag is used to display the specified picture within the table cell for the current record. The product name, cost, and shipping charge are also displayed within the table cell. If the `CustomerID` field has been found, a link is placed in each table cell to allow the customer to order the specific product. The link contains a query string that specifies the customer ID and the current `ProductID` field from the `Products` table. The link invokes the `Order` method, which is discussed next.

After all the records in the `Products` table have been added to the HTML table, the method finishes up the HTML coding, closes the database, and exits.

The `Order` method is not fully implemented in this example. It merely produces an output page informing users that the widget they ordered is in the mail. It expects the `ProductID` and `CustomerID` fields to be provided in the query string. These are used to obtain the product name of the product ordered and the ordering customer's name.

Listing 10.6. The code for BROWSE.CLS.

```
Public Sub MakePage(request As String, response As String)

    On Error GoTo MakePageErr

    Dim lHTML$      'local variable to hold the HTML
    Dim lsql$
    Dim lTxt$
```

continues

Listing 10.6. continued

```
    lHTML$ = "Content-Type: text/html" & vbCrLf & vbCrLf
    lHTML$ = lHTML$ & "<html><head><title>"

    'parse the parameters
    ' replace any CrLf characters w/ empty spaces (everything is one line)
    lTxt$ = tReplaceChars(request, Chr$(13), "")
    lTxt$ = tReplaceChars(lTxt$, Chr$(10), "")
    ParseQuery lTxt$

    'open the database
    DBOpen

    'get the customer ID if provided
    CustID$ = ""
    If ParamPresent("CustomerID") And Len(GetParam("CustomerID")) Then
        CustID$ = GetParam("CustomerID")
        'validate the customer ID
        If ValidateCustomerID(lHTML$, db) = False Then
            response = lHTML$
            db.Close
            Exit Sub
        End If
    End If

    lHTML$ = lHTML$ & "Catalog Contents</title></head><body>"
    lHTML$ = lHTML$ & "<H1>Catalog Contents</H1><CENTER>"

    'open the Products table
    Dim snap As Recordset
    Set snap = db.OpenRecordset("Products", dbOpenSnapshot)
    If snap.RecordCount Then
        'format as a table
        lHTML$ = lHTML$ & "<table border = 2>"
        While Not snap.EOF
            'start a new row
            lHTML$ = lHTML$ & "<tr><td>"
            'if there's a picture, display it
            lPicture$ = chknull(snap!PictureURL, "")
            If Len(lPicture$) Then
                lHTML$ = lHTML$ & "<img src=""" & lPicture$ & """ align=left>"
            End If
            lHTML$ = lHTML$ & snap!ProductName & "<br>"
            lHTML$ = lHTML$ & "Cost: " & Format$(snap!Cost, "$ 0.00") & "<br>"
            lHTML$ = lHTML$ & "Shipping: " & Format$(snap!Shipping, "$ 0.00")
            'is this for a customer?
            If Len(CustID$) Then
                'yes, provide an Order link
                lHTML$ = lHTML$ & "<br><a href=""" & OLEISAPI_PATH
                lHTML$ = lHTML$ & "/CATALOG.Browse.Order?ProductID="
                lHTML$ = lHTML$ & snap!ProductID
                lHTML$ = lHTML$ & "&CustomerID=" & CustID$
                lHTML$ = lHTML$ & """>Order Item</a>"
            End If
            lHTML$ = lHTML$ & "</td></tr>"
            snap.MoveNext
        Wend
        lHTML$ = lHTML$ & "</table>"
```

```
    Else
        lHTML$ = lHTML$ & "<H2>Catalog Database is Empty!</H2>"
    End If
    lHTML$ = lHTML$ & "</center></body></html>"
    response = lHTML$
    Exit Sub

MakePageErr:
    response = ProduceError("Browse", "MakePage")
    Exit Sub

End Sub

Public Sub Order(request As String, response As String)
    On Error GoTo OrderErr

    Dim lHTML$      'local variable to hold the HTML
    Dim lsql$
    Dim lTxt$

    lHTML$ = "Content-Type: text/html" & vbCrLf & vbCrLf
    lHTML$ = lHTML$ & "<html><head><title>"

    'parse the parameters
    ' replace any CrLf characters w/ empty spaces (everything is one line)
    lTxt$ = tReplaceChars(request, Chr$(13), "")
    lTxt$ = tReplaceChars(lTxt$, Chr$(10), "")
    ParseQuery lTxt$

    'open the database
    DBOpen

    'get the user's name
    lsql$ = "Select FirstName & ' ' & LastName from Customers where "
    lsql$ = lsql$ & "CustomerID = " & GetParam("CustomerID")
    lCustName$ = tExecAndAnswer(lsql$, db, lStatus%)

    'get the name of the product they ordered
    lsql$ = "Select ProductName from Products where ProductID = "
    lsql$ = lsql$ & GetParam("productID")
    lProductName$ = tExecAndAnswer(lsql$, db, lStatus%)

    lHTML$ = lHTML$ & "Thanks!</title></head><body>"
    lHTML$ = lHTML$ & "Thanks for the order, " & lCustName$ & ".<br>"
    lHTML$ = lHTML$ & "A " & lProductName$ & " is in the mail!"
    lHTML$ = lHTML$ & "</body></html>"
    response = lHTML$
    Exit Sub

OrderErr:
    ProduceError "Browse", "Order"
    Exit Sub

End Sub
```

Compiling the OLE Object

After all the code has been entered and the project saved, it's time to create the OLE object's DLL file. Select File | Make OLE DLL File. When the Make OLE DLL File dialog appears, select a location to store the DLL and click the OK button.

If you are compiling the object on the same machine it will be accessed from (that is, on the IIS machine that will invoke the object), you can choose any directory. After it is compiled, Visual Basic registers the OLE object with the operating system. This registration information includes the path to the DLL file so the DLL can be placed anywhere on the system.

If you will be copying the DLL file to another system, select a location that you'll remember. Also, you must manually register the DLL on the target system before it can be used. You do so using the DOS shell command:

```
regsvr32 myobject.dll
```

In addition, keep in mind that you must have all the necessary VB support files on the target machine so that the DLL can be executed.

Testing the Application

After compiling the OLE DLL, check the following points before attempting to test the application.

1. Have you created `catalog.htm` and `create.htm` and placed them in your server's document root directory? The HTML for these files is given in Listings 10.1 and 10.2.
2. Have you created the database `catalog.mdb` and placed it in a directory accessible to applications running on your server machine? Also, does the path to the database match the `DB_PATH` constant found in `GENERAL.BAS`?
3. Have you copied `OLEISAPI.DLL` to a directory your server considers to be an executable directory? Does the server-relative path match the `OLEISAPI_PATH` constant found in `GENERAL.BAS`?

4. Have you entered some product information into the products table of the `Customers` database? Pictures make a nice addition to the catalog; do you have any entered and are they properly referenced in the `PictureURL` field? Several "widget" pictures are included on the CD-ROM if you'd like some to play with.

NOTE:

Picture files used on Web pages should be in either GIF or JPEG format. Almost all graphical Web browsers support these two formats. There are many commercially available packages that can convert graphics files to and from the GIF and JPEG formats. The GIF format should be used if high picture quality is not a great concern because the

files are much smaller and, therefore, load much faster on the user's browser. If you have high-quality photographs and you want to preserve that quality, use the JPEG format. You'll be sacrificing Web page loading time, however.

After you're satisfied with the preceding points, you can begin testing. The application is not difficult to test. If any problems occur, they're pretty simple to narrow down. You can determine which method is being invoked by examining the URL of the link that has been clicked or the `action` element of the `<FORM>` tag for the form that has been being filled in.

So, to begin testing the application, follow these steps:

1. Load your favorite Web browser and point it to your server and the `catalog.htm` page. For example, if the host name for your server is `www.myhost.com`, you would browse the location `http://www.myhost.com/catalog.htm`.
2. Because you're the first customer to come along, you should create a customer record. Click the `Create Your Customer Record` link to load the Create form.
3. On the Create form, enter at least a user name, e-mail address, password, and verified password. Then click the Submit button. If the record is created properly, you will see a page similar to Figure 10.8.

Figure 10.8.

The new user name page.

4. Click the `Browse Catalog` link. A catalog page similar to Figure 10.5 appears, but with the product information from your database, of course.
5. Reload the entry page. Select the `Browse the Catalog` link. The catalog page should be identical to the one produced by step 4 but without the `Order` links.
6. Reload the entry page again. Enter your user name and password in the fields provided. Click the Log-On button. You should see a page similar to Figure 10.4.

7. Click the `Browse` link. The page produced should be identical to the page produced in step 4.
8. Now return to the entry page again. Run through the system entering invalid information to test the validation code. For example, enter a user name that is not in the database or a password that doesn't match the password you entered.
9. Back on the create page, try to create a record with the same user name you used previously. Also, enter different values in the password and verify fields to make sure the password verification code is working.
10. Continue testing the system until you're satisfied.

NOTE:

If you ever have to recompile the Visual Basic code, you must stop the IIS Web server before using File | Make OLE DLL File. Otherwise, you'll probably get a `Permission Denied. Another process is using the file` error message when you attempt to make the DLL. Although the OLEISAPI DLL should be freeing the objects when it is finished with them, it didn't do so on my system.

You may also have to turn off the Cache Extensions option of the Web service. Doing so ensures that the DLL is not kept in memory by the server. This option, as of this writing, must be manually changed in the system registry using `REGEDT32.EXE`. The registry key is `HKEY_LOCAL_MACHINE\SYSTEM\CurrentControlSet\Services\W3SVC\Parameters\CacheExtensions`. The value for this key should be either `0` (don't cache extensions) or `1` (cache extensions). Set it to `0` while debugging your applications. When you're ready for production, return this key to `1`.

After you have recompiled the DLL, restart the IIS Web server.

Summary

This chapter has presented the VB programmer with a high-performance method of programming Web extensions for the Microsoft Internet Information Server. Although Win/CGI applications can still be used (see Appendix C), they are extremely slow compared to ISAPI applications. Even using the OLEISAPI DLL to invoke objects that you create in Visual Basic is markedly faster than executing a Win/CGI application on the same server.

The drawback to using the OLEISAPI DLL as it is shipped with the IIS is that most of the standard Win/CGI variables are not made available to the OLE objects. This could easily be remedied by creating a standard set of object properties to which the OLEISAPI DLL would assign the CGI variables before invoking the object's methods. However, it is well beyond the scope of this book to begin mucking around in C++ code, especially C++ code that accesses OLE Automation objects!

Chapter 11

A Brief Introduction to Web Spiders and Agents

- Terminology
- How Robots Work
- Potential for Problems
- Robot Exclusion
- Basic Algorithms for Search Robots
- Examples of Existing Web Robots

A *spider*, or *robot* as they are commonly called, is a program that automatically traverses Web space. By this, we mean that the program automatically requests a series of URLs, picks new URLs to traverse, and continues traversing until some programmer-defined condition is met.

Consider these tools as incredibly fast, efficient Netscape users. Instead of manually navigating the Web, these robots can load and parse the received data and return to the user its results. For example, if you wanted to keep tabs on an online bookstore and be notified by e-mail whenever a new book written by your favorite author is published, a robot can do that for you.

The benefits of spiders can be seen by their applications. A few more popular implementations of spiders include these uses:

- As search engines
- Finding out the growth of the WWW
- Obtaining the current size of the WWW
- Downloading a site's HTML files for offline browsing
- Notifying a user of changes to a specified Web page

As more people find more uses for the Web, more robots and spiders will come up. Right now their use has been pretty well limited to academic research. The main language for programming these tools has been a mix of C/C++ and Perl.

In this chapter, we go over the ideas behind spider programming, the guidelines to follow, and in the following chapters, we'll go through some Visual Basic programs that act as spiders.

First, let's define the different terms that fall loosely under the "agent" or "spider" category.

Terminology

As with everything Internet related, a lexicon has developed to describe client-side applications and server-side resources. Most of the early work on the Internet was performed at universities and military organizations. Both are notorious for clever naming schemes. This section defines some of the terms used in this and later chapters.

Robot—This is the first term used to define the program whose activity was recurring WWW pages, looking for information. More or less, all spiders, agents, and crawlers can be called robots.

Spiders—The media-friendly term for robot.

Agent—Another term for the same concept, although some derivatives of agent have come up: intelligent agents, autonomous agents, and so forth.

Worms—A worm formerly meant a program that would replicate and distribute itself over a server. To my knowledge, WWW Worms are nothing like that; the original developers just chose a bad term to describe their robot.

Web Crawlers—There is a search engine called WebCrawler (`http://www.webcrawler.com`), but some have used the term Web Crawler, or just crawler to describe the actions of robots.

Web Ants—These are multiple robots usually running on different servers that work cooperatively.

New terms for these robots are sure to pop up as they become more popular and easier to program, but for this chapter, we'll stick to robot. If you hear of, or invent a new term, please e-mail it to me (haasch@execpc.com).

How Robots Work

The key to what makes robots work is the 'Web' in the term World Wide Web. The word Web in this case makes reference to the connectedness of the URLs that exist.

Figure 11.1 is a somewhat unrealistic, but possible spider's web. Each point where two threads of spider silk touch represents a Web page, and a single strand of silk to the next intersection is a URL. The threads become anchors between the pages.

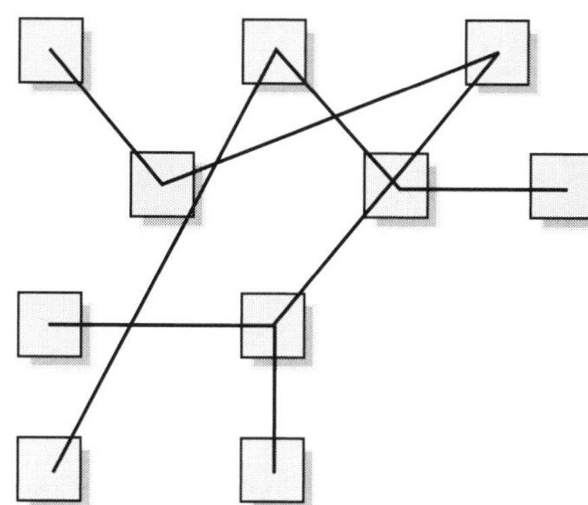

Figure 11.1.
The World Wide Web viewed as a "spider's web."

The one shortcoming of this analogy is that unlike two intersections in a spider's web, where one leads to another and vice versa (you can travel in either direction), URLs usually don't have anchors back to all URLs that anchor to them.

In Figure 11.2, arrows show the direction of the anchor. The arrow originates on the URL that has the anchor and points to the URL that it is anchored to.

A robot is a program that traverses these links automatically. Taking an arbitrary number of root URLs, the program follows the anchors and repeats this process until it is told by an exit condition to stop.

These *exit conditions* are usually the time elapsed during the traversal, number of levels of recursion that have occurred, number of pages loaded, or the discovery of a search parameter.

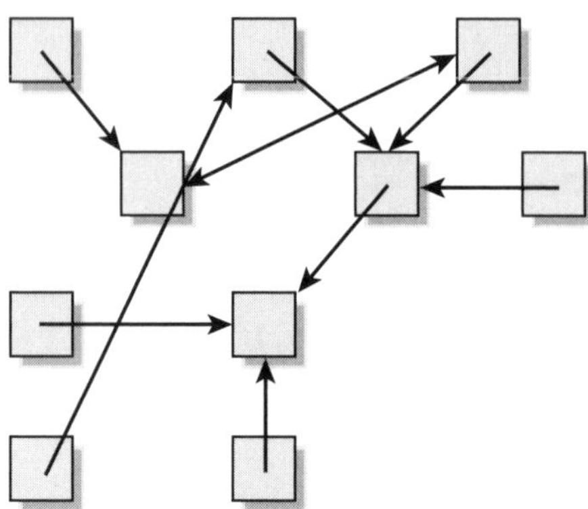

Figure 11.2.
Web diagram with arrows showing direction of anchors.

Choosing the Root URL(s)

Let's consider each step of the process—first, choosing the root URL. Currently, there are no less than a dozen *search engines* that exist on the Internet. Some function as robots, such as WebCrawler, that search for pages matching the text you submit to them. Others, such as Yahoo!, are large databases of URLs with descriptions that are categorized. These sites are visited millions of times a day and are general purpose, broad-based tools to find what you're looking for on the Internet.

A possible application using these mega search engines would be a client-side application that takes a user-entered keyword, submits that keyword to a group of search engines, takes their responses, and formats them uniformly. This would save the user from going to Yahoo!, then to InfoSeek, then to WebCrawler, and so forth—all for the same keyword search.

Another application would be a group of URLs pertaining to one topic, for instance, law. This group of URLs would need some external links to traverse. From there, the program would load the first user-defined set of URLs, search for the keyword, and traverse any links until it met an exit condition.

These are just two search type tools that robots can perform. A few other robots that have been implemented and their descriptions are described later in the chapter.

Traversing the Links

A variety of algorithms describe this traversal process. Two of the most common are breadth-first and depth-first traversals.

With a URL or group of URLs to use as a staring point, let's look at traversal issues.

The fact that the World Wide Web can be viewed as nodes and links lends itself very well to graph theory and graphing algorithms. The two methods of traversal we want to consider are depth-first and breadth-first searching.

Depth-First Searching

Given the following group of nodes and directed anchors, a depth-first search would start with the root node A, then move to H, I, K, J, B, C, E, F, D, G. As you trace the path followed by this progression, you notice that it goes as deep as it can to find nodes, then backs up a step, checks for any other children nodes, moves to them, and repeats for all paths. There is no one correct way on this and many graphs to do a depth-first search. Another valid search would start again at A, then move through the following path, backing up as necessary: B, D, G, C, E, F, H, I, K, J.

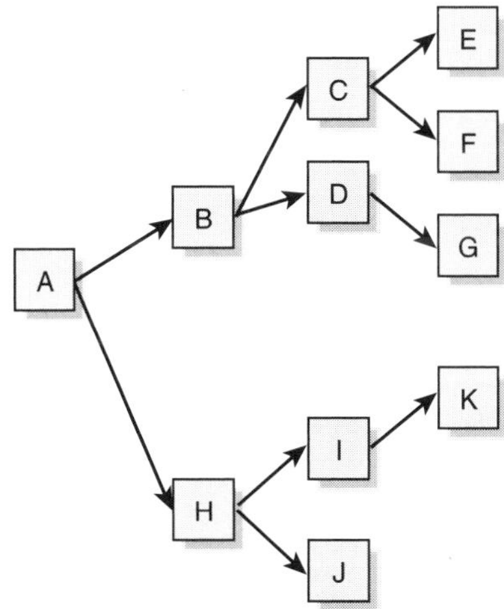

Figure 11.3.
Navigating a depth-first search.

Breadth-First Searching

Consider the graph in Figure 11.3: A is the root node, with B and H as its children; C, D, I and J are its grandchildren; E, F, G, and K as its great-grandchildren. The breadth-first search is done by first searching the root, then all of its children, then all of its grandchildren, and finally its great-grandchildren. A possible breadth-first search path would be A, B, H, C, D, I, J, E, F, G, K. As with the depth-first search, there usually is no one correct way of navigating the links in a breadth-first search. Another possible path could be A, H, B, C, D, I, J, K, G, F, E.

In Chapter 14, "WebSearcher: A Simple Search Tool," you'll implement a Web search tool that uses a breadth-first searching method of traversing Web hyperlinks.

Traversal Design Considerations

It's easy to get caught up in the wonderful way a robot works—pulling down pages, searching, getting anchors, searching some more, pulling more pages, and on and on. One important thing is consideration for the Webmaster whose server you're hitting.

As you know, the ability to serve Web pages depends on three factors: amount of bandwidth, speed of the Web server, and the amount of data being transferred. So, when your robot rifles off a few hundred requests per minute at one Web server, the Web server will definitely feel the effects.

Consider the diagram in Figure 11.4. A root page is indicated by the singular uppermost block in the diagram. Having the robot recur the anchors in that root page would generate requests for its ten children. If the robot is programmed to recursively traverse its children's links, then you're up to its 100 grandchildren now. This cycle could continue as long as there are more anchors to traverse, but the performance impact if all of these pages reside on one Web server would be extreme, to say the least.

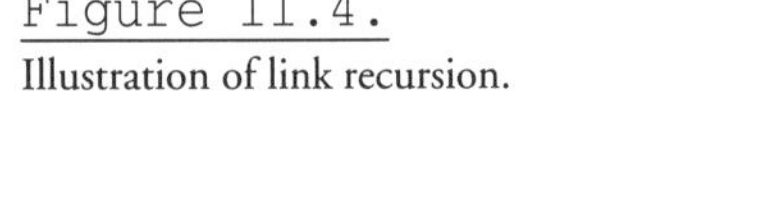
Figure 11.4.
Illustration of link recursion.

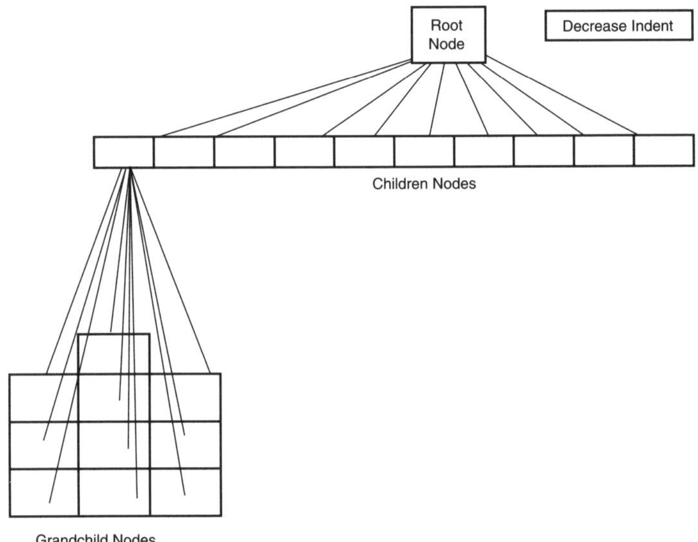

An easy solution to this problem is to slow down with the requests. Although there are no hard and fast numbers about how slow, try the robot against a site where you are the administrator, or know the administrator, and find the results. Then slow it down by increasing the time between requests until it's not a very noticeable depreciation in server performance.

Another feature that makes breadth-first searching attractive is that you hit alternate servers during the operation of your robot, rather than concentrating on the depth within one server.

Potential for Problems

Spiders are a controversial topic among Web site administrators, mostly because unwary programmers have made spider programs that make too many requests in too short a time span. This is called *rapid fire.* At best it slows the performance of the server, and the worst case scenario would be a Web server crash.

This, combined with the fact that more and more sites are adding forms for user feedback (which a robot wouldn't need to look at, much less submit blank forms), CGI scripts with side effects (voting, submitting forms), and deep nesting and interlinking of pages have brought about a movement for the ability for a site administrator to limit or exclude robots from their sites.

The fact that robots can and have caused server slowdowns and crashes makes them a controversial tool. Some people love them for their information searching capabilities; some people hate them because of the performance hits' effects on their Web servers.

Due to this potential for problems, a standard for robot exclusion is under development. This document is summarized here.

Robot Exclusion

http://web.nexor.co.uk/mak/doc/robots/norobots.html

As an evolving standard for robot exclusion, this document can be found at `http://web.nexor.co.uk/mak/doc/robots/norobots.html`. Currently, the standard is to place a file called `robots.txt` in the server's root directory so it is accessible by the URL `http://www.yourwebsite.com/robots.txt` if the server's host name is `www.yourwebsite.com`. The robot (if it conforms to this evolving standard) will read the file and check to see if it is excluded from or limited at the site.

The `robots.txt` file is structured as a series of records that indicate the HTTP user agent of the robot and any number of disallow fields that limit or exclude that user agent.

Entries are case-sensitive, and comments can be added using the Borne shell style `# <comment>` format.

Listing 11.1 is an example of a `robots.txt` file.

Listing 11.1. An example of a robot exclusion file.

```
User-agent: *
Disallow: /temp
Disallow: /bin
Disallow: /usr

User-agent: InfoSeek Robot
Disallow: /
```

In this example you see two records: In the first, the `*` indicates that the following conditions apply to all robots, and disallows them from the `/temp`, `/bin`, and `/usr` directories. The second record disallows the InfoSeek robot from the entire Web site.

The number of record entries and disallow statements per record is up to the site administrator.

Compliance with this standard for exclusion is not mandatory, but unless the robot author wants his e-mail box filled with flames from angry Webmasters and site administrators, compliance is recommended.

Basic Algorithms for Search Robots

A popular implementation for spiders is to search for information. WebCrawler and InfoSeek are two search engines that provide the user feedback from a spider-type program.

Algorithm for a Search Engine

A search engine starts off with a user query, usually a keyword or two. The server-side program then takes the query and sends it to the robot. The robot starts with a set of starter pages and parses the starting pages for anchors and the keywords. It then traverses the anchors, looks for keywords there, and recurs this process until either a maximum depth of anchors is reached, a timeout period is reached, or a specified number of matches is met.

The titles are returned to the user as hypertext links, and are often ranked by the occurrence of the query words.

Search engines, such as WebCrawler, actually assign a *rank* to each page it finds for you. Most of these ranking systems assign a higher rank for a higher incidence of keywords found, so if your keyword is `"HTML"` and a document has the string `"HTML"` in it 100 times, that document would be ranked higher than a different document containing the string `"HTML"` only 40 times.

A searching spider can be implemented with these steps:

1. With a database of root pages, search for the keyword. If the keyword is found, rank the page on the number of occurrences of that keyword, and add it to a temporary list. Check for timeout and number of matches requirements; keep going if necessary; otherwise, wrap the results in HTML and return the results to the user.
2. Go to the anchors of the root pages; load their children; again search for the keyword. Again, if the keyword is found, add it and its rank to the temporary list. Check for timeout, search depth, and number of matches, repeat this step as many times as necessary, continually building the list of matches.
3. After one of the conditions is met, the list of URLs, their titles, and their rankings according to number of keywords per page can be translated to HTML. After this page is built, it can be returned to the user as the search results.

TIP

A few tips: First, don't forget to look for the `robots.txt` file, and search for the user-agent field that matches your browser. With this, you know where and where not to aim your robot.

Another good idea if using a robot that takes in a number of root nodes that access different servers is to use a round-robin type schedule to increase the amount of time the robot successively hits one server. A hit every few seconds, or better yet, every few minutes, is much more polite to the owner of the server than making a few thousand requests in a minute or two.

With this and a good parsing program, you can build a Visual Basic front end that enables the user to specify the root URLs, the number of times to recur, and the information the user seeks.

Behind this program, you need to set up a system of requesting, parsing, and analyzing pages for content, as well as a system to determine if the search, timeout, and depth conditions and restrictions have been met. Tack on the results into a textbox or a browser custom control, add a status bar indicating the progression of the search, and you've built a full-featured Web robot.

See Chapter 14 for a Visual Basic implementation of a simple Web searching tool.

Generating a Report on Invalid Links

A continual headache for Webmasters and site maintainers is the constant moving and deleting of Web resources. The innerconnectiveness of the World Wide Web encourages sites to link to other sites via hypertext references.

One problem with these external links is that when the page pointed to by the external link is moved, the person who linked to it is not notified, thus creating a `404 URL Not Found` error message or a message similar to `"Thanks for visiting, but this page has moved to http://www.newurl.com"`.

This is very similar to an old address book of people you occasionally call. If the people move and change their phone numbers, you get that familiar phone company voice telling you the number has changed or has been disconnected.

Currently, there is no such method for a page, when it changes location or disappears, to notify all linking pages of the change. The lack of this facility causes these all-too-often error and "We have moved here…" messages.

The idea to find out what percent of links result in this behavior is somewhat difficult to implement. Here is a basic plan of attack for designing this application:

1. Choose a root URL that contains at lease one anchor.
2. Select the number of recursions you want the robot to perform.

3. Retrieve the root URL.
4. Check the information within the URL. If it returns an `Error Code 404 (Text Description Here)`, increment a variable that contains the number of bad URLs. Otherwise, increment a variable that contains the number of valid URLs. Also increment the number of recursions that have occurred.
5. If the number of recursions is `0`, then the percentage is either `0` or `100`, depending on the validity of the root URL. In either case, report back to the user and exit.
6. If the number of recursions is greater than zero, parse the URLs of the anchors within the previously retrieved page. Retrieve these URLs, collecting their anchors also. At this step, you also need to increment the counters that store the number of invalid and valid links, and the number of recursions that have taken place.
7. Check for the number of recursions. If it has been met, report to the user, and then exit. Otherwise, retrieve the child URLs of the URLs that were retrieved in step 6.
8. Continue the process until the number of recursions has been met.

Again, with any spider, it is suggested that the standard for robot exclusion be implemented and that the servers are hit in a round-robin fashion, so as not to overload any single Web server.

Examples of Existing Web Robots

Although there are no known robots written in Visual Basic currently running regularly on the Web, they will pop up. Currently, most Web robots are being written in Perl, C, and C++.

WebCrawler

http://www.webcrawler.com

WebCrawler at `http://www.webcrawler.com` (see Figure 11.5) is one of the major search engines on the World Wide Web. It started in 1994 as a project at the University of Washington and is currently hosted by America Online. You can tell if your server has been hit by this search engine by checking the log files of the Web server for the http user-agent of `WebCrawler/2.0 libwww/3.0` that was run from a machine named spidey.webcrawler.com.

Figure 11.5.
Opening screen for WebCrawler.

MOMSpider

http://www.ics.uci.edu/WebSoft/MOMspider/

Multi-Owner Maintenance spider (MOMSpider) is a project from Roy Fielding at the University of California-Irvine. The MOMSpider was written to deal with the maintenance of Web sites. MOMSpider and its accompanying documentation address the important issue of continually changing page locations and URLs as it relates to managing a Web site. In other words, by utilizing a program such as MOMSpider, you can help eliminate users seeing the `File Not Found` message when clicking a link on your Web page. Documentation and the MOMSpider program itself are available at `http://www.ics.uci.edu/WebSoft/MOMspider/`.

Summary

This chapter demonstrated that there are many uses for the Web other than just browsing. The ability to use a World Wide network full of information is a massive opportunity. Be it searching, validating links, or reporting on the status of a set of pages, robots can make these tasks easier for the user of the World Wide Web.

What's Next?

From here, you can go on to Chapter 15, "Link Checker: A Spider That Checks for Broken Links." There, we'll go through the design and construction of a link-verifying robot. In Chapter 14 you build a client-side Web search tool.

Chapter 12

QuoteWatcher: An Interactive Web Agent

As the Internet in general and the Web in particular grow in popularity and usage, more and more financial institutions are finding them to be very effective means of distributing and collecting financial data. This is true for everything from electronic banking packages to stock brokerages that allow trades to be conducted using a Web browser. This chapter guides you through the process of creating an interactive Web agent that harnesses a small piece of the financial data available on the Web: stock quotes.

http://www.pcquote.com

The quotes are retrieved from a server run by PC Quote, Inc., a provider of real-time securities quotations and news. Its home page is located at `http://www.pcquote.com`, and there, you'll find background information about the company as well as information on its subscription-based services and Visual Basic market data controls. The quotes that QuoteWatcher accesses are 20-minute delayed quotes, but because the application is for educational purposes, I think we can all live with that limitation.

Another feature of QuoteWatcher is that it runs as a *tray icon* application. In proper Windows 95 lingo, this "tray" I'm speaking of is the taskbar notification area (see Figure 12.1) where applications can place icons to indicate their status or allow users to perform basic functions. The taskbar notification area is the area at the end of the Windows 95 taskbar that appears sunken (on the right end, if the taskbar is oriented horizontally; it's at the bottom, if the taskbar is oriented vertically). Because of the sunken appearance, it looks like a tray, hence the term tray icon. Figure 12.1 shows four icons in the tray, in addition to the current time. The icons can even have a dynamic tooltip to provide further feedback to the user.

Figure 12.1.
The Windows 95 taskbar notification (tray icon) area.

Because QuoteWatcher is designed to automatically update stock prices at a predetermined interval, it's a natural to become a tray icon application. When the application launches, it creates the tray icon and makes itself invisible. The user right-clicks the tray icon to pop up a shortcut menu, which provides a way to restore the window for viewing and editing. As quotes are retrieved, the tooltip and icon change to provide an updated status.

This chapter builds on the material covered in Chapter 5, "Retrieving Information from the Web." Most of the code presented here closely resembles the code from Chapter 5. A few routines have been added to handle the HTML results obtained from the PC Quote server. If you haven't read Chapter 5 yet, it would probably help to skim the sections covering the `dsSocket` control. This is the TCP/IP control used in this chapter to communicate with the HTTP server that provides the quotes.

QuoteWatcher's Functionality

The QuoteWatcher application's basic task is to retrieve and display stock and mutual fund price quotes to the user. Figure 12.2 shows a screen shot with some sample stocks and mutual funds and their prices at the time. Figure 12.3 shows the QuoteWatcher taskbar notification area icon (the wristwatch) and default tooltip.

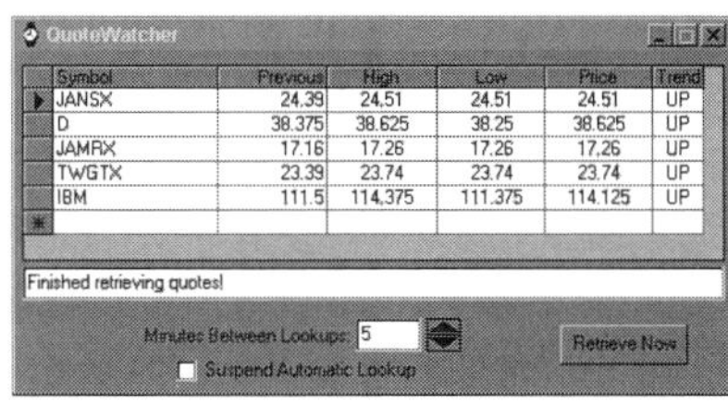

Figure 12.2.
The QuoteWatcher application in action.

Figure 12.3.
The QuoteWatcher tray icon.

As Figure 12.2 shows, the pricing data is presented to the user with a grid control. The application is built around a simple Microsoft Access database that stores the names of the symbols to be retrieved and the pricing information retrieved. The Symbol column can be edited; the other columns are read-only. The grid displays the symbol, the previous closing price, high and low prices for the day, the latest price, and the trend—whether the stock price is up, down, or unchanged from the previous closing price. The user is allowed to add, edit, and delete symbols to modify the list of stock and mutual fund prices to retrieve.

The user specifies how often to check for prices using the Minutes Between Lookups textbox and spin button. Automatic checking can be suspended if desired. There is also a button which, when pressed, manually starts the retrieval process. The textbox in the middle of the screen provides status feedback as quotes are being retrieved.

If the application performs a pricing retrieval while the main window is hidden and there is a change in one of the prices, the tray icon changes to a light bulb. This alerts the user to the fact that the price of at least one of the symbols being tracked has changed. The icon reverts to its initial value when the user displays the main window.

A hidden menu serves as the tray icon's popup menu. It contains options for showing or hiding the main window, suspending or activating the retrieval process, manually starting a retrieval, and exiting the program. The tray icon's tooltip displays information about the current state of the program.

Implementing Tray Icons in Visual Basic

Ever since I first installed Windows 95, I have marveled at taskbar notification area applications. In my opinion, they are one of the best user interface enhancements Microsoft made in Windows 95. As soon as Microsoft Press published *Programmer's Guide to Microsoft Windows 95*, I bought a copy in hopes of creating hundreds of these tray icon applications.

I was quickly disappointed, however, after reading the chapter covering the taskbar notification area. The taskbar notification area was named that for a reason: Windows 95 wants to *notify* those applications whenever mouse events take place within their spots in the notification area. This, of course, meant that my programs would have to intercept a callback message from Windows 95. As most experienced VB programmers know, Visual Basic does not provide a direct mechanism for capturing these messages. It seemed that I'd have to dust off my copy of Visual C++ and actually try to do something useful with it if I wanted to write a tray icon application. Most of the programs I wanted to add tray icon functionality to were written in Visual Basic, though.

All hope seemed lost for this lowly VB programmer. My hopes had been quickly dashed on the rocks of the Windows 95 messaging system. That is, until the *Microsoft Systems Journal* published an article in the February, 1996 issue titled "Create Tray Icons In Visual Basic." This article, written by Joshua Trupin, was the answer to my dilemma. Joshua provided the missing piece to the puzzle: a callback control that creates an invisible window, which can receive those elusive callback messages. The control then fires a Visual Basic event, which is where the code for handling the tray icon's user interaction is placed.

The next section discusses the `CallBack` control. The section following, "The Basics of Programming for the Taskbar Notification Area," covers the basics of the taskbar notification area interface and provides some routines to make life easier when writing tray icon applications.

The **CallBack** OLE Control

In this section, I'll cover the basics of using the `CallBack` control. The best source of information about the `CallBack` control is, of course, the original published article, mentioned in the preceding section.

NOTE:

The `CallBack` control is provided in OCX form on the CD-ROM. The original C++ source code can be found in the *Microsoft Systems Journal* article mentioned earlier.

After you have the control installed on your system, it is simple to use. The control has one useful method (`WatchMsg`), one useful property (`hWnd`), and one event (`CallBack`).

The `WatchMsg` method is used to register the Windows messages that, when they are received by the control, cause the `CallBack` event to fire. As you'll see in the next section, the taskbar notification area interface requires you to specify which message Windows 95 is to use when notifying the tray icon application that an event has occurred. The message specified for this notification purpose should also be registered with the `CallBack` control using `WatchMsg`. Because this message is a user-defined message, it should be assigned a value greater than the Windows API constant `WM_USER` (`&H400`). Other than that restriction, the message number assigned can be any value and doesn't have to be particularly unique in any way. Using a value greater than `WM_USER` ensures that you won't conflict with any existing Windows messages.

The `hWnd` property is the window handle of the control's window. The control makes itself invisible when it is created, but it still has a window handle.

The `CallBack` event fires whenever a message registered using `WatchMsg` is received by the control. The parameters of the event are `msg`, `wParam`, and `lParam`. These are the original `msg`/`wParam`/`lParam` that the control's message handler received from Windows 95. They are the message received, the short parameter, and the long parameter. For example, when a window receives a "left mouse button down" notification message, the value of `msg` is `WM_LBUTTONDOWN` (`&H201`). The value of `wParam` specifies which, if any, special keys were down at the same time the message was sent, and `lParam` specifies the X and Y coordinates of the cursor when the button was pressed. These parameters are used by the VB code to determine what action should be taken.

The Basics of Programming for the Taskbar Notification Area

When an application wishes to register a tray icon for itself or modify an existing tray icon, the `Shell_NotifyIcon()` API function is called. This function handles all the tasks related to tray icons: adding, deleting, or modifying them. The VB declaration for this function is:

```
Declare Function Shell_NotifyIcon Lib "shell32.dll" Alias "Shell_NotifyIconA"
                    (ByVal dwMessage As Long, lpData As NOTIFYICONDATA) As Long
```

where `dwMessage` is a value that specifies the operation to perform (add, modify, or delete), and the `lpData` value is a variable whose type is the user-defined type `NOTIFYICONDATA`.

The `dwMessage` parameter can have one of three values: `NIM_ADD` (`&H0`), `NIM_DELETE` (`&H1`), or `NIM_MODIFY` (`&H1`).

The `NOTIFYICONDATA` structure shown in Listing 12.1 specifies the information Windows requires to handle a tray icon application. This includes the handle to the window that receives the notification messages (you'll be using the `CallBack` control's `hWnd` property) and an application-defined identifier for the tray icon. The value of the callback message to be used when notifying the application is also specified within the structure. A handle to the pictorial representation of the icon to be displayed and the text of the tooltip are also in this structure, and this is how you'll modify them within your applications. Finally, a flag variable indicates which of the three modifiable properties (callback message, icon, and tooltip) are currently valid (this is used when you modify the tray icon's properties). The flag consists of an `OR`'ed combination of the following constants: `NIF_MESSAGE` (`&H1`), `NIF_ICON` (`&H2`), and `NIF_TIP` (`&H4`). There is also a size element (`cbSize`) that should be set to **`Len`**`(`*`myStructure`*`)`, if *`myStructure`* is the name of your `NOTIFYICONDATA` structure.

Adding and Deleting Icons

To add an icon to the tray, you first must fill a variable of type `NOTIFYICONDATA` with the appropriate information. You must specify the application-defined identifier, the window handle, the size, and a handle to the icon to be displayed. You do not have to specify the tooltip or the callback message. If you do not specify the callback message, Windows 95 will not notify the `CallBack` control specified of any mouse events. After the structure has been filled with data, you then call `Shell_NotifyIcon()` with `NIM_ADD` as the `dwMessage` parameter.

To delete an icon, you need only to specify the size, the window handle, and the application-defined identifier elements. You then call `Shell_NotifyIcon()` with `NIM_DELETE` as the `dwMessage` parameter.

TIP:

Be sure you delete any icons you create before exiting the application. Windows 95 does not clean up after the tray icon applications until the user moves the mouse over the area the icon occupies. This obviously isn't disastrous but does leave the user wondering whether or not the application has really ended.

Modifying Icons

To modify an existing icon, fill in the required information of the `NOTIFYICONDATA` structure (handle, identifier, and size) and then whichever combination of message, icon handle, and tooltip you want to modify. Next, set the flag element to match the combination of properties being modified. Finally, call `Shell_NotifyIcon()` with `NIM_MODIFY` as the `dwMessage` parameter. For example, if you wanted to change the icon being displayed and the tooltip, you would set those elements in the `NOTIFYICONDATA` structure and call `Shell_NotifyIcon()` with `dwMessage` equal to `NIF_ICON + NIF_TIP`.

Receiving Mouse Events

When the `CallBack` control receives a taskbar mouse event notification message, it passes the parameters of that message straight to its `CallBack` event. The `wParam` parameter contains the application-defined identifier for the particular tray icon that received the event (in case there are more than one such icons attached to the application). The `lParam` parameter specifies which mouse event occurred (mouse move, left button down, etc.). The `msg` parameter contains the callback message specified when the tray icon was created.

Typically, the application will use only the `lParam` parameter. If the application has created multiple tray icons, or changes the callback message being used, however, it does become necessary to examine the contents of the other parameters.

Coding and Using the VBTRAY.BAS Module

The *Microsoft Systems Journal* article discussed earlier provides a small module named `VBTRAY.BAS` that contains the function declaration, the definition of the `NOTIFYICONDATA` structure, and the constants used when creating tray icon applications. I have expanded that module to add some useful procedures. This section describes `VBTRAY.BAS`, all of which is shown in Listing 12.1. This module is used in the QuoteWatcher application. It doesn't include all the procedures that could be defined when using tray icons, but it does have enough to get through the development of QuoteWatcher.

Listing 12.1. The `VBTRAY.BAS` module.

```
Public Const WM_USER = &H400

Public Const NIF_ICON = &H2
Public Const NIF_MESSAGE = &H1
Public Const NIF_TIP = &H4

Public Const NIM_ADD = &H0
Public Const NIM_DELETE = &H2
Public Const NIM_MODIFY = &H1

Public Const WM_MOUSEMOVE = &H200
Public Const WM_LBUTTONUP = &H202
Public Const WM_LBUTTONDOWN = &H201
Public Const WM_LBUTTONDBLCLK = &H203
Public Const WM_RBUTTONDOWN = &H204

Type NOTIFYICONDATA
        cbSize As Long
        hwnd As Long
        uID As Long
        uFlags As Long
        uCallbackMessage As Long
```

continues

Listing 12.1. continued

```
        hIcon As Long
        szTip As String * 64
End Type

Declare Function Shell_NotifyIcon Lib "shell32.dll" Alias "Shell_NotifyIconA" _
                 (ByVal dwMessage As Long, lpData As NOTIFYICONDATA) As Long


Public Sub RemoveIcon(CBWnd As CallBack, puID as Long)
Dim tnd As NOTIFYICONDATA

    tnd.uID = puID
    tnd.cbSize = Len(tnd)
    tnd.hwnd = CBWnd.hwnd
    rc = Shell_NotifyIcon(NIM_DELETE, tnd)

End Sub

Public Sub UpdateTip(CBWnd As CallBack, puID as Long, ptNewTip$)
    Dim tnd As NOTIFYICONDATA

    tnd.uFlags = NIF_TIP
    tnd.uID = puID
    tnd.cbSize = Len(tnd)
    tnd.hwnd = CBWnd.hwnd
    tnd.szTip = ptNewTip$ & Chr$(0)
    rc = Shell_NotifyIcon(NIM_MODIFY, tnd)

End Sub

Public Sub ChangeIcon(pvNewIcon, CBWnd As CallBack, puID as Long)
    Dim tnd As NOTIFYICONDATA

    ' Fill the data structure with necessary information
    tnd.uFlags = NIF_ICON
    tnd.uID = puID
    tnd.cbSize = Len(tnd)
    tnd.hwnd = CBWnd.hwnd
    tnd.hIcon = pvNewIcon

    rc = Shell_NotifyIcon(NIM_MODIFY, tnd)

End Sub

Public Sub CreateIcon(CBWnd As CallBack, puID as Long, _
       plMsg As Long, ptInitTip$, pzInitIcon)
    Dim tnd As NOTIFYICONDATA ' The Shell_NotifyIcon data structure

            ' Fill in tnd with appropriate values
    tnd.szTip = ptInitTip$ & Chr$(0)
            ' Flags: the message, icon, and tip are valid and should be
            ' paid attention to.
    tnd.uFlags = NIF_MESSAGE + NIF_ICON + NIF_TIP
    tnd.uID = puID
    tnd.cbSize = Len(tnd)
            ' The window handle of our callback control
    tnd.hwnd = CBWnd.hwnd
            ' The message CBWnd will receive when there's an icon event
```

```
    tnd.uCallbackMessage = plMsg
    tnd.hIcon = pzInitIcon
            ' Make the callback window wait for our defined message
    CBWnd.WatchMsg (plMsg)
            ' Add the icon to the taskbar tray
    rc = Shell_NotifyIcon(NIM_ADD, tnd)

End Sub
```

The declarations section contains the `Shell_NotifyIcon()` function declaration, the type definition for `NOTIFYICONDATA`, the flag and `dwMessage` constants, and some useful mouse event message constants.

The `RemoveIcon` procedure is used to remove the icon from the tray. The parameters specify the `CallBack` control and the application-defined identifier. The procedure builds the `NOTIFYICONDATA` structure and calls `Shell_NotifyIcon()` using `NIM_DELETE`.

The `UpdateTip` procedure is used to change the tray icon's tooltip. It takes the `CallBack` control, the identifier, and the new text for the tooltip as parameters. It builds the structure, setting the flags parameter to `NIF_TIP` because the tooltip is being changed, and calls `Shell_NotifyIcon()` using `NIM_MODIFY`.

The `ChangeIcon` procedure changes the icon being displayed in the tray. The parameters to the procedure are a reference to the new icon (the `Picture` or `Icon` properties of picture boxes and forms can be sent as the parameter), the `CallBack` control, and the identifier. The procedure fills a `NOTIFYICONDATA` variable, setting the flag element to `NIF_ICON`, and calls `Shell_NotifyIcon()` using `NIM_MODIFY`.

Finally, the `CreateIcon` procedure does all the work of creating a tray icon. It takes the necessary parameters, builds the `NOTIFYICONDATA` structure, and calls `Shell_NotifyIcon()` using `NIM_ADD`.

`CreateIcon` also invokes the `CallBack` control's `WatchMsg` method, specifying the callback message as the method's parameter. This instructs the `CallBack` control to fire its `CallBack` event whenever it receives the callback message from Windows.

Setting Up the QuoteWatcher Database

As mentioned in the section "QuoteWatcher's Functionality" near the beginning of this chapter, QuoteWatcher stores the pricing information for the funds and stocks being tracked in an Access database. The database is very simple, consisting of a single table named `Symbols`, which only has a few fields. The final section of this chapter, "Modifying the Application," discusses how the application and database can be expanded to create a much more useful application. For the purposes of this chapter, however, the simple one-table database is quite suitable.

The table's layout is shown in Table 12.1. This table shows field names, data types, and field length. Because the user will probably not track a large list of prices and because there are no related tables, a primary key is not really necessary for this table.

Table 12.1. The QuoteWatcher `Symbols` table.

Field Name	*Data Type*	*Length*
`Symbol`	`Text`	10
`PrevClose`	`Numeric`	Double
`High`	`Numeric`	Double
`Low`	`Numeric`	Double
`Price`	`Numeric`	Double
`Trend`	`Text`	2

The two text fields are set to allow zero-length strings. The `Symbol` field is the only required field. No validation rules are defined, and the numeric fields all default to zero.

You can use whatever means you like to create this database and table—Microsoft Access 95, through JET engine code, or by using the Data Manager add-in that ships with VB. The remainder of this section guides you through the process of creating the database and table using the Data Manager. You can skip to the next section if you already know how to do this.

To use the Data Manager add-in, start Visual Basic (if it isn't already running). Select the Add-Ins | Data Manager menu option to start the Data Manager. After the Data Manager has started, follow these steps to create the database and the `Symbols` table:

1. Select the File | New Database menu option. In the New Database dialog that appears, locate or create the directory you'll be using for the application.
2. Enter **`quotes.mdb`** in the File Name textbox and click Save. After the Data Manager creates the database file, you'll be presented with a screen that looks similar to Figure 12.4. The database is, obviously, empty.

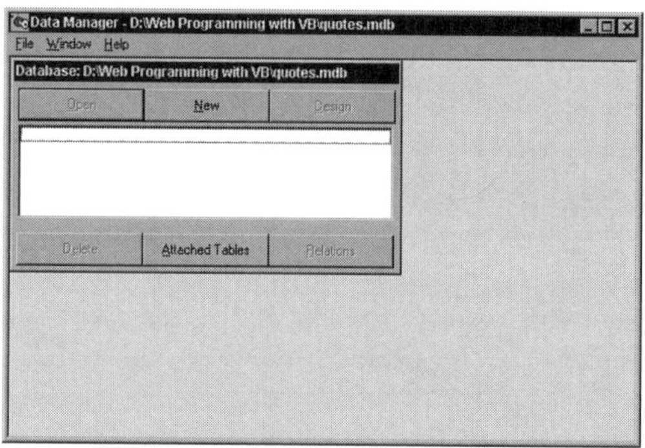

Figure 12.4.
The Data Manager with the new `QUOTES.MDB`.

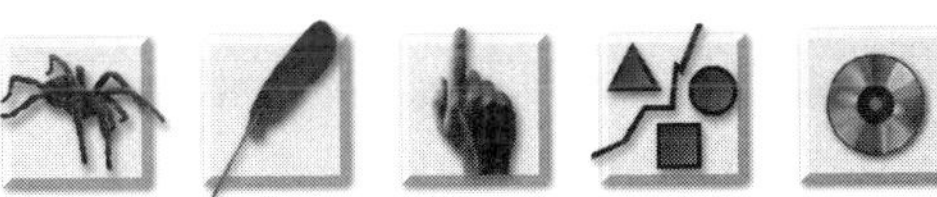

3. The next step is to add the table. In the database window, click the New button. The Add Table dialog box appears. This dialog (shown in Figure 12.5) enables you to name the table and add all its fields.

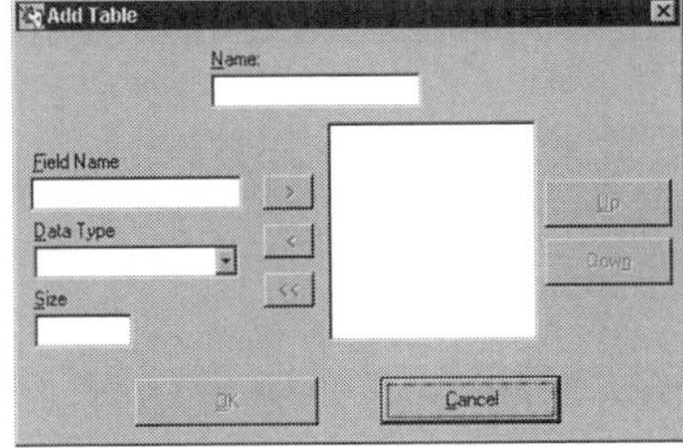

Figure 12.5.
Data Manager's Add Table dialog box.

4. Enter **Symbols** in the Name textbox. Press the Tab key to move to the Field Name textbox.
5. Type **Symbol** in the Field Name box. Select Text in the Data Type drop-down listbox. The Size box defaults to 10, which is the correct size for the `Symbol` field.
6. Click the button labeled with a right arrow (>) to add the `Symbol` field to the table.
7. Click in the Field Name box. Enter **PrevClose**. Select Double as the data type. Click the right-arrow (>) button.
8. Repeat step 7 for the `High`, `Low`, and `Price` fields.
9. Click in the Field Name box. Enter **Trend**. Select Text as the data type and enter `2` in the Size box. Click the right-arrow button.
10. Click the OK button. The database window now shows the `Symbols` table in its listbox, and a SQL Statement window has been opened.
11. Select the `Symbols` table in the database window. Click the Design button.
12. The Table Editor dialog box shown in Figure 12.6 appears. Double-click in the Symbol column.

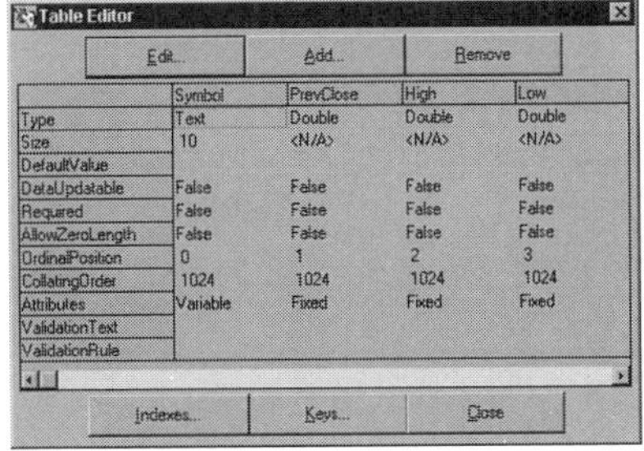

Figure 12.6.
Data Manager's Table Editor dialog box.

13. The Edit Field dialog appears. This is where additional properties of the fields can be specified. For the `Symbol` field, check the boxes labeled Required and AllowZeroLength. Click OK.
14. Find the Trend column (it's the right-most column of the grid). Double-click the column and check the AllowZeroLength box. Click OK. Click Close on the Table Editor dialog.
15. Now that the database and table have been created, you can close the Data Manager. Select the File | Exit menu item.

Creating the Project

Now that the database has been created, it's time to create the actual Visual Basic project. Because it is assumed that you have experience with creating Visual Basic applications, I won't present step-by-step instructions in this section. Instead, I'll just discuss the components necessary for the project.

Start a new project. Then, go to the Custom Controls dialog and remove all the controls except for the Apex Data Bound Grid, the `CallBack` OLE Control Module, the Dolphin Systems `dsSocket` TCP/IP control, and the Outrider SpinButton control. If any of these controls are missing from the dialog's listbox, they are probably not installed. A demo version of the `dsSocket` control and a working version of the `CallBack` control are included on the CD-ROM accompanying the book. The other controls are shipped with Visual Basic.

A demo version of the `dsSocket` control and a working version of the `CallBack` control are included on the CD-ROM accompanying the book.

NOTE:

If the controls on the CD-ROM haven't been installed, simply copy the OCX files to your Windows System directory. Then use `regsvr32 callback.ocx` to properly register the `CallBack` control (the `dsSocket` control doesn't need to be registered). On the VB Custom Controls dialog use the Browse button, if necessary, to locate the controls.

The project uses just one form, which you can name anything you desire. Next, add the `VBTRAY.BAS` module discussed earlier in this chapter. It can be found on the CD-ROM with the code accompanying this chapter.

Save the project in the same directory that you used when you created the quotes database. Name the project `quotes.vbp`.

Designing QuoteWatcher's Form

The user interface design comes next. The screen shot in Figure 12.7 shows all the controls on the form, as well as the Visual Basic Toolbox and the Properties window for the form.

In describing the user interface, I'll move from the top of the form to the bottom. When there are multiple controls horizontally, I'll move from left to right.

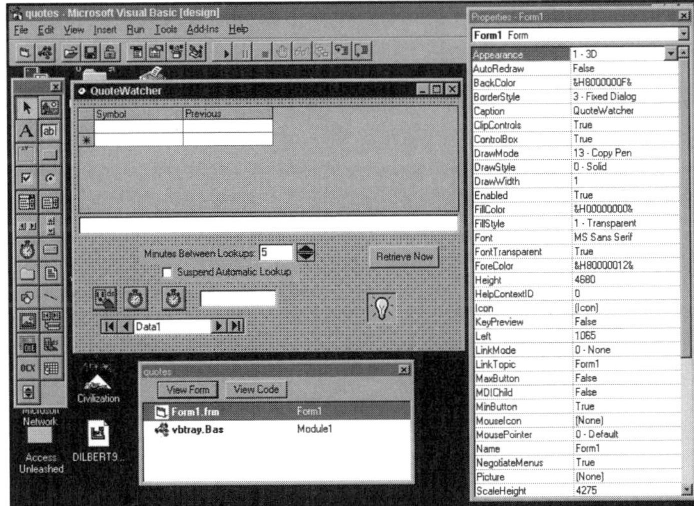

Figure 12.7.
QuoteWatcher's user interface in design mode.

The first control to add is the Data Bound Grid control. Add it with roughly the size and position as shown in Figure 12.7. When you first add the control, it has two columns with no headings. That's fine for now; you'll come back to the grid control after you add the data control. Name the grid `dbgQuotes`, and for now, leave the rest of the properties at their default values.

Next, add the textbox that appears below the grid. This will be used as a status box and is named `txtStatus`. Size it to the width of `dbgQuotes` and position it just below the grid. Set its `Locked` property to `True` to prevent the user from typing in it.

Add the Minutes Between Lookups: label below the status box. All properties except for the `Caption` can be left at their default values. Then, add the textbox to the right of the label. Name it `txtDelay` and set its `Text` property to `5` and its `MaxLength` property to `4`. This sets the initial time delay to five minutes between price checks and allow for up to 9999 minutes between checks.

Immediately to the right of the `txtDelay` textbox, place a SpinButton control. After it is properly sized, you can leave the rest of its properties at their default values.

Further to the right of the form but at the same horizontal position, add a command button. Name the button `cmdRetrieve` and set its caption to Retrieve Now.

Below the Minutes Between Lookups: label place a checkbox control. Leave its name at the default value (`Check1`) and set its caption to Suspend Automatic Lookup.

This is the last of the controls that the user will have access to. When you're ready to run the application, you'll shrink the form's height so that only these controls are visible. A few controls still need to be added but the user doesn't have access to these.

Add a `dsSocket` control and leave its name as `dsSocket1`. Add two time controls. Name one `tmrCheckQuotes` and the other `tmrTimeOut`. Set the `Interval` property of both to `60000`. This means that the timer will fire at one minute intervals. Set the `Enabled` property for `tmrTimeOut` to `False` (leave `tmrCheckQuotes` enabled).

Add another textbox. Name this one `txtInternalStatus` and set its `Text` property to an empty string. This control will be used in the application's state machine to trigger a change of state. As you'll see in the next section, there are several states in which the application can be while quotes are being retrieved. Each state is represented by a string constant. When the application is ready to change state, the next state's string constant is assigned to the `Text` property of this textbox. This fires the textbox's `Change` event, which contains the code that makes the state machine work (and is actually where half of the program's code resides). Because the textbox is in a portion of the form that won't be visible to the user, you can leave the `Visible` property set to `True`.

Next, add a data control. Set the `DatabaseName` property to point to the database you created earlier in this chapter. Then, set the `RecordSource` property to `Symbols` to point to the `Symbols` table. Leave the default name (`Data1`) intact.

Finally, add a picture box control. Set its name to `picLight` and set the `AutoSize` property to `True`. I used the file `lighton.ico` as the `Picture` property for this control. If you installed the icon files when Visual Basic was installed, this icon was installed in the `\icons\misc` directory beneath the directory Visual Basic was installed to (it is also included on the CD-ROM). Obviously, you can use any picture you wish. The `Picture` property of this control will be used as the tray icon when a quote has changed since the last retrieval.

If you installed the icon files when Visual Basic was installed, this icon was installed in the `\icons\misc` directory beneath the directory Visual Basic was installed to (it is also included on the CD-ROM). Obviously, you can use any picture you wish. The `Picture` property of this control will be used as the tray icon when a quote has changed since the last retrieval.

The last control to be added is the `CallBack` control. It's an invisible control, which is why it can't be seen in Figure 12.7. Select the tool labeled OCX in the Toolbox and place it on the form. Or, simply double-click the tool, and it will be placed on the form for you. Change its name to `CBWnd`.

Now that you have all the controls in place, you can finish setting the design properties of the grid. Select the `dbgQuotes` control again. Set its `DataSource` property to `Data1`. Open the control's property page by clicking the `Custom` property and then clicking the button with the ellipses. On the property page, select the Columns tab. With `Column1` selected in the Column drop-down listbox,

type **Symbol** in the Caption box. Select Symbol from the DataField drop-down listbox. Then, select Column2 in the Column listbox. Enter **Previous** in the Caption box and select PrevClose in the DataField listbox. Select Center in the Alignment listbox. Click OK to save the property changes. The grid should now appear as in Figure 12.7.

Finally, select the form so that you can modify its properties. First, shrink the form so that it hugs the user interface controls. Size it so that it resembles Figure 12.2.

Set the BorderStyle property to 3 - Fixed Dialog. This sets the MinButton and MaxButton properties to False. That's OK for MaxButton because you don't want the user to maximize the application (there is no resize support in this version), but you do want the user to minimize the application. Set the MinButton property back to True. When the user clicks the Minimize button, the code hides the form, making it appear that the application has returned to its tray area.

Set the form's caption to QuoteWatcher.

The form's icon will be used as the default tray icon. I used the file watch02.ico, which is in the same directory as the picLight icon. Of course, you are free to choose your own icon.

Finally, it's time to create the menu that appears when the user right-clicks over the tray icon's spot in the tray area. Table 12.2 lists the menu captions, names, and indention levels for the menu.

Table 12.2. The QuoteWatcher menu structure.

Caption	*Name*	*Indention Level*
Main	mnuMain	0
Suspend	mnuSuspend	1
Show	mnuShow	1
Retrieve Now	mnuRetrieve	1
Exit	mnuExit	1

An indention level of one means that you should click the right arrow on the Menu Editor dialog for that menu entry. This makes the menu item a subitem of the previous menu item whose indention level is one less. In this application, all menu items are subitems of mnuMain.

Make mnuMain invisible by unchecking its Visible checkbox on the Menu Editor dialog box. This is the top-level menu that will be used with the PopupMenu statement executed when the user right-clicks on the tray icon.

Finally, the user interface is finished. It's now time to move on and actually attach some code to all these objects.

Coding the Application

This section delves into the details of the code behind the QuoteWatcher application. All the code is available on the accompanying CD-ROM in addition to being presented in this chapter. I don't go into a lot of details when describing most of the code because it's pretty self-documenting.

The database interface is handled almost exclusively by the Data Bound Grid control. The `Form_Load` load event sets `Data1.DatabaseName` to either the value of the command-line parameter (if provided) or to `quotes.mdb` (if the command-line parameter is not provided). The `dsSocket1_Close` event is responsible for editing the recordset and updating the values for each symbol as it is retrieved from the server. Finally, code in the `dbgQuotes_BeforeColUpdate` event prevents the user from editing any column except the Symbol column.

All QuoteWatcher's HTTP messaging code is taken from the `dsSocket` sample application in Chapter 5. The only difference is that instead of enabling the user to enter the URL of a Web-based resource, the application uses a hard-coded URL that executes a query on PC Quote's Web server.

There are some differences in the code in the `dsSocket`'s `Receive` and `Close` events as well. Because QuoteWatcher is concerned only with the pricing information contained in the HTML document that the PC Quote server returns, the `Receive` event ignores any received characters that aren't part of the pricing information. When it is receiving the portion of the document that relates to pricing, the event appends the received characters to a form level variable named `gtQuote`. Upon the closing of the connection by the PC Quote server, QuoteWatcher parses the data in `gtQuote` to pull out the information that will be displayed in the `dbgQuotes` grid. This is done with two new functions: `szStripHTML()`, which removes the HTML tags from the data, and `Extract()`, which extracts a substring from a larger string based on the parameters provided.

To see just what the HTML document the PC Quote server returns look like, run either sample application from Chapter 5 and enter `http://www.pcquote.com/cgi-bin/getquote.exe?TICKER=x` where *x* is the ticker symbol for any stock or fund. You can also get the latest Dow Jones Industrials Average by using the ticker symbol `$INDU`. Figure 12.8 shows the HTML received when I requested the latest price for the Janus Mercury Fund (JAMRX).

As you can see, there are a few pieces of the HTML text that you can use as delimiters to separate the pricing information. The `<H3>...</H3>` tags on the second line of the displayed HTML are

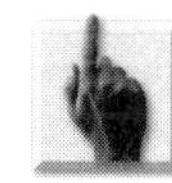

the first occurrence of these tags. This line always ends with the `</H3>` tag. In the `Receive` event, you can use their presence to indicate the beginning of the pricing information. Note also the `<PRE>` tag. This marks the actual beginning of the pricing information. There is a corresponding `</PRE>` tag at the end of the pricing information. You'll use the `</PRE>` tag to signal the end of the `Receive` event's need to keep received characters.

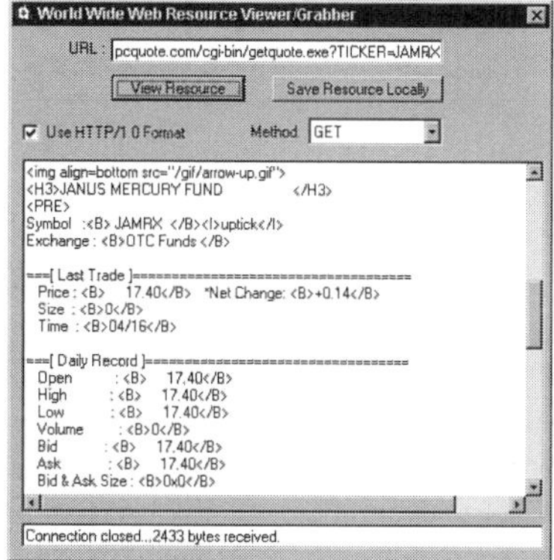

Figure 12.8.
The HTML received from the PC Quote server.

We're lucky the folks at PC Quote have made it easy to parse the desired pricing information out of the HTML document their server returns. Each piece of data is on its own line, and the numeric data is separated from the label by a colon character. You can use these facts when you call `Extract()`.

As I've mentioned several times, QuoteWatcher uses a state machine paradigm when it's retrieving quotes. Figure 12.9 shows a flow chart of the state machine and what happens during each state. The `STATUS_x` constants are defined in the form's declarations section. They represent each of the possible states that can be entered. When the application wishes to enter a new state, it simply sets `txtInternalStatus.Text` to the constant representing the state to be entered. For example, when the user clicks the Retrieve Now button, the application sets `txtInternalStatus.Text` to `STATUS_START`, which kicks off the retrieval process.

All the code for the form is presented in Listing 12.2. The remainder of this section explains the code behind some of the routines found in Listing 12.2. The procedures that are not discussed here are well commented and should be self-explanatory.

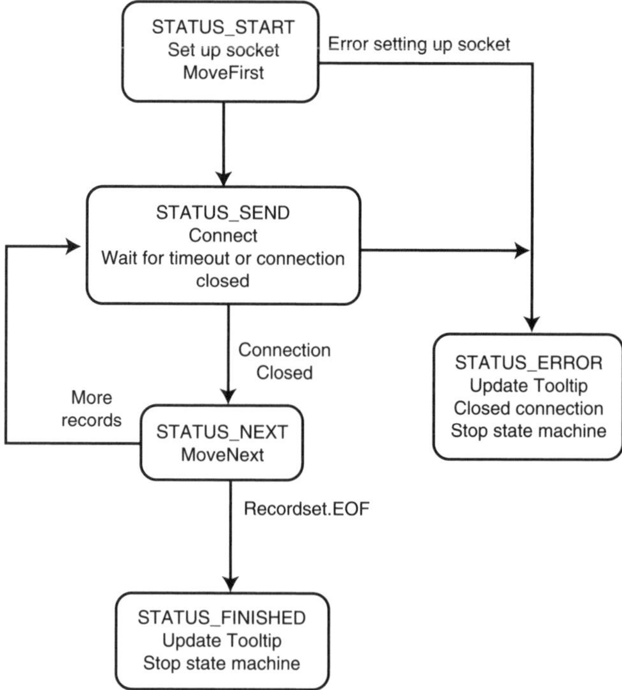

Figure 12.9.
A flow chart showing the QuoteWatcher state machine.

The `CallBack` Event

The `CallBack` control's `CallBack` event is fired whenever the tray icon receives a mouse event notification message from Windows. The event's `lParam` parameter specifies which message has been received.

QuoteWatcher responds to right mouse button clicks and double-clicks in its tray icon area. When a right button click is detected, `lParam` will be `WM_RBUTTONDOWN`. The application then displays the popup menu (`mnuMain`). The menu is displayed at the current mouse position. The `mnuShow` subitem is displayed as the default menu item—its caption is displayed in bold typeface.

When the user double-clicks the tray icon, QuoteWatcher executes the code for the `mnuShow_Click` event. This event toggles the visible state of the form.

The `tmrCheckQuotes_Timer` Event

This event occurs once per minute (the `tmrCheckQuotes.Interval` property is set to `60000`) whenever the timer is enabled. The procedure uses a `static` variable as a loop counter. This counter keeps track of the number of minutes that have passed since the end of the last retrieval.

When the value of the loop counter matches the value in the `txtDelay` textbox and there are symbols in the database, the procedure starts the retrieval process. First, the timer disables itself to prevent it from firing while a retrieval is in process. Then the application sets `txtInternalStatus.Text` to `STATUS_START`. Setting the textbox to this value starts the retrieval state machine, described in the next section.

The `txtInternalStatus_Change` Event

The textbox `txtInternalStatus` is used to store the current state of the retrieval state machine and to trigger a change of state. By setting the `Text` property to a new value, the state is changed. The valid values of the `Text` property are `STATUS_START`, `STATUS_NEXT`, `STATUS_FINISHED`, `STATUS_SEND`, and `STATUS_ERROR`. This section discusses what happens in each state. Figure 12.9 shows a flow chart documenting the state machine.

The initial state of the retrieval process is `STATUS_START`. When this state is entered, the procedure first checks to make sure there is not an open connection. If a connection is open, the state is changed to `STATUS_ERROR`, and the procedure exits. If no connection is open, the procedure sets up the socket control to prepare it to connect to the PC Quote server. If no error occurs during this process, the procedure moves the data control's record pointer to the first record, updates the tray icon tooltip, and changes the state to `STATUS_SEND`. If an error does occur while setting up the connection, the state changes to `STATUS_ERROR`, and the procedure exits.

The next state is `STATUS_SEND`. The status box and tray icon tooltip are updated to reflect the current symbol being retrieved. The `gtQuote` variable is reset to the empty string in preparation for new pricing information. Then the `Connect` method of `dsSocket1` is invoked. This starts the connection to the server. If no errors occur while attempting to open the connection, some status flags are reset, and the timeout timer (`tmrTimeOut`) is enabled. The procedure then enters a `Do Until...` loop. This loop continues until one of the other procedures sets either `gfClosed` or `gfTimeout` to `True`. If `gfClose` gets set, the connection has closed properly. If `gfTimeout` gets set, a timeout has occurred. In this case, the procedure updates the status controls to show that a timeout has occurred and then changes the state to `STATUS_ERROR`. If the loop ends because the connection has closed, the procedure turns off the timeout timer and changes the state to `STATUS_NEXT`.

The `STATUS_NEXT` state is used to move to the next symbol in the database. If there are no more symbols to be retrieved, the procedure moves the record pointer back to the first record and changes the state to `STATUS_FINISHED`. If there are more symbols, the state is changed back to `STATUS_SEND` to retrieve that symbol's pricing information.

The `STATUS_FINISHED` state updates the status box, enables the disabled controls, and stops the state machine. Likewise, the `STATUS_ERROR` state closes the connection if it's still open, updates the status box, enables the disabled controls, and stops the state machine.

The `dsSocket1_SendReady` Event

After the state machine starts the connection process, it is up to the server to accept the connection. If the server does allow the connection, the `dsSocket`'s `Connect` and `SendReady` events are fired.

The `SendReady` event is where QuoteWatcher creates and sends the request message that retrieves the quote information for the current symbol.

The dsSocket1_Receive Event

The `Receive` event is used to capture the incoming characters that the PC Quote server sends in response to the `GET` request message generated in the `SendReady` event. The procedure discards all data until it has received a line containing an `<H3>` HTML tag. This marks the beginning of the pricing information. From that point on, the procedure appends any received data to the `gtQuote` variable. This continues until a line that contains the `</PRE>` HTML tag is received. After this line is received, the procedure ignores any further data received.

The `Receive` event fires whenever a complete line is received from the server (`dsSocket1.LineMode` is set to `True`). This continues until the PC Quote server closes the HTTP connection, firing the `dsSocket`'s `Close` event.

The dsSocket1_Close Event

The `Close` event is where all the pricing information is parsed from the `gtQuote` variable. The procedure first calls `szStripHTML()` to remove all the HTML tags from `gtQuote`. The variable now resembles text shown in the Debug window in Figure 12.10. The remainder of the procedure extracts the desired information from `gtQuote` and updates the database accordingly. If the new current price is different from the previously retrieved price and the form is not visible, the tray icon is changed to the contents of the `picLight` picture box. This indicates a change in price for at least one symbol.

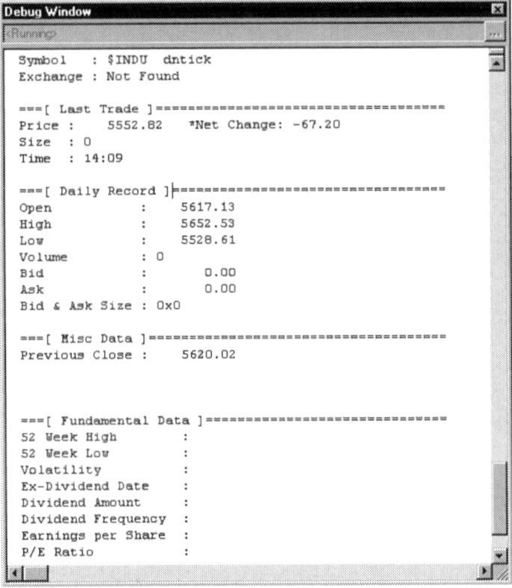

Debug Window
<Running>
Symbol : $INDU dntick
Exchange : Not Found
===[Last Trade]===================================
Price : 5552.82 *Net Change: -67.20
Size : 0
Time : 14:09
===[Daily Record]=================================
Open : 5617.13
High : 5652.53
Low : 5528.61
Volume : 0
Bid : 0.00
Ask : 0.00
Bid & Ask Size : 0x0
===[Misc Data]====================================
Previous Close : 5620.02
===[Fundamental Data]=============================
52 Week High :
52 Week Low :
Volatility :
Ex-Dividend Date :
Dividend Amount :
Dividend Frequency :
Earnings per Share :
P/E Ratio :

Figure 12.10.
An example of `gtQuote`'s contents.

After the database is updated for the current symbol, the procedure sets the `gfClosed` flag to `True`. This causes the `Do Until` loop in the `txtInternalState_Change` event to end.

Listing 12.2. The code for QuoteWatcher's form.

```
' where pricing information is stored as it is retrieved
Dim gtQuote As String
' a flag signifying that the connection has been closed
Dim gfClosed As Integer
' a flag signifying that a price has changed since the last retrieval
Dim gfChange As Integer
' a flag signifying that a timeout has occurred
Dim gfTimeout As Integer

Const TIMEOUT_MINUTES = 2   'how long to wait for timeout to occur

' state machine constants
Const STATUS_START = "1"        'start
Const STATUS_NEXT = "2"         'move to the next symbol
Const STATUS_FINISHED = "3"     'all done!
Const STATUS_SEND = "4"         'send the message
Const STATUS_ERROR = "5"        'oops!

' dsSocket State property constants
Const SOCK_STATE_CLOSED = 1
Const SOCK_STATE_CONNECTED = 2
Const SOCK_STATE_LISTENING = 3
Const SOCK_STATE_CONNECTING = 4
Const SOCK_STATE_ERROR = 5
Const SOCK_STATE_CLOSING = 6
Const SOCK_STATE_UNKNOWN = 7
Const SOCK_STATE_BUSY = 8

' dsSocket Action property constants
Const SOCK_ACTION_CLOSE = 1
Const SOCK_ACTION_CONNECT = 2
Const SOCK_ACTION_LISTEN = 3

Private Sub CBWnd_CallBack(ByVal msg As Integer, _
            ByVal wParam As Long, ByVal lParam As Long)
    ' this event is fired when our tray icon receives a
    ' mouse event message from Windows

    If (lParam = WM_RBUTTONDOWN) Then
        ' the right mouse button was pressed,
        ' display the menu
        PopupMenu mnuMain, , , , mnuShow

    ElseIf lParam = WM_LBUTTONDBLCLK Then
        ' the left mouse button was double-clicked,
        ' execute mnuShow_Click
        Call mnuShow_Click
    End If

End Sub
```

continues

Listing 12.2. continued

```
Private Sub Check1_Click()
    ' this is for enabling/disabling the automatic retrieval
    ' enable/disable timer based on checkbox setting
    tmrCheckQuotes.Enabled = (Check1.Value = 0)

    ' if the box is checked,
    If Check1.Value = 1 Then
        'update the tooltip to show suspended state
        Call UpdateTip(CBWnd, 100, "QuoteWatcher Suspended")
        ' change the menu caption
        mnuSuspend.Caption = "Activate"
    Else    'otherwise
        ' update the tooltip to show active state
        Call UpdateTip(CBWnd, 100, "QuoteWatcher Active")
        ' update the menu caption
        mnuSuspend.Caption = "Suspend"
    End If

End Sub

Private Sub cmdRetrieve_Click()

    ' if the state machine isn't already running and there are symbols
    If (Len(txtInternalStatus) = 0) And Data1.Recordset.RecordCount Then
        ' kick off the retrieval process
        txtInternalStatus.Text = STATUS_START
    End If

End Sub

Private Sub dbgQuotes_BeforeColUpdate(ByVal ColIndex As Integer, _
            OldValue As Variant, Cancel As Integer)
    ' if the user edited any column but the Symbol column
    ' (column 0), cancel the update
    If ColIndex <> 0 Then
        Cancel = True
    Else
        Cancel = False
    End If

End Sub

Private Sub dsSocket1_Close(ErrorCode As Integer, ErrorDesc As String)

    Dim ltTemp$
    ' strip all of the HTML tags from gtQuote
    gtQuote = szStripHTML(gtQuote)

    ' edit the recordset
    Data1.Recordset.Edit
    ' get the Price field from gtQuote
    ltTemp$ = Extract(gtQuote, "PRICE", ":", "*")
    ' if fraction is present - convert to decimal
    If InStr(ltTemp$, "/") Then
        ltTemp$ = Str$(ConvertFraction(ltTemp$))
    End If
```

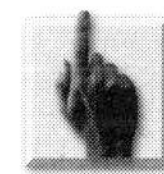

```
    'if the price has changed AND the change hasn't already
    ' been recognized AND the form is invisible,
    ' update the tray icon to the lighbulb
    If (Val(Trim$(ltTemp)) <> Data1.Recordset("Price")) _
       And (gfChange = False) And (Me.Visible = False) Then
        gfChange = True
        Call ChangeIcon(picLight.Picture, CBWnd, 100)
    End If
    ' update the field
    Data1.Recordset("Price") = Val(Trim$(ltTemp$))

    ' repeat most of that for the PrevClose field
    ltTemp$ = Extract(gtQuote, "PREVIOUS CLOSE", ":", Chr$(13))
    If InStr(ltTemp$, "/") Then
        ltTemp$ = Str$(ConvertFraction(ltTemp$))
    End If
    Data1.Recordset("PrevClose") = Val(Trim$(ltTemp$))

    ' and the High field
    ltTemp$ = Extract(gtQuote, "HIGH", ":", Chr$(13))
    If InStr(ltTemp$, "/") Then
        ltTemp$ = Str$(ConvertFraction(ltTemp$))
    End If
    Data1.Recordset("High") = Val(Trim$(ltTemp$))

    ' and the Low field
    ltTemp$ = Extract(gtQuote, "LOW", ":", Chr$(13))
    If InStr(ltTemp$, "/") Then
        ltTemp$ = Str$(ConvertFraction(ltTemp$))
    End If
    Data1.Recordset("Low") = Val(Trim$(ltTemp$))

    ' set the Trend field based on the current price and
    ' the previous closing price
    If Data1.Recordset("Price") > Data1.Recordset("PrevClose") Then
        ' price has gone up
        Data1.Recordset("Trend") = "UP"
    ElseIf Data1.Recordset("Price") < Data1.Recordset("PrevClose") Then
        ' price has gone down
        Data1.Recordset("Trend") = "DN"
    Else
        ' price is unchanged
        Data1.Recordset("Trend") = "—"
    End If
    ' udpate the recordset
    Data1.Recordset.Update
    ' set the connection closed flag
    gfClosed = True

End Sub

Private Sub dsSocket1_Connect()

    txtStatus = "Connected..."

End Sub
```

continues

Listing 12.2. continued

```
Private Sub dsSocket1_Receive(ReceiveData As String)
    Static bReceivingQuote

    txtStatus = "Receiving data..."
    'send everything to the Debug window for testing
    Debug.Print ReceiveData

    ' are we in the middle of the pricing data?
    If bReceivingQuote Then
        ' yes:
        ' append the current data to gtQuote
        gtQuote = gtQuote & ReceiveData
        ' check to see if this is the last line
        If InStr(UCase$(ReceiveData), "</PRE>") Then
            ' it is the last line, clear he bReceivingQuote flag
            bReceivingQuote = False
        End If
    End If

    ' if we're not in the middle of the pricing data, see if
    ' the line we just received contains the start marker (<H3>)
    If Not (bReceivingQuote) And InStr(UCase$(ReceiveData), "<H3>") Then
        ' the line does contain <H3>, turn on bReceivingQuote
        bReceivingQuote = True
    End If

End Sub

Private Sub dsSocket1_SendReady()
    'after a successful connect, the SendReady event fires

    Dim ltSendStr$

    ' create the HTTP request message:
    ltSendStr$ = "GET /cgi-bin/getquote.exe?TICKER="
    ' the Symbol field contains the ticker symbol
    ltSendStr$ = ltSendStr$ & UCase$(Trim$(Data1.Recordset("Symbol")))
    ' finish the message
    ltSendStr$ = ltSendStr$ & " HTTP/1.0" & vbCrLf
    ' and send it
    dsSocket1.Send = ltSendStr$ & vbCrLf

    ' now we wait for the Receive event to kick in

End Sub


Private Sub Form_Load()

    Dim i%

    ' add the additional columns to the grid
    Call AddColumn("High", 1000)
    Call AddColumn("Low", 1000)
    Call AddColumn("Price", 1000)
    Call AddColumn("Trend", 500)
    ' adjust the width of the Previous Close column
```

```
    dbgQuotes.Columns(1).Width = 1000

    ' the database name can be specified on the command line
    If Len(Command$) Then
        Data1.DatabaseName = Command$
    ' or we can use the default name
    Else
        Data1.DatabaseName = App.Path & "\quotes.mdb"
    End If

    ' do a refresh to make sure DatabaseName is valid,
    ' Err will be > 0 if it's not valid
    On Error Resume Next
    Data1.Refresh
    If Err Then
        MsgBox "Error opening quotes database:" & Chr$(13) & Err.Description
        End
    End If

    ' if there are records in the database, move to the first one
    If Data1.Recordset.RecordCount Then Data1.Recordset.MoveFirst

    'create the tray icon for QuoteWatcher
    Call CreateIcon(CBWnd, 100, WM_USER + 1, "QuoteWatcher Active", Me.Icon)

    ' hide until the user wants to see me
    Me.Visible = False

End Sub

Public Function Extract(ptBigString$, ptAfter$, ptBegin$, ptEnd$) As String

    ' get the substring from ptBigString$
    Extract = ""
    ' look for the substring after we find ptAfter$
    liAfterPos% = InStr(UCase$(ptBigString), UCase$(ptAfter$))
    If liAfterPos% Then
        ' get the position of ptBegin$
        liPos2% = InStr(liAfterPos%, ptBigString, ptBegin$)
        If liPos2% Then
            ' get the position of ptEnd$
            liPos3% = InStr(liPos2%, ptBigString, ptEnd$)
            ' if end was found, extract the substring
            If liPos3% Then
                Extract = Trim$(Mid$(ptBigString, liPos2% + 1, _
                        liPos3% - 1 - liPos2%))
            End If
        End If
    End If

End Function

Private Sub Form_QueryUnload(Cancel As Integer, UnloadMode As Integer)

    Call RemoveIcon(CBWnd, 100)

End Sub
```

continues

Listing 12.2. continued

```
Private Sub Form_Resize()
    ' if the user clicked minimize
    If Me.WindowState = 1 Then
        ' hide once again
        Me.Visible = False
        ' reset to NORMAL
        Me.WindowState = 0
        ' update the menu caption
        mnuShow.Caption = "Show"
    End If
End Sub

Private Sub Form_Unload(Cancel As Integer)

    Call RemoveIcon(CBWnd, 100)

End Sub

Private Sub mnuExit_Click()

    ' remove the tray icon
    Call RemoveIcon(CBWnd, 100)
    ' end
    End

End Sub

Private Sub mnuRetrieve_Click()

    'menu item equivalent to Retrieve Now
    ' if not visible,
    If Me.Visible = False Then
        ' show myself
        Call mnuShow_Click
    End If
    ' click the Retriev Now button
    Call cmdRetrieve_Click

End Sub

Private Sub mnuShow_Click()

    ' if the caption is "Show" then the form
    ' is invisible and should be shown
    If mnuShow.Caption = "Show" Then
        ' show the form
        Me.Show
        ' change the caption
        mnuShow.Caption = "Hide"
        ' if a price has changed since last time
        ' form was visible, reset the tray icon
        If gfChange Then
            gfChange = False
            Call ChangeIcon(Me.Icon, CBWnd, 100)
        End If

    Else
```

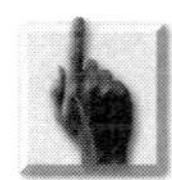

```
        ' the form must be visible, hide it & update caption
        Me.Visible = False
        mnuShow.Caption = "Show"
    End If

End Sub


Private Sub mnuSuspend_Click()

    ' if the caption is "Suspend", check the box
    If mnuSuspend.Caption = "Suspend" Then
        Check1.Value = 1
    Else
        ' otherwise the caption was "Activate",
        ' un-check the box
        Check1.Value = 0
    End If

End Sub

Private Sub SpinButton1_SpinDown()

    ' spinning down, smallest value allowed is 1
    If Val(txtDelay) > 1 Then
        txtDelay = Val(txtDelay) - 1
    Else
        Beep
    End If

End Sub

Private Sub SpinButton1_SpinUp()

    ' spinning up, largest value allowed is 9999
    If Val(txtDelay) < 9999 Then
        txtDelay = Val(txtDelay) + 1
    Else
        Beep
    End If

End Sub


Private Sub tmrCheckQuotes_Timer()

    'define a static loop counter
    Static iLoopCount%

    ' increment the loop counter
    iLoopCount% = iLoopCount% + 1
    ' if the loop counter exceeds the user-defined
    ' time between retrievals
    If iLoopCount% > Val(txtDelay) Then
        ' if there are symbols to retrieve
        If Data1.Recordset.RecordCount Then
            ' disable this timer
```

continues

Listing 12.2. continued

```
            tmrCheckQuotes.Enabled = False
            ' kick off the state machine
            txtInternalStatus.Text = STATUS_START
        End If
        ' reset the loop counter
        iLoopCount% = 0
    End If

End Sub


Private Sub tmrTimeout_Timer()

    ' define a static loop counter
    Static iLoopCount%

    ' increment the loop counter
    iLoopCount% = iLoopCount% + 1
    ' if the loop counter matches the timeout value
    If iLoopCount% = TIMEOUT_MINUTES Then
        ' reset the loop counter
        iLoopCount% = 0
        ' disable this timer
        tmrTimeout.Enabled = False
        ' set the gfTimeout flag to signal the timeout
        ' (the state machine is checking for this flag
        '  being set to True to signal a timeout)
        gfTimeout = True
    End If

End Sub

Private Sub txtDelay_KeyPress(KeyAscii As Integer)

    ' only allow numbers
    If KeyAscii < Asc("0") Or KeyAscii > Asc("9") Then
        KeyAscii = 0
    End If

End Sub


Private Sub txtDelay_LostFocus()

    ' if the value is zero, set it to 1
    If Val(txtDelay) = 0 Then txtDelay = 1

End Sub

Private Sub txtInternalStatus_Change()

    Select Case txtInternalStatus.Text
    Case STATUS_START
        'let's rock-and-roll!
        ' if the socket is alread connected, error!
        If dsSocket1.State = SOCK_STATE_CONNECTED Then
            txtInternalStatus.Text = STATUS_ERROR
```

  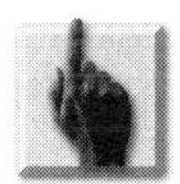  

```
            Exit Sub
        End If

        'disable some controls
        dbgQuotes.Enabled = False
        cmdRetrieve.Enabled = False
        tmrCheckQuotes.Enabled = False

        ' set up the socket's properties
        dsSocket1.LineMode = True
        dsSocket1.EOLChar = 10
        dsSocket1.RemoteHost = "www.pcquote.com"
        dsSocket1.RemotePort = 80

        ' do a forward lookup to get the IP address
        On Error Resume Next
        dsSocket1.FwdLookup
        If Err Then
            txtStatus = "Error connecting: " & Error$
            txtInternalStatus.Text = STATUS_ERROR
        End If

        ' move to the first symbol
        Data1.Recordset.MoveFirst
        ' update the tray icon tooltip
        Call UpdateTip(CBWnd, 100, "Retrieving Quotes")

        ' move to the next state
        txtInternalStatus.Text = STATUS_SEND

    Case STATUS_SEND
        ' time to connect

        ' if the Symbol field is NULL, move to the next record
        ' (this shouldn't happen if the database is set up properly)
        If IsNull(Data1.Recordset("Symbol")) Then
            txtInternalStatus.Text = STATUS_NEXT
            Exit Sub
        End If

        ' update the status box and tray icon tooltip
        txtStatus = "Retrieving " & Data1.Recordset("Symbol") & "..."
        Call UpdateTip(CBWnd, 100, "Retrieving " & Data1.Recordset("Symbol"))

        ' reset the gtQuote string
        gtQuote = ""

        'connect to the server
        On Error Resume Next
        dsSocket1.Connect
        If Err Then
            txtStatus = "Error connecting: " & Error$
            txtInternalStatus.Text = STATUS_ERROR
        End If

        'reset the connection flags
        gfClosed = False
```

continues

Listing 12.2. continued

```
        gfTimeout = False

        ' enable the timeout timer
        tmrTimeout.Enabled = True

        ' loop here until the connection closes
        ' or a timeout occurs
        Do Until gfClosed Or gfTimeout
            DoEvents
        Loop

        ' did a timeout occur?
        If gfTimeout Then
            ' yes, update status and tooltip
            txtStatus = "Timeout occurred..."
            Call UpdateTip(CBWnd, 100, "Suspended due to timeout")
            ' suspend further retrievals
            Check1.Value = 1
            ' go to the error state
            txtInternalStatus = STATUS_ERROR
        Else
            ' no timeout, move to the next symbol
            tmrTimeout.Enabled = False
            txtInternalStatus = STATUS_NEXT
        End If

    Case STATUS_NEXT
        On Error Resume Next
        ' get the next symbol
        Data1.Recordset.MoveNext

        ' have we reached the end?
        If Data1.Recordset.EOF Then
            ' yes, reset to the first record
            Data1.Recordset.MoveFirst
            ' and move to the finished state
            txtInternalStatus.Text = STATUS_FINISHED
        Else
            ' no, retrieve the new symbol
            txtInternalStatus.Text = STATUS_SEND
        End If

    Case STATUS_ERROR
        ' ERROR!!!!

        On Error Resume Next
        ' close the socket if it's open
        If dsSocket1.State = SOCK_STATE_CONNECTED Then
            dsSocket1.Close
        End If
        ' stop the state machine
        txtInternalStatus = ""
        ' enable the controls and update the tooltip
        Call ToggleControls
        Call UpdateTip(CBWnd, 100, "QuoteWatcher Active")
```

```
    Case STATUS_FINISHED
        ' Whew, we made it!

        txtStatus = "Finished retrieving quotes!"
        txtInternalStatus = ""
        Call ToggleControls
        Call UpdateTip(CBWnd, 100, "QuoteWatcher Active")

    End Select


End Sub



Public Function szStripHTML(szString As String) As String

    Dim szTemp As String
    Dim szResult As String
    Dim nPos As Integer
    Dim nMarker As Integer

    '-- Copy the argument into a local
    '   string so the original does not
    '   get whacked.
    szTemp = szString

    '-- Remove HTML codes
    Do
        nPos = InStr(szTemp, "<")
        If nPos = False Then
            Exit Do
        Else
            '-- szResult contains the final
            '   product of this routine.
            szResult = szResult & _
                Left$(szTemp, nPos - 1)
            '-- szTemp is the working string,
            '   which is continuously
            '   shortened as new codes
            '   are found
            szTemp = Mid$(szTemp, nPos + 1)
            nPos = InStr(szTemp, ">")
            If nPos = False Then
                '-- No complimentary arrow
                '   was found.
                Exit Do
            Else
                '-- Shorten the working
                '   string
                szTemp = Mid$(szTemp, _
                    nPos + 1)
            End If
        End If
    Loop
```

continues

Listing 12.2. continued

```
    '-- Find a marker byte by looking for
    '   a char that does not already exist
    '   in the string.
    For nMarker = 255 To 1 Step -1
        If InStr(szResult, Chr$(nMarker)) _
            = 0 Then
            Exit For
        End If
    Next

    '-- Remove carriage returns
    Do
        nPos = InStr(szResult, Chr$(13))
        If nPos Then
            szResult = Left$(szResult, _
                nPos - 1) & Mid$(szResult, _
                nPos + 1)
        Else
            Exit Do
        End If
    Loop

    '-- Replace linefeeds with Marker bytes
    Do
        nPos = InStr(szResult, Chr$(10))
        If nPos Then
            szResult = Left$(szResult, _
                nPos - 1) & Chr$(nMarker) _
                & Mid$(szResult, nPos + 1)
        Else
            Exit Do
        End If
    Loop

    '-- Replace marker bytes with CR/LF pairs
    Do
        nPos = InStr(szResult, Chr$(nMarker))
        If nPos Then
            szResult = Left$(szResult, _
                nPos - 1) & Chr$(13) & Chr$(10) _
                & Trim$(Mid$(szResult, nPos + 1))
        Else
            Exit Do
        End If
    Loop

    '-- Thats all for this routine!
    szStripHTML = szResult


End Function

Private Function ConvertFraction(ptNumber$, Optional ptSep) As Double

    ' converts a string containing fraction to a decimal
    ' ptSep can be specified if the fraction part of the
    ' string ptNumber$ is separated from the whole number
```

```
    ' with any character besides a space

    Dim ltSep$, ltString$, liSepPos%, liDivPos%
    Dim lNumerator%, lDenominator%
    Dim ldTemp As Double

    If IsMissing(ptSep) Then
        ltSep$ = " "
    Else
        ltSep$ = ptSep
    End If

    ltString$ = Trim$(ptNumber$)
    'find the separator
    liSepPos% = InStr(ltString$, ltSep$)
    'find the fraction sign
    liDivPos% = InStr(ltString$, "/")

    If (liSepPos% = 0) Or (liDivPos% = 0) Then
        ConvertFraction = Val(ltString$)
        Exit Function
    End If

    'get the whole number portion
    ldTemp = Val(Left$(ltString$, liSepPos% - 1))

    lNumerator% = Val(Trim$(Mid$(ltString$, liSepPos%, liDivPos% - liSepPos%)))
    lDenominator% = Val(Trim$(Mid$(ltString$, liDivPos% + 1)))
    If lDenominator% = 0 Then
        'invalid fraction!
        ConvertFraction = ldTemp
    Else
        ConvertFraction = ldTemp + lNumerator% / lDenominator%
    End If

End Function

Private Sub ToggleControls()

    'reset the control states
    tmrCheckQuotes.Enabled = True
    dbgQuotes.Enabled = True
    tmrTimeout.Enabled = False
    cmdRetrieve.Enabled = True

End Sub

Public Sub AddColumn(ptCaption As String, pdWidth As Double, _
        Optional ptDataField)
    Dim ptField$

    'check for the option parameter
    If IsMissing(ptDataField) Then
        'if not present, use the ptCaption parameter
        ptField$ = ptCaption
    Else
        ptField$ = ptDataField
```

continues

Listing 12.2. continued

```
    End If

    ' add the column as the right-most column
    dbgQuotes.Columns.Add (dbgQuotes.Columns.Count)
    ' set the new column's properties
    With dbgQuotes.Columns(dbgQuotes.Columns.Count - 1)
        .Visible = True
        .Caption = ptCaption
        .Locked = True
        .DataField = ptField$
        .Width = pdWidth
    End With

End Sub
```

Testing the Application

If you've entered all the code or, better yet, copied it from the CD-ROM, you can now test the application. QuoteWatcher is simple to use.

First, make sure you have a solid connection to the Internet. QuoteWatcher won't get very far if it can't communicate with the PC Quote Web server. After your connection is established, run the application.

At first it will appear that nothing has happened. However, if you look at the taskbar notification area (the tray), you'll notice that the QuoteWatcher icon has been added. To make the window visible, double-click the QuoteWatcher icon. The QuoteWatcher form appears with an empty grid (see Figure 12.11).

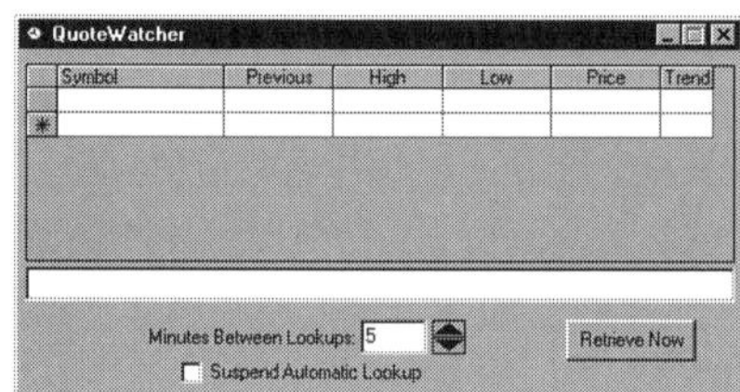

Figure 12.11.
Running QuoteWatcher for the first time.

Enter some symbols in the database by clicking in the first column of the grid row that has an asterisk in the row header column. Type a ticker symbol for a stock or mutual fund for which you'd like to retrieve the pricing information. As soon as you start typing, the grid moves the text to the first row of the grid. After you've entered all the ticker symbols, press the Enter key and then the down arrow. This permanently stores that symbol into the database. Enter other symbols in the same manner.

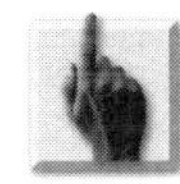

After you have all the symbols entered, click the Retrieve Now button. The retrieval process starts, and you should see the status textbox get updated as the state machine operates. The rows of the grid will update after each symbol's pricing information is retrieved. While executing the application within Visual Basic, the `Receive` event sends all the received data to the Debug window for you to view. This is useful in case you're having connection or timeout problems—you can see exactly what has been received by the application.

Now, adjust the Minutes Between Lookups value to a smaller number. Click the form's Minimize button. The form disappears. Move the mouse pointer over the QuoteWatcher tray icon. Leave it stationary until the tooltip appears. The tooltip should read QuoteWatcher Active. Right-click the icon. The popup menu appears. Click the Suspend menu item. Right-click again. The Suspend menu item has changed to Activate. Select the Show menu item. The form appears, and now the Suspend Automatic Lookup checkbox is checked. Click the checkbox again to enable automatic checking. Minimize the form and wait.

After the time interval specified in Minutes Between Lookup, the retrieval process starts again. Note how the tooltip is updated to show which symbol is currently being retrieved. After the retrieval is completed, the tray icon may change to a different picture. This indicates that one of the prices has changed. Double-click the icon to view the form. The tray icon changes back to the default icon. However, if you are doing this after market hours or if your list of symbols only includes mutual funds, you probably won't see the different icon because it is unlikely that the price will change.

When you've finished testing the application, select Exit from the popup menu or click the form's Close button.

Modifying the Application

The QuoteWatcher application is a very simple agent. However, the code can be easily expanded to add new features. It's also easy to add new columns to the database table and grid in order to use more of the data retrieved from the PC Quote server.

For example, you may wish to add a history table that allows you to track the prices through time. You could even create graphs of that historical data and display those to the user.

Another useful addition would be the ability to set price break points. The user could specify a high and low price limit for each symbol. Then, when the application detects that these limits have been exceeded, it could change the tray icon to reflect this fact. You could even program the application to e-mail your broker with a buy or sell order in such cases. However, you'll probably want to obtain a subscription account from PC Quote so you can retrieve real-time quotes. The server that QuoteWatcher accesses supplies quotes on a twenty minute delay basis.

The possibilities are almost limitless for QuoteWatcher. After you know how to retrieve the data from the Web server, you can do whatever you desire with it.

Summary

This chapter walked you through the process of creating an interactive Web agent. The QuoteWatcher application is just the beginning in Web agent development. Such a vast amount of information is present on the Web that it will be a long time before all possible information agents have been written. By that time, the world of interactive multimedia will present the application developer with an even wider variety of needed information processing applications.

The remaining chapters in this book present more complicated Web-based agents. I hope this chapter has given enough background to assist you in understanding these advanced applications.

Chapter 13

Building an E-Mail Signature Generator

Although use of the World Wide Web is growing by leaps and bounds, the Internet's main use is for electronic mail. E-mail and Usenet News readers allow people who are sending or posting messages to append a signature to the message. This signature (also called a *tag line*) shows clearly (outside the often garbled header) who sent or posted the message.

This signature, which is usually stored as a text file, gets appended to the bottom of the message; it may look something like this:

```
---------------------------------------------------------------------
Brad Haasch                         "Let's go Rangers!"
Sams Publishing
haasch@execpc.com
---------------------------------------------------------------------
```

This is an easy way to identify yourself to the recipient of your e-mail or the reader of your posting on a Usenet group. It's much easier to figure out who sent what via a signature file than to sort through the often large and confusing header attached to mail and Usenet messages.

Originally, not much went into a signature file; usually one like the following would suffice:

```
(End of e-mail body)
Brad Haasch
haasch@execpc.com
(End of e-mail)
```

Then people began to spice up their signatures a bit, add a nifty quote, some cool line art, and before long you might see this:

```
/\/\/\/\/\/\/\/\/\/\/\/\/\/\/\/\/\/\/\/\/\/\/\/\/\/\/\/\/\/\/\/\/\/\/\
|  Brad Haasch                "Problems are only opportunities       |
|  SAMS Publishing             in work clothes."                     |
|  haasch@execpc.com               -- Henry J. Kaiser                |
VVVVVVVVVVVVVVVVVVVVVVVVVVVVVVVVVVVVVVVVVVVVVVVVVVVVVVVVVVVVVVVVVVVVVV
```

So, now, not only does the signature convey who sent the message, the sender's title, e-mail address, and often employer's name, it might also include some cool ASCII line art, and a witty quote.

This chapter discusses how and where signature files are stored and provides an application that accesses a Web page to retrieve quotations to be placed into your signature file. This allows you to easily generate signature files that not only provide your basic contact information but also provide an interesting quote for the reader of your e-mail or postings.

Where Signature Files Reside

The storage of signature files varies depending on the operating system on which the e-mail program or newsreader operates. This section describes those locations for both UNIX and Windows operating systems.

UNIX Signature Files

For you non-UNIX people, let me explain the placement and use of the signature file. In UNIX, the signature file is held in a file called `.signature`. The period (.) before the filename indicates that the file isn't important to the everyday UNIX user on a day-to-day basis, and that on a directory command (`ls` in UNIX), these period files are skipped, as you can see in Figure 13.1.

Figure 13.1.
The average user's UNIX home directory.

As you can see, no files beginning with a period (including the `.signature` file) appear, but we know they exist. Add the `-a` flag to the `ls` command to see these period files, as shown in Figure 13.2.

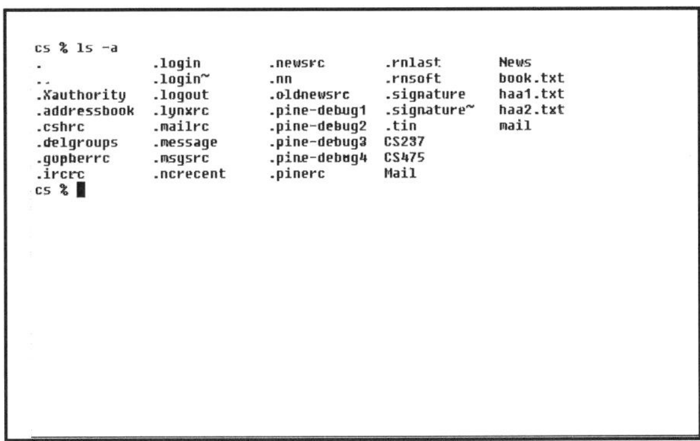

Figure 13.2.
UNIX home directory exposed with `ls -a`.

Here you see a bunch of UNIX user files that take care of things such as login scripts, e-mail, subscribed newsgroups, and so on. The file we're concerned about is `.signature`.

Windows Signature Files

Now that Windows e-mail programs working via a PPP connection have come to market and have gained wide use, the signature file is stored in a different place for each different e-mail program.

For instance, Eudora stores your signature file in a file called `signatur.pce` in the root Eudora directory. These files are standard text, so you can generate a replacement for signature files quite easily.

Web Sources for Quotes

http://www.yahoo.com

By using Yahoo! (`http://www.yahoo.com`), I searched for `tag lines`. The first site returned by Yahoo! was named Taglines Galore and is described in the next section. Some other sites that have quotes suitable for this type of application are also featured in the following sections.

Taglines Galore

http://www.brandonu.ca/~ennsnr/Tags/Welcome.html

This is the root of several quote pages. One has a different set of 100 random quotes every day. This site also includes the computer archive, which is used in the application presented here, as well as other sites.

A Quote from Mr. Spock

http://www.cs.ubc.ca/spock

Every time this page is reloaded, it not only provides you with a new quote from the great Vulcan himself, but a neat picture as well.

Quote of the Moment

http://spidey.usc.edu/www-bin/quote

This is another CGI script that returns a random quote. This script was produced by Andrew N. Marshall at the University of Southern California.

Quotes from Steven Wright and Jack Handy

http://www.hooked.net/users/davew/bin/stevenwright

http://www.hooked.net/users/davew/bin/deepthoughts

Provided by `davew@hooked.net`, these two URLs are for obtaining a Steven Wright quote and bringing you a 'deep thought' from Jack Handy.

Random Quotes

http://www.nova.edu/Inter-Links/quotes.html

This site, maintained by Andrew Tong, has several anchors to quote sites.

Keep in mind you should get the permission of the site Webmaster to use such a site in any application. Imagine the Webmaster who finds his access logs go from 100 hits per day to a few thousand due to a distributed application using his site as a source for quotes.

Overview of the Application

Due to the difficulty of coming up with a witty quote, I present a program that will, given user information, connect to a Web site, pick out a quote at random, and write a new signature file to the user-specified location.

The program provides space for users to enter their name, e-mail address, and title. With that information in place, the program will present the quote, get a different one if the user doesn't like the one suggested, and then allow the user to save the new signature file.

The signature generator program goes through these steps:

1. Connects to the Web server and retrieves the list of quotes.
2. Selects one at random from the list, ignoring the HTML tags.
3. With the given user information, writes the new file to disk.

To start, you'll design the user interface to include the following: textboxes with labels for the user information and the suggested quote; command buttons to connect to the quote server or grab a different quote if the first one isn't acceptable; a button to save the file; and an exit button.

The other controls you'll use are the common dialog for saving the file, the `dsSocket` control from Dolphin Systems for connecting to the Web server and retrieving the information, and a listbox for holding the complete list of quotes. Figure 13.3 shows the arrangements of the elements for the E-Mail Signature Generator application.

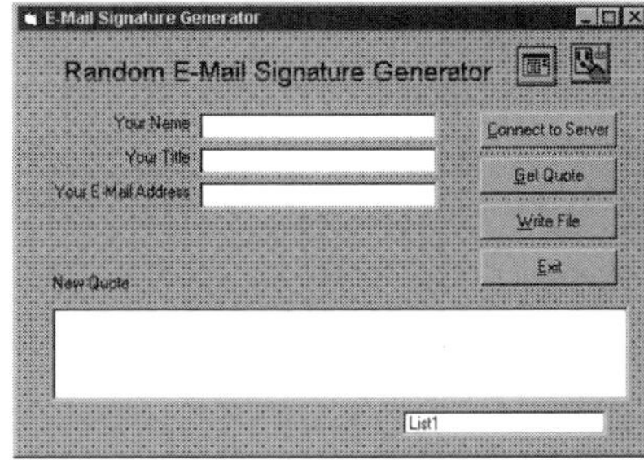

Figure 13.3.
Design-time view of the application.

Using the **dsSocket** Control

You can start by examining the code to configure and use the `dsSocket` control. This control is used to connect to the Web server and then to retrieve the quotes. In the `Form_Load` procedure, the following lines define some of the properties of the `dsSocket` control:

```
dsSocket1.RemoteHost = "www.brandonu.ca"
dsSocket1.RemotePort = 80
dsSocket1.LineMode = True
dsSocket1.EOLChar = 10
```

The `RemoteHost` property of the `dsSocket` control is set to the server name, *not* the URL of the quotes. The URL is specified later when you issue the `GET` command to the server. The `RemotePort` is specified to `80`, which is the default of the control, and the standard port that is used for HTTP communications. The `LineMode` property is set to `True`, indicating that the `dsSocket` control will trigger the receive events when the EOL character (defined by `dsSocket.EOLChar`) is reached. The `EOLChar` property is set to `10`, which is the ASCII code for the linefeed character.

To actually retrieve the page, you must issue a command to the Web server specified in the `dsSocket`'s properties. The command button `cmdGo` (captioned Connect to Server) contains the following lines of code:

```
dsSocket1.Connect
dsSocket1.Send = "GET /~ennsnr/Tags/COMP_hype.html" & vbCrLf & vbCrLf
```

The `Connect` method of the `dsSocket` property connects the control to the specified Web server. Then use the `Send` method to issue a command to the Web server.

`GET`, followed by the URL, requests the document from the server. The two carriage-return/line-feed combinations issue the command.

Once the request is sent, the server starts sending back the contents of the requested URL. This fires the `Receive` event of the `dsSocket` control. The code for the `Receive` event is

```
list1.AddItem ReceiveData
list1.ListIndex = list1.ListCount - 1
```

The line received is added to the hidden listbox on the form, and the index is set to the next usable value (`list1.ListCount -1`). The `Receive` event fires repeatedly, adding each line of the URL to the listbox, until the page is completely downloaded.

Selecting and Formatting the Quote

Now that you have a list of quotes and a few HTML tags in your listbox, you can choose one at random and place it in the `txtQuote` textbox, with the following code:

```
num_quotes = list1.ListCount - 18
Randomize
random_quote_index = Int((num_quotes * Rnd) + 11)
list1.ListIndex = random_quote_index
iTemp1 = Len(list1.Text)
txtQuote = Left(list1.Text, iTemp1 - 1)
```

You subtract 18 from the list count to account for the number of lines used for HTML tags. This varies depending on the site you use as a source for quotes. You then initialize the random number generator, and choose a random number based on the modified list count. With this, you copy the selected line into the `txtQuote` textbox, removing the last character, which is the vertical bar, representing the linefeed character.

With the first quote in place, the user then can select different quotes by repeatedly pressing the Get Quote button. This action chooses another random number within the constraints of the modified list length and displays that quote.

Formatting the Strings and Writing to Disk

After the user has settled on a quote and entered his or her name, title, and e-mail address, the user can press the Write File button to save the new quote to disk.

The code to format the user information and the quote is a good example of string manipulation in Visual Basic.

The desired format for the signature is

```
-=-=-=-=-=-=-=-=-=-=-=-=-=-=-=-=-=-=-=-=-=-=-=-=-=-=-=-=-=-=-=-=-=-=-
User Name
User Title      "Insert cute quote here"
User E-Mail
-=-=-=-=-=-=-=-=-=-=-=-=-=-=-=-=-=-=-=-=-=-=-=-=-=-=-=-=-=-=-=-=-=-=-
```

or, if the quote is too big to fit on one line:

```
-=-=-=-=-=-=-=-=-=-=-=-=-=-=-=-=-=-=-=-=-=-=-=-=-=-=-=-=-=-=-=-=-=-=-
User Name       "Insert cute quote here, but it's long, so we'll
User Title      have to use part of the second line also."
User E-Mail
-=-=-=-=-=-=-=-=-=-=-=-=-=-=-=-=-=-=-=-=-=-=-=-=-=-=-=-=-=-=-=-=-=-=-
```

The code to do this is rather involved. Let's start with the first and last lines—the alternating -= pattern to offset the signature from the message. These lines create the pattern:

```
For x = 1 To 40
            sTemp1 = sTemp1 & "-"
            sTemp1 = sTemp1 & "="
Next x
```

This generates a separator line 80 characters long, of minus and equal signs.

Two different cases you have to take into account are when the quote fits on one line, and when a quote requires two lines.

You may be wondering about long quotes that would take three or more lines. Because this is an Internet book, not a string processing book, I only cover up to two-line quotes. However, it's not a horrible task to convert my code that breaks a quote into two lines into a routine that would handle three- or four-line quotes as well.

To know if you need to break the quote apart, you need to know the length of the longest user field. The code to determine that is a series of `If-Then` blocks:

```
left_min = Len(txtUser(0).Text) + 6
If left_min < Len(txtUser(1).Text) Then
     left_min = Len(txtUser(1).Text) + 6
End If
If left_min < Len(txtUser(2).Text) Then
     left_min = Len(txtUser(2).Text) + 6
End If
```

The `txtUser(0)` through `txtUser(2)` textboxes correspond to the name, title, and e-mail address of the user. The six is added to the `left_min` value as an offset. Later, you'll use the `left_min` as a starting point for the starting character of the quote for that line, and the six spaces provide some room between the longest user field and the quote.

Now that you know how much room is taken up on the left side by the user information, you can look at the length of the string and see if it needs to be broken apart. You can handle each case and format the strings used for output:

```
quote_len = Len(txtQuote.Text)
```

`quote_len` is used as a placeholder for the length of the quote. Then you check against the value given by `80 - left_min`. `left_min` is the number of characters the longest user information field uses; eighty is the total number of columns available. The difference becomes the amount of available characters per line for the quote.

```
If (quote_len > (80 - left_min)) Then
```

If this condition is satisfied, you need to break the string into two parts. You start by finding the first space that occurs after the halfway point in the quote:

```
iTemp2 = (quote_len / 2)
iTemp2 = InStr(iTemp2, txtQuote, " ")
```

You then copy the first part to `subStr1` and the second part to `subStr2`:

```
subStr1 = Left(txtQuote, (quote_len - iTemp2))
subStr2 = Right(txtQuote, iTemp2)
```

Now you can build the strings used for user output. `sTemp1` contains the top and bottom separator bars (`-=-=-=--=`). `sTemp2` holds the user's name and first line of the quote if the quote is multiline.

1. Start with the user's name:

   ```
   sTemp2 = txtUser(0)
   ```

2. Add whitespace for padding:

   ```
   sTemp2 = sTemp2 & Space(left_min - Len(txtUser(0)))
   ```

3. Now add the first line of the quote:

   ```
   sTemp2 = sTemp2 & subStr1
   ```

The same procedure for the first line is applied to the second—this time using the user's title and the second half of the quote, as follows:

```
sTemp3 = txtUser(1)
sTemp3 = sTemp3 & Space(left_min - Len(txtUser(1)))
sTemp3 = sTemp3 & substr2
```

The `Else` condition, in this case, generates the strings for a one-line quote. It first gets the user's information, then adds the whitespace padding, and finally the quote:

```
Else
'sTemp2 gets the user name...
  sTemp2 = txtUser(0)
'sTemp3 gets the title...
  sTemp3 = txtUser(1)
  sTemp3 = sTemp3 & Space(left_min)
  sTemp3 = sTemp3 & txtQuote.Text
End If
```

That's all there is to it. Now that the strings for the signature are formatted, all you have to do is write them to disk.

Writing the New Signature to Disk

The time has come to write the signature to a file. The following code shows just how easy it is to do this using the common dialog control and simple file I/O code.

```
commondialog1.filename = ""
commondialog1.ShowSave
If commondialog1.filename = "" Then Exit Sub
Open commondialog1.filename For Output As #1
    Print #1, sTemp1       'border
    Print #1, sTemp2       'name + quote if 2 line quote
    Print #1, sTemp3       'title + quote
    Print #1, sTemp4       'e-mail address
    Print #1, sTemp1       'border again
Close #1
```

You use the check on a zero-length filename to see if the user pressed Cancel. If not, open the file as text, write to it, and close the file.

Controlling the Order of User Events

Timing is everything, and event-driven programming drives that fact home. You might have noticed and wondered when looking at the form, "What happens if the user clicks on Get Quote before clicking on Connect to Server?" Because one is dependent on the other, set the `Enabled` property of the `GetQuote` to `False` at form load, and on the `Click` event of the Connect to Server button, set it back to `True`. This ensures that no error occurs because a connection to the Web server wasn't made first.

Modifying the Code for Use with Other Quote Servers

One limitation of this program is that, if it were to be distributed, the server name and URL are hard-coded. The application also assumes that there won't be any HTML tags within the body of quotes, and the HTML tags take up approximately the first 10 lines and the last 8 lines of the file.

You could instead use a drop-down listbox filled with known quote sites. The sites you choose should have a consistent format for displaying the quotes so your code can pick them out. Then, when the user selects a different site from the list, your code would adjust the expected formatting in order to retrieve the quote correctly. See the section titled "Selecting and Formatting the Quote" for the code that you'll have to modify to make this change.

Shortcomings of the Signature Generator

Another potential shortcoming is handling server-returned error messages that are returned as HTML files. The possible error codes and messages are discussed in Chapter 2, "HTTP: How to Speak on the Web." One way to handle errors is to have an expected listcount number, and if the number returned is substantially less than that number, to show the user an error message.

Summary

This is a basic example of using Web-based information to provide an added service to the end user. By incorporating the Web into the application, updates to the quote database can be made, and the user can take advantage of them, without modifying the client program. Programs using information such as stock quotes (see Chapter 12, "QuoteWatcher: An Interactive Web Agent"), book prices, and other information subject to change can greatly benefit from hosting the data on a Web server rather than distributing database files on a periodic basis.

Chapter 14

WebSearcher: A Simple Search Tool

- Designing the Application
- Coding the Application
- Testing the Application
- Other Directions

The vast amount of information available on the World Wide Web is its greatest strength. Millions of resources scattered across the world are available any day, at any time, to anyone with a connection and a browser...great, right?

Try finding something you need. Since the creation of the World Wide Web, search tools have gone from nonexistent to extremely prevalent. I can think of ten different ones off the top of my head, and I'm sure many more exist.

Search engines provide the compass to the Web traveler. Either by going through a series of narrower and narrower categories, or by just typing in a keyword.

The search engine then looks through its database of registered URLs and returns to the user a listing of what it found that lines up with the keywords entered.

Right now most search engines depend on the use of a Web browser such as Netscape Navigator: You go to the site of the search engine, enter your query, and in a moment or two, the browser displays a set of pages that match your request.

Now, using a custom control such as the Sax Webster control described in Chapter 4, "Using Web Browser Custom Controls," you can put this search engine on the user's desktop.

Designing the Application

There are a few basic capabilities you'll want this search engine to have:

- Allow the user to specify base URLs to be searched, place these base URLs in a listbox, and make sure that any pages linked to these root URLs are searched also.
- Show the pages in a Webster control as they're received. The Webster control is used because it provides a `GetLinkURL` method, which allows you to iterate through an array containing the URLs of all of the hypertext links on a specified page.

http://www.microsoft.com/kb/peropsys/win95/q138789.htm

http: //www.microsoft.com/kb/peropsys/win95/q153038.htm

NOTE:

For some reason the Webster control seems to have trouble communicating over certain dial-up TCP/IP stacks, including the stack included with Internet in a Box. If at all possible, use the Microsoft TCP/IP stack that ships with Windows 95. It is very easy to configure the Dial-Up Networking feature of Windows 95 to work with just about any

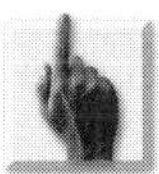

Internet service provider. There are two Microsoft Knowledge Base articles available at the Microsoft Web site that explain how to do this. Point your browser to `http://www.microsoft.com/kb/peropsys/win95/q138789.htm` and `http://www.microsoft.com/kb/peropsys/win95/q153038.htm` to view these articles.

- Show any hypertext links found on the base pages in a listbox, using the aforementioned `GetLinkURL` method.
- Take a user-specified keyword and record the URL of any pages that contain the keyword in a listbox.
- When the search engine isn't performing a search, allow the user to view a URL in the Webster control by double-clicking a URL in any of the listboxes.
- Keep the user informed of the status of the Internet activity (connecting, sending, and receiving of information) using the status bar control.

With these ideas in place, you can start thinking about the processes involved in setting up the form and the flow of the program.

Knowing the base functionality of the program, you can choose the controls for the program. Figure 14.1 shows how the form should look when you're finished with this section.

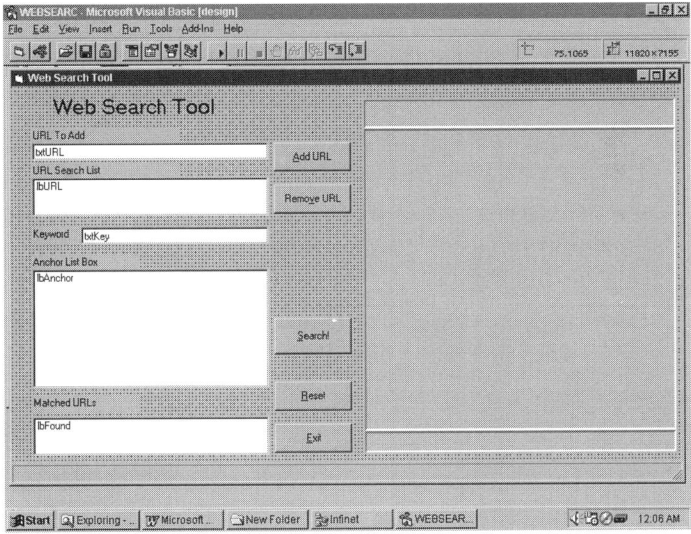

Figure 14.1.
Design-time view of the Web search application.

NOTE:

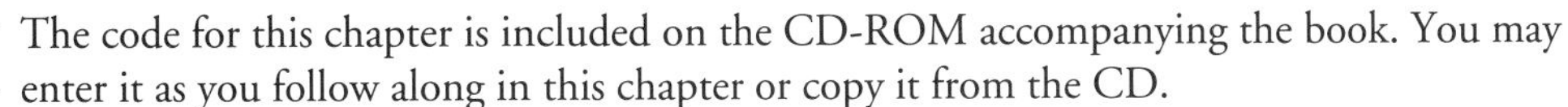

The code for this chapter is included on the CD-ROM accompanying the book. You may enter it as you follow along in this chapter or copy it from the CD.

To create this form, follow these steps:

1. Start a new project in Visual Basic. Add the Webster control using Tools | Custom Controls. You'll use this control to load the URLs and parse the links found on the loaded pages.
2. Increase the form's size to allow enough room for all the controls.

NOTE:

This application was originally designed on a monitor set at 800 × 600 resolution. If you are limited to, or prefer, 640 × 480, you'll probably have to shrink some of the controls on the left-hand side of the form to get everything to fit.

3. Add a Webster control to the form, positioning it so it takes up the right half of the form.
4. Set the `HomePage` property to an empty string. Set the `LoadImages` property to `False` because the program is only searching for text.
5. Set the `PagesToCache` property to `1` to remove any page caching. This is necessary to ensure that Webster loads and parses each page. Otherwise, a cached page would not be properly searched because Webster merely re-displays cached pages without firing the `LoadComplete` event, or any event for that matter.
6. Using the control's custom properties page (select the `Custom` property in VB's Property Window and click the button with the ellipses), select the Display tab and turn off all the Buttons checkboxes except for the Back/Forth checkbox. The tab should appear as in Figure 14.2.

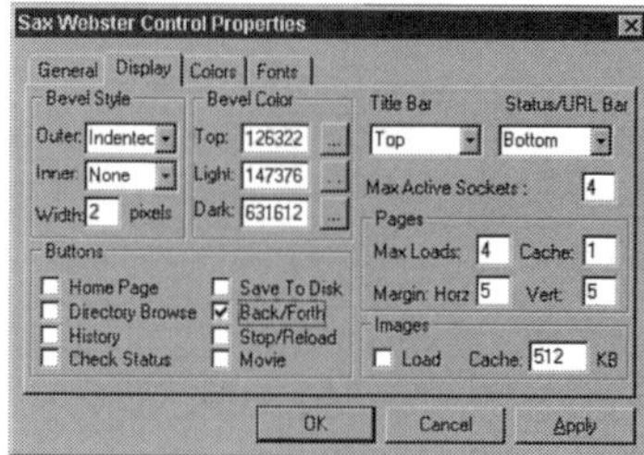

Figure 14.2.
Webster's custom properties Display tab.

NOTE:

You can leave more of the buttons enabled if you wish, but you must make sure that while the application is performing a search, the user is unable to change the URL that Webster is attempting to load. The best method for doing so is to modify the control's `ButtonMask` property right before a search to turn off all buttons. Then, upon completion of a search, turn your buttons back on using the same property.

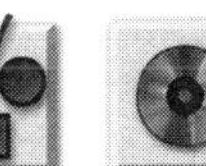

7. Add a status bar (`Status1`) and two textboxes: one for entering URLs (`txtURL`) and one for entering the keyword for the search (`txtKey`).
8. Add three listboxes: one for the user-specified URLs to search (`lbURL`), another for the anchors found within those user-specified URLs (`lbAnchor`), and one listbox for URLs of pages containing the keyword specified (`lbFound`).
9. Add the labels as shown in Figure 14.1.
10. Add command buttons for adding (`cmdURL, Index = 0`) and deleting (`cmdURL, Index = 1`) user-specified URLs, starting the search (`cmdSearch`), resetting the application (`cmdReset`), and exiting (`cmdExit`).

With these controls in place, the form should look like Figure 14.1. If so, you can start adding code to the project. Otherwise, retrace your steps and make it look similar.

Coding the Application

Now that the form's controls are in place, it's time to add some code. This section provides all the code necessary to make the search application operate.

The **Declarations** Section

There are a few form-level variables defined in the `Declarations` section of our form's code. Open the form's code module by clicking the View Code button on the VB Project window or by pressing the F7 key. In the `Declarations` section, enter the following lines:

```
Option Explicit

Dim fPageLoaded%          'set true when a page is loaded
Dim LBFlag As Integer     'which list box to process
```

The first line specifies that all variables within the application must be declared before they can be used. The first variable defined is a flag that is used to determine if a page is loaded in the Webster control. Because Webster caches pages, if the first searched page is the current page loaded in the Webster control, Webster won't reload the page. If Webster doesn't reload the page, the `LoadComplete` event won't fire and the program won't process the page.

The second variable, `LBFlag`, is a flag that tracks which URL listbox is being processed. The application only searches the URLs specified by the user and then any URLs linked on those pages. If you're processing URLs from the user-specified list, you'll load the anchor listbox with all the links found on the pages. If you're processing the anchor listbox, you'll only be searching for text, not links.

The AddMatch Subroutine

This subroutine adds the URL of a page containing the search string to the `lbFound` listbox. The URL to be added is provided as a string parameter to the subroutine. The code, shown in Listing 14.1, first searches all the URLs currently in the listbox to verify that the URL specified doesn't already exist in the list. If a duplicate URL is not found, the URL is added to the listbox.

Listing 14.1. The `AddMatch` subroutine.

```
Sub AddMatch(sMatchURL As String)

Dim x As Integer

For x = 1 To lbFound.ListCount
    lbFound.ListIndex = lbFound.ListCount - 1
    If lbFound.Text = sMatchURL Then
        Exit Sub
    End If
Next x

lbFound.AddItem sMatchURL

End Sub
```

Specifying the URLs to Search

Let's start off by coding the adding and removing of user-specified URLs from the `lbURL` listbox. Each of the URLs the user adds is searched for the keyword when the Search command button is pressed.

The Add URL and Remove URL buttons are in a control array. The code behind the `Click` event is found in Listing 14.2.

Listing 14.2. The `cmdURL_Click` event code.

```
Private Sub cmdURL_Click(Index As Integer)
'allows user to build URL listbox
    Select Case Index
          Case 0  'add url
            If Trim(txtURL.Text) = "" Then
                Exit Sub
            End If
            lbURL.AddItem (txtURL.Text)
            txtURL.Text = ""
         Case 1  'remove url
            If lbURL.ListIndex < 0 Then
                Exit Sub
            Else
```

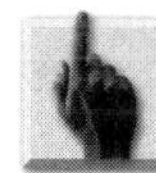

```
            lbURL.RemoveItem (lbURL.ListIndex)
        End If
    End Select
End Sub
```

The `Case 0` section handles the click event for the Add URL button. It verifies that the user actually typed something in the `txtURL` textbox, and then adds the contents of the textbox to the URL listbox. It then empties the contents of the `txtURL` textbox. The verification of the URL is handled during the breaking apart of the host name and filename.

`Case 1` handles the removal of any user-specified URLs. It verifies that a URL is actually highlighted and then removes it from the list.

The Reset Button

The Reset button performs the following functions:

- Clear the contents of the listboxes and textboxes
- Enable the Search button
- Cancel any page load the Webster control may be performing
- Set the status bar to "Ready"

Listing 14.3 contains the code for the `Click` event of the Reset button.

Listing 14.3. The `cmdReset_Click` event code.

```
Private Sub cmdReset_Click()
    txtURL.Text = ""
    lbURL.Clear
    txtKey.Text = ""
    lbAnchor.Clear
    lbFound.Clear
    cmdSearch.Enabled = True
    StatusBar1.SimpleText = "Ready"
    Webster1.Cancel
End Sub
```

The Search Button

The main program flow is handled through two events. After the user inputs the URLs and the keyword, the next step is to click on the Search button. The code for the `cmdSearch_Click` event is shown in Listing 14.4.

Listing 14.4. The `cmdSearch_Click` event.

```
Private Sub cmdSearch_Click()

Dim x As Integer
Dim URL_Index As Integer
Dim Anchor_Index, Last_Anchor_Index As Integer

'verify that we have at least one URL to search:
If lbURL.ListCount = 0 Then
    MsgBox "Please enter a URL into the URL Search List!"
    Exit Sub
End If

'verify that there's some text to search for:
If Len(Trim$(txtKey)) = 0 Then
    MsgBox "Please enter a search key into the Keyword text box!"
    Exit Sub
End If

'disable the search button
cmdSearch.Enabled = False

'clear any existing stuff:
lbAnchor.Clear
lbFound.Clear
If fPageLoaded% Then Webster1.DismissPage ""

'start retrival of user specified url's here
LBFlag = 0

For URL_Index = 0 To lbURL.ListCount - 1

    'select index here.
    lbURL.ListIndex = URL_Index

    StatusBar1.SimpleText = "Loading " & lbURL.Text
    Webster1.LoadPage lbURL.Text, False

    'wait till the page is loaded
    While Choose(Webster1.LoadStatus + 1, 0, 1, 1, 1, 1, 0, 0)
        DoEvents
    Wend

Next URL_Index

'ok, have anchors from user specified URL's now get those
LBFlag = 1

For Anchor_Index = 0 To lbAnchor.ListCount - 1

    'select index here.
    lbAnchor.ListIndex = Anchor_Index
    StatusBar1.SimpleText = "Loading " & lbAnchor.Text
    Webster1.LoadPage lbAnchor.Text, False

    'wait till the page is loaded
    While Choose(Webster1.LoadStatus + 1, 0, 1, 1, 1, 1, 0, 0)
        DoEvents
```

   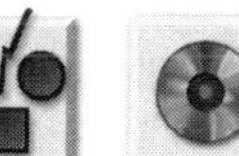

```
    Wend

Next Anchor_Index

'turn the search button back on
cmdSearch.Enabled = True
StatusBar1.SimpleText = "Ready"

End Sub
```

These first lines do a few essential tasks: First, you verify that the user has entered at least one URL to search as well as a string to search for. If either of these are missing, a message box is displayed and the routine exits. Next, you disable the Search button so the user doesn't keep clicking it. Because the response time varies from a few seconds to a few minutes depending on the number and which URLs are specified, you don't want the event fired more than once before the whole procedure is completed.

Next, the result listboxes (`lbAnchor` and `lbFound`) are cleared. If a page has previously been loaded, the Webster control is also cleared.

You then set the `LBFlag` (listbox flag) to zero. This is used in the Webster control's `LoadComplete` event to determine if the page that was just loaded was from the user-specified list (`lbURL`) or from the list of anchors that are retrieved from the user-specified URLs (`lbAnchor`).

The first loop (starting with the line `For URL_Index = 0 To lbURL.ListCount - 1`) loops through all the URLs the user entered using the Add URL button. The `ListIndex` property of the `lbURL` listbox is set to the current loop index. The status bar text is updated. Finally the page load is started by invoking the Webster control's `LoadPage` method. After the load is started, it's time to sit back and wait for the Webster control to finish loading the page. This is done with the `DoEvents` loop that immediately follows the `LoadPage` method.

The `While` loop condition contains a seldom-used Visual Basic function: `Choose()`. The syntax for `Choose()` is

```
Choose(index, choice-1[, choice-2, ... [,choice-n]])
```

The function returns a value from the list of choices based on the value of `index`. If `index` is 1, `Choose()` evaluates to the first choice in the list; if `index` is 2, it evaluates to the second choice, and so on. Note that if `index` is less than 1 or greater than the number of given choices, the function will return `Null`.

The `LoadStatus` property of the Webster control has the following possible values:

0	Page load is complete
1	Connecting to host
2	Connected, waiting
3	Page text is loading
4	Images are loading

5 Load failure
6 Unknown—URL failed to load

The application needs to wait until either the page has completely loaded (`LoadStatus = 0`) or some error condition has occurred (`LoadStatus = 5` or `LoadStatus = 6`). The expression `Choose(Webster1.LoadStatus + 1, 0, 1, 1, 1, 1, 0, 0)` returns the value `1` until either of these conditions are met. This keeps the `While` loop active. When either of the conditions is met, `Choose()` returns `0` and the code drops out of the loop.

After the `DoEvents` loop has been exited, the application loops to the next URL in the `lbURL` listbox and performs the above operations on that URL.

Part of the processing that's done while the above loop is loading pages is to fill the `lbAnchor` listbox with all the links found on the pages specified in `lbURL`. The next section of code in Listing 14.4 loads the URLs from the `lbAnchor` listbox.

The first step is to set the `LBFlag` (listbox flag) to `1`. This informs the `LoadComplete` event that it no longer needs to load the `lbAnchor` listbox with the links contained in the pages that get loaded.

Next, the application loops through all the URLs in the `lbAnchor` listbox. The code within the loop is identical to the code within the `lbURL` loop described above.

After the `lbAnchor` loop has completed, the Search button is turned back on and the status bar displays the Ready message. The application is now ready to begin a new search!

Parsing Loaded Pages

As pages are loaded by the loops described in the preceding section, the `LoadComplete` event is fired for the Webster control. This section describes the code of the `LoadComplete` event and demonstrates one of the more powerful features of the Webster control. The code for this event is given in Listing 14.5.

Listing 14.5. The `Webster1_LoadComplete` event.

```
Private Sub Webster1_LoadComplete(URL As String, ByVal Status As Integer)
    Dim i%, PageText$, lSize%

    fPageLoaded% = True

    'if search button is on, we're not searching
    ' so don't process the page
    If cmdSearch.Enabled Then Exit Sub

    'check to see whether we're loading
    ' a top level page or a subordinate
    If LBFlag = 0 Then      'top-level
        'fill the anchor list box with all
        ' the URLs on this page
```

```
        For i% = 0 To Webster1.GetLinkCount("") - 1
            URL$ = Webster1.GetLinkURL("", i%)
            If UCase$(Left$(URL$, 4)) = "HTTP" Then lbAnchor.AddItem URL$
        Next
    End If

    'Get the text on the page
    lSize% = Webster1.GetTextSize("")
    PageText$ = Webster1.GetText("", 0, lSize%)
    'If it matches the search string, add the URL
    'if the search string wasn't in the text,
    '  check the page title
    If InStr(UCase(PageText$), UCase(txtKey)) Then
        AddMatch (Webster1.PageURL)
    ElseIf InStr(UCase$(Webster1.PageTitle), UCase$(txtKey)) Then
        AddMatch (Webster1.PageURL)
    End If

End Sub
```

The event provides two parameters, `URL` and `Status`, both of which are ignored in this application. The code within the event will work regardless of the `Status` indicated.

The first line of code sets the `fPageLoaded%` flag to `True` to inform the rest of the application that at least one page has been loaded in the Webster control.

The next line of code checks to see whether the Search button is enabled. If the button is enabled, a search is not currently in progress and the code has no reason to parse the page's contents, so the routine exits.

The code next checks the value of the listbox flag, `LBFlag`, to determine whether the page just loaded should have any links it placed into the anchor's listbox (`lbAnchor`). If the value of this flag is `0`, then links are placed into the `lbAnchor` listbox. Otherwise, the code continues.

When the user-specified pages are being loaded (`LBFlag = 0`), any HTTP links found on those pages are placed into the `lbAnchor` listbox. The Webster control has a property named `GetLinkCount` that returns the number of links found on a specified page. Using an empty string as the parameter to the method as is done in Listing 14.5 returns the number of links for the currently loaded page. The control also provides an array of the URLs for these links. This array is accessed using the `GetLinkURL` property and specifying the parent URL (in this case, an empty string to specify the currently loaded page), and the index to retrieve from the array.

The `For...Next` loop iterates through all of the links on the page that was just loaded. Only the HTTP links are added to the `lbAnchor` listbox, though, because you'll be using the Webster control to load each of the URLs that gets added to that listbox.

After links are loaded, the procedure moves on to actually search the loaded page for the string the user entered into the `txtKey` textbox. The Webster control provides two methods that make this possible. First, determine the size of the text using the `GetTextSize` method. Again, providing an empty string as the parameter indicates that you're interested in the text size for the current page.

The method returns the size of the *pure* text contained on the page. Any characters contained within HTML tags or occurring outside the `<BODY>` tags are not considered pure text, and you're also not interested in searching them either. Once the size is determined, the `GetText` method is used to retrieve all the pure text from the current page. The code then uses the `Instr()` function to determine if the search string is contained within the text. If the search string is found, `AddMatch` is called to add the current URL to the found listbox (`lbFound`). If the string is not found within the text, the code checks for the string in the page's title. Again, if the search string is found, the URL is added to `lbFound` using `AddMatch`.

And that, finally, concludes the majority of our search engine.

Viewing Pages

Another feature of the Web Search Tool is that it allows you to load any of the URLs from any of the listboxes into the Webster browser. If a search is not in progress, you can double-click a URL in any of the listboxes and it will be loaded by the Webster control. The code to make this happen is contained in Listing 14.6 but doesn't bear much explanation.

Also, because the Webster control allows the user to click on hypertext links and load the page the link points to, you'll want to disable this feature while a search is in progress. The best way to do this is by using the Webster control's `DoClickURL` event. Setting the `Cancel` parameter to `True` within the event's code is done if the Search button is disabled, you prevent the Webster control from loading the page pointed to by the URL that was clicked. Although not applicable for this application, this event can also be used to trap URLs that you want to prevent the user from accessing.

Listing 14.6 Code to load pages from the listboxes.

```
Private Sub lbURL_DblClick()
    If cmdSearch.Enabled Then Webster1.LoadPage lbURL.Text, False
End Sub

Private Sub lbAnchor_DblClick()
    If cmdSearch.Enabled Then Webster1.LoadPage lbAnchor.Text, False
End Sub

Private Sub lbFound_DblClick()
    If cmdSearch.Enabled Then Webster1.LoadPage lbFound.Text, False
End Sub
```

```
Private Sub Webster1_DoClickURL(SelectedURL As String, Cancel As Boolean)

    'if the search button is off, don't allow clicks
    '  (the program is still searching)
    If Not (cmdSearch.Enabled) Then Cancel = True

End Sub
```

Testing the Application

This application is simple to test. After all the code is entered or copied from the CD-ROM, run the application. Make sure you have either an active Internet connection or have a Web server running locally.

NOTE:

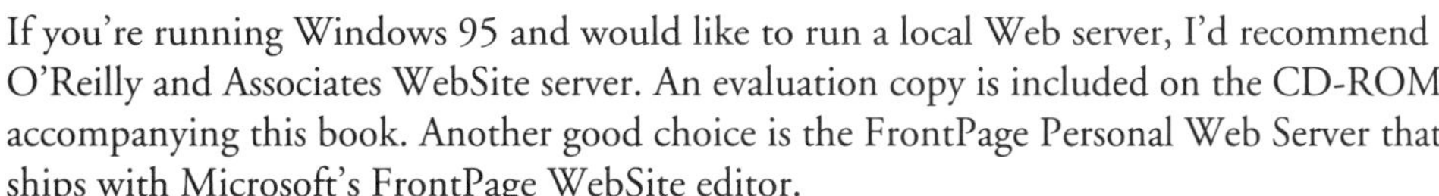

If you're running Windows 95 and would like to run a local Web server, I'd recommend O'Reilly and Associates WebSite server. An evaluation copy is included on the CD-ROM accompanying this book. Another good choice is the FrontPage Personal Web Server that ships with Microsoft's FrontPage WebSite editor.

Enter a URL into the URL To Add textbox and click the Add URL button. Next, enter a string to search for on the page specified by the URL.

Click the Search button and watch the action. You should see the page you specified load into the Webster browser. Then, if there are any links on that page, the Anchor List Box is filled with them and each page is loaded and searched. The URLs for any pages with matches are added to the Matched URLs listbox.

Once the search is completed (the Search button turns back on), you can double-click any of the URLs to load the page into the Webster control. Then, use the Webster browser just like any other Web browser to surf to your heart's content.

For example, Figure 14.3 shows the results of searching the URL `http://www.infi.net` for the string `cool`. After the search filled the listboxes, I double-clicked the URL in the URL Search List box to reload the starting page into the Webster control.

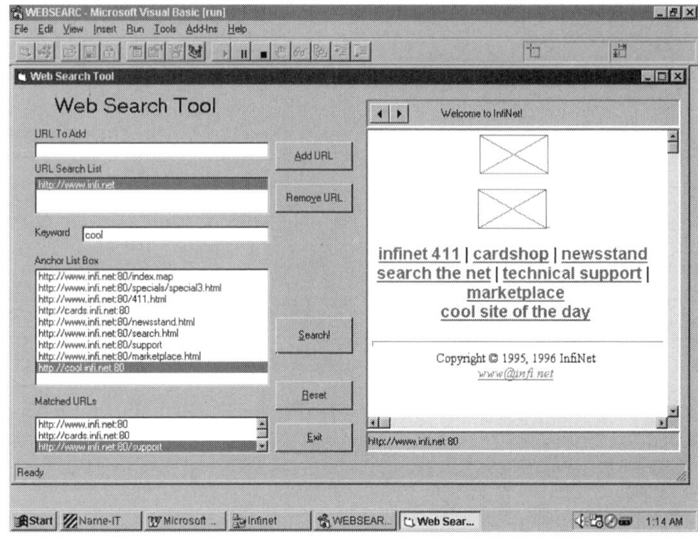

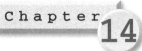

Figure 14.3.
The Web Search Tool in action.

Other Directions

This sample application is not meant to be a fire-and-forget solution for searching the Web. Quite a few areas could be pursued, and I leave a few suggestions—ideas you can add.

- `Robots.txt` support—This would allow you to target any server and find out whether it permits robots (such as this one) and what directories are off-limits (see Chapter 11, "A Brief Introduction to Web Spiders and Agents").
- Merciful timing—As discussed in Chapter 12, you should not rapid fire requests to servers. This may or may not happen during the execution of this sample application depending on the URLs you specify and the links contained within those URLs.
- Recursion—Add the functionality to dig as deep as you want. This application recurs the users' specified links and the links within those pages. Without too much effort, you could add a textbox that takes a number, and instructs the program to search that many levels deep into the user-specified URL's anchors.
- Ranked searching—Add the ability to perform Soundex and other types of searches so that matches can be made based on criteria other than just finding the exact text within the document. Note that this is a very advanced topic but mastery of such a searching mechanism can have very high rewards.

Summary

From here you go on to a client-side application (Chapter 15, "LinkChecker: A Spider that Checks for Broken Links") that verifies all of the local links within the page. The Web Search and Link Checker chapters are very similar and share quite a bit of code. With a knowledge of how the processes work, you can expand the ideas presented in this and the next chapter to your own applications.

Chapter

15

LinkChecker: A Spider that Checks for Broken Links

If I had a dime for each `404 Not Found`, `This page has moved to http://www.new-and-better.com`, or simply, `This URL does not have a DNS entry` message, I'd be sipping rum on a beach in St. Thomas instead of writing this book.

One of the problems people have with the Web is the so-called *invalid link*. This crops up in search engines where the links are out of date, in user home pages that list a thousand "cool" sites (and the maintainer never checks them more than once), or other sources of external links.

When you add a link to a page maintained by someone else, that person has no idea that you've added a link. Therefore, when the other site moves, its author/administrator can't be expected to notify everyone with such links to inform them of the page's new location.

And because it's not uncommon for a site to change servers, the invalid link message is very prevalent, and for the foreseeable future, it's here to stay.

This chapter presents a Windows client tool that verifies links of a specified URL. Given a URL, this program verifies that all the hyperlinked URLs actually exist on the Web.

So, first let's look at the different types of invalid links that exist.

Bad Links

So far, I've been generically calling "invalid links" all links that don't take us where we want to go. This is because for each time I typed "invalid links," I didn't want to go through this list. The following are the types of invalid links and what could cause them:

1. The `Unable to locate the Server` error—This most often happens when a host name is mistyped in the browser URL field. Figure 15.1 shows what happens when the browser goes to resolve the DNS name and no entry is found for the host name.
2. `File Not Found`—This error occurs when the host name is OK, but the filename or directory contained in the URL doesn't exist. The server replies with a small page that looks like Figure 15.2.
3. `This link has moved`—This error is perhaps the most difficult to diagnose. The requested host and file both exist, but the error serves as a pointer to a new location. The syntax involved in the HTML code for a `This link has changed` situation is not standard—usually just a brief explanation and a hypertext link to the new page.

With these conditions in mind, you can write a simple Visual Basic application that takes a root URL and checks the links on the page. You can also make sure that the referenced images are present.

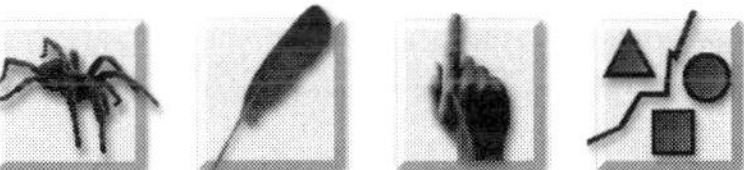

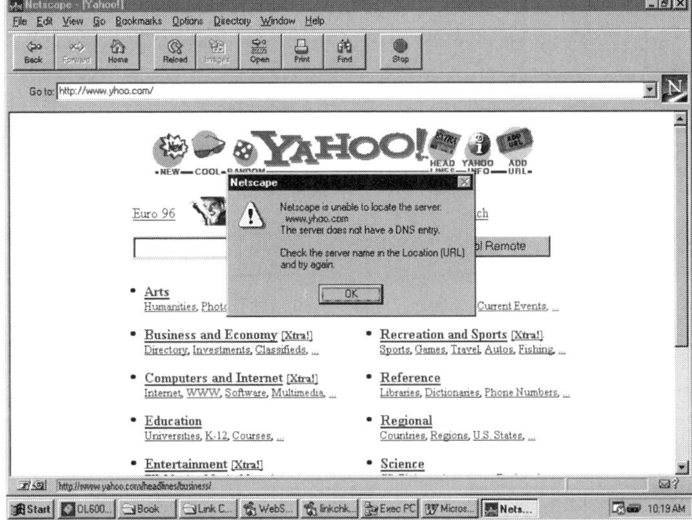

Figure 15.1.
Unable to Locate Server error in Netscape.

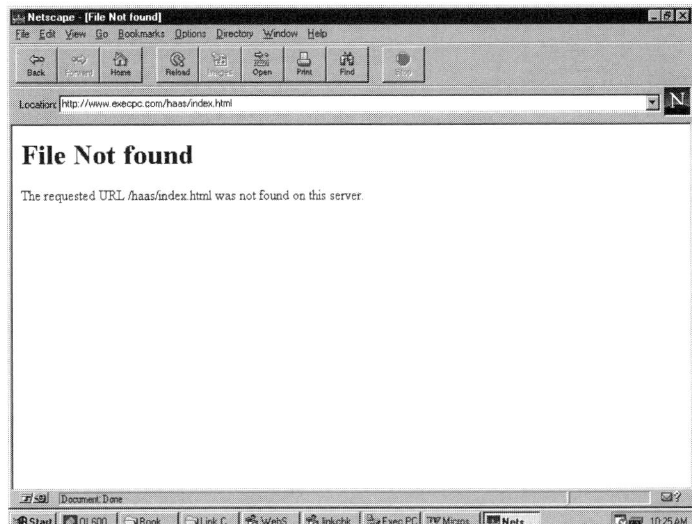

Figure 15.2.
File Not Found error.

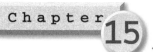

Figure 15.3.
This link has moved.

Designing the LinkChecker Application

The usual flow of the application would look like this: The user enters a URL to validate. The app loads that URL into a Sax Webster control (first described in Chapter 4, "Using Web Browser Custom Controls") and parses all of its anchors using the control's `GetLinkCount` and `GetLinkURL` methods as described in Chapter 14, "WebSearcher: A Simple Search Tool." Then the Microsoft Internet Control Pack's HTTP client control is used to retrieve the HTTP header information for the anchors (see Chapter 2, "HTTP: How to Speak on the Web," for information on HTTP messages, and Chapter 5, "Retrieving Information from the Web," for information on the HTTP client control).

If you don't have access to the Sax Webster control, there's a short section at the end of this chapter describing how to accomplish the link checking using the Microsoft Internet Control Pack's HTML control (also introduced in Chapter 4). Using the Microsoft control requires a good deal more code, so this chapter only describes how to modify the Webster-based code to work with the Microsoft control.

Each response received by the HTTP client control is then checked for the previously listed error conditions, and if present, the URL should be marked as not valid. If a valid HTTP header information response is received for the link, the link is marked as valid. Also, if the Web server associated with the link provides the Last-Modified HTTP response header field, the field's value is displayed in the grid.

NOTE:

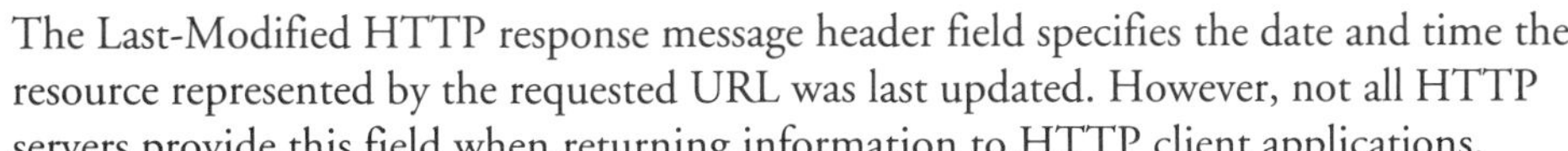

The Last-Modified HTTP response message header field specifies the date and time the resource represented by the requested URL was last updated. However, not all HTTP servers provide this field when returning information to HTTP client applications.

You'll also want the user to be able to specify whether to check only links local to that site or all links referenced within the page. You add this functionality via a frame and two option buttons.

The form has a tab control (see Figures 15.4 and 15.5) that allows the user to select either Link View or Web View: The Link View is where the grid is placed; the Web View is where the Webster control is placed. There is also a checkbox on the Web View to enable and disable loading of embedded images by the Webster control. By turning the load images off, the page to be verified will load faster.

Designing the User Interface

The final result of this section is shown in Figure 15.4, which shows the Link View tab, and Figure 15.5, which shows the Web View tab. Most of the controls use the default properties, but a few have their properties modified to meet the needs of this application.

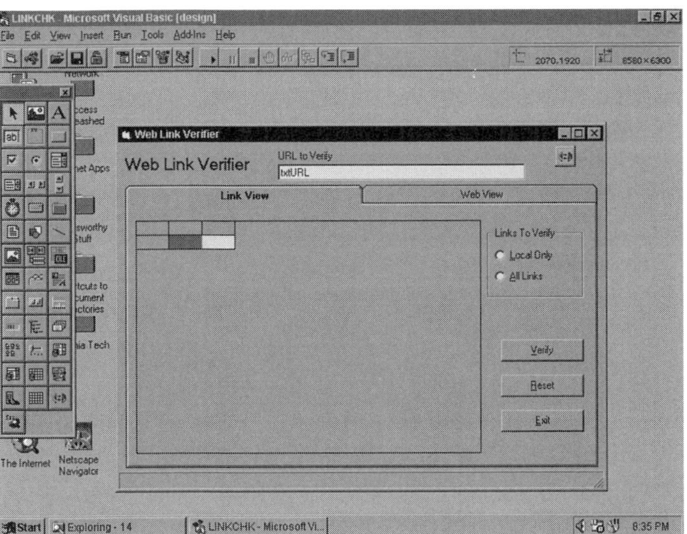

Figure 15.4.

Design-time view of the Link View tab.

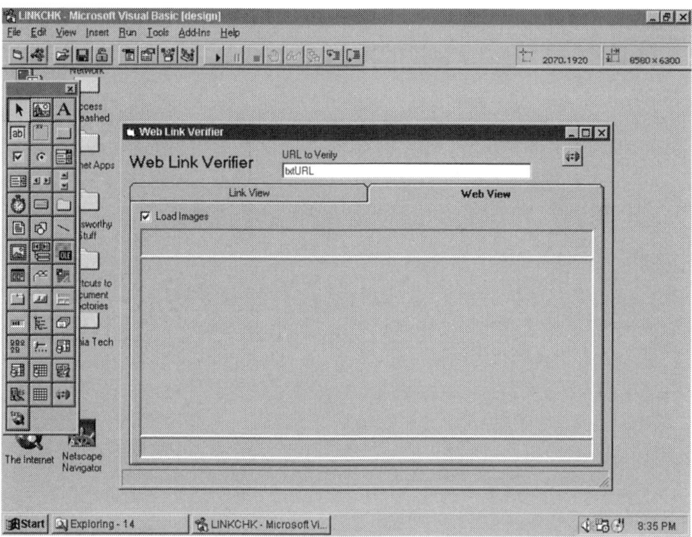

Figure 15.5.
Design-time view of the Web View tab.

http://www.microsoft.com/icp

Start a new project in Visual Basic. View the currently available custom controls by selecting the Tools | Custom Controls menu item. This project requires the following controls be included in the list:

- Microsoft Grid Control (GRID32.OCX)
- Microsoft HTTP Client Control (HTTPCT.OCX)—this is available in the Microsoft Internet Control Pack (ICP) discussed in Chapter 5. The ICP is available on the Web at `http://www.microsoft.com/icp`.
- Microsoft Windows Common Controls (COMCTL32.OCX)
- Sax Webster Control (WEBSTER.OCX)
- Sheridan Tabbed Dialog Control (TABCTL32.OCX)

All controls except the Webster control and the HTTP client control ship with the Visual Basic Professional Edition. After you add the controls, you must also add a reference to the Microsoft Internet Support Objects. Use the Tools | References menu and select this item in the list. If it is not in the listbox, click the Browse button and locate the file `NMOCOD.DLL`. If you can't find this file on your system, you probably need to re-install the Microsoft Internet Control Pack.

Once the proper controls have been added to the project, you can begin to populate the form. To create the controls directly on the form, follow these steps:

1. Add a label to the top-left corner and give it a `Caption` of `Web Link Verifier`. Set its `FontSize` to `13.5` and its `BackStyle` to `0` (transparent).

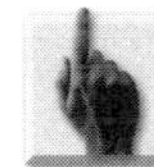

2. Add the label for the URL textbox near the top-center of the form. Set its `Caption` to `URL to Verify` and its `BackStyle` to `0`.
3. Add a textbox below this label. Set its `Name` to `txtURL`.
4. Add the HTTP client control. It's not visible at runtime, so it can be placed anywhere. In Figure 15.4 and 15.5 it's in the top-left corner. Set its `Method` property to `2` (HEAD method). The default control name, `HTTP1`, is used in the code. If this is not the name provided as the default, change the control's `Name` property to `HTTP1`.
5. Add a StatusBar control. Set `Align` to `2` (align bottom) and `Style` to `1` (single pane simple text). The control's name should default to `StatusBar1`. If it doesn't, change it so that it matches the code.
6. Add an SSTab control above the status bar control. Size it similar to what's shown in Figure 15.4. Set its `Tabs` and `TabsPerRow` properties to `2`. Select `Custom` on the VB Properties window and click the button with the ellipses to access the tab control's custom properties page (shown in Figure 15.6). On the General tab, enter `Link View` as the `TabCaption` for tab 0. Click the button with the ">" symbol to change the current tab to 1. Enter `Web View` as the caption and click the OK button. Again, the default name should be `SSTab1`. If it's not, change the control's `Name` property to `SSTab1`.

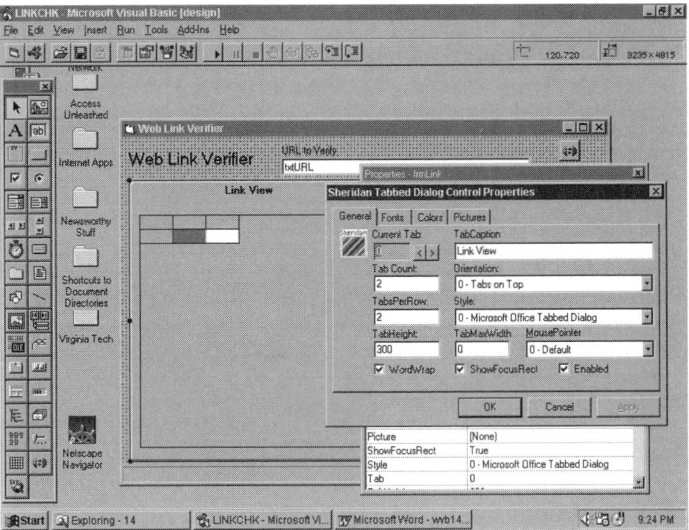

Figure 15.6.
The SSTab control's custom properties page.

Now that the form's shell has been created, it's time to add controls to the tabs. Bring the tab back to the Link View by clicking on its tab caption. Refer to Figure 15.4 for control placement. Follow these steps to add the controls for this tab:

1. Add the Verify command button. Set its `Caption` to `&Verify`. Set its name to `cmdVerify`. Because you don't want the user to be able to start a verification without a URL entered in `txtURL`, set the button's `Enabled` property to `False`.

2. Add the Reset button. Set its `Caption` to `&Reset`. Set its name to `cmdMain`.
3. Add the Exit button by copying and pasting the Reset button. When asked by Visual Basic if you wish to create a control array, answer Yes. Set the new button's `Caption` to `&Exit`.
4. Add the Microsoft grid control. Set its `Cols` property to `3`. Leave the rest of its properties set at their default values. The `Name` property should be `Grid1`.
5. Add the frame that appears above the command buttons. Set its `Caption` to `Links To Verify`. The default name, `Frame1`, should be used.
6. Add an option button to the frame. Set its `Name` to `optLocal` and its `Caption` to `&Local Only`.
7. Copy and paste the option button to the frame, below the first. Answer Yes when asked to create a control array. Set the new option button's `Caption` to `&All Links`.

You're almost there. Click the Web View tab caption to move to the other tab. To add the controls, refer to Figure 15.5 and follow these steps:

1. Add a CheckBox control. Assign `chkImages` to its `Name` property. Set `Value` to `1` and its `Caption` to `Load &Images`.
2. Add a Webster control and size it to fill most of the tab. Change the `PagesToCache` property to `1` and the `HomePage` property to an empty string. The `Name` should default to `Webster1` but if not, change the `Name` property to `Webster1`.

Now that the controls are in place, it's time to start entering some code. The next section covers all the code necessary to make the Link Verifier work.

Coding the Application

The task of this application is to retrieve the user-specified URL, gather all the anchors out of that page, add those anchors to the grid, and then for each URL in the grid, attempt to retrieve the HTTP header information. Finally, the app marks the URL verified or not verified accordingly.

A lot of the code here is also used in Chapter 14. The linkchecker, as you will see, is a customized version of the Web search tool. There, instead of looking for the invalid link conditions, you look for a user-specified keyword.

The `Declarations` Section

The `Declarations` section contains the following code:

```
Option Explicit

Dim Conn_Done As Integer
Dim Grid_Pos as Integer
```

The `Conn_Done` variable is a flag used by the HTTP control to signal the end of an HTTP request. The `Grid_Pos` variable stores the row in the grid where the next URL checked will be inserted.

The AddAnchor Subroutine

The `AddAnchor` subroutine is used to add URLs to the grid control. The routine goes through the grid row by row, making sure that the URL to be added doesn't already exist. If the URL doesn't exist in the grid, the routine adds it to the grid. The code is shown in Listing 15.1.

Listing 15.1. `AddAnchor` subroutine.

```
Sub AddAnchor(sNewAnchor As String)
Dim X As Integer
For X = 1 To Grid_Pos
    Grid1.Row = X
    Grid1.Col = 0
    If Grid1.Text = sNewAnchor Then
        Exit Sub
    End If
Next X

Grid1.AddItem sNewAnchor
Grid_Pos = Grid_Pos + 1
End Sub
```

The GetHostFromURL Function

This routine was first introduced in Chapter 5. It is taken from the dsWeb sample that ships with the Dolphin Systems `dsSocket` control discussed in that chapter. The function is used to parse the host name from a URL. The function depends on the URL being valid. If the URL is invalid, it returns an empty string.

The `GetHostFromURL()` function (see Listing 15.2) retrieves the host name from the URL. The host name is the portion of the URL that occurs between the "//" and the first "/" characters. If the "//" is not present, `GetHostFromURL()` considers the URL to be invalid and returns an empty string.

Listing 15.2. `GetHostFromURL() Function.` z

```
Private Function GetHostFromURL(szURL As String) As String
    '   parse out the hostname from a valid URL
    '   the URL should be of the format: http://www.microsoft.com/index.html
    '   the returned hostname would then be: www.microsoft.com

    Dim szHost      As String
    Dim lPos%
```

continues

Listing 15.2. continued

```
    szHost = szURL
    '   invalid URL
    If InStr(szHost, "//") = 0 Then
        GetHostFromURL = ""
        Exit Function
    End If
    szHost = Mid(szHost, InStr(szHost, "//") + 2)
    lPos% = InStr(szHost, "/")
    If lPos% = 0 Then
        GetHostFromURL = szHost
        Exit Function
    Else
        GetHostFromURL = Left(szHost, lPos% - 1)
        Exit Function
    End If
End Function
```

The Form_Load Event

The Form_Load event is where you take care of all the startup activity for the application. The code is provided in Listing 15.3.

The grid format is set up, including column widths and captions. Then the local only option button is selected as the default. Finally, the Reset command button's Click event is fired.

Listing 15.3. Form_Load event code.

```
Private Sub Form_Load()

    'Set up grid headers
    Grid1.Row = 0
    Grid1.Col = 0
    Grid1.Text = "URL"
    Grid1.ColWidth(0) = 5000
    Grid1.Col = 1
    Grid1.Text = "Verified?"
    Grid1.ColWidth(1) = 900
    Grid1.Col = 2
    Grid1.Text = "Updated"
    Grid1.ColWidth(2) = 1200

    optLocal(0).Value = True

    Call cmdMain_Click(0)

End Sub
```

User Interface Support Subroutines

There are two routines that provide some simple user interface functionality. The first, `GridClear`, clears the grid in preparation for a new verification. The second, `ToggleControls`, enables and disables some of the controls on the form based on the `pState%` flag that is passed as a parameter. The code for both routines is in Listing 15.4.

Listing 15.4. `GridClear` and `ToggleControls` Subroutines.

```
Public Sub GridClear()
    Dim X

    For X = 1 To Grid_Pos - 1
        Grid1.RemoveItem 1
    Next

    Grid1.Row = 1
    For X = 0 To 2
        Grid1.Col = X
        Grid1.Text = ""
    Next
    Grid_Pos = 1

End Sub

Public Sub ToggleControls(pState%)

    Frame1.Enabled = pState%
    cmdVerify.Enabled = pState%
    Me.MousePointer = IIf(pState%, vbDefault, vbHourglass)
    If pState% = False Then SSTab1.Tab = 0
    SSTab1.Enabled = pState%

End Sub
```

The code behind the textbox and the load images checkbox is equally straightforward. The code for these two controls is provided in Listing 15.5.

When the text entered into the `txtURL` textbox changes, the code application sets the `Enabled` property of the `cmdVerify` command button to `True` if there are any characters in the textbox. It is set to `False` otherwise.

The `chkImages` checkbox merely changes the value of the Webster control's `LoadImages` property based on whether or not the checkbox is checked.

Listing 15.5. Code for `txtURL` and `chkImages`.

```
Private Sub txtUrl_Change()

    cmdVerify.Enabled = (Len(Trim$(txtUrl)) > 0)

End Sub

Private Sub chkImages_Click()

    Webster1.LoadImages = chkImages.Value

End Sub
```

The cmdMain Command Buttons

For ease of explanation, I put the Exit and Reset buttons in one control array, and left the Verify button on its own. The code for the `Click` event of the Reset/Exit button control array is found in Listing 15.6.

There's nothing too special about this code—all you want to do is allow the user to clear the results by pressing the Reset button. This clears the form-level variables, as well as the URL textbox and the results grid. It also cancels the Webster control's page load, if one is in progress.

The Exit button simply unloads the form, causing the application to end.

Listing 15.6. The `cmdMain_Click` event code.

```
Private Sub cmdMain_Click(Index As Integer)

    Select Case Index
        Case 0      'Reset
            txtUrl.Text = ""
            Webster1.Cancel
            GridClear
            StatusBar1.SimpleText = "Ready..."

        Case 1      'Exit
            Unload Me

    End Select

End Sub
```

The cmdVerify Code

When the user enters a URL into `txtURL` and clicks on the Verify button, it's time for the real action to begin. The `cmdVerify_Click` event is where the action gets kicked off, as you'll see.

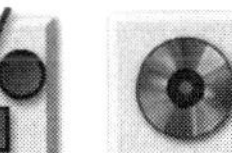

The code for the event is given in Listing 15.7. The first few lines of code clear the grid and disable some of the buttons and the tab control. Then the host name of the machine on which the URL entered resides is extracted from the URL by calling `GetHostFromURL()`. Next, the status bar caption is updated to reflect the page being loaded.

The Webster control's `LoadPage` method is used to load the URL to be verified. The Visual Basic `Choose()` function is used as the switch for a `DoEvents` loop. This function was discussed in detail in Chapter 14, but basically, the value returned is the value from the list provided that corresponds to the integer value of the first parameter. In this case, the value returned will be based on the current value of the Webster control's `LoadStatus` property each time through the loop. The loop continues until either the URL is completely loaded or an error occurs.

After the loop finishes, the URL is entered into the grid. If an error occurred while loading the URL (`LoadStatus >= 5`), the `Verified?` column in the grid is set to `No` and the routine exits.

If the URL was loaded successfully, the `Verified?` column in the grid is set to `Yes` and the routine proceeds to extract all the links from the page. This is accomplished using the Webster control's `GetLinkCount` and `GetLinkURL` methods. These methods allow you to iterate through a list of all the links found on the loaded Web page. The code checks to make sure a link is an HTTP link (as opposed to a `mailto:` or `news:` link, for example, which aren't accessed using the HTTP protocol and therefore can't be verified by this application). If it is an HTTP link and the user has selected the Local Links only option button (`optLocal(0).Value = True`), the code further checks to make sure the link is to a URL on the same host as the URL being verified. If it is, the link is added to the grid using `AddAnchor`. If `optLocal(0).Value = False`, then the URL is automatically added to the grid.

After all the links on the page being verified are added to the grid, the HTTP client control is used to retrieve the header information for each of the links in the grid. The original URL is also checked again, but this time to retrieve the HTTP header fields for the URL since the Webster control doesn't provide properties for most of them (it does provide properties for the Content-Type and Content-Size headers).

The code loops through each item in the grid, using the variable `Grid_Pos` as the count of the number of rows in the grid. The `Conn_Done` variable is used as a flag to indicate that the current header information request has completed. In `cmdVerify_Click` the flag is set to `0`. The flag is set to `1` within the `HTTP1_DocOutput` event discussed in the next section. The URL is extracted from the grid, the status bar is updated, the URL is assigned to the HTTP control's `URL` property, and finally the HTTP control's `GetDoc` method is invoked to retrieve the header information (recall that the HTTP control's `Method` property is set to `2` (HEAD method) at design time). Another `DoEvents` loop waits until `Conn_Done` is set before continuing to the next URL in the grid.

After all the URLs have been processed, the command buttons and tab are enabled once again, allowing the user to enter another URL to verify or to use Webster control to view the URL entered in `txtURL`.

Listing 15.7. The `cmdVerify_Click` event code.

```
Private Sub cmdVerify_Click()

    Dim lHostName$, i%, URL$, X

    GridClear
    ToggleControls False

    lHostName$ = GetHostFromURL(txtUrl.Text)

    StatusBar1.SimpleText = "Loading " & txtUrl.Text
    Webster1.LoadPage txtUrl.Text, False

    'wait till the page is loaded
    While Choose(Webster1.LoadStatus + 1, 0, 1, 1, 1, 1, 0, 0)
        DoEvents
    Wend

    Grid1.Row = 1
    Grid1.Col = 0
    Grid1.Text = txtUrl.Text
    'if an error occurred loading the page,
    ' add it to the grid and exit
    If (Webster1.LoadStatus >= 5) Then
        Grid1.Col = 1
        Grid1.Text = "No"
        ToggleControls True
        Exit Sub
    End If

    'add this link to the grid as verified:
    Grid1.Col = 1
    Grid1.Text = "Yes"

    'now get all of the links on the page:
    For i% = 0 To Webster1.GetLinkCount("") - 1
        URL$ = Webster1.GetLinkURL("", i%)
        'is it an HTTP link?
        If UCase$(Left$(URL$, 4)) = "HTTP" Then
            'are we verifying only local links?
            If optLocal(0).Value = True Then
                If InStr(UCase$(URL$), "HTTP://" & UCase$(lHostName$)) Then
                    AddAnchor URL$
                End If
            Else
                AddAnchor URL$
            End If
        End If
    Next

For X = 1 To Grid_Pos

    Conn_Done = 0
    Grid1.Row = X
    Grid1.Col = 0

    StatusBar1.SimpleText = "Loading " & Grid1.Text
```

```
    HTTP1.URL = Grid1.Text
    HTTP1.GetDoc

    While Conn_Done = 0
        DoEvents
    Wend

Next X

ToggleControls True

End Sub
```

The HTTP Client Control's Event Code

The responses to the HEAD request messages generated in `cmdVerify` (described in the previous section) are handled by the HTTP control's `DocOutput` and `Error` events. The code for these events is given in Listing 15.8.

The `DocOutput` event (described in detail in Chapter 5) is fired whenever the HTTP control receives data from the HTTP server it's connected to. This data can be in the form of HTTP header fields such as Content-Type or Server (these are discussed in Chapter 2) or content data (such as the HTML markup code or an image file). The event is also fired at the start and end of a received message and in the event of an error. The event provides a parameter named `DocOutput` which is an object containing all the information about the received message. The object's `State` property indicates the reason that the `DocOutput` event was fired and is used in a `Select Case` construct to determine what course of action to take.

The available states are:

`icDocHeaders`	HTTP header fields have been received
`icDocBegin`	Retrieval started
`icDocEnd`	Retrieval ended
`icDocData`	Content data is being received
`icDocError`	An error has occurred

Because you're not interested in knowing when the retrieval starts or what the content data looks like (there shouldn't be any content data returned because the request message used the `HEAD` method), these two states have no code associated with them in Listing 15.8.

The `icDocHeaders` state is entered whenever all the HTTP response message header fields have been received. The `DocOutput` object provides a collection aptly named `Headers`, which contains all the header fields received. The `Headers` collection has a `Count` property and an `Items` collection. There is one entry in the `Items` collection for each header field received. Each item has a `Name` and a `Value` property. You're going to be displaying only the Last-Modified header, so the code loops through all the available header fields (there won't be more than a few). If the Last-Modified header is found, its value is placed in the Updated column of the grid.

The `icDocEnd` state is entered when the connection with the Web server terminates. If the `Conn_Done` flag was not previously set by an error condition, the code marks the current URL as verified and sets the `Conn_Done` flag to signal the end of the verification process for the current URL. Note that even if an error such as `URL not located` occurs, the `icDocEnd` state is still entered

The `icDocError` state is entered whenever an HTTP server returns an error code. The application places the HTTP control's `ReplyCode` property (the error code received from the HTTP server) into the status bar, marks the current URL as not verified, and marks the end of the verification for this URL by setting `Conn_Done` to `1`.

The `Error` event is fired whenever an error occurs that causes the HTTP request/response messages to be invalid. This event is handled the same way as the `icDocError` state discussed in the previous paragraph.

Listing 15.8. The HTTP control's event code.

```
Private Sub HTTP1_DocOutput(ByVal DocOutput As DocOutput)
    Dim i%
    Select Case DocOutput.State
    Case icDocHeaders
        With DocOutput.Headers
            For i% = 1 To .Count
                If .Item(i%).Name = "Last-Modified" Then
                    Grid1.Col = 2
                    Grid1.Text = .Item(i%).Value
                End If
            Next
        End With

    Case icDocBegin

    Case icDocEnd
        'if the done flag is already set, exit:
        If Conn_Done Then Exit Sub

        StatusBar1.SimpleText = "Done... "
        Grid1.Col = 1
        Grid1.Text = "Yes"
        Conn_Done = 1

    Case icDocData

    Case icDocError
        'if the URL doesn't exit, we'll get an error...
        StatusBar1.SimpleText = "Reply Code: " & HTTP1.ReplyCode
        Grid1.Col = 1
        Grid1.Text = "No"
        Conn_Done = 1

    End Select
```

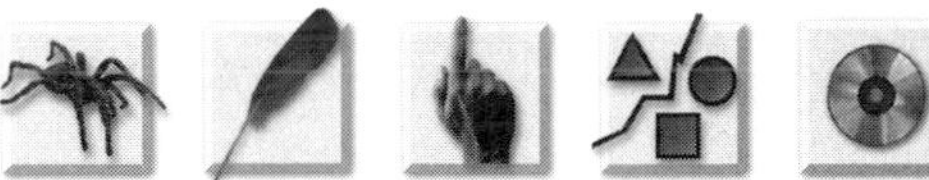

```
End Sub

Private Sub HTTP1_Error(Number As Integer, Description As String, Scode As Long,
➥Source As String, HelpFile As String, HelpContext As Long, CancelDisplay As Boolean)

    Conn_Done = 1
    Grid1.Col = 1
    Grid1.Text = "No"

End Sub
```

Testing The Application

Now that all the code is entered, it's time to test the application. Either connect to the Internet or start a local Web server, and then run the application. Enter a URL in the `txtURL` textbox and click the Verify button. You should see the status bar indicate the page being loaded, then the grid fills with all the local links on the page you specified. Finally, all of those links are checked and the status bar is updated as each link is checked.

Figure 15.7 shows the application after it was run against a local Web server using the default Web page (note that no filename is specified in the URL textbox, only the server name). I selected All Links in the Links To Verify frame in order to show the two external links as not verified (the machine was not connected to the Internet at the time the verification was performed).

Figure 15.8 shows the application after it was run against a server that provides the Last-Modified HTTP header field. I re-sized the columns at runtime in order to display all three columns on-screen.

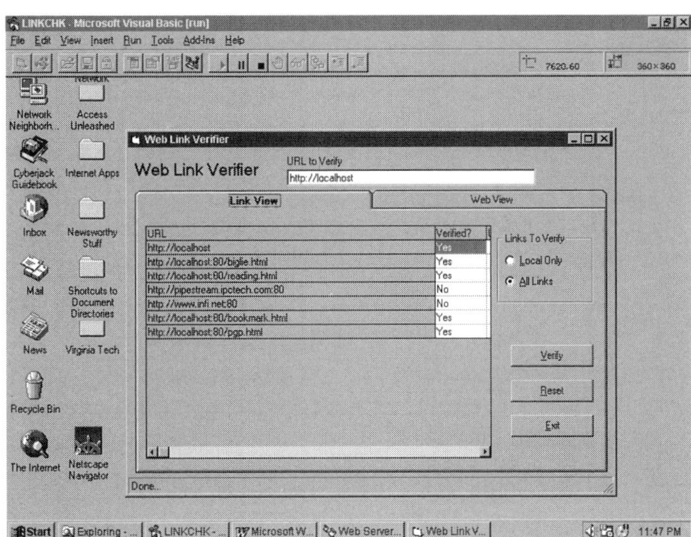

Figure 15.7.
Verifying a local server.

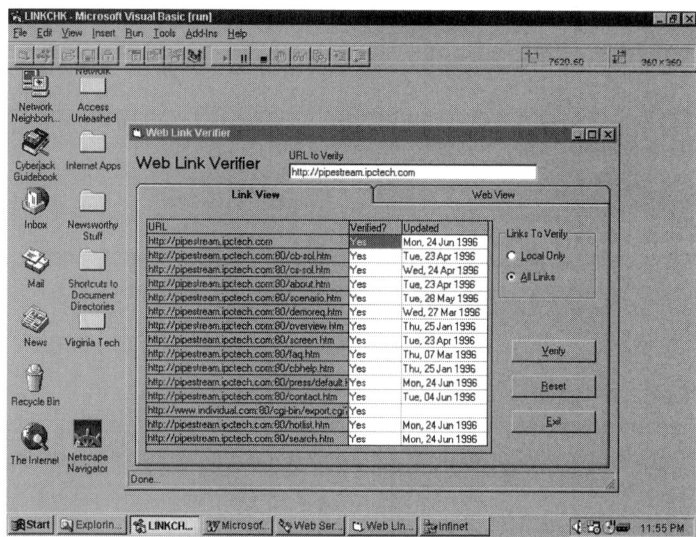

Figure 15.8.

Verifying on a server that provides Last-Modified.

Using the Microsoft HTML Control

If you don't wish to use the Sax Webster control, or if you're looking for a programming challenge to wind up this book, rewrite the application using the Microsoft Internet Control Pack's HTML client control.

NOTE:

If you have the Webster control and are modifying the project created above, you must remove the Webster control from the new project. For some reason, if both controls are in the project, the Microsoft HTML control is unable to connect to an HTTP server.

The Microsoft control lacks the `GetLinkCount()` and `GetLinkURL()` methods provided by the Webster control but makes up for this by providing an event named `DoNewElement`. If the control's `ElemNotification` property is set to `True`, this event is fired for each new HTML element parsed as the page to be verified is loaded. You can check the event's `ElemType` parameter to determine if the element is a link anchor (in which case `ElemType` will be `A`) and if it is, use a modified `AddAnchor` procedure to add the link to the grid control. `AddAnchor` must be modified because the HTML control does not resolve relative URLs to the absolute URLs that are necessary for the HTTP control. I'll leave these modifications to you as a code challenge.

Sample code for the `DoNewElement` event is provided in Listing 15.9. Chapter 4 and the Internet Control Pack's help file describe this event and its parameters in more detail.

Listing 15.9. Sample `DoNewElement` event code.

```
Private Sub HTML1_DoNewElement(ByVal ElemType As String, _
        ByVal EndTag As Boolean, ByVal Attrs As HTMLAttrs, _
        ByVal Text As String, EnableDefault As Boolean)
    Dim i%
    'is this a link anchor?
    If UCase$(ElemType) = "A" Then
        'yes, find the HREF element:
        For i% = 1 To Attrs.Count
            If UCase$(Attrs.Item(i%).Name) = "HREF" Then
                AddAnchor Attrs.Item(i%).Value
            End If
        Next
    End If

End Sub
```

NOTE:

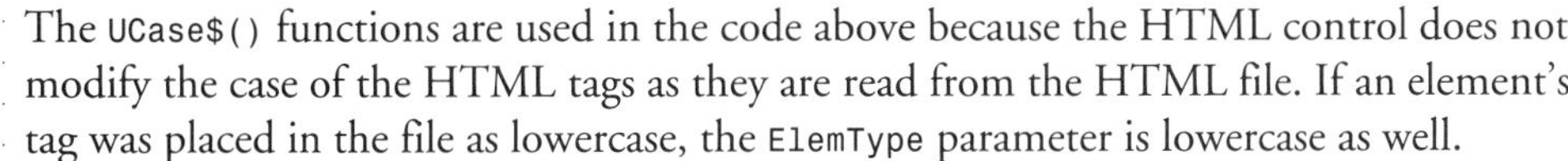

The `UCase$()` functions are used in the code above because the HTML control does not modify the case of the HTML tags as they are read from the HTML file. If an element's tag was placed in the file as lowercase, the `ElemType` parameter is lowercase as well.

You will also have to modify the code for `cmdVerify_Click` to use the HTML control to load the initial page. You should use the `Conn_Done` flag to signal the end of the page load by placing `Conn_Done = 1` in the HTML control's `EndRetrieval` event and `Conn_Done = -1` in the control's `Error` and `Timeout` events. Sample code for `cmdVerify_Click` is provided in Listing 15.10.

Listing 15.10. Sample `cmdVerify_Click` code.

```
Private Sub cmdVerify_Click()

    Dim lHostName$, i%, URL$, X

    GridClear
    ToggleControls False

    lHostName$ = GetHostFromURL(txtUrl.Text)

    StatusBar1.SimpleText = "Loading " & txtUrl.Text
    Conn_Done = 0
    HTML1.ElemNotification = True
    HTML1.RequestDoc txtURL.Text

    'wait till the page is loaded
    While Conn_Done = 0
        DoEvents
    Wend
```

continues

Listing 15.10. continued

```
    Grid1.Row = 1
    Grid1.Col = 0
    Grid1.Text = txtUrl.Text
    'if an error occurred loading the page,
    ' add it to the grid and exit
    If (Conn_Done = -1) Then
        Grid1.Col = 1
        Grid1.Text = "No"
        ToggleControls True
        Exit Sub
    End If

    'add this link to the grid as verified:
    Grid1.Col = 1
    Grid1.Text = "Yes"

    'now check all the links in the grid
    For X = 1 To Grid_Pos

        Conn_Done = 0
        Grid1.Row = X
        Grid1.Col = 0

        StatusBar1.SimpleText = "Loading " & Grid1.Text

        HTTP1.URL = Grid1.Text
        HTTP1.GetDoc

        While Conn_Done = 0
            DoEvents
        Wend

    Next X

ToggleControls True

End Sub
```

The last major change you'll have to make is to correct the code for the `chkImages_Click` event. The HTML control uses a property named `DeferRetrieval` to indicate whether embedded documents should be loaded by the control. Change the line of code for this event to read

```
HTML1.DeferRetrieval = (chkImages.Value = 0)
```

You'll also have to modify other code that references `Webster1` to reference `HTML1` (or whatever name you give the HTML control). Note that the HTML control does support the `Cancel` method, so in the `cmdMain_Click` event code you simply replace `Webster1.Cancel` with `HTML1.Cancel`.

The code for the HTTP control's events can be left intact as long as the link URL resolution is handled in `AddAnchor` as described above.

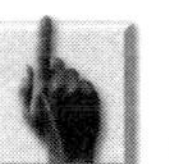

Summary

Being the last chapter in the book, this chapter was designed to incorporate information from several of the previous chapters. If you hadn't done so already, hopefully this chapter prompted you to read some of the earlier chapters. Probably the most important chapter to help you grasp this chapter is Chapter 2, which discusses the HTTP protocol and HTTP header fields in detail.

The book concludes with several appendixes that discuss how to create HTML files (Appendix A, "Basic HTML Tags"), Microsoft's new VB Script programming language (Appendix B, "VBScript—VBA for the Web"), and programming Win/CGI applications for the Microsoft Internet Information Server (Appendix C, "Win/CGI on the Microsoft Internet Information Server"). The final appendix, Appendix D, "Bibliography and Cool Web Sites," provides a good listing of resources both on and off the Net to assist you in your Web programming endeavors.

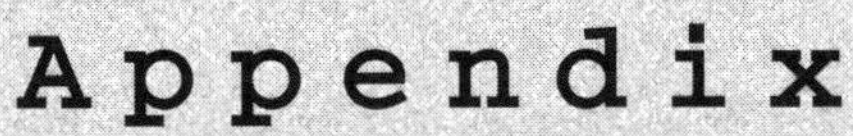

Basic HTML Tags

- General Tags
- Formatting HTML
- Text Alignment
- Embedding Images Within Web Pages
- Linking to other Documents and Sites
- Tables
- Forms
- Netscape 2.x/Microsoft Internet Explorer 3.x Frames

This appendix is not meant to be an HTML tutorial. Instead, it provides brief descriptions of what the authors think are the most useful tags, as well as all the tags used in the book. For a comprehensive tutorial guide to HTML, we suggest *Teach Yourself Web Publishing with HTML 3.0 in a Week* by Laura Lemay (Sams Publishing, 1995).

General Tags

<HTML> </HTML>

The <HTML> and </HTML> tags mark the beginning and end of the HTML file respectively.

<TITLE> </TITLE>

The text enclosed in the <TITLE> and </TITLE> tags is displayed by the browser in the title area—most often the browser's application title bar.

<HEAD> </HEAD>

Descriptive information, such as the title and document type, are enclosed in the HEAD tags.

<BODY> </BODY>

The BODY tags mark the beginning and end of the document body. These tags are not required for the document to look correct on most browsers, but it is proper HTML practice to put them at the beginning and end of the document, respectively. A number of attributes can be set in the body tags.

```
<BODY BACKGROUND = "back.gif">
```

The BACKGROUND attribute sets the background to a tiled series of the image back.gif. You can also set the color of the document text, links that have or have not been visited, and active links, as shown in the following lines:

```
<BODY TEXT = "#rrggbb">
<BODY LINK = "#rrggbb">
<BODY ALINK = "#rrggbb">
<BODY VLINK = "#rrggbb">
```

http://www.biola.edu/cgi-bin/colorpro/

This sets the text, link, activated link, and visited link to the color where *rr* as the amount of red, *gg* as the amount of green, and *bb* as the amount of blue. The numbers provided are hexadecimal in the range of `00` — `FF`. Many utilities generate the values of these values automatically from a color dialog box, or sliders for the red, green, and blue colors. A wonderful online resource for color setting is the ColorServer Pro site at http://www.biola.edu/cgi-bin/colorpro/.

```
<BODY BACKGROUND = "back.gif" TEXT = "#rrggbb" LINK = "#rrggbb"
ALINK = "#rrggbb" VLINK = "#rrggbb">

(Insert HTML document here)
</BODY>
```

NOTE:

Microsoft Internet Explorer 3.0 supports named colors wherever a color attribute can be used. For example, `<BODY TEXT=TEAL>` causes the text in the document to be teal.

Formatting HTML Text

HTML provides many ways to format the look of text appearing in your Web documents. Table A.1 lists many of the tags for formatting textual information.

Table A.1. Tags for formatting text.

Tag	*Description*
`<B> </B>`	Applies boldface to text between tags.
`<BLINK> </BLINK>`	Causes any text between the tags to blink.
`<CITE> </CITE>`	Used to offset a citation from a book or magazine article. Browsers typically display citations in italics.
`<CODE> </CODE>`	Offsets a source code program listing. The browser usually displays this in a smaller monospaced font.
`<DFN> </DFN>`	Styles a definition of a term. Browsers typically display definitions in italics.
`<EM> </EM>`	The text between these tags is emphasized. Most browsers use italic to show emphasized text.
`<FONT SIZE = #> </FONT>`	Sets the font size (#) used to display the HTML appearing between the tags. Default is 3; the range is 1 to 7.

continues

Table A.1. continued

Tag	Description
<H#> </H#>	The # in the <H#> tag specifies the heading level—a number between 1 and 6, with 1 as the largest size and 6 as the smallest.
<I> </I>	Text occurring between the tags is displayed in italics.
<KBD> </KBD>	The Keyboard tag is used to represent keyboard keys such as the Del or Enter keys. On most browsers this is displayed in a smaller monospaced font.
<PRE> </PRE>	Preformatted text is displayed without any special formatting. This is a good tag to use if you want to maintain spacing over several lines; it's also an easy way to put tabs into your document.
<MARQUEE> </MARQUEE>	(Microsoft Internet Explorer 2.0/3.0 only.) This tag causes the text within to scroll by default from left to right across the screen. The attributes of the MARQUEE element are as follows:
ALIGN	Specifies that the text around the marquee should align to the TOP, MIDDLE or BOTTOM of the marquee.
BEHAVIOR	The valid settings for this attribute are SCROLL, SLIDE, and ALTERNATE.
SCROLL	The default, repeatedly scrolls the text from one side of the screen to the other, then repeats.
SLIDE	Scrolls the text across the screen, and when it hits the margin, stops.
ALTERNATE	Bounces the text from margin to margin.
BGCOLOR	This sets the background color of the marquee.
DIRECTION	The direction can be either the default LEFT, or RIGHT. This specifies the start direction either left to right, or right to left, of the marquee.
HEIGHT	Sets the height of the marquee either in pixels (HEIGHT = *n*) or in a percentage of the screen (HEIGHT = *n*%).
WIDTH	Similar to the HEIGHT attribute, but applies to the width of the marquee.
HSPACE	Sets the left and right margins for the outside of the marquee in pixels.
LOOP	Specifies the number of times the marquee should scroll.

Tag	Description
	If left undefined, set to `-1` or `INFINITE`, and the marquee scrolls until the user leaves the page.
`SCROLLAMOUNT`	Sets the number of pixels to move the text between redrawing of the marquee text.
`SCROLLDELAY`	The number of milliseconds between movements of the marquee text.
`VSPACE`	Sets the top and bottom margins of the outside marquee in pixels.
`<SAMP> </SAMP>`	Shows a group of literal characters. Most browsers display this as a monospaced font.
`<STRIKE> </STRIKE>`	Text enclosed in these brackets appears struckout (~~Example~~).
`<STRONG> </STRONG>`	Another way of drawing attention to a special section of text; `<STRONG>` usually is displayed in bold by most browsers.
`<TT> </TT>`	Displays in a typewriter style (monospaced) font.
`<U> </U>`	Text occurring between the tags is displayed underlined.

Figures A.1 through A.4 demonstrate how Netscape Navigator and Microsoft Internet Explorer display various headings and text formatting tags.

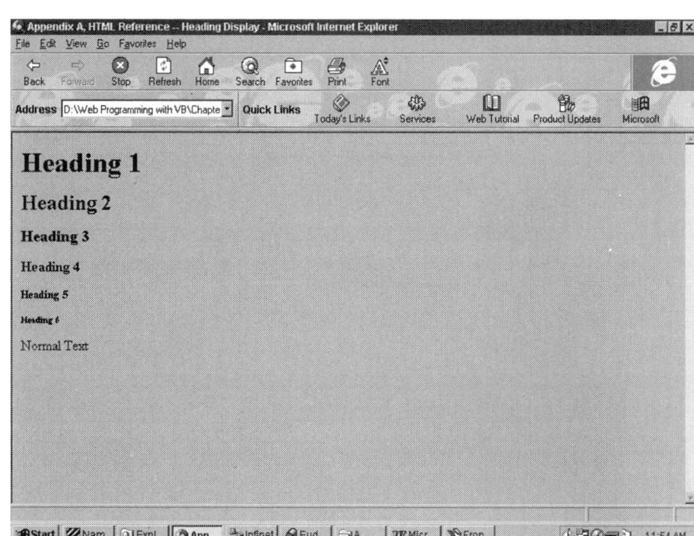

Figure A.1.
Headings displayed by Microsoft Internet Explorer.

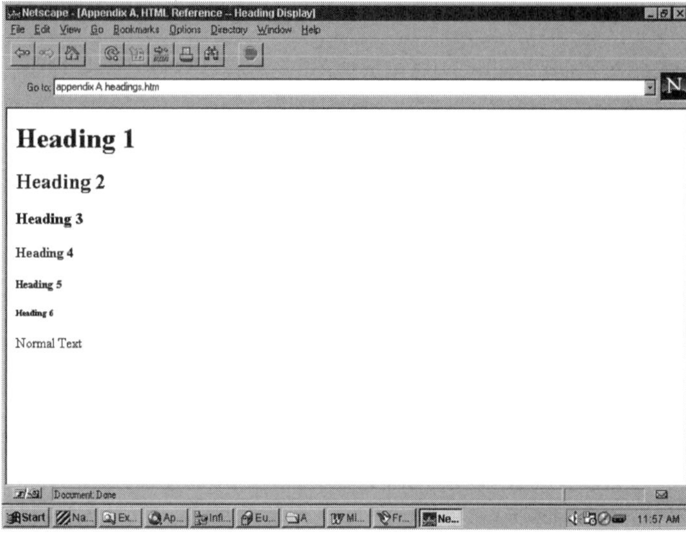

Figure A.2.
Headings displayed by Netscape Navigator.

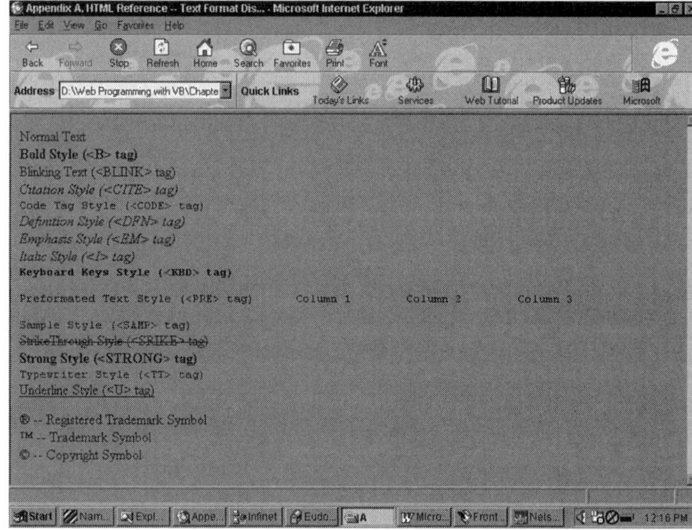

Figure A.3.
Text formats displayed by Microsoft's Internet Explorer.

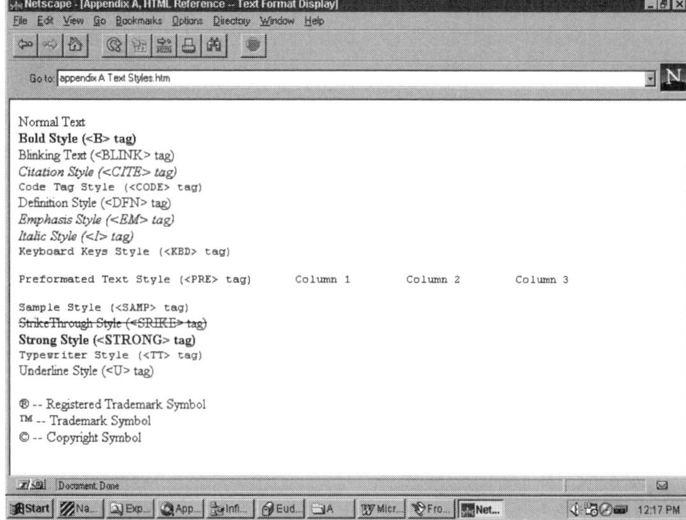

Figure A.4.
Text formats displayed by Netscape Navigator.

NOTE:

As you can see from Figure A.4, Navigator does not correctly render the <U> tag. The same HTML file was used for both Figure A.3 and A.4.

Text Alignment

<CENTER> </CENTER>

These tags center the text or image enclosed in the tags.

<P ALIGN=LEFT¦CENTER¦RIGHT> </P>

This aligns the text to the left, center, or right of the browser display.

<H# ALIGN=LEFT¦CENTER¦RIGHT> </H#>

This aligns the enclosed text to the left, center, or right and gives the text the heading level of the number that replaces the two # symbols.

Embedding Images Within Web Pages

To insert an image into a Web page, simply use the <IMG> tag. The tag has the following elements:

SRC=*URL* The URL that points to the image file.

ALIGN The ALIGN element specifies how the image will be aligned relative to text and other elements near the image. Many values are available and won't be covered here.

ALT=*text* Specifies the text (typically placed within quotation marks) to be displayed if the Web browser is incapable of displaying images or if the image was not loaded correctly for some reason.

HEIGHT=*h* WIDTH=*w* Specifying the height and width of the image allows the Web browser to set aside enough space for the image before it actually retrieves the image. This aides the Web browser in rendering the entire document when all images haven't yet been retrieved.

An example of embedding an image into a Web page is

```
<IMG SRC=Picture.gif HEIGHT=100 WIDTH=65 ALIGN=TOP ALT="A Picture">
```

Linking to other Documents and Sites

HTML documents are hypertext documents. This means that they can contain links to other documents. The anchor (<A> </A>) tag is used to specify a link to another document or resource to be loaded when the user clicks the link. The text and any other HTML appearing between the anchor tags appears to the user as a hotlink, usually colored differently than regular browser text or underlined. The following sections describe the attributes of the anchor tag.

HREF

HREF = "*URL*" specifies the URL of the resource to be displayed after the user clicks on the anchor. As an example, <A HREF="http://www.microsoft.com"> specifies a link to the Microsoft Web site.

NAME

The NAME attribute specifies the name of a location within the current HTML document that can be linked to by a link from another page. This enables other documents to reference the specific anchor in a page. To reference a named anchor, the URL of the page is specified, then a #, followed by the name of the anchor. For example, <a name="Copyright"> defines a link named Copyright within the current document.

TITLE

This attribute, although not required, allows the page designer to include the title of the page that the anchor references.

URN

This specifies a URN (Universal Resource Name) for the target document.

Tables

Tables are implemented in both Internet Explorer 2.0 and 3.0, as well as Netscape 1.1 and later. Tables are a good way to logically group information that would otherwise appear in a spreadsheet. Using tables is also, in some cases, a convenient way to display database records.

The following code contains an example of a basic table:

```
<TABLE BORDER = 5>
<TR>
<TD>1</TD> <TD>2</TD> <TD>3</TD> <TD>4</TD>
</TR>
<TR>
<TD>5</TD> <TD>6</TD> <TD>7</TD> <TD>8</TD>
</TR>
</TABLE>
```

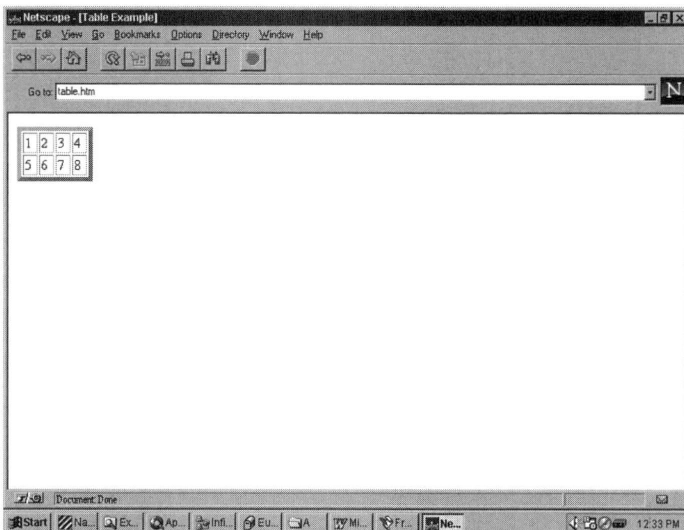

Figure A.5.
Simple table as displayed by Netscape Navigator.

<TABLE> </TABLE>

The following are the attributes of the TABLE tag and their effects on the table.

BORDER

The BORDER attribute sets the width of the border as displayed by the browser. Experiment with the browser you use and the information within to find the optimum setting.

CELLSPACING

The CELLSPACING attribute determines the amount of space the browser places between each individual cell and the space between the cell and the border (if the cell is on the outer edge of the table). Again, experimentation works well to find an appropriate value.

CELLPADDING

The CELLPADDING attribute determines the amount of space the browser places between the data in the table cell and the border around the cell. The greater the value in CELLPADDING is, the more room around the actual value in the cell. Within the table tags, three other tags define the header, rows, and cells. These tags are the table header <TH>, table row <TR>, and table data <TD>.

The following are the attributes of the <TABLE> element.

WIDTH

The WIDTH attribute can be set either as a number defining the absolute width in pixels, or as a percentage of the browser's viewing space. The browser can stretch the table, but it does not compress the table if the size of the browser window is smaller than that of the table.

ALIGN

With ALIGN, you can specify left, center, or right alignment of the table.

BGCOLOR

As with the <BODY> tag, you can set the background color of tables using the BGCOLOR attribute, you can either use the *#rrggbb* color definition, or, if you're designing for Internet Explorer, you can specify the color by name (for example, <TABLE BGCOLOR = RED>). The *#rrggbb* color values follow those of the <BODY> tag as described at the beginning of this appendix.

BORDERCOLOR (Microsoft Internet Explorer 2.0/3.0 Only)

This works similarly to the BGCOLOR attribute but applies to the tables external and internal borders.

BORDERCOLORLIGHT (Microsoft Internet Explorer 2.0/3.0 Only)

This setting is optional and sets the color of the thin line around the top and left sides of the entire exterior of the table and the bottom right sides of the interior of the table. These colors can be modified to enhance or change the default 3-D appearance.

BORDERCOLORDARK (Microsoft Internet Explorer 2.0/3.0 Only)

This setting functions as the exact opposite of BORDERCOLORLIGHT, coloring the bottom and right sides of the exterior and the upper and left sides of the interior cells of the table.

<TH> </TH>

The table header element functions the same as the table data <TD> element, except the table header element is displayed in a bold font. The valid attributes for the table header element are ROWSPAN, COLSPAN, ALIGN, VALIGN, NOWRAP, BGCOLOR, BGCOLORDARK, and BGCOLORLIGHT. The attributes function similarly to the table elements but affect only the header cell that they are set in.

<TD> </TD>

The table data element marks the beginning and end of each cell in the table. The valid attributes for the table data element are ROWSPAN, COLSPAN, ALIGN, VALIGN, NOWRAP, BGCOLOR, BGCOLORDARK, and BGCOLORLIGHT. These elements are described in the following sections.

ROWSPAN

This attribute specifies the number of rows the cell should stretch; for instance, if ROWSPAN is set to 3, that cell will span three normal rows in the table.

COLSPAN

This attribute specifies the number of columns the cell should stretch; for instance, if COLSPAN is set to 3, that cell will span three normal columns in the table.

NOWRAP

Inserting the NOWRAP attribute keeps the text of the cell all on one line.

<TR> </TR>

The table row element marks the beginning and end of each row in the table. The valid attributes of the table row element are ALIGN, VALIGN, BGCOLOR, BGCOLORDARK, and BGCOLORLIGHT.

<CAPTION> </CAPTION>

The CAPTION tags are placed within the table tags, but not within row, heading, or cell tags. The text in the CAPTION tags defines the associated caption of the table. The following are the valid attributes of the CAPTION tag.

ALIGN

The valid settings for the ALIGN attribute for Netscape are TOP and BOTTOM; Microsoft's Internet Explorer includes TOP, BOTTOM, LEFT, RIGHT, and CENTER.

VALIGN

With VALIGN, you can specify the vertical alignment of the data within the table cells. This attribute is set within the <TD> tag of the cell to be aligned. Valid settings are TOP, MIDDLE, and BOTTOM. Not specifying the tag results in center aligned (MIDDLE) text. For example, <TD VALIGN=TOP>Top Aligned</TD> specifies a cell that will be aligned with the top of the row.

Forms

Forms are the way to get feedback from the visitors to your Web site. Beginning and ending with the <FORM> and </FORM> tags, the fields within these determine the size and type of input fields. Although you can have multiple forms on a page, you cannot nest forms.

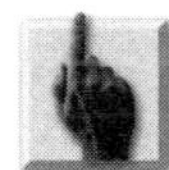

The <FORM> Tag

The attributes of the form element are described in the following sections.

ACTION

This specifies the URL of the resource that will carry out the action on the form data, and give the user a response.

```
ACTION = "http://www.execpc.com/~haasch/search"
```

METHOD

This can either be the default `GET` or `POST`. Using `GET`, the query appends the form data to the end of the URL; using `POST`, the data is sent via an HTTP post transaction.

Elements Contained Within a Form

The following sections describe the various elements that can be placed within a form.

INPUT

The `INPUT` element specifies the user interface to enter information. The following are the attributes for the `INPUT` tag.

CHECKED

For checkboxes and radio buttons, this attribute can be set to `TRUE` (checked) or `FALSE` (unchecked).

MAXLENGTH

`MAXLENGTH` indicates the maximum number of characters that can be entered into a textbox.

NAME

This specifies the name of the form control. This is used to identify the data elements on the form to the resource that processes those elements. It's also used by VBScript (described in Appendix B, "Visual Basic Script Reference") to provide similar functionality to control names in Visual Basic.

SIZE

This specifies the size of the form control. This can either be specified in a single value, representing the width in characters of the control, or in a width/height pair.

SRC

This specifies the image to be displayed with the control.

TYPE

This sets the type of control to use. The following is a list of available controls:

CHECKBOX The checkbox control is a simple TRUE/FALSE control, where checked is TRUE, and empty indicates FALSE.

HIDDEN This control is not displayed to the viewer of the page. It can be used to send state information back to the form-processing program.

IMAGE This causes the form data to be submitted immediately, and the value passed back from the image is the x, y coordinates in pixels.

PASSWORD This functions the same as a textbox, but the text is echoed as asterisks instead of the letters typed.

RADIO This functions much like the CHECKBOX control, but only one option button in the group may be selected at a time.

RESET When a RESET button is clicked, the form data returns to the initial values specified in the form's data element definitions. The VALUE attribute can be set to give the RESET button a label.

SUBMIT Clicking this button submits the form data to the FORM ACTION URL.

TEXT This control is used to gather a single line of text. SIZE and MAXLENGTH attributes can be set to restrict the size of user input and the appearance of the text control.

TEXTAREA This control is used for multiline text input. The SIZE and MAXLENGTH attributes have the same function as the TEXT control.

SELECT

The SELECT tags mark the beginning and end of the data in a listbox or a drop-down selection list. The following are the attributes for the SELECT element.

MULTIPLE The multiple attribute enables the user to select more than one item from the listbox. The user holds the CTRL button and clicks on the different items to select them.

NAME	This specifies the name of the SELECT element.
SIZE	This sets the height of the list control.

OPTION

The OPTION element sets off each selection in the textbox or listbox. The following are the attributes of the OPTION element:

SELECTED	This attribute sets the default value of the text- or listbox.
VALUE	This is the return value of the element that is selected.

Netscape 2.x/Microsoft Internet Explorer 3.x Frames

With Netscape 2.0 and above, the browser is able to display frames that contain different sets of HTML code.

<FRAMESET> </FRAMESET>

The FRAMESET element is the container element for a group of frames. Its two attributes are ROWS and COLS.

ROWS

The ROWS tag specifies the amount of space given to each row. The number can be specified in pixels, in percent by placing a % after the value, or as a relative value by placing an asterisk (*) in place of the value.

COLS

The syntax for the COLS attribute is the same as that of the ROWS attribute.

<FRAME>

The FRAME element specifies the properties for each individual frame in the frameset. Because it contains no text, there is no corresponding end-tag. The attributes of the FRAME tag are as follows.

SRC

The SRC attribute specifies the URL source for the frame.

NAME

The NAME attribute is used to assign a name to the frame, so it can act as a target from other URLs.

MARGINWIDTH

This allows the page designer to specify the width of the frame border in number of pixels.

MARGINHEIGHT

This works the same as MARGINWIDTH except it affects the height of the margin.

SCROLLING

The valid settings for the SCROLLING attribute are YES, NO, and AUTO. If set to YES, a scrollbar is provided for the frame; NO results in no scrollbar; and AUTO provides a scrollbar if the document size exceeds the size of the frame.

NORESIZE

Specifying this attribute prevents the user from dragging the margins of the frame to cause them to resize. Default is to allow the user to resize the frames.

<NOFRAMES> </NOFRAMES>

The data within the NOFRAMES tags is ignored by form-capable browsers. This set of tags allows information to be displayed to non-forms capable browsers.

Appendix

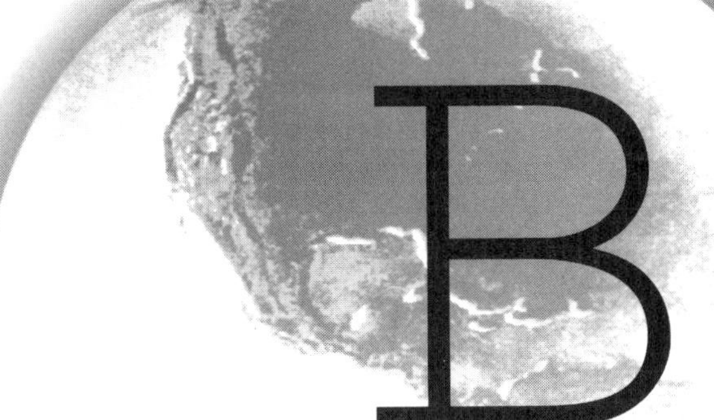

VBScript—VBA for the Web

- Variables
- Operators
- Control Constructs
- Using Subroutines and Functions
- Visual Basic Script Statement Overview
- Visual Basic Script Functions Overview
- The Err Object's Properties and Methods
- Visual Basic Script Examples

Visual Basic Script, herein referred to as VBScript or VBS, is Microsoft's answer to Sun's JavaScript. Both are meant to be intertwined in HTML code; both are meant to expand on the client side functionality of the Web, and neither of the two are fully released products. (VBScript is in beta with MS-Internet Explorer 3.0. JavaScript was first implemented in Netscape 2.0.)

http://www.microsoft.com/vbscript

The resource for information on Visual Basic Script is the Microsoft Web site (http://www.microsoft.com/vbscript). Here you can find complete documentation, some sample snippets of VBScript code, and links to sites using VBScript.

Variables

In most languages, variables are an important part of the language, its structure, and its implementation. In VBScript, the variables are all of the same type, Variant.

The Variant type is an "all things to all people" generic data type. Assign it a string, and it acts as a string; assign it a number, and it acts like a number. The following lines are an example of declaring a Variant in VBScript:

```
<SCRIPT LANGUAGE="VBScript">
Option Explicit
Dim vUserName, vUserNumber, vUserString
</SCRIPT>
```

The SCRIPT LANGUAGE tag is a proposed addition to the HTML standard and is first implemented in the Microsoft Internet Explorer 3.0 It informs the browser that code, which must be interpreted, is coming and of what type it is. The usual as Variant, (like you would see in a regular Visual Basic program) is omitted because the Variant type is the only one available. Multiple variables per line are allowed—the procedure is to separate each by a comma. The Option Explicit keyword is implemented in Visual Basic Script, and if used, it should appear as the first statement after the <SCRIPT LANGUAGE = "VBScript"> tag.

Naming Restrictions

The naming constraints in VBScript are similar to those of Visual Basic. Note that these rules apply to function names, constant names, and variable names. The name must begin with an alphabetic character. It cannot contain an embedded period, must be less than 255 characters, and it must be unique in the scope in which it is declared.

Scope Rules for VBScript Variables

Two scopes are available in VBScript: the script level and procedure level. Variables at the script level are instantiated at the time the script is run, and exist until the script has completed running.

   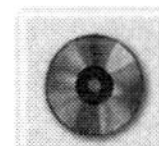

Procedure level variables exist from the beginning of the procedure they are declared in until the end of that procedure.

The `Static` keyword is supported when using persistent procedure level variables.

Arrays with multiple dimensions are also supported in VBScript:

```
Dim aSums(10) 'single dimension
Dim aTable (10, 10) 'two dimension
```

As you can see, the declaration is just as in Visual Basic, except again there is no as <Variable Type>.

The `ReDim` and `ReDim Preserve` keywords are also supported in the creation and recreation of arrays. They function in the same way as their Visual Basic counterparts.

Operators

VBScript includes all the operators found in Visual Basic: arithmetic (+, -, and so on), logical (`And`, `Or`, `Not`, etc.), and comparison (=, < >, and so on). VBScript also obeys the same rules for operator precedence as Visual Basic.

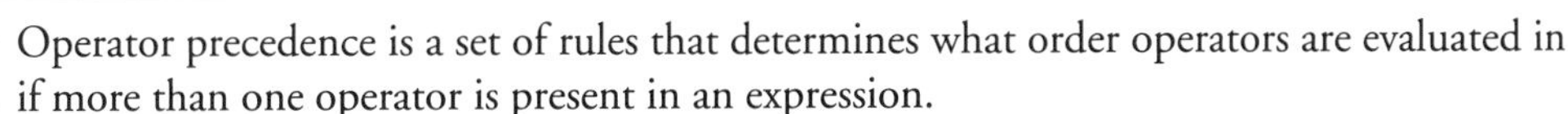

NOTE:

Operator precedence is a set of rules that determines what order operators are evaluated in if more than one operator is present in an expression.

Control Constructs

The `If-Then-Else`, `Do-Loop`, `While-Wend`, `For-Next`, and `For Each-Next` control constructs are supported, just as they are in standard Visual Basic syntax.

Using Subroutines and Functions

Like its Visual Basic cousin, VBScript supports the `Sub` and `Function` procedures. Within the HTML file, the subroutines and function bodies must be placed before the code that calls them. It's advisable to put the VBScript functions and subroutines in the beginning of the <HEAD> portion of the HTML document. Then, following the subroutines and procedures, place the remainder of the VBScript code.

Visual Basic Script Statement Overview

Visual Basic Script supports a subset of the Visual Basic statements. The following list are the functions supported:

`Call` statement
`Dim` statement
`Do-Loop` statement
`Erase` statement
`Exit` statement
`For-Next` statement
`For Each-Next` statement
`Function` statement
`If-Then-Else` statement
`Let` statement
`LSet` statement
`Mid` statement
`MsgBox` statement
`On Error` statement
`Private` statement
`Public` statement
`Randomize` statement
`ReDim` statement
`Rem` statement
`RSet` statement
`Set` statement
`Static` statement
`Sub` statement
`While-Wend` statement

Visual Basic Script Functions Overview

The following is a list of functions and objects that are supported by Visual Basic Script and operate similarly to the VB counterparts:

`Abs` function
`Asc` function
`Atn` function
`Chr` function

Cos function
Date function
DateSerial function
DateValue function
Day function
Exp function
Hex function
Hour function
InputBox function
InStr function
Int, Fix functions
LBound function
LCase function
Left function
Len function
Log function
LTrim, RTrim, and Trim functions
Mid function
Minute function
Month function
MsgBox function
Now function
Oct function
Right function
Rnd function
Second function
Sgn function
Sin function
Sqr function
Str function
StrComp function
String function
Tan function
Time function
TimeSerial function
TimeValue function
UBound function
UCase function
Val function
VarType function
Weekday function
Year function

The following sections provide information regarding new functions or functions that behave differently than their VB counterparts.

The Array Function

The Array function returns a variant that contains an array. The following is an example:

```
Dim aNums as Variant
aNums = Array(1, 2, 3, 4, 5)
```

This would create an array with five values, 1 through 5. If no arguments are passed to the Array function, the array created is of zero length.

Accessing the elements of an array is done the same way in VBScript as in Visual Basic. For instance,

```
X = aNums(3)
```

would assign the value of the third position in the array aNums to the variable X.

Data Conversion Functions

The data conversion functions listed in Table B.1 take one Variant variable as an argument and return that value as the Variant subtype of that function.

For example, the CBool function would take a normal Variant as an argument and return a value into a Variant with the subtype Boolean.

Table B.1. VBScript's data conversion functions

Function	*Description*
CByte	Variant to subtype byte
CDate	Variant to subtype date
CDbl	Variant to subtype double
CInt	Variant to subtype integer
CLng	Variant to subtype long
CSng	Variant to subtype single
CStr	Variant to subtype string
CVErr	Variant to subtype error

The values passed to these conversion functions must be in the valid range for the type being converted to. For example, the argument passed to the CVErr function must be a valid error number.

The `Is` and `Isx` Functions

The `Is` functions determine whether the variable is of that data type. The `IsArray` function returns `True` if the `Variant` type variable passed to the function is of subtype `array`. The other `Is` functions (`IsDate`, `IsEmpty`, `IsError`, `IsNull`, `IsNumeric`, and `IsObject`) behave in the same way.

The `Err` Object's Properties and Methods

At this point, VBScript supports only the `Err` object. This contains any information about runtime errors during the processing of the script.

`Description` Property

The `Description` property can return or be set to a string that is displayed to the user when a runtime error occurs.

`HelpContext` Property

The `HelpContext` property returns or sets the help context ID used to find a topic in a help file.

`HelpFile` Property

`HelpFile` specifies or can be set to any path that contains the help file.

`Number` Property

This corresponds to the error number of the `Err` object. It can be read or set at runtime.

`Source` Property

The `Source` property returns or sets the object or code that caused the error.

`Clear` Method

This clears all properties of the `Err` object.

Raise Method

To generate a runtime error, use the Raise method on the Err object. The arguments to the Raise method are number, source, description, helpfile, and helpcontext.

These correspond to the properties of the Err object and enable the programmer to set these properties at the time the error is raised.

Visual Basic Script Examples

Currently, the only browser that supports VBScript is Microsoft's Internet Explorer 3.0 Beta. For the latest updates to the Internet Explorer and for VBScript examples, see Microsoft's Web site (http://www.microsoft.com), the Visual Basic Script page from Microsoft (http://www.microsoft.com/vbscript/), and the Internet Explorer page at (http://www.microsoft.com/ie/).

Listing B.1 provides the HTML for a quick and dirty Hello World VBScript application. If you have Internet Explorer 3, you can enter this into Notepad or load it from the CD-ROM included with this book.

Listing B.1. The Hello World VBScript example

```
<HTML>
<HEAD><TITLE>VBScript Hello World Example</TITLE></HEAD>
<BODY>

<CENTER><H2>Hello World Example</H2>
<INPUT TYPE=TEXT VALUE="Insert Name Here" NAME="txtName"><p>
<INPUT TYPE=BUTTON VALUE="Click Here" NAME="BtnHello">
</CENTER>

<SCRIPT LANGUAGE="VBScript">
<!—
Sub BtnHello_OnClick
    MsgBox "Hello, world!", 0, "From " + txtName.Value
End Sub
—>
</SCRIPT>
</BODY></HTML>
```

The HTML in Listing B.1 is pretty straightforward. The first <INPUT> tag defines a text box with an initial value of Insert Name Here and a Name of txtName. The second <INPUT> tag defines a button named BtnHello that has a caption reading Click Here (a button's caption is defined by the Value element of the <INPUT> tag). The page produced is shown in Figure B.1.

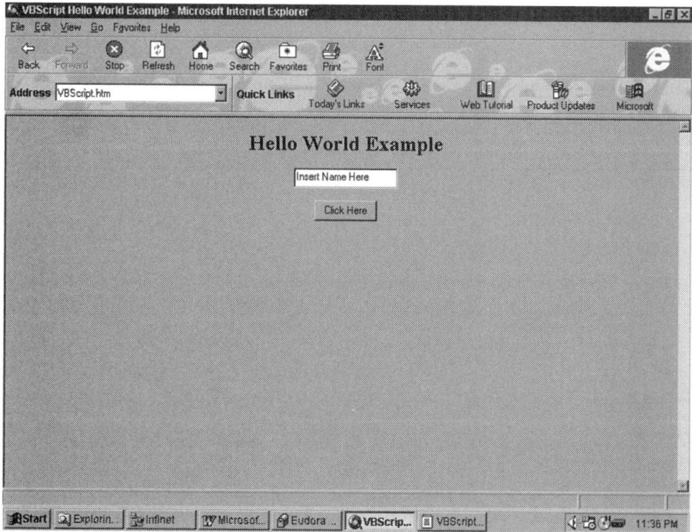

Figure B.1.

The Hello World VBScript Web page.

The VBScript portion begins with the `<SCRIPT>` tag. Note that outside of the `<SCRIPT>` tags, the actual script is placed within an HTML comment (`<!` – ... –`>`). This is to prevent Web browsers that are not script-compliant from attempting to interpret or display the code that is contained within the script.

The `Sub` defined in the script is the event procedure that is executed whenever `BtnHello` is clicked. This concept is identical to the event-driven nature of Visual Basic. The procedure executes the `MsgBox` statement. The text in the message box is `Hello, world!` and the title for the message box is the string `From` concatenated with the text contained in the `txtName` textbox.

A simple example, I know, but it demonstrates the ease-of-use and integration with HTML that VBScript provides.

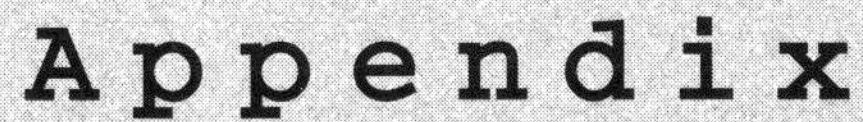

C

Win/CGI on the Microsoft Internet Information Server

- Introduction to IS2SWCGI.DLL
- Examining and Compiling the IS2WCGI.DLL Code
- Installing and Referencing IS2WCGI.DLL

The Microsoft Internet Information Server (IIS) is Microsoft's entry into the Web server arena. Being a Microsoft product, it is closely knit with the Windows NT operating system as well as Microsoft's BackOffice family of products.

The IIS supports CGI scripting applications but does not directly support the Win/CGI interface. This means that input and output take place using the standard input and standard output for an NT console application. This is something I've never been able to accomplish using Visual Basic (not that I ever had the desire to give it a serious effort).

Like most Microsoft products, the IIS is supported by an API. This API is known as the Internet Server API, or ISAPI. The IIS provides the capability of running DLLs as server extensions. The advantages of using DLLs versus standard executables are discussed in Chapter 10, "Using OLEISAPI with the Microsoft Internet Information Server." However, they can be summed up by stating that using a DLL instead of an EXE greatly improves the server's and the extension's performance. Microsoft's position is that your Win/CGI applications should be converted to ISAPI applications when used on the IIS. I second this recommendation.

Obviously, the previous two paragraphs create a quandary for the Webmaster who has a lot of Win/CGI applications written in VB but wants to switch Web servers to use the IIS. That's where Jim Schmidt, a support engineer at Microsoft Developer Support, came to the rescue. He authored the `IS2WCGI.DLL` sample application contained in Microsoft's ActiveX SDK (formerly known as the Internet SDK).

CAUTION:

Please don't throw tomatoes my way, but you're about to encounter some C++ code. You probably realized that when I started talking about DLLs, but I like to warn the unsuspecting anyway.

Introduction to **IS2SWCGI.DLL**

Just when I had about given up hope of being able to use VB to code applications for the IIS, I stumbled upon a reference to the `IS2WCGI` sample server extension. Everywhere else in the IIS documentation, I saw those three dreaded letters: DLL, also spelled C++.

The `IS2WCGI` sample allows you to use your existing Win/CGI applications on the Internet Information Server. It is an ISAPI-compliant DLL that takes the data received from the IIS, puts it into a Win/CGI-compliant format, and launches the Win/CGI executable. `IS2WCGI` then sends all the Win/CGI application's output data back to the IIS to return it to the client.

The `IS2WCGI` application was developed to allow existing applications to be used on the IIS. However, keep in mind that the reason the IIS does not directly support the Win/CGI is that the specification is very inefficient. The ISAPI provides a very efficient means of launching the server extension and providing it with the necessary data from the client. Therefore, the IS2WCGI method should only be used until your applications can be ported to ISAPI or converted to an OLE server to use the OLEISAPI extension discussed in Chapter 10.

The `IS2WCGI` sample also includes a sample Web page (see Figure C.1) and a C++ application that returns all the Win/CGI data to the client, similar to the application developed in Chapter 7, "Creating CGI Applications in Visual Basic."

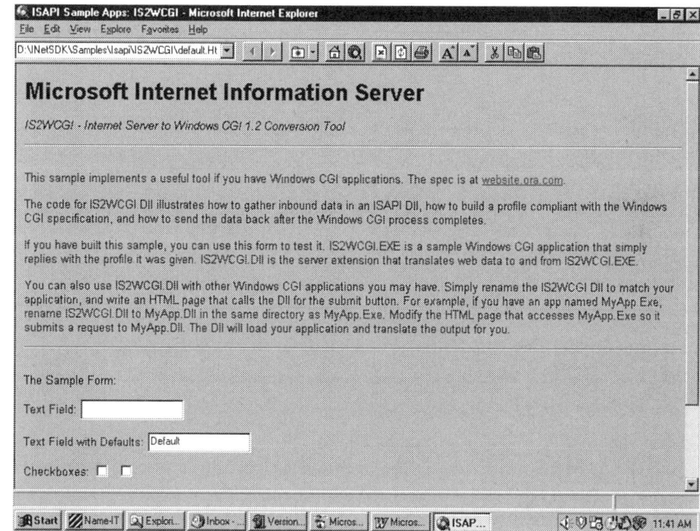

Figure C.1.
The Web page included with the IS2WCGI sample.

The remainder of this appendix consists of an elementary discussion of the code (being C++-impaired, that's all I'm capable of anyway) and some instructions on installing and referencing the `IS2WCGI.DLL` on your Internet Information Server.

Examining and Compiling the `IS2WCGI.DLL` Code

The code for the `IS2WCGI` sample, even though it's written in C++, is pretty easy to follow. As I said earlier, I won't rehash the entire application here. Instead, I'll touch some of the highlights and areas you may wish to modify for your applications.

The ISAPI specification requires that extension DLLs provide and export two functions: `GetExtensionVersion()` and `HttpExtensionProc()`. These functions must be present in every ISAPI-compliant DLL you code.

When the server loads the DLL, it calls the DLL's `GetExtensionVersion()` to retrieve the version of the specification on which the extension is based and a description for administrators. Every time a client requests the URL specifying the extension DLL, the `HttpExtensionProc()` function is called. This is where the bulk of the work in an ISAPI extension is performed. It's identical to the `Sub Main` procedure of the Win/CGI applications developed in this book.

As explained in Chapter 10, the server communicates with the DLL using a structure of the type `EXTENSION_CONTROL_BLOCK`. This structure contains information about the current request message and about the server itself. A pointer to an `EXTENSION_CONTROL_BLOCK` structure is provided as the parameter to the `HttpExtensionProc()` function.

The `IS2WCGI` sample performs all of its work within `HttpExtensionProc()`. The DLL creates a temporary file to store the CGI data, fills the profile's key names, retrieves the encoded form data, and writes the data to either the profile file or to an external file (depending on the format of the data). The DLL then creates a child process used to execute the actual CGI application and waits for the process to finish execution. After the CGI application ends, the DLL writes the data back to the Web client and cleans up after itself.

Possible Changes to IS2WCGI.CPP

While the `IS2WCGI.DLL` functions just fine as provided with the ActiveX SDK, you may wish to make a few changes to the C++ code. To recompile the code, however, requires Visual C++. The Microsoft Developer Studio included with VC++ 4 makes working with C++ code almost bearable for the VB programmer. It's easy to move around in your C++ projects by using the Studio's class view, and the online books are very helpful. So, if you're going to commit to the Internet Information Server platform and want to write some extensions for your Web server, invest in a copy of VC++ 4.

The first thing I noticed when using the `IS2WCGI` extension was that the `User Agent` request message field was missing from the `[CGI]` section of the profile file. The first section to follow discusses adding this to the `[CGI]` section of the Win/CGI profile file. The sections that follow discuss increasing the timeout period that `IS2WCGI` waits for your CGI application to complete and how to change `IS2WCGI` to use the Win/CGI Debug mode.

Adding User Agent to the [CGI] Section of the Win/CGI Profile File

`IS2WCGI` has a subroutine named FillCGI which creates the `[CGI]` section of the profile file. However, the `FillCGI` procedure is missing the `[CGI]` section's `User Agent` field. This field is returned, instead, in the `[Extra Headers]` section with the key name `"USER_AGENT"`. If your applications expect to find the `User Agent` field in the `[CGI]` section, it's a simple matter to add it there.

To add this field to the `[CGI]` section, locate the `FillCGI` subroutine in the `IS2WCGI.CPP` source code. Add the following line at the bottom of the routine:

```
GetVarAndWriteKey (pParam, szSection, TEXT("HTTP_USER_AGENT"),
➥             TEXT("User Agent"));
```

Fortunately, the code has been documented well enough to make such modifications easy to identify and easy to code.

Extending the Time Period for Timeout Errors

Another modification you might want to make is to change the value of the `WAIT_EXT_TIMEOUT` constant. This constant defines how long the DLL will wait for the CGI application to complete before flagging a timeout error. If you know your application can take longer than the defined value (120 seconds), locate the line

```
#define WAIT_EXT_TIMEOUT 120000     // 120 secs
```

within `IS2WCGI.CPP`. Adjust the value defined to a reasonable value for your application. However, don't set the constant too high or you'll risk leaving the user in limbo for extended periods of time should your CGI application actually not exit properly.

Placing the Server in Debug Mode

The `IS2WCGI.DLL`, by default, deletes all the CGI files it creates and also the output file your CGI application creates. If you want to run your application in Debug mode and leave these files intact, you need to remove the `DeleteFile` calls that appear in `HTTPExtenionProc()`.

To do so, open the `IS2WCGI.CPP` source code file. Locate `HTTPExtensionProc()` and scroll to near the end of the routine. Find the following comment:

```
//
// Clean Up
//

// Delete the temp files made in form decoding
```

and comment out all the code between the last comment and the comment that reads

```
// Clean up key list resources & delete content file
```

Leave all the code that appears after this comment intact. Comment out the following line:

```
DeleteFile (param.lpszContentFile);
```

Be very careful not to comment out the line immediately following this one, which begins with `HeapFree`.

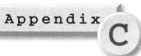

Also comment out the two lines:

```
DeleteFile (param.szProfielName);
DeleteFile (param.szOutputFileName);
```

Finally, move to the beginning of the source file. In this line,

```
static TCHAR gszDebugMode[] = TEXT("No");
```

replace the `"No"` with `"Yes"`.

After you rebuild the DLL, it leaves all the temporary files intact. Note that this should be a temporary measure on your part. Once you have the CGI application working properly, change the code back to its original state. If you want to get really fancy, you can place an entry in the system registry to control whether or not the DLL should be run in Debug mode. My C++ skills are not up to that level, so I chose not to pursue this route.

Building **IS2WCGI.DLL** to Accomplish a Direct Return

A compile-time flag in `IS2WCGI.CPP` determines whether or not the DLL recognizes a *direct return* CGI application. A CGI application that is using direct return is responsible for creating the HTTP response message headers. A typical CGI application would allow the Web server to create the HTTP response message headers. In this case, the CGI application is responsible only for the *contents* of the response (typically the HTML text).

There are cases, however, when you want to control the response message headers. These include returning error conditions to the client and redirecting the client to another resource.

For example, I have a Web page that contains a link to a demo copy of an application. Instead of providing the ZIP filename in the link, I provide the name of a CGI application. When the application executes, it places the query string from the link as well as other CGI fields into a database and redirects the user's Web browser to the ZIP file. The code to perform the redirection (using variables and routines from `CGI32.BAS`) is

```
OutputString "HTTP/1.0 301 REDIRECT"
OutputString "Location: /newpage.htm"
OutputString ""
```

To change the IS2WCGI extension to allow direct returns from your applications, remove the comment from the line that reads

```
//#define CONFORMANT_HEADER
```

which can be found near the top of the `IS2WCGI.CPP` source file. Rebuild the DLL and rename it something that you'll recognize as supporting the direct return. If you attempt to use this version of the DLL with a CGI application that does *not* return all of the HTTP response headers, your application will not return a valid HTTP message to the client.

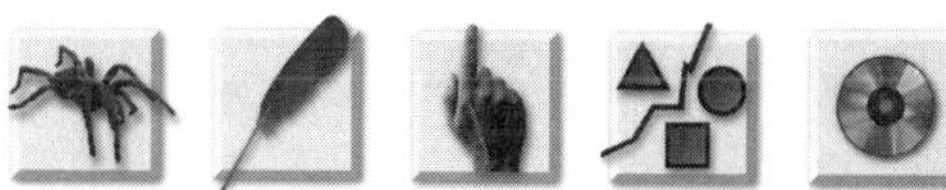

Installing and Referencing IS2WCGI.DLL

After you have compiled `IS2WCGI.DLL`, you are ready to install it alongside your Win/CGI application. The `IS2WCGI.DLL` file must be renamed to match the name of your executable because it uses its filename when it executes the `CreateProcess()` function to launch the Win/CGI application. So, if your executable is named `entry.exe`, you can make a copy of `IS2WCGI.DLL`, name it `entry.dll`, and place it in the same directory as `entry.exe`. This directory needs to be a directory that allows execution but does not allow reads. Figure C.2 shows the setup screen for such a directory in the IIS Administration Tool.

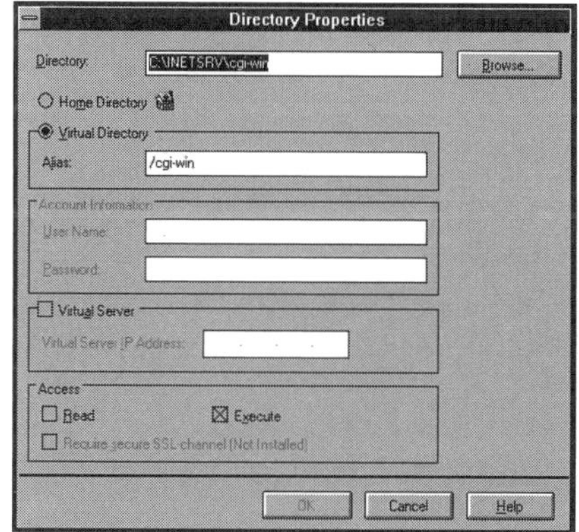

Figure C.2.
The `/cgi-win` directory setup for the IIS.

The second step to using the `IS2WCGI.DLL` on your Web site is to properly refer to it in your HTML documents. Instead of your documents referencing the executable file, as is the case for other Web servers running Win/CGI applications, if you're using IIS, you should reference the DLL file. For example,

```
<form method="POST" action="/cgi-win/entry.dll">
```

will `POST` the form's data to the resource located at `/cgi-win/entry.dll`. This is the copy of the `IS2WCGI.DLL` server extension you just created. When the Submit button is clicked, the IIS loads the DLL which creates the Win/CGI temporary files and launches `entry.exe`, the original Win/CGI application.

A hyperlink that performs a `GET` request would look similar:

```
<A HREF="/cgi-win/entry.dll?QueryString">Query</A>
```

This link, when clicked, follows the same chain of events as the form submit just discussed.

Appendix D

Bibliography and Cool Web Sites

- Chapter-by-Chapter Bibliography
- General Publications of Interest to Web Programmers
- Web Sites for the Visual Basic Web Programmer

This appendix lists bibliographic information for some of the sources that have been used in developing this book, as well as some resources we have just stumbled upon in our travels on the Web. We hope you'll find these resources as helpful as we have in our Web programming adventures.

Chapter-by-Chapter Bibliography

Chapter 2, "HTTP: How to Speak on the Web"

Cheong, Fah-Chun., *Internet Agents: Spiders, Wanderers, Brokers, and Bots.* New Riders, 1996; (Chapter 6).

Cope, Ken and Kris Jamsa. *Internet Programming.* Jamsa Press, 1995; (Chapter 19).

Marchuk, Michael. *Building Internet Applications with Visual Basic.* Que, 1995; (Chapter 17).

On the Internet Engineering Task Force (IETF) Web site (`http://ietf.cnri.reston.va.us/`):

- `http://www.ietf.cnri.reston.va.us/ids.by.wg/http.html`, a page containing links to many HTTP-related documents.
- `ftp://ietf.cnri.reston.va.us/internet-drafts/draft-ietf-http-v10-spec-05.txt`, the most recent Internet-Draft for HTTP.

Chapter 3, "Interfacing to the Web with DDE and OLE"

De Bruijn, Michiel. "Hook into Browsers for the Web," *Visual Basic Programmer's Journal.* Fawcette Technical Publications, February, 1996.

Chapter 4, "Using Web Browser Custom Controls"

Jackson, Steve. "Internet Control Pack," *Microsoft Interactive Developer*, Fawcette Technical Publications, Spring, 1996.

Chapter 5, "Retrieving Information from the Web"

Jackson, Steve. "Internet Control Pack," *Microsoft Interactive Developer*, Fawcette Technical Publications, Spring, 1996.

The Dolphin System's Home Page:

`http://www.dolphinsys.com/`

The Microsoft ActiveX Internet Control Pack Web site:

`http://www.microsoft.com/icp`

Chapter 6, "The Win/CGI Interface"

General introduction to CGI:

`http://hoohoo.ncsa.uiuc.edu/cgi/`

The Windows CGI Interface specification:

`http://website.ora.com/wsdocs/32demo/windows-cgi.html`

The HTML Form-Testing Home Page:

`http://www.research.digital.com/nsl/formtest/home.html`; provides information on how popular Web browsers handle HTML forms.

Chapter 9, "Connecting to OLE Servers: Using the Web as a Front-End to Schedule Plus"

Gilbert, Mike. "Building Activity Management Applications with Schedule+ and OLE," Found on Microsoft Tech-Ed 95 (ML304) on recent Microsoft Developer's Network CDs.

"Microsoft Schedule+ Programmer's Guide," *BackOffice Software Development Kit.*

Chapter 10, "Using OLEISAPI with the Microsoft Internet Information Server"

"A Specification for Writing Internet Server Applications," included with the Microsoft ActiveX SDK.

Franklin, Carl. "Serving Up the Web," *Visual Basic Programmer's Journal*, Fawcette Technical Publications, April, 1996.

Schmidt, Jim. "ISAPI: Writing Internet Information Server Extensions Is No Day at the Zoo," *Microsoft Interactive Developer*, Fawcette Technical Publications, Spring, 1996.

The Process Software Corporation provides a link to its Web server's programmer's guide which includes ISAPI information: `http://www.process.com/news/spec.htp`

Chapter 12, "QuoteWatcher: An Interactive Web Agent"

"Visual Programmer: Create Tray Icons in Visual Basic," *Microsoft Systems Journal*: Miller Freeman, February, 1996.

Appendix A, "Basic HTML Tags"

"A Beginner's Guide to HTML"

`http://www.ncsa.uiuc.edu/General/Internet/WWW/HTMLPrimer.html`

"Composing Good HTML"

`http://www.cs.cmu.edu/~tilt/cgh/`

"Guides to Writing Style for HTML Documents"

`http://union.ncsa.uiuc.edu:80/HyperNews/get/www/html/guides.html`

Appendix B, "VBScript—VBA for the Web"

Pleas, Keith. "Visual Basic Script," *Microsoft Interactive Developer*, Spring, 1996.

Templeman, Michael. "Collision Course: JavaScript and VBScript," *Visual Basic Programmer's Journal*, April, 1996.

The Microsoft VBScript Home Page:

`http://www.microsoft.com/vbscript`

Appendix C, "Win/CGI on the Microsoft Internet Information Server"

Schmidt, Jim. "ISAPI: Writing Internet Information Server Extensions Is No Day at the Zoo," *Microsoft Interactive Developer*, Fawcette Technical Publications, Spring, 1996.

General Publications of Interest to Web Programmers

Microsoft Interactive Developer, a magazine published by Fawcette Technical Publications. (Half of the articles appearing in the premier issue are listed above. Need I say more?)

Microsoft Systems Journal, a magazine published by Miller Freeman.

Visual Basic Programmer's Journal, a magazine published by Fawcette Technical Publications (the quintessential VB magazine).

Web Techniques, a magazine published by Miller Freeman. (An excellent new magazine chock full of Web programming information.)

WEBsmith Magazine, a magazine published by Specialized Systems Consultants, Inc. (SSC). (This provides mostly UNIX articles, but the basic concepts apply regardless of platform.)

Web Sites for the Visual Basic Web Programmer

"Carl and Gary's Visual Basic Home Page:"

`http://www.apexsc.com/vb` (My favorite jump-off site!)

Avatar: The Interactive Developers' Online Magazine:

`http://www.avatarmag.com/`

Microsoft's Visual Basic Page:

`http://www.microsoft.com/vbasic`

The Development Exchange:

`http://www.windx.com`

The Microsoft Systems Journal Page:

`http://www.msj.com/`

Index

Symbols

A

B

C

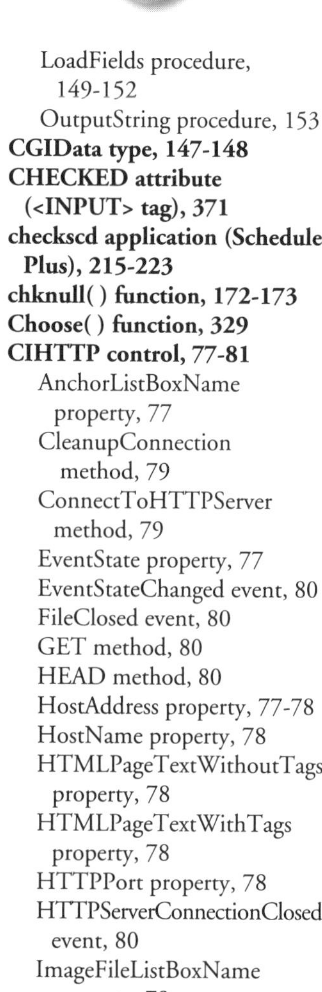

I

S

T

U

Tricks of the Visual Basic 4 Gurus

— James Bettone, et al.

Microsoft is betting that the new release of Visual Basic 4 will create a mass migration from other compilers including its own, Visual Basic 3 compiler. In expectation of that migration, *Tricks of the Visual Basic Gurus* presents tips and secrets from programmers who work inside Microsoft—giving developer's the "inside scoop" on the latest shortcuts and techniques to VB programming. Both 16-bit and 32-bit developing is covered, in addition to tips on OLE and OCX programming.

CD-ROM contains source code from the book and the complete referenced applications

Covers Windows 32-bit programming for Windows 95

Teaches about OLE and the Win32 API

Programmers learn to port between 16-bit OCX controls and 32-bit OLE controls

$49.99 USA/$67.99 CDN | *User Level: Accomplished - Expert*
ISBN: 0-672-30929-7 | *744 pages*

CGI Developer's Guide

— Eugene Eric Kim

This book is one of the first books to provide comprehensive information on developing with CGI (the Common Gateway Interface). It covers many of the aspects of CGI including interactivity, performance, portability, and security. After reading this book, the reader will be able to write robust, secure, and efficient CGI programs.

CD-ROM includes source code, sample utilities, and Internet tools

Covers client/server programming, working with gateways, and using Netscape

Readers will master forms, image maps, dynamic displays, database manipulation, and animation

$45.00 USA/$63.95 CDN | *User Level: Accomplished - Expert*
ISBN: 1-57521-087-8 | *600 pages*

Tricks of the Java Programming Gurus

— Glenn Vanderburg, et al.

This book is a guide for the experienced Java programmer who wants to take his Java skills beyond simple animations and applets. It will show the reader how to streamline his Java code, how to achieve unique results with undocumented tricks, and how to add advanced level functions to his existing Java programs.

CD-ROM includes all the source code from the book

Skilled Java professionals show how to improve garbage collection before and after compilation for improved performance

Provides a fast-paced guide to advanced Java programming

Covers Java 1.1

$49.99 USA/$70.95 CDN | *User Level: Accomplished - Expert*
ISBN: 1-57521-102-5 | *888 pages*

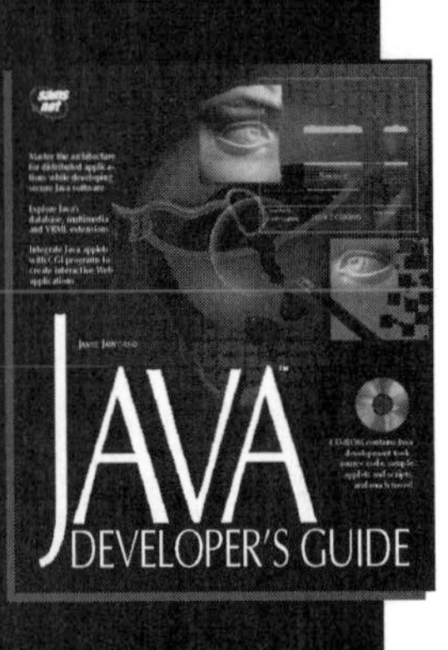

Java Developer's Guide

— Jamie Jaworski & Carie Jardean

Java is one of the major growth areas for developers on the World Wide Web. It brings with it the ability to download and run small applications called applets from a Web server. *Java Developer's Guide* teaches developers everything they need to know to effectively develop Java applications.

CD-ROM includes source code from the book and valuable utilities

Covers Java interface, VRML extensions, security, and more

Explores new technology and future trends of Java development

Covers Java 1.1

$49.99 USA/$67.99 CDN *User Level: Accomplished - Expert*
ISBN: 1-57521-069-x *768 pages*

Database Developer's Guide with Visual Basic 4, Second Edition

— Roger Jennings

This book shows developers how to optimize their applications for desktop and client/server databases, write queries in ANSI SQL and Access SQL with Visual Basic code, and create front-end databases using MIDI forms.

CD-ROM contains a data dictionary application, cross tab query generator, multiplatform graphical front end, and DDE and OLE applications with Excel 5

Provides in-depth coverage of networking issues surrounding databases

Explains how to use third-party, data-aware custom controls to add flexibility to applications

Covers latest version for Windows

$59.99 USA/$81.95 CDN *User Level: Accomplished - Expert*
ISBN: 0-672-30652-2 *1,152 pages*

Windows NT 4 Web Development

— Sanjaya Hettihewa

Windows NT and Microsoft's newly developed Internet Information Server is making it easier and more cost-effective to set up, manage, and administer a good Web site. Since the Windows NT environment is relatively new, there are few books on the market that adequately discuss its full potential. *Windows NT 4 Web Development* addresses that potential by providing information on all key aspects of server setup, maintenance, design, and implementation.

CD-ROM contains valuable source code and powerful utilities

Teaches how to incorporate new technologies into your Web site

Covers Java, JavaScript, Internet Studio, and VBScript

Covers Windows NT

$59.99 USA/$84.95 CDN *User Level: Accomplished - Expert*
ISBN: 1-57521-089-4 *800 pages*

Teach Yourself VBScript in 21 Days

— *Keith Brophy & Tim Koets*

Readers learn how to use VBScript to create living, interactive Web pages. This unique scripting language from Microsoft is taught with clarity and precision, providing the reader with the best and latest information on this popular language.

CD-ROM contains all the source code from the book and examples of third-party software

Teaches advanced OLE object techniques

Explores VBScript's animation, interaction, and mathematical abilities

Covers VBScript

$39.99 USA/$56.95 CDN *User Level: New - Casual*
ISBN: 1-57521-120-3 *550 pages*

Visual Basic 4 Developer's Guide

— *Boyle, et al.*

This book shows programmers who are already well-versed in the programming basics how to get the most out of Visual Basic. It teaches programming techniques and strategies as well as how to implement Visual Basic in a network setting.

CD-ROM contains complete source code for all the programs in the book

Teaches developers how to exploit the new features of the latest version of Visual Basic

Covers implementation of Visual Basic in a network setting and in conjunction with other technologies and software

Covers Latest Version for Windows

$55.00 USA/$74.95 CDN *User Level: Accomplished - Expert*
ISBN: 0-672-30783-9 *1032 pages*

Add to Your Sams.net Library Today with the Best Books for Internet Technologies

ISBN	Quantity	Description of Item	Unit Cost	Total Cost
0-672-30929-7		Tricks of the Visual Basic 4 Gurus (Book/CD-ROM)	$49.99	
1-57521-087-8		CGI Developer's Guide (Book/CD-ROM)	$45.00	
1-57521-102-5		Tricks of the Java Programming Gurus (Book/CD-ROM)	$49.99	
1-57521-069-X		Java Developer's Guide (Book/CD-ROM)	$49.99	
0-672-30652-2		Database Developer's Guide with Visual Basic 4, Second Edition (Book/CD-ROM)	$59.99	
1-57521-089-4		Windows NT 4 Web Development (Book/CD-ROM)	$59.99	
1-57521-120-3		Teach Yourself VBScript in 21 Days (Book/CD-ROM)	$39.99	
0-672-30783-9		Visual Basic 4 Developer's Guide (Book/CD-ROM)	$55.00	
		Shipping and Handling: See information below.		
		TOTAL		

Shipping and Handling: $4.00 for the first book, and $1.75 for each additional book. If you need to have it NOW, we can ship product to you in 24 hours for an additional charge of approximately $18.00, and you will receive your item overnight or in two days. Overseas shipping and handling adds $2.00. Prices subject to change. Call between 9:00 a.m. and 5:00 p.m. EST for availability and pricing information on latest editions.

201 W. 103rd Street, Indianapolis, Indiana 46290

1-800-428-5331 — Orders 1-800-835-3202 — FAX 1-800-858-7674 — Customer Service

Book ISBN 0-672-106-8

What's on the Disc

The companion CD-ROM contains software developed by the authors, plus an assortment of third-party tools and product demos. The disc is designed to be explored using a CD-ROM Menu program. Using the Menu program, you can view information concerning products and companies, and install programs with a single click of the mouse. To run the Menu program, follow these steps:

Windows 3.1 and Windows NT Installation Instructions:

1. Insert the CD-ROM into your CD-ROM drive.
2. From File Manager or Program Manager, choose Run from the File menu.
3. Type `<drive>\setup` and press Enter, where `<drive>` corresponds to the drive letter of your CD-ROM. For example, if your CD-ROM is drive D:, type `D:\SETUP` and press enter.

Windows 95 Installation Instructions

1. Insert the CD-ROM into your CD-ROM drive.
2. If Windows 95 is installed on your computer, and you have the AutoPlay feature enabled, the Menu program starts automatically whenever you insert the disc into your CD-ROM drive.
3. If Autoplay is not enabled, using Explorer, choose Setup from the CD drive.

NOTE

For best results, set your monitor to display between 256 and 64,000 colors. A screen resolution of 640×480 pixels is also recommended. If necessary, adjust your monitor settings before using the CD-ROM.